A HISTORY OF THE 'ALAWIS

A HISTORY OF THE 'ALAWIS

*

From Medieval Aleppo to the Turkish Republic

STEFAN WINTER

PRINCETON UNIVERSITY PRESS
PRINCETON AND OXFORD

Copyright © 2016 by Princeton University Press

Published by Princeton University Press,
41 William Street, Princeton, New Jersey 08540
In the United Kingdom: Princeton University Press,
6 Oxford Street, Woodstock, Oxfordshire OX20 1TR
press.princeton.edu

Cover art courtesy of the author

All Rights Reserved

Library of Congress Cataloging-in-Publication Data

Names: Winter, Stefan, 1970– author.
Title: A history of the 'Alawis : from medieval Aleppo to the Turkish republic / Stefan Winter.
Description: Princeton ; Oxford : Princeton University Press, [2016] | Includes bibliographical references and index.
Identifiers: LCCN 2016005146 | ISBN 9780691167787 (hardcover : alk. paper) | ISBN 9780691173894 (pbk. : alk. paper)
Subjects: LCSH: Nosairians—Syria—History. | Nosairians—History.
Classification: LCC DS94.8.N67 W56 2016 | DDC 297.8/25109—dc23 LC record available at http://lccn.loc.gov/2016005146
British Library Cataloging-in-Publication Data is available

This book has been composed in Sabon Next LT Pro

Printed on acid-free paper. ∞

Printed in the United States of America

10 9 8 7 6 5 4 3 2 1

FOR
Ahmet Bilgin

CONTENTS

List of Illustrations ix
Acknowledgments xi

INTRODUCTION *1*

Classical Perceptions of 'Alawism, Nomenclaturism, and Dissimulation * *Sources and Argument*

* 1 *

THE NUSAYRIS IN MEDIEVAL SYRIA: FROM RELIGIOUS SECT TO CONFESSIONAL COMMUNITY (TENTH–TWELFTH CENTURIES CE) *11*

Ghulat *Shiʻi Origins* * *The Nusayri (Khasibi)* Daʻwa * *The Conversion of the Syrian Highlands* * *Between the Ismailis and the Crusaders* * *Makzun al-Sinjari* * *Conclusion: The Birth of a Minority*

* 2 *

BEYOND THE MOUNTAIN REFUGE: 'ALAWISM AND THE SUNNI STATE (THIRTEENTH–FIFTEENTH CENTURIES) *43*

The Defeat of the Ishaqis and the Hululi-Thamina Controversy * *Relations with the State Authorities and the Ismailis* * *Ibn Taymiyya and the Politics of Persecution* * *The Uprising of 1318* * *Mamluk Fiscal Policies toward the 'Alawis* * *Conclusion: The Persecution Syndrome*

* 3 *

SURVEY AND PUNISH: THE 'ALAWIS' INTEGRATION INTO THE OTTOMAN EMPIRE (1516–1645) *74*

The Ottoman Conquest * *The 'Alawi Rebellion* * *The* Dirhemü'r-Rical *and the Tax Districts of the Coastal Highlands* * *The Province of Jabala under Ottoman Rule* * *Conclusion: From Rebels to* Reaya

* 4 *
THE AGE OF AUTONOMY: 'ALAWI NOTABLES AS OTTOMAN TAX FARMERS (1667–1808) *119*

'Alawi Tribalism, Tribalization, and Gentry * *The Shamsins and the Mukataa of Safita* * *The Bayt al-Shillif* * *The Rise of Latakia* * *Population Pressure and Migration toward Antioch* * *The Townships* (Hillas) *of Safita and the Barakat and Raslan Families* * *Saqr ibn Mahfuz* * *The War with the Ismailis* * *Conclusion: The Economics of Anarchy*

* 5 *
IMPERIAL REFORM AND INTERNAL COLONIZATION: 'ALAWI SOCIETY IN THE FACE OF MODERNITY (1808–1888) *161*

The Disappearance of Ottoman Tripoli * *Conversion and Sectarianization* * *Shaykh al-Moghrabi* * *The Egyptian Occupation, 1831–1841* * *A World Restored* * *The Struggle over Schooling* * *The Plight of the Minorities* * *Administrative Modernity* * *Conclusion: 'Alawi Ottomanism and Compatriotism*

* 6 *
NOT YET NATIONALS: ARABISM, KEMALISM, AND THE ALAOUITES (1888–1936) *218*

Hamidian Reeducation * *Loyalty and Control* * *The 'Alawi Awakening* * *Salih al-'Ali and the Güney Cephesi (Southern Front)* * *Mandate vs. Republic* * *Conclusion: The Double Disservice*

CONCLUSION *269*

From the Sectarian to the Local

Bibliography *275*
Index *295*

ILLUSTRATIONS

MAPS

1. Overview of region 79
2. 'Alawi-populated tax districts 82
3. Safita and associated tax districts 91
4. Northern tax districts and 'Alawi revolt area, 1519 107

FIGURES

1.1. Frieze from the central hall of the shrine of Khidr, Balis 24
1.2. Ba'rin, with ruins of old village in foreground 29
1.3. Shrine of Shaykh Hasan, Kafrun 37
1.4. Abu Qubays castle 38
1.5. Entrance to the shrine of Shaykh Musa al-Rabti, Abu Qubays 40
2.1. Qadmus 55
2.2. Cenotaph of Shaykh Mahmud al-Qusayr, al-Hatiriyya 56
2.3. Shrine of Shaykh Ibrahim al-'Idda, al-Harif 57
3.1. Detail from Tahrir Defteri 68:316 81
3.2. View of Safita 88
4.1. Tobacco fields near Salma 132
4.2. Qal'at al-Muhalaba (ancient Platanus) 144
4.3. *Iltizam* contract for Ubin, 1778 148
4.4. Shrine of Nabi Yusuf ibn 'Abdallah, Ba'rin 155
5.1. Port of Latakia, early nineteenth century 166
5.2. Ottoman spy report on the 1834 uprising HAT 22354 C 187
5.3. French sketch map of Latakia province, 1870 201
6.1. Blueprints of planned police station in Qardaha 233
6.2. Shaykh Salih al-'Ali 246
6.3. Salih al-'Ali's letter to Mustafa Kemal, 17 July 1921 254
6.4. Ruins of French barracks near Shillif (Latakia) 259
6.5. Pro-unionist petition signed by 'Ali Sulayman al-Asad, 1936 261

ACKNOWLEDGMENTS

This project developed out of a long-standing interest in the political history of 'Alawism in Syria and several years' worth of prior engagement with early modern Ottoman rural society in the archives of Istanbul and Tripoli. In its present form the book, originally conceived as a quick, general introduction to the 'Alawis under Ottoman rule, was begun during a sabbatical year at the Institut français du Proche-Orient (IFPO) in Aleppo in 2010–11. The discovery of several exciting new sources, the realization that virtually all the previous literature was single-mindedly obsessed with the 'Alawis' religious beliefs, to the exclusion of their social and economic environment, and finally, of course, the outbreak of what already then had all the trappings of a civil war persuaded me that a new, evidence-based, long-term narrative of the community and its relationship with wider Syrian and Middle Eastern society was not only necessary but even a matter of some urgency. The following is therefore offered both as an object-oriented, academic contribution to our knowledge of 'Alawi and Syrian (and Turkish) history and, in view of the catastrophe that has since transpired in Syria, as my own coming-to-grips with a land, a society, and a history that will never be the same again.

Over the years I have accumulated many debts, both institutional and intellectual, which it is my duty and pleasure to acknowledge here. I am grateful to my colleagues from the history department at the Université du Québec à Montréal (UQÀM) for repeatedly affording me the opportunity to spend time researching abroad, and for providing a congenial academic environment back home. Financial support was derived from several different projects funded by the Conseil de recherche en sciences humaines (CRSH) of Canada and the Fonds de recherche du Québec Société et Culture (FRQSC), none of whose initial description actually bore much of a resemblance to the final result (which suggests once again how vital a role institutional state sponsorship of curiosity-driven, noncommercial research must continue to play in the social sciences). Additional funding toward a sabbatical year in Ankara in 2014–15 was generously provided by the Scientific and Technological Research Council of Turkey (TÜBİTAK), for which I likewise express my appreciation. In Ankara I have had the good fortune to be attached to the history department of Bilkent University as an

A HISTORY OF THE 'ALAWIS

INTRODUCTION

The 'Alawis are doubtless one of the most conspicuous, talked-about confessional groups in the Middle East today. Considered a branch of Imami Shi'ism and referred to in much of the classical literature as "Nusayris," the 'Alawis represent perhaps 11 percent of the population in Syria (approximately two million people), with important regional concentrations in the province of Antioch (Hatay) as well as in Adana and Mersin in southern Turkey,[1] and in the 'Akkar district and the city of Tripoli in northern Lebanon. There is also a single 'Alawi village in southern Lebanon, Ghajar, half of which was sectored off and has remained under Israeli occupation even after the IDF's withdrawal from most of the country in 2000. Whatever Ghajar's eventual status (as of September 2015 it is still occupied), a small population of 'Alawis can thus also be said to have come under de facto Israeli sovereignty. But it is above all their role in the modern history of Syria that has attracted attention: long deprecated as a heterodox mountain "sect" living on the geographic and social margins of the state, the rise of a new class of 'Alawi officers in the army of independent Syria, their dominant position within the Ba'th Party and the outright seizure of power by the 'Alawi general Hafiz al-Asad in 1970, his lengthy reign as president followed by that of his son Bashar in 2000, and the disproportionate role since played by 'Alawis in the state, especially marked since Syria's descent into civil war and sectarian chaos in 2011, have all served to put the spotlight on the putative origins, development, and political identity of the community as such.

Despite (or rather because of) the current interest they have generated, however, the older history of the 'Alawis is often treated in essentialist terms and reduced to a single overarching theme of religious deviance, marginality, and oppression. Whether in Western or Arab Gulf media, hardly any report on Syria today fails to specify that 'Alawism is a "minority" regarded by other Muslims as heretical, and that the entire community has therefore been "historically persecuted." According to this metanarrative, which is also shared

---

[1] Not to be confused with the "Alevis" of Turkey, with whom they share a similar name and confessional basis but who constitute an entirely distinct, or even several distinct, ethnic and religious communities.

by a good number of academics, a fatwa that was given by the well-known fundamentalist scholar Ibn Taymiyya in the fourteenth century and which calls for their extermination would also sum up their actual lived experience under Muslim rule, such that they survived only by remaining holed up in their "mountain refuge" of northwestern Syria, before emerging from isolation in the French mandate period and ultimately "capturing power" over the whole country. The concealment, self-defense, and clannishness of the ceaselessly persecuted sect would thus go a long way toward explaining the current regime's nature. Ironically, Asad proponents have begun to play on this view themselves and stoke fears among the 'Alawis and other groups of the Sunni majority's unbridled historical hatred, as a means of enforcing loyalty to the regime.[2]

The problem with the notion of "historical persecution" and other such blanket assessments is that they are not borne out by the historical evidence. In basing their perception on fatwas, theological treatises, and narrative chronicles, historians have always tended to concentrate on the 'Alawis' normative separation from the rest of society and on episodic, inherently rare cases of communal conflict. The focus on confessional difference—part of a wider pattern of interpretation which assumes that religion is really the only thing that matters in the Middle East—is not only unsatisfying in scholarly terms but also indefensible in light of the sectarianist myths being mobilized on all sides of the civil war in Syria. Numerous sources exist that point to the 'Alawis' integration within wider Syrian society throughout history. In particular, a wealth of Mamluk administration manuals, Ottoman and Turkish archival documents, and the 'Alawis' own prosopographical literature challenge the notion that the 'Alawi "community," if there even was one such thing, was cut off from the world around it, differentiated from other rural populations, or subjected to systematic discrimination. This study aims to provide a less essentializing, more material account of 'Alawi history by focusing not on its confessional underpinnings but on the origins and spread of the 'Alawi mission in Syria, on the 'Alawis' specific situation under successive Muslim empires and their relations with other communities, and on regional and class differences within 'Alawi society itself. It proposes a "secular" approach to this history in the double sense of the word (as in French *séculier* and *séculaire*): by privileging the socioeconomic, political, and administrative context of modern 'Alawism's development over its purely religious traits, and by adopting a *longue-durée*, multicentury perspective in order to take stock of the necessarily profound transformation of 'Alawi communal identity over time.

---

[2] See the recent analyses in Michael Kerr and Craig Larkin, eds., *The Alawis of Syria: War, Faith and Politics in the Levant* (London: Hurst, 2015).

CLASSICAL PERCEPTIONS OF ʿALAWISM, NOMENCLATURISM, AND DISSIMULATION

In terms of doctrine, ʿAlawism or Nusayrism is a secret mystical revelation of the true nature of God, the cosmos, and the "imamate" (i.e., the belief, common to all Shiʿis, that ʿAli ibn Abi Talib and his lineage were the Prophet Muhammad's only legitimate successors), passed down from Muhammad Ibn Nusayr, a scholar and companion of the last two visible Shiʿi Imams in the ninth century. Because of the concealed, esoteric nature of the teaching, which, much like in a Sufi order, is transmitted only to select initiates, pious ʿAlawis have naturally been loath to divulge the details of their faith and cult to outsiders, and it has thus become a common cliché to present ʿAlawism as obscure, mysterious, and insufficiently studied.[3] In fact, its very fascination has spawned a huge literature in modern times that belies its supposed obscurity. Some of the first European travelers to the region did not actually meet any ʿAlawis and were content simply to rely on their local interlocutors for their breathless depictions of the sect; even renowned orientalist scholars have repeated outrageous claims to the effect that the ʿAlawis are pagans, that they worship the sun, dogs, and female genitalia or partake in night-time sex orgies as part of their cultic practices—things that have of course formed part of the standard register of accusations against sectarian groups, both Christian and Muslim, throughout history. At the same time, the increasing presence of Europeans in the Middle East and the expansion of oriental studies at Western universities in the nineteenth century also produced a large number of sober, text-critical or empirical studies that early served to establish ʿAlawism as a privileged subject of academic inquiry.

Classical scholarship on ʿAlawism, much like on other Eastern religions, has concentrated for the most part on its hypothetical origins and allegorical teaching. Joseph Simon Assemani's *Bibliotheca Orientalis* (1717–28), a compendium of oriental texts translated into Latin, which contains a somewhat deprecatory account of the sect's beginnings, long served as the basis of European knowledge about the ʿAlawis;[4] among the first critical examinations of the community, however, is that offered by Carsten Niebuhr (d. 1815), a member of a Danish-funded expedition to Arabia and the Far East in the 1760s. Niebuhr's account is based on information obtained from sympathetic local contacts as well as on a Nusayri treatise apparently seized by the Ottoman authorities, and it already contains in essence what is known about

---

3 For a state-of-the-art overview, see Heinz Halm, "Nusayriyya," *Encyclopaedia of Islam*, new ed. [*EI2*] (Leiden: Brill, 1995), 8:145–48; İlyas Üzüm, "Nusayrîlik," *Türkiye Diyanet Vakfı İslam Ansiklopedisi* (Istanbul: İSAM, 2007), 33:270–74.

4 Cited in Constantin-François Volney (d. 1820), *Travels through Egypt and Syria in the Years 1783, 1784, and 1785* (New York: Evert Duyckinck, 1798), 2:3–5.

the religion today. Niebuhr stands out among early writers for his attempt to explain 'Alawism rationally, noting that the "Nusayris" prefer to refer to themselves as "Mûmen" (believers), accurately summarizing their belief structure, and suggesting that accusations regarding their supposed worship of the sun and other celestial bodies might result from a misinterpretation of their catalog of symbolic names and terms.[5] Subsequent orientalists and missionaries explored at great length the sect's possible grounding in Neoplatonism, Gnosticism, and Eastern Christianity. Studies by Olaus Gerhard Tychsen (1784, 1793) and Heinrich Gottlob Paulus (1792), for example, debated whether the Nusayris were to be identified with the Mandaeans, whose syncretic beliefs and similar-sounding alternate name of "Nazoraeans" proved a source of lasting confusion;[6] a number of later authors followed Ernest Renan (d. 1892) in assuming that "Nusayri" was the Arabic diminutive of "Nasara" (Christians) and that the 'Alawis were hence a long-lost Christian sect.[7] Though easily disproven, this notion does bespeak the fact that Nusayri thought had several features in common with early Christian Gnosticism and that on a popular level, the 'Alawis of the Syrian highlands often participated in or even adopted the religious holidays of their Christian neighbors. Even today, the degree of Christianity's and other religions' possible influences on 'Alawism continues to be a subject of much interest and debate among specialized scholars.[8]

The fascination with 'Alawism's roots and doctrines has also brought attention to bear on two aspects of 'Alawi identity of concern here, namely, the lack of a uniform historical term for the group, and the supposed practice of *taqiyya* or dissimulation. The name "Nusayri" is first encountered in medieval Muslim heresiographies and has never been used by 'Alawi scholars in their own writings. On the other hand, the 'Alawi populace did in many cases identify themselves vis-à-vis others as Nusayris (or, in the contracted colloquial pronunciation of the Arabic plural, *an-Nusayriyya*, which was then consecrated in European travel reports as "Ansarie," "Ansairy," etc.), so that one can presume that, as with other heterodox groups, they eventually appropriated a term that had originally been applied to them by others in

---

5 Carsten Niebuhr, *Reisebeschreibung nach Arabien und anderen umliegenden Ländern* (Copenhagen: Nicolaus Möller, 1778), 2:439–44.

6 Olaus Gerhard Tychsen (d. 1815), "Die Syrischen Nassairier und ihre Itame," in *Memorabilien*, vol. 4 (1793), 185–88; Heinrich Eberhard Gottlob Paulus (d. 1851), in *Memorabilien: Eine philologisch-theologische Zeitschrift der Geschichte und Philologie der Religionen dem Bibelstudium und der morgenländischen Litteratur gewidmet*, ed. H. Paulus (Leipzig: Siegfried Lebrecht Crusius, 1793), 3:111–22.

7 René Dussaud (d. 1951), *Histoire et religion des Nosairîs* (Paris: Bouillon, 1900), xxxi, 9, 14.

8 Meir Bar-Asher and Aryeh Kofsky, *The Nusayri-'Alawi Religion: An Enquiry into Its Theology and Liturgy* (Leiden: Brill, 2002); Yaron Friedman, *The Nusayri-'Alawis: An Introduction to the Religion, History and Identity of the Leading Minority in Syria* (Leiden: Brill, 2010).

a pejorative sense.[9] The name "'Alawi," while serving occasionally in medieval times to distinguish Imami from Ismaili Shi'is (see chapter 1), was not adopted until the very end of Ottoman rule; by way of self-identification, Syrian 'Alawis were more liable to refer to themselves as *fellahin* ("peasantry") or as followers of the "Khasibi" path, in distinction to other currents within the early Shi'i movement. The use of the term to designate and construct a single overarching sectarian community for the first time, typified in the publication of Muhammad Amin Ghalib al-Tawil's *Tarikh al-'Alawiyyin* in 1924,[10] to date the only complete history of the 'Alawis per se, as will be argued in chapter 6, was in itself a historical process proper to the dislocation of the Ottoman Empire.

The other aspect of 'Alawism that has received considerable, often undue, attention in Western studies is the practice of dissimulation, known in Islamic terminology as *taqiyya*, by which 'Alawis as well as members of other sectarian minorities could conceal or at least downplay their identity in order to avoid discrimination. The principle of *taqiyya* is firmly anchored in Islamic jurisprudence but has historically played a particular role in Shi'ism and certain Sufi rites, where it can also have the meaning of keeping the mystery of one's secret knowledge hidden from outsiders.[11] Nusayri initiates thus certainly practiced *taqiyya* as regards their religious precepts, but their Sunni disparagers as well as Western observers have often claimed that this extended to lying about their identity too: "It is their principle to adhere to no certain religion," the seventeenth-century English voyager Henry Maundrell remarked, "but chameleonlike, they put on the color of that religion, whatever it be, which is reflected upon them from the persons with whom they happen to converse."[12] Not insisting on the nonconformist elements of their faith, or on questions of religion in general, will have come naturally to members of heterodox minorities when traveling or dealing with the authorities over

---

9 Samuel Lyde (d. 1860), *The Asian Mystery. Illustrated in the History, Religion, and Present State of the Ansaireeh or Nusairis of Syria* (London: Longman, Green, Longman and Roberts, 1860), 1. The term 'Alawi will be used when discussing the community and its history in a general sense, but the term Nusayri will also be used without prejudice when referring more precisely to its religious doctrines or when quoting from primary sources. "Nusayri" has gained some acceptance in Syria and Lebanon when used in a historical context; see Muhammad Ahmad 'Ali, *Al-'Alawiyyin fi'l-Tarikh: Haqa'iq wa-Abatil* (Beirut: Mu'assasat al-Nur, 1997), 259–61. In Turkey, where the term is not subject to the same political taboo, it is commonly used to distinguish the "Arap Aleviliği" (Arab 'Alawism) of Hatay and adjoining regions from the larger Turkish "Alevi" denomination.

10 Muhammad Amin Ghalib al-Tawil (d. 1932), *Tarikh al-'Alawiyyin*, 3rd ed. (Beirut: Dar al-Andalus, 1979).

11 Etan Kohlberg, "Some Imamī-Shī'ī Views of Taqīya," *Journal of the American Oriental Society* 95 (1975): 395–402; Friedman, *Nusayrī-'Alawīs*, 13–14, 143–47.

12 Henry Maundrell (d. 1701), *A Journey from Aleppo to Jerusalem at Easter, A.D. 1697* (Boston: Samuel Simpkins, 1836), 21.

more worldly matters; on the other hand, in a time when different segments of society were even more clearly distinguishable by dress and dialect[13] than today, it is highly unlikely that 'Alawis and other mountaineers were not immediately recognizable for what they were. Mamluk chancery manuals and Ottoman administrative documents, as will be seen, demonstrate that the authorities usually had a precise, well-informed idea of their taxable subjects' sectarian identities, if only very little concern with their actual confessional beliefs. The capture and execution of certain 'Alawis in Latakia in the early nineteenth century (see chapter 5) belie the notion that they could merely hide their identity. *Taqiyya* was, historically speaking, simply never a factor in their interaction with the state or with members of other communities.

SOURCES AND ARGUMENT

This study is predicated on the understanding that most literary sources, including the 'Alawis' own theological writings as well as Sunni heresiographies, fatwas, medieval chronicles, and essentially any text that names the 'Alawis (Nusayris) as such, will concentrate on their religious identity and therefore overemphasize their otherness and irreconcilability with the rest of Muslim or Syrian society. The result is that almost all previous studies of the 'Alawi past either have been too concerned with theology or have provided only *histoire événementielle*, emplotting a handful of references to seemingly ubiquitous, but in fact very rare, instances of sectarian strife, discrimination, and violence of the sort favored in the narrative chronicles, to produce a story of apparently unremitting conflict. The following chapters, on the other hand, will concentrate precisely on the less conspicuous—but ultimately more typical—historical evidence of mundane, uneventful, everyday interaction between the 'Alawis, their neighbors, and the state authorities. In particular, they will bring to light a wealth of administrative documents from both Istanbul and Tripoli that, among other reasons because they do not support the usual narrative of persecution, have never been used before: tax cadastres and executive orders which show that both the Mamluks and Ottomans recognized and integrated the 'Alawis as a taxpaying category of subjects; tax farm contracts from the *shar'iyya* court archives in Tripoli which show that the region was dominated by an autonomous class of Ottoman-'Alawi landed gentry that owed its success to the development of commercial tobacco farming in the eighteenth century; records of school construction by the state and other social disciplining efforts in the nineteenth and early twentieth centuries; and a new series of documents from the military archives

---

13 Even in modern times 'Alawis are often distinguished by their pronunciation of the letter q, which is silent in most other Syrian spoken dialects.

of Ankara revealing the functional ties between an 'Alawi revolt against the French at the very end of the Ottoman Empire and Kemalist forces in Anatolia.

These sources will be complemented, especially for the two opening chapters on the medieval period, with a unique, unpublished 'Alawi biographical dictionary (of which the master copy now appears to be inaccessible on account of the civil war) that contains numerous incidental references to 'Alawis interacting on an ordinary, day-to-day level with Ayyubid or Mamluk officials and with their Ismaili neighbors. The *Khayr al-Sani'a fi Mukhtasar Tarikh Ghulat al-Shi'a* by Husayn Mayhub Harfush (d. 1959) has not yet been the object of a systematic study, even though its corpus has begun to inform a broad new, prosopography-based 'Alawi historiography in recent decades.[14] The final two chapters will furthermore incorporate extensive materials from the French Foreign Ministry (La Courneuve) and military (Vincennes) archives that reflect France's growing interest in, and finally authority over, the 'Alawi community in the late nineteenth and early twentieth centuries. The book will close with a consideration of early Turkish republican documents from the National Archives in Ankara, which detail the efforts of Atatürk's Cumhuriyet Halk Partisi (Republican People's Party; CHP) to recast the 'Alawis of southern Turkey as ethnic Turks. By privileging secular over religious sources throughout, this study aims not to discredit the pertinence of 'Alawi religious identity and of the 'Alawi sectarian community as a subject of analysis but to demonstrate that its rapport with its neighbors, rulers, and presumed oppressors can be examined, in all its historical depth, only on a significantly wider documentary basis than has previously been used.

Chronologically this book begins with the establishment of the Shi'i Hamdanid dynasty in Aleppo in 947, under whose patronage the 'Alawi teaching was originally disseminated in geographic Syria. Chapter 1 argues that 'Alawism was not an "offshoot" of "mainstream" Iraqi Twelver Shi'ism but rather constituted one of its central tendencies and was only retrospectively cast as a "heterodox" variant or heresy with the institutionalization of a literary Twelver Shi'ism in the eleventh century. Moreover, its spread throughout the Euphrates valley and into northern Syria, Aleppo, Hama, and finally the coastal highlands from Acre to Latakia (in that order) was the result not of some imagined flight from oppression but rather of a sustained missionary effort (*da'wa*). This *da'wa* was in competition with that of the Ismailis, the Ishaqis, and various other Shi'i subgroups but was not clearly distinct from

14 See 'Ali 'Abbas Harfush (d. 1981), *Al-Maghmurun al-Qudama' fi Jibal al-Ladhiqiyya* (Damascus: Dar al-Yanibi', 1996); Dib 'Ali Hasan, *A'lam min al-Madhhab al-Ja'fari "al-'Alawi,"* 3 vols. (Beirut: Dar al-Sahil li'l-Turath, 1997–2000); 'Ali Muhammad al-Musa, *Al-Imam 'Ali wa'l-'Alawiyyun: Dirasa wa-Tarikh wa-Tarajim* (Damascus: Dar al-Fatat, 2002); and Amil 'Abbas Al Ma'ruf, *Tarikh al-'Alawiyyin fi Bilad al-Sham: Mundhu Fajr al-Islam ila Tarikhina al-Mu'asir khilal Jami' al-'Usur wa'l-Duwaylat illati Marrat 'ala'l-Mintaqa al-'Arabiyya wa'l-Islamiyya*, 3 vols. (Tripoli: Dar al-Amal wa'l-Salam, 2013).

Imami Shi'ism until later medieval times, which explains why 'Alawi and Twelver Shi'i territory in Syria and Lebanon are to the present day perfectly contiguous without overlapping. The 'Alawi *da'wa* was probably the most important of these missions up to the early eleventh century, having the support of various local dynasties including the Hamdanids, the Tanukhids, and even the Fatimids, and therefore developed historically not as a "marginal" sect but as one of the most important currents in all of Islam; its cantonalization in the mountains of western Syria was above all the product of the Crusades, which spelled the effective end of the *da'wa* and increasingly forced the 'Alawis to organize themselves along tribal lines and seek the protection of their erstwhile competitors, the Nizari Ismaili emirs.

This process of inward turning, as chapter 2 will attempt to show, brought on an important internal debate about the limits of 'Alawi religious authority and orthodoxy, which were far more formative of the community than any supposed conflict with other Shi'i or Sunni tendencies; the medieval Arabic chronicles almost never mention the 'Alawi community, which, according to its own biographical sources, benefited from the indifference if not outright tolerance on the part of Ayyubid and Mamluk officials in the later Middle Ages. This chapter will furthermore focus on a punitive campaign against the 'Alawis of the Jabala region in 1318, which has often been taken as representative of general Mamluk policy against the 'Alawis, but which was in fact caused by a local tax revolt and only reinterpreted in later, "piety-minded" Sunni literature as a religious conflict. Ibn Taymiyya's famous fatwa, being one of the only Sunni sources to even mention the sect in this period, has come to be seen today as expressing the one and unchanging Muslim orthodox position on 'Alawism, when in fact Ibn Taymiyya himself was an outcast and his opinions demonstrably had no influence on Mamluk or Ottoman thought until the eighteenth century. A far better source on Mamluk "policy" toward the 'Alawis, I will argue in closing, would be early Ottoman tax cadastres, which perpetuated and institutionalized the Mamluk practice of levying 'Alawi-specific taxes, thereby formally recognizing the community.

The Ottoman cadastres are then examined in detail in chapter 3, both to demonstrate the extent of the Ottoman state's control over the region in the sixteenth century and to show that the Ottomans did not attempt to annihilate the 'Alawi population (as is claimed in local folklore) but rather to maximize their tax revenues, maintaining 'Alawi-specific dues but also emending or even forgiving taxes in areas in need of economic revival. The second part of the chapter will draw mainly on Ottoman executive orders to show that the imperial government perceived of brigandage in the coastal mountains committed by 'Alawis as a social and not a religious problem, repeatedly casting "uneducated" 'Alawi subjects as the victims of manipulation by more powerful figures and not discriminating against them on the basis of their religion.

Continuing in the same vein, chapter 4 will show that with the decentralization of Ottoman provincial rule in the eighteenth century, the authorities were happy to employ known 'Alawi families as government tax farmers in the region, who in turn benefited from the unprecedented development of commercial tobacco cultivation to become a veritable landed gentry; the chapter will argue that growing social disparities within the community, rather than oppression from without, led both to the increasing "tribalization" of 'Alawi society and to widespread 'Alawi migration toward the coastal and interior plains as well as to the colonization of the Hatay district in what is now Turkey.

Chapter 5 tackles the long nineteenth century and the period of Ottoman reform. It begins by showing that the 'Alawi notability increasingly came into conflict with semiautonomous local officials during the breakdown of Ottoman imperial authority at the start of the century, causing the community as a whole to be cast as heretics and outcasts from Ottoman society for the first time. Faced with increasing discrimination and abuse by provincial officials, 'Alawi feudal leaders nonetheless continued to support the diffuse authority of the Ottoman Empire over the intrusive statism of the Egyptian regime between 1832 and 1840. We go on to argue that the 'Alawi community was then increasingly subjected to repressive social engineering measures under the Tanzimat and the reign of Abdülhamid II, including military conscription and conversion. At the same time, however, while resisting efforts at assimilation, the 'Alawis nevertheless also began to avail themselves of the benefits of modern public schooling and proportional representation on newly instituted municipal councils, thereby finding their voice as a political community for perhaps the first time.

Finally, chapter 6 traces the continuing ambivalence of late Ottoman, French mandatory, and Turkish republican efforts to integrate the 'Alawi population into the modern state. After examining both Hamidian and Young Turk concepts of citizenship as applied, or not applied, to the 'Alawis, the chapter highlights the literary and intellectual "awakening" (*yaqza*) led on behalf of the community by a new class of 'Alawi intellectuals on the eve of World War I. Arising out of this watershed communal moment, it will be argued, the great 'Alawi resistance against the French occupying forces in 1918–21, far from constituting a parochial rejection of foreign authority or a local variant of Arab nationalism, as the literature alternately claims, was a coordinated effort with Turkish Kemalist forces and should therefore be understood as part of the "southern front" campaign (Güney Cephesi) of the Turkish "War of Liberation." The book closes with a comparative look at the different fates of the 'Alawi communities in postwar Syria and Turkey and suggests that 'Alawis in Syria were fundamentally divided over support for, and resistance against, the constitution of a separate "Alaouites" state under French rule, a dichotomy with important consequences during the treaty negotiations between France and Syria in 1936, with which this chronological purview ends, and arguably with echoes down to the present day. The 'Alawi population in southern Turkey, on the other hand, was subjected to radical, even racialized assimilation policies under the iron fist of the CHP, perhaps with the somewhat paradoxical long-term effect that they now constitute a more secure, self-aware sectarian minority within Turkey than do the 'Alawis in Syria.

There is obviously not one, linear progression of 'Alawi destiny from the arrival of the Khasibi *da'wa* in Hamdanid Aleppo to the independence of the modern Syrian and Turkish republics. The lived experiences of the 'Alawi community or communities, over a period of ten centuries and in countless distinct regional and political contexts, from the collapse of Fatimid rule over southern Syria to the Crusades, early state modernization under the Mamluks, the Ottoman conquest, integration into a world system economy and finally modern colonialism, were necessarily diverse. Rather than trying to impose a single interpretative framework or theme on this history, or treating it in isolation, this study aims to bring out the complexity, contingency, and changeability of factors affecting the 'Alawis' secular and multisecular rapport with Middle Eastern, Ottoman, and Syrian society at large. The sources emphasized here tell of fiscal exploitation, war, and migration but also of alliances between Bedouin and 'Alawis, promotions to government office, and intercommunal friendship. As all Syrians today will, in the medium to long term, have no alternative but to rebuild their country as well as their national community in one form or another, the lesson that 'Alawi relations with other groups and individuals were not historically determined by uniform animosity and inescapable oppression but were repeatedly characterized by accommodation, cooperation, and trust may yet be an important one.

* 1 *
THE NUSAYRIS IN MEDIEVAL SYRIA
FROM RELIGIOUS SECT TO CONFESSIONAL COMMUNITY (TENTH–TWELFTH CENTURIES CE)

The Nusayris or ʿAlawis constitute one of the oldest and most established confessional communities in what is today northwestern Syria and adjoining regions, but their history in premodern times is often conceived of in terms of the anomalous and the exotic. In the literature they are generally branded as an "extremist" branch or "offshoot" of more normal Shiʿism; members of a "heterodox" and covert "sect" who practice a "syncretic" religion with admixtures of Christianity, Zoroastrianism, and other belief systems, a "survival" from the past who suffered continuous "persecution" and thus took "refuge" in the coastal mountains, where they maintained themselves for centuries in "concealment" and through *taqiyya* (dissimulation). While each of these notions can be investigated on its own merits, it is the way in which they are linked and emplotted, usually to the exclusion of more prosaic historical themes, that has produced a narrative in which the ʿAlawi community's past appears wholly determined by religion, secrecy, and otherness.

The purpose of this chapter is to reexamine the early development of the ʿAlawi community and its situation in western Syria in the medieval period in the wider context of what might be termed Islamic provincial history. It starts from the premise that the conventional image of the "Nusayris" has largely been fashioned by elite historical sources whose discourse on nonorthodox groups is a priori negative but which, when read against the grain and compared with other sources, can yield a less essentializing, less conflictual account of the community's development. In particular, this chapter aims to show that the ʿAlawi faith was not the deviant, marginal phenomenon it has retrospectively been made out to be but, on the contrary, constituted, and was treated by the contemporary authorities as, a normal mode of rural religiosity in Syria. The first part will trace the genesis and early diffusion of Nusayri thought, mainly on the basis of secondary literature, but will attempt to situate this thought in the wider stream of Shi'i history and argue that Nusayrism simply represented the Syrian variant of medieval Twelver Shi'ism rather than a radical departure from it. The second part will take a closer look at the constitution of Nusayri/'Alawi society in geographic Syria. Drawing on a little-known 'Alawi biographical dictionary, it will examine the community's struggle with its Druze and Ismaili neighbors, its internal conflicts, and its reorganization along tribal lines following the intervention of Makzun al-Sinjari in the early thirteenth century.

GHULAT SHI'I ORIGINS

There is no self-evident starting point for writing the history of the 'Alawi community of Syria. Modern writers who equate 'Alawism wholeheartedly with Shi'ism tend to begin with the conflict over the Prophet Muhammad's succession and the battle of Siffin in the seventh century;[1] Western orientalists sometimes took the term "Nusayri" to be the Arabic diminutive of "Christian" (Arabic *Nasara*) and thus fondly conceived of the 'Alawis as a long-lost Christian tribe whose origins would of course predate Islam. While not accurate, this last view does raise the question of why the history of a given population need necessarily begin with its adoption of a particular religious creed, which is only one event on the timeline of its social and political evolution. This book will nevertheless take a conventional stand and begin with Muhammad ibn Nusayr and his teaching in the ninth century—not because these intellectual foundations should be seen as the one defining essence of 'Alawi identity throughout history but because, right or wrong, it is as "Nusayris" that they were usually perceived by outsiders, categorized, discriminated against, ruled, taxed, and written into the historical record.

The doctrine subsequently labeled Nusayri can be traced back to the ninth-century Baghdadi scholar and mystic Muhammad ibn Nusayr al-Namiri (d. 883), a close disciple of 'Ali al-Hadi (d. 868), the tenth Imam of the Imami (Twelver) Shi'i tradition, and of his son Hasan al-'Askari (d. 874), the eleventh and final visible Imam. According to the Nusayri/'Alawi creed, the latter entrusted Ibn Nusayr with a secret revelation of the true nature of God, of the imamate and of the created cosmos, and anointed him as the *bab* or "gateway" through which believers could arrive at the same mystical comprehension. Ibn Nusayr's doctrine, like the other *ghulat* or "ultra-Shi'i" ideas current in Iraq at the time, revolved around the belief that 'Ali ibn Abi Talib had not merely been the Prophet Muhammad's chosen successor but was

---

1 Al-Tawil, *Tarikh al-'Alawiyyin*, 120ff.; al-Musa, *Al-Imam 'Ali wa'l-'Alawiyyun*, 47–72; Al Ma'ruf, *Tarikh al-'Alawiyyin fi Bilad al-Sham*, 1:51–74.

in fact himself God. In the beginning of time the souls of the faithful had been celestial points of light worshipping 'Ali, but at one point they were cast down to earth and incarnated in physical bodies as punishment for refusing to obey Him. The objective of the true believer is thus to recognize 'Ali and return to his side in heaven; to this end 'Ali appeared to mankind in various forms through the eons, whereby his true essence (*ma'na*) was accompanied in each eon by a more outwardly prominent face (*ism* or *hijab*) as well as by a *bab*. In the Islamic cycle this triad was represented by the corporeal 'Ali, the Prophet Muhammad, and their (probably legendary) Persian companion Salman al-Farisi and continued in the line of twelve Imams and their respective associates, including and ending with Ibn Nusayr himself.[2]

Ibn Nusayr's deification of 'Ali and the Imams earned him the rejection of Hasan al-'Askari and later Shi'i theologians and legists, who branded his thought as *ghulat* or beyond the pale of acceptable Shi'ism and thus relegated Nusayrism to the rank of heresy with which it has been identified ever since. As is frequently the case in the study of religions, however, the orthodox mainstream, in this case of Twelver Shi'ism, was nowhere near completely formed in his time, and it is precisely in the period of Twelver Shi'ism's consolidation as an Islamic "church" in its own right, under the protection of the Shi'i Buyid dynasty in Baghdad in the eleventh century, that the first heresiographies defining Nusayrism and distinguishing it from correct Shi'ism make their appearance. Historically, Ibn Nusayr and other *ghulat* did not "split from" or "part ways with" the mainstream Shi'a, the views they espoused being no more or less heterodox at the time than those which were then—retroactively—made part of the normative Imami tradition. The term *ghulat*, as Marshall Hodgson observed, was a convenient label for any form of early Shi'i speculation that did not make it into the later canons, while many of the central features of Twelver Shi'ism, including the condemnation of the "two shaykhs" (i.e., the two caliphs) Abu Bakr and 'Umar, the refusal to admit the death of the last Imam, and the expectation of his return, were in fact *ghulat* beliefs before the wider community adopted them.[3] Conversely, the research of Mohammed Ali Amir-Moezzi suggests that many of the doctrines later identified with *ghulat* excess, such as the incarnation of God (*hulul*) or the transmigration of souls (*tanasukh*), were probably shared by the contemporary Imams themselves, who condemned the likes of Ibn Nusayr not for the content of their teaching but for disclaiming it publicly when it should have been kept secret (the fundamental meaning of *taqiyya*). Sects such as

---

2 Halm, "Nusayriyya," 8:145–48; Üzüm, "Nusayrîlik," 33:270–74.

3 Marshall Hodgson (d. 1968), "How Did the Early Shî'a Become Sectarian?," *Journal of the American Oriental Society* 75 (1955): 1–13; see also Wadad al-Qadi, "The Development of the Term Ghulāt in Muslim Literature with Special Reference to the Kaysāniyya" in *Akten des VII. Kongresses für Arabistik und Islamwissenschaft, Göttingen*, ed. Albert Dietrich (Göttingen: Vandenhoeck & Ruprecht, 1976), 295–319.

the Nusayris, Amir-Moezzi posits, may well hold the key to understanding what constituted "original" Shi'ism.[4]

If the formation of Twelver Shi'i orthodoxy has to be seen in terms of a historical process, the same is also true for Nusayrism itself. Many of the fundamental texts of Nusayri doctrine were also shared by other *ghulat* currents and predate Ibn Nusayr, such as the famous *Kitab al-Haft wa'l-Azilla* (Book of the Fall and the Shadows), while other elements such as the belief in seven cycles of cosmic time and the distinction between exoteric and esoteric meaning have cognates in, or are derived from, Neoplatonic philosophy and Eastern Christian Gnosticism.[5] Still other features of Nusayrism, most notably its ritual calendar, show Zoroastrian influences and were incorporated only subsequently by Ibn Nusayr's successors.[6] It has for these reasons become a common theme in the literature to describe Nusayrism disparagingly as "syncretistic," as if more established religions were not also historical amalgams of various older belief systems and influences. What is perhaps particular in the case of Nusayrism is that it would remain distinctive enough to not be absorbed into the general synthesis of Twelver Shi'ism (even though Ibn Nusayr himself continues to be cited as a legitimate source for some Imami hadith) but never acquired the sort of patronage that would have allowed it to institutionalize a Nusayri "college" and fix its own orthodoxy along the lines of the better-known Shi'i sects.

Ibn Nusayr's thought originated in the still amorphous confessional context of ninth-century Baghdad, where the Imams of the 'Alid line were venerated but viewed with suspicion by the 'Abbasid caliphs and surrounded by intimates who alternately saw them as emanations of the divine or potential leaders of a millenarian revolt. Ibn Nusayr's claim to be the true deputy of the eleventh and later the twelfth Imams was certainly considered plausible, seeing as he was their contemporary and associate; again it was only a century later under the Buyids that the idea of four "envoys" maintaining contact with the hidden Imam during the "lesser occultation" became the official and exclusive Imami dogma. Ibn Nusayr seems in particular to have been supported in his claim by the Banu Numayr (or Namir), a bedouin confederation based around Baghdad with which he himself was affiliated, and as such his mission was originally labeled "Namiri" and seen as a tribal as much as a religious movement. Despite the sectarian nature of his pro-Imami doctrine, he also had the support of the al-Furat family, a key pillar of 'Abbasid court and intellectual life in ninth-century Baghdad. Ibn Nusayr's

---

4 Mohammed Ali Amir-Moezzi, *Le guide divin dans le Shî'isme originel: aux sources de l'ésotérisme en Islam* (n.p.: Verdier, 1992), esp. 313–17.

5 Heinz Halm, *Die Islamische Gnosis: Die Extreme Schia und die 'Alawiten* (Zurich: Artemis, 1982).

6 Rudolf Strothmann, "Festkalender der Nusairier: Grundlegendes Lehrbuch im syrischen Alawitenstaat," *Der Islam* 27 (1946); Bar-Asher and Kofsky, *The Nusayrî-'Alawî Religion*, 112–13.

main opponents were neither the Sunni rulers nor what later coalesced into the Twelver Shi'a but rather another *ghulat* gnostic of Hasan al-'Askari's inner circle, Ishaq ibn Muhammad al-Nakha'i (d. 899) and his followers. Like the Nusayris, the Ishaqis deified 'Ali and considered their own leader his rightful deputy or *bab*; as such they were serious rivals for the loyalties of the early Shi'a, and this animosity carried over into Syria, where both sects eventually took root.[7]

The struggle between different *ghulat* currents to define correct belief was a key factor in their early diffusion but also raises the question of what historically constitutes "true" Nusayrism. After Ibn Nusayr's excommunication and death his teaching was perpetuated by Husayn ibn Hamdan al-Khasibi (d. circa 957). Khasibi openly embarked on a mission to convert the faithful throughout the region and is thus usually considered to be the founder of the "Nusayriyya" as an organized religious group. At the same time, seeking the patronage of the Buyids, he also cast himself as a regular Imami scholar and rejected some of the most basic *ghulat* doctrines, including the physical incarnation of God and the transmigration of souls. He furthermore took a clear stand against antinomianism, insisting that the allegorical interpretation of Islam inherent in Nusayrism does not dispense the believer from also conforming to the outward letter of the law and from praying, fasting, and so forth. Yaron Friedman, whose recent monograph provides the most complete account of the religion's development to date, has traced the many different and sometimes contradictory traditions represented in 'Alawi theological literature and argued that many key precepts were not at variance with Muslim orthodoxy: thus the manifestation of the divine in human form has to be, and indeed was, understood docetically (i.e., as being in appearance only), while accusations of heresy or antinomianism or the use of the label *ghulat* generally resulted from a superficial or facile comprehension of Nusayri mysticism on the part of its detractors.[8]

Nevertheless, it would be wrong to conclude that the accusations leveled against the Nusayris were simply baseless. While a part of Nusayrism's scriptural tradition may formally have rejected its more *ghulat* aspects, there is plenty of historical and anthropological evidence that various heterodox beliefs and practices were carried over into 'Alawi religiosity on the popular level. Medieval, early modern, and contemporary observers attest to the widespread enjoyment of wine, which Friedman states was restricted to small amounts at especially important religious ceremonies, and certainly the Ottomans made a point of controlling and taxing the Nusayris' wine production and distribution in the region (see chapter 3). This undercuts the notion that the Nusayris consistently denied or concealed their sectarian leanings; moreover

---

7 Halm, *Islamische Gnosis*, 278–82; Friedman, *The Nusayrī-'Alawīs*, 8–13.
8 Friedman, *Nusayrī-'Alawīs*, esp. 5, 61, 82–89, 194.

it raises the question of what sort of religion the average Nusayri actually observed on a daily basis. In particular, the theological treatises that have been passed down make little or no reference to the visitation of shrines and the veneration of holy figures such as the pre-Islamic prophet and fertility saint Khidr (Hızır), which then as now can be said to have been the basis of popular 'Alawi religiosity.[9] Anecdotes about the Nusayris using mosques which the Mamluk authorities built for them as stables (see chapter 2), even if exaggerated for effect, and numerous later observations that 'Alawis shunned mosque worship do indicate that pious Sunni Muslims throughout history found cause to criticize not only the mountaineers' theoretical ideas but also their concrete religious practices.

Beyond the anecdotal and anthropological indications that 'Alawi popular religion did not necessarily always conform to "orthodox" Nusayri thought, which was in any event reserved to the initiated elite, there is also biographical evidence that the community remained divided over what constituted correct belief even long after its establishment in northwestern Syria. The unpublished biographical dictionary *Khayr al-Sani'a fi Mukhtasar Tarikh Ghulat al-Shi'a*, while compiled in the early twentieth century, draws on a wealth of apparently authentic religious treatises and mystical poetry that have been preserved locally and whose authors' tombs are in part still extant and known; already of interest is that the name *ghulat* used in the title was obviously not always considered to be pejorative but could indeed be used as a mark of distinction by 'Alawis themselves.[10] The *Khayr al-Sani'a* contains numerous entries on both medieval and Ottoman-period scholars, the details of whose lives can sometimes provide a more day-to-day, personal impression of the debates and cleavages within 'Alawi society at the time. Among the conflicts these materials point to in the medieval period is one with the so-called Thamina, a branch otherwise unattested (or long-since silenced) in the more formal literature and which preached, or was accused of preaching, the incarnation of God in both living creatures and inanimate objects. In the early thirteenth century, as will be seen in the following chapter, this controversy over *hulul* (incarnation) resulted in one of the sharpest intracommunal conflicts in 'Alawi history. However, further splits such as the Murshidiyya movement in the early twentieth century also suggest that

---

9 Patrick Franke, *Begegnung mit Khidr: Quellenstudien zum Imaginären im traditionellen Islam* (Beirut: Franz Steiner, 2000); Hüseyin Türk, *Nusayrilik (Arap Aleviliği) ve Nusayrilerde Hızır İnancı* (Ankara: Ütopya, 2002); Procházka-Eisl and Procházka, *Plain of Saints and Prophets*; Laila Prager, "Alawi Ziyāra Tradition and Its Interreligious Dimensions: Sacred Places and Their Contested Meanings among Christians, Alawi and Sunni Muslims in Contemporary Hatay (Turkey)," *Muslim World* 103 (2013): 41–61.

10 Husayn Mayhub Harfush (d. 1959), *Khayr al-Sani'a fi Mukhtasar Tarikh Ghulat al-Shi'a* (Library of the Institut français du Proche-Orient, Damascus: photocopy of ms. dated 1991).

the social and intellectual evolution of 'Alawism remained ongoing and not constrained to any one period.

Ultimately there is little point in trying to determine, solely on the basis of religious texts, what constitutes "true" 'Alawism or which subcurrent of thought is closest to "original" Shi'ism. The formation of what would eventually be seen as the Nusayri sect of Syria was a long historical process, stemming from the ferment of *ghulat* thought and propaganda in ninth-century Baghdad and rooted, at least on an intellectual level, in even older gnostic and neoplatonic traditions. The categorization of "Nusayris" as a derivation, and therefore a heresy, occurred only ex post facto, as Shi'ism and Islam in general congealed into a few large churches defined by their 'Abbasid, Buyid, or Fatimid backers as canonical; Nusayrism nonetheless retained its attraction in some circles and was able to establish itself in parts of Iraq and Syria, as we will see presently. Its lack of direct political sponsorship, however, meant that it remained malleable and open to competing *ghulat* claims, local variations, and popular religious influences that are ignored in the formal theological literature and only hinted at indirectly in historical and biographical sources. This lack of institutionalization would play an important role not only in the Nusayri/'Alawi community's internal affairs but also in its relations with the (Sunni) Muslim state in Syria down to modern times.

THE NUSAYRI (KHASIBI) *DA'WA*

After Ibn Nusayr's death the nascent sect was led by Muhammad ibn Jandab, who still holds a place in the 'Alawi hierarchy of saints but is historically obscure and finds no mention in the *Khayr al-Sani'a*. He in turn was succeeded by 'Abdallah al-Jannan al-Junbulani (d. 900), a native of southern Iraq described as a Persian ascetic, who is also remembered as the teacher of several key scholars of the Imami tradition. While the Nusayris (or Namiris) at this point were only a small confrérie of *ghulat* gnostics trying to come to terms, like other Shi'is, with the occultation of the Twelfth Imam, this would change significantly under the leadership of one of Junbulani's students and compatriots, the already mentioned Husayn ibn Hamdan al-Khasibi. As with the more established Imami and Ismaili schools of Shi'ism, and again with parallels in the formation of other major religions, the disappearance of the last direct link with the divine, while experienced as a spiritual misfortune, actually had a liberating effect on the sect itself. In essence Khasibi was free to reformulate Nusayrism on his own cognizance, furthering its claim to represent the Imam's mystical heritage while appearing at least outwardly to bring it more in line with mainstream Shi'i thought, and also introducing new elements such as the observance of the Persian New Year celebration that would help win converts among the *mawali* (acculturated Arab-Persianate) society of Iraq and western Iran. Presenting the Nusayris as the one and only true Shi'a (*Shi'at al-Haqq*), Khasibi's missionary efforts can be seen as the origin of the 'Alawi confessional community as such.[11]

In their quest to assume the Imam's succession, the Nusayris of course had competition. This book has already referred to the Twelver Shi'a, whose leading *'ulama* (religious scholars) began to exercise a sort of communal deputyship in Baghdad, ultimately reminiscent of Sunnism itself, through the classification of hadith and the elaboration of a distinctive legal system. This, however, implied deferring the Imam's return to a hypothetical distant future and working within the parameters of the Sunni caliphate; it is certainly not fortuitous that the Twelver Shi'i–leaning Buyid dynasty could seize power in Baghdad and put the 'Abbasids under tutelage only after the "greater occultation" in 941 formally removed the threat of his return and intervention in state affairs. Not all Shi'is were prepared to give up their idealism, however, and it is precisely in this context that the Ismaili movement gathered force. The Ismailis were another *ghulat*-inspired dissident group which believed the true Imam had actually been Ja'far al-Sadiq's late son Isma'il, whose own son in turn would come back to lead the community to justice. Like the Nusayris, theirs was a mystical initiatory path, and their esoteric (*batini*) interpretation of Islam remains a defining feature of the religion down to the present day. However, the Ismaili movement, led by the obscure 'Abdallah of Khuzistan, quickly grew out of the socially disadvantaged *mawali* milieu in the late ninth century and started to crystallize wider political opposition against the 'Abbasids. From its headquarters in Salamya, near Hama on the edge of the Syrian desert, Ismaili propagandists spread the religio-political *da'wa* (call; mission) to the far corners of the empire, making new converts especially among the disenfranchised minorities in the mountains of northern Iran, Yemen, and North Africa. In 909 the chief missionary 'Ubayd Allah, claiming descent from 'Ali's wife Fatima and declaring himself to be the awaited Mahdi (Messiah), launched a successful Berber revolt against the 'Abbasids in Tunisia, which laid the basis for the establishment of an Ismaili Shi'i Empire over Egypt and parts of Syria that would last until 1171.

The Fatimid *da'wa* thus stood in direct opposition to that of Nusayrism, and indeed the Ismailis as well as the Druze, a derivation of Fatimid Ismailism, would constitute the Nusayris' most formidable challengers in western Syria in the following centuries. However, the political and intellectual climate created by the Buyids in Baghdad, on the one hand, and the Fatimids in Cairo, on the other, could only be favorable to the dissemination of various strands of Shi'i thought and calls to action. If the concept of *da'wa* has today become overwhelmingly identified with the Fatimids, lesser groups such as

---

11 Halm, *Islamische Gnosis*, 295–97; Friedman, *Nusayrī-'Alawīs*, 16–21; Al Ma'ruf, *Tarikh al-'Alawiyyin fi Bilad al-Sham*, 1:56.

the Nusayris, Ishaqis, and, one may speculate, the Hululis or Thamina were equally active in carrying their message of refusal and millenarian expectation to the masses. Khasibi, according to Nusayri tradition, had initially been imprisoned for several years by the governor of Baghdad before escaping to northern Mesopotamia and establishing a new center in the city of Harran. He returned to Baghdad shortly after the Buyids' seizure of power in 945 to organize the local community there, presenting himself as an Imami scholar but also addressing what would become one of the key texts of Nusayri doctrine, the *Risala Rastbashiyya*, to the Buyid prince Bakhtiyar. Despite (or because of) his success in Iraq, Khasibi left again a few years later to extend his mission to Aleppo in northern Syria. The religious-political testament he left to his deputy in Baghdad, 'Ali ibn 'Isa al-Jisri, constitutes another fundamental text for the 'Alawi faith.[12]

Aleppo proved to be particularly fertile ground for the expansion of the Nusayri *da'wa* in the later tenth century. Since 947 the city and its province had constituted a nearly autonomous emirate in the hands of the Hamdanids, an Arab tribal dynasty based in Mesopotamia that already held the governorship of Mosul. Much like the Buyids, the Hamdanids were using their military power to shore up the 'Abbasid caliphate even though they themselves had pronounced Shi'i leanings or were "Shi'is in some vague sense."[13] The Hamdanids had first made their name by fighting the Khariji sect as well as the Qarmatians, a radical dissident Ismaili faction that represented the greatest direct threat to the Sunni caliphs, and in seeking the Hamdanids' patronage Khasibi likely also hoped they would adopt Nusayrism as their official brand of Shi'ism. The court of Sayf al-Dawla al-Hamdani (d. 967) was certainly one of the most brilliant of the time, drawing poets and philosophers such as the famous Abu'l-Tayyib al-Mutanabbi from all over the Islamic world, and it is here that Khasibi completed his theological oeuvre, which would define the Nusayri religious canon. According to Moojan Momen's survey of Shiite biographical sources, Aleppo was a leading place of origin of Imami *'ulama* in the tenth–eleventh century (even surpassing Baghdad in the twelfth and still ranking third overall, after Hilla and Jabal 'Amil, as late as the fourteenth),[14] and it is likely the 'Alawis continued to flourish here as Imamism's elite mystical branch. Khasibi died in 957 or 969. His tomb, situated just outside

---

12 Halm, *Islamische Gnosis*, 296–97; al-Musa, *Imam 'Ali*, 99–103; Friedmann, *Nusayrī-'Alawīs*, 28–35; Al Ma'ruf, *Tarikh al-'Alawiyyin fi Bilad al-Sham*, 1:195–207.

13 Albert Hourani, *A History of the Arab Peoples* (Cambridge, MA: Harvard University Press, 1991), 39; Marius Canard, "Hamdānids," *Encyclopaedia of Islam*, new ed. (Leiden: Brill, 1971), 3:125–31.

14 Moojan Momen, *An Introduction to Shi'i Islam* (New Haven, CT: Yale University Press, 1985), 76, 84, 91, 97. On Shi'ism in medieval Aleppo, see also Ibrahim Nasrallah, *Halab wa'l-Tashayyu'* (Beirut: Mu'assasat al-Wafa', 1983), 17–110.

Aleppo to the north, while generally identified now with an Ottoman-era Muslim shaykh, was revered by ʿAlawis down to modern times.

There is no conclusive evidence that the Hamdanid dynasty itself embraced Nusayrism, but from their base in Aleppo Khasibi and his successor Muhammad ibn ʿAli al-Jilli (d. 1009) were able to spread the *daʿwa* throughout the Middle East. Bruno Paoli, the first historian to have studied the *Khayr al-Saniʿa* in some detail, has used the biographical entries of Khasibi's and Jilli's disciples to retrace the Nusayri mission in the tenth century and show that it was far more ramified than often assumed.[15] The community kept in contact with its branches in Harran and Baghdad but was also able to win adepts or establish cells in Cairo, Jerusalem, Hebron, Nablus, Ascalon, Gaza, ʿAyntab, Raqqa, Diyarbekir, Mardin, Tikrit, Rahba, ʿAna, Hilla, Najaf, and as far away as Iran and Yemen. Far from being restricted to marginal or rural groups, Nusayrism gained a significant following among the urban artisan classes, and Nusayri missionaries were also responsible for converting numerous Christians and Jews to Islam. Most important, the *Khayr al-Saniʿa* also suggests these missionaries were able to recruit a number of "secret disciples" among the political elite of the time, possibly even within the Hamdanid, Buyid, and Fatimid households. While not as visible as the more politically entrenched Imami and Ismaili Shiʿis, Nusayrism may at one point have constituted one of the principal or most influential sects of all Islam.

The following section will look at the consolidation of the Nusayri/ʿAlawi community in the mountain hinterland of Syria; here we can ask what happened to it in other areas reached by the *daʿwa*. In Baghdad as in Cairo, the Shiʿi heyday did not actually last very long. In 1055 Baghdad was taken over by the Sunni Saljuqs, whom the caliphs were glad to award the title of "sultan" or worldly ruler and thus finally be rid of the Shiʿi Buyids' influence. By now Imami Shiʿism was nonetheless sufficiently institutionalized as a religion and, in the shrine cities of Kazimayn (Baghdad), Najaf, and Qom, continued to spawn its own scholarly and legal tradition. There is no more word of the Nusayri community in Iraq, but it seems likely that it eventually melded into the mainstream of Imami Shiʿism. In Cairo, the Fatimids' capital after 972, the strength of the Ismaili *daʿwa* probably precluded the further development of Nusayrism, particularly after al-Hakim bi-Amriʾllah's (d. 1021) attempts to reform the religion with himself at its head gave rise to a new missionary movement, out of which the Druze sect was born. At the same time, in order to function as a legal system, Ismailism had had to shed some of its more esoteric aspects and incorporate much of the methodology of the Maliki school of jurisprudence, such that Egypt reverted rather easily to Sunnism after the fall of the Fatimid dynasty in 1171. Somewhat remarkably,

---

15 Bruno Paoli, "La diffusion de la doctrine nusayrie au IVe/Xe siècle d'après le Kitāb Hayr al-sanī'a du šayh Husayn Mayhūb Harfūš," *Arabica* 58 (2011): 19–52.

however, one of the leading government functionary families in late Fatimid Cairo seems to have been Nusayri-'Alawi. Tala'i' ibn Ruzzik (d. 1168), one of several successive Fatimid vezirs of Armenian origin, converted to Islam in the Lake Urmia region before entering the Fatimid dynasty's service around 1144. Both he and the "Banu Ruzzik," that is, his sons, brothers, and nephews with whom he exercised power as a team, first as governor of Ushmunayn and later as vezir, are noted in contemporary chronicles to have practiced Nusayrism and sponsored 'Alid shrines. Their close friend the Fatimid emir Abu'l-Hasan 'Ali ibn Zubd was also considered to be Nusayri.[16]

There is some evidence that Shi'ism continued to survive in Egypt after the Fatimid period on a popular level,[17] but it is unlikely in this context that Nusayrism was widespread or that it was preserved as a distinct, elite mystical initiatory path. Damascus and other urban centers in Syria, meanwhile, had been controlled only intermittently by the Fatimids, and they had been even less successful in imposing Shi'ism there than in Egypt.[18] Again there is nothing to suggest the Nusayri presence here effectively outlasted the so-called Shi'i century, as the unprecedented period of Fatimid, Buyid, and Hamdanid ascendancy over the Middle East has come to be known.

The areas where Nusayrism or other nonorthodox teachings were most likely to withstand the homogenizing effect of the institutionalization of both Shi'i and Sunni schools of law were those far from the Fatimid and 'Abbasid capitals of Cairo and Baghdad or other leading centers of Islamic scholasticism. Harran, for one, where Khasibi had established the first Nusayri cell outside of Baghdad, continued to play an important role for the community throughout the tenth century. Many Nusayri missionaries, including Jisri and Jilli, had been part of Khasibi's circle in Harran, and the Shu'ba family of scholars based in Harran were among the last whose religious authority was recognized throughout the Nusayri community in Syria and Iraq.[19] Around 962, however, Sayf al-Dawla removed the entire Shi'i population of the city in order to repopulate Aleppo, after a Byzantine attack had left his capital devastated, and this may also have hastened the end of Harran's Nusayri presence. The rural population around Harran, on the other hand, appears to have continued to subscribe to some form of Shi'ism and mounted a series of chiliastically inspired uprisings as the decline of Hamdanid authority began to throw the entire region into disarray in the first half of the eleventh century. The leaders of the largest of these revolts, which followed upon a particularly

---

16 Seta Dadoyan, *The Fatimid Armenians: Cultural and Political Interaction in the Near East* (Leiden: Brill, 1997), 10, 156–61.

17 Devin Stewart, "Popular Shi'ism in Medieval Egypt: Vestiges of Islamic Sectarian Polemics in Egyptian Arabic," *Studia Islamica* 84 (1996): 35–66.

18 Thierry Bianquis, *Damas et la Syrie sous la domination fatimide* (Damascus: IFÉAD, 1986–89), 211–12, 340–42, 684.

19 Friedman, *Nusayrī-'Alawīs*, 25, 45–47.

severe winter in 1032–33 and which was directed against Harran's Muslim and Sabean aristocracy, are not fully identifiable but are characterized in the sources as either *ashraf* or "'Alawis."[20]

In other rural areas it is even more difficult to ascertain to what extent 'Alawism survived. In the mountains of western Iran, Azerbaijan, and northern Iraq, the Ahl-i Haqq, whose existence as a religious community can be traced to the eighteenth century but whose origins go back much further and are evidently grounded in *ghulat* Shi'ism, may have had a connection with the Nusayri *da'wa*. Sharing many basic beliefs regarding the eons of cosmic time, the theophany of God, and the transmigration of souls, the Ahl-i Haqq and other similar groups in the region, labeled by their detractors as "'Ali-Ilahis" (deifiers of 'Ali), were frequently assimilated to the Nusayris in later texts.[21] Their divine avatars and religious rites differ somewhat from those of 'Alawism, with elements drawn from Zoroastrian and possibly Yezidi traditions, and no doubt reflect the influences of their Persian and Kurdish cultural milieu. While the two sects can thus not be equated, their common belief structure, eschatology, and veneration of the Twelve Imams suggest they developed out of the same general movement to bring *ghulat* Shi'ism to the disenfranchised rural populace in the tenth–eleventh century. Local Armenians such as the Banu Ruzzik who converted to Islam in this period almost all joined the Nusayris, Ali-Ilahis, or other sub-Shi'i sects.[22] Under the Saljuqs in the fourteenth century, the governors of both Erzincan and Bidlis in what is now eastern Turkey were reported to have been of the Nusayri *madhhab*.[23] While difficult to corroborate, the embrace of Nusayrism-'Alawism by Emir Makzun al-Sinjari and his army, who moved from the northern Iraqi borderland region to support and take control of the Syrian 'Alawi community in the thirteenth century (see below), was likely possible only if these populations already shared a close religious affinity.

The entire Middle Euphrates, a key conduit for the movement of people and ideas between Iraq, northern Mesopotamia, and Syria, likely came under the direct influence of 'Alawism. The *Khayr al-Sani'a* refers, for instance, to one of al-Jilli's spiritual heirs, Abu'l-Hasan ibn Kulayb, who was *naqib al-ashraf* (head of the corporation of 'Alid descendants) in an unnamed fortress on the Euphrates (most plausibly in northern Mesopotamia, since he died in Diyarbekir) in the eleventh century. When a local Sunni, so the

---

20 Stefan Heidemann, *Die Renaissance der Städte in Nordsyrien und Nordmesopotamien: Städtische Entwicklung und wirtschaftliche Bedingungen in ar-Raqqa und Harrān von der Zeit der beduinischen Vorherrschaft bis zu den Seldschuken* (Leiden: Brill, 2002), 56, 82, 91–93.

21 Vladimir Minorsky, "Ahl-i Hakk," *EI2*, 1:260–3; see also Matti Moosa, *Extremist Shiites: The Ghulat Sects* (Syracuse, NY: Syracuse University Press), 185–254.

22 Dadoyan, *Fatimid Armenians*, 14, 156, 159.

23 Ibn Fadlallah al-'Umari (d. 1349), *Al-Ta'rif bi'l-Mustalah al-Sharif*, ed. Samir al-Durubi (Karak: Mu'ta University, 1992), 44–45.

story goes, began to insult the *ashraf*, accuse 'Ali of having raped 'A'isha, and claim the 'Abbasids were better than the 'Alids, Abu'l-Hasan had him killed, dismembered, and thrown in the river.[24] Doubtless a better indication of the extent and influence of the Shi'i missions in the medieval period, of course, is the high concentration of (now largely forgotten) 'Alid sanctuaries in the region. According to the *Kitab al-Ziyarat* (pilgrimage manual) of 'Ali ibn Abi Bakr al-Harawi (d. 1215), alone in what is now Syrian territory there were shrines dedicated to 'Ali and/or his companions at al-Rahba, Busayra, Raqqa, and of course Siffin, site of the epic seventh-century battle between 'Ali and the Umayyads. At both Nusaybin (across the border in today's Turkey) and Raqqa there were additional sites where 'Ali's handprints or Husayn's severed head were thought to have been kept, and still others dedicated to the born and stillborn sons of Husayn.[25] Perhaps the most impressive of these monuments was the Mashhad of Khidr, one of several 'Alid shrines at Balis (on the Euphrates near present-day al-Maskana), which was constructed in 1076–77. Dominique Sourdel and Janine Sourdel-Thomine have argued that the invocation of the Twelve Imams on the highly ornate interior central hall frieze (which is preserved today in the National Museum in Damascus) proves the shrine was an Imami rather than a Fatimid-Ismaili site;[26] its dedication to the prophet-saint Khidr, at the height of the Nusayri-Khasibi *da'wa* in the region, however, raises the question if it should not be identified especially with the 'Alawi current of Imami Shi'ism.

The one place outside of geographic Syria (that is, the classical Roman province of Syria west of the Euphrates, not including today's Jazira) where Nusayrism per se unquestionably survived past the medieval period is 'Ana. Situated on the Euphrates approximately 100 km inside what is today Iraq, 'Ana had a Nusayri cell since at least the eleventh century, when some of Khasibi's disciples settled there from Aleppo.[27] In a thirteenth-century theological dispute pitting more orthodox 'Alawi scholars against the Hululi or "incarnationist" sect (see chapter 2), the latter's adherents are noted in part to have been merchants from 'Ana as well as from Basra and Mosul.[28] Hasan al-Ajrud, a scholar based near Latakia in the fourteenth century who is not mentioned in the *Khayr al-Sani'a* but whose introduction to an older

24 Harfush, *Khayr al-Sani'a*, 179.
25 'Ali ibn Abi Bakr al-Harawi, *Guide des lieux de pèlerinage*, trans. Janine Sourdel-Thomine (Damascus: Institut français de Damas, 1957), 136–44.
26 Dominique Sourdel and Janine Sourdel-Thomine, "Un Sanctuaire chiite de l'ancienne Balis," in *Mélanges d'Islamologie*, ed. Pierre Salmon (Brill: Leiden: 1974), 247–53. Other shrines dedicated to Khidr were located at Manbij and Dara. See also Stephennie Mulder, "Sunnis, Shi'is and the Shrines of the 'Alids in the Medieval Levant" (PhD diss., University of Pennsylvania, 2008), 20–60.
27 Harfush, *Khayr al-Sani'a*, 161, 164; Paoli, "La diffusion de la doctrine nusayrie," 32.
28 Harfush, *Khayr al-Sani'a*, 371; see also Harfush, *Al-Maghmurun*, 229.

FIGURE I.I. Frieze from the central hall of the shrine of Khidr, Balis (National Museum, Damascus)

treatise is included in the recently published *Silsilat al-Turath al-'Alawi*, was also originally from there.[29] 'Ana was ravaged during the Mongol invasions and later came under the effective rule of the Abu Rish bedouin emirate. Surprisingly, however, there are still references in Ottoman-era sources to an 'Alawi presence in the seventeenth century: the Cihannüma of the famous Ottoman geographer and bureaucrat Katib Çelebi (d. 1657) describes 'Ana as prosperous and home to many scholars and people of refinement and notes that "previously Nusayris lived in this area but today they are very few in number."[30] This would also substantiate the observations of Pietro Della Valle, who traveled through 'Ana on his way to India in the fall of 1616 and reported the existence of "an extravagant sect" native to the city whose members mixed in with the rest of the population but who neither prayed nor fasted and who kept their true beliefs hidden. He repeats his local informant's claim that the adherents of this sect secretly worshipped the sun and practiced communal incest, and he surmises (much like other Europeans) that they might thus be

---

29 Abu Musa and Shaykh Musa, eds., *Majmu'a al-Ahadith al-'Alawiyya, Silsilat al-Turath al-'Alawi* (Diyar 'Aql, Lb.: Dar li-Ajl al-Ma'rifa, 2008), 8:166; see also al-Tawil, *Tarikh al-'Alawiyyin*, 379–80.

30 Katib Çelebi, *Kitab-ı Cihannüma*, English trans. ed. Gottfried Hagen (New Haven, CT: Yale University Press, forthcoming). According to Gottfried Hagen, this portion of the text was composed by Abu Bakr Bahram al-Dimashqi (d. 1691). This might indicate that there was an 'Alawi presence in 'Ana even as late as the late seventeenth century, a time when the Ottoman imperial government was beginning to reassert more direct control over the region.

remnants of the Persian "Magi," but he does not appear to be aware that they might have been related to a much larger community in Syria. According to Della Valle, the sect was reviled by the Muslims of 'Ana, and its members were "severely punished" whenever they were unmasked. He cites one case where the Abu Rish emir has a book that had been seized from them burned in public, but it is not clear whether Della Valle learned this from hearsay or witnessed it himself during his stay in 'Ana.[31]

At the height of the "Shi'i century" the geographic reach of the Nusayri *da'wa* was thus quite significant. From its center first at Baghdad and later at Aleppo, the self-professed "true Shi'a" spread out everywhere the more mainstream forms of Imamism as well as Ismailism had taken hold or were making new inroads as the authority of the 'Abbasid caliphate weakened. This included impoverished rural and mountain areas where the radical, antinomian message of *ghulat* Shi'ism gave expression to prevalent social grievances, but also in more urban settings and even within some Shi'i dynasties where the initiatory path of Nusayri mysticism appealed to the highest educated elites. In many places this distinct teaching did not survive the normalization of Imami Shi'i theology and law, and with the upheavals wrought by the decline of Hamdanid rule, the coming of the Saljuqs, and finally the Mongol invasions, many 'Alawi communities lost touch with one another or were absorbed into the larger Shi'i tendencies. The fact that the Nusayri *da'wa* was part of the same great movement of Shi'i outreach as the Imamis, Ishaqis, Qarmatians, Fatimids, Druze, and others in the tenth and eleventh centuries, however, suggests not only that it was not as unusual or marginal in that time as it was later made out to be but that in the areas where it did take hold, 'Alawism might also be seen historically as the original local variant of "mainstream" Shi'ism rather than a schismatic departure from it.

THE CONVERSION OF THE SYRIAN HIGHLANDS

If the spread of the Nusayri *da'wa* from Baghdad to Aleppo and other urban centers can be traced with some precision, its dissemination in the highlands of northwestern Syria is considerably more obscure. For one, the nature of our textual sources does not provide much insight into the assimilation or adaptation of complex doctrines by a largely illiterate rural population, which probably occurred over a longer period of time and with more local variations and compromises than later historians allow. Just as important is the fact that the question of the 'Alawis' and other minorities' supposed

---

[31] Pietro Della Valle (d. 1652), *Voyages de Pietro della Vallé, Gentilhomme romain, dans la Turquie, l'Egypte, la Palestine, la Perse, les Indes Orientales & autres lieux* (Rouen: Robert Machuel, 1745), 2:202–4.

provenance has become extremely politicized in the modern era, as various groups have sought to construct themselves an ethno-confessional genealogy and assert their claims to a particular national identity in what is today Syria, Lebanon, and Turkey. In attempting to portray the 'Alawis as nothing other than Twelver Shi'is, native 'Alawi historians have by and large subscribed to the myth, first expounded by Shi'i writers in Lebanon in the early twentieth century, that the Shi'i community in Syria was originally established by the Prophet's companion Abu'l-Dharr al-Ghifari and can therefore be considered as one of the oldest in the Islamic world. In Muhammad Amin Ghalib al-Tawil's seminal *History of the 'Alawis*, first published in Beirut in 1924, not only Latakia but also the city of Antioch are presented as ancient centers of the community to which the 'Alawis have always longed to return, while Adana, Tarsus, and the Cilician plain are described as essentially 'Alawi settlements.[32] More recently, and partially in response to claims by opponents of the Asad regime that 'Alawis are fundamentally Iranian in origin (and therefore in political loyalty), Syrian writers such as Hashim 'Uthman or Amil 'Abbas Al Ma'ruf have sought to demonstrate their Arab tribal roots. Aside from again reinforcing the idea that 'Alawis are simply part of the wider Shi'a, this argument also mirrors the general trend among Lebanese Shi'i historians of recent years to insist on the ethnic Arab derivation of the entire community.[33]

Another problem arises from the confusing political situation in western Syria at the time of the Nusayri *da'wa*'s advent. Modern 'Alawi historiography has generally credited the Tanukhi dynasty with facilitating the implantation of the Shi'i/'Alawi community in the coastal highlands behind Latakia after the decline of the Hamdanids of Aleppo in the late tenth and early eleventh centuries.[34] The Tanukhis, one of the oldest Arab tribal confederations in the region, appear to have been invested with the governorship of Ma'arrat al-Nu'man (an important provincial center south of Aleppo) and Latakia by the 'Abbasids after their relatively late conversion to Islam in the eighth century. Little is actually known of the Tanukhis' reign in Latakia, other than that they too played host to al-Mutanabbi in the early tenth century, and that one of their branches later became a leading Druze dynasty in the Gharb mountains further south along the coast near Beirut. Around 930, however, al-Mutanabbi himself is thought to have launched a tribal-cum-religious revolt from Latakia, which then spread to Homs and the desert interior before

---

32 Al-Tawil, *Tarikh al-'Alawiyyin*, 382–86, 438; see also Cahit Aslan, *Fellahlar'ın Sosyolojisi: Arapuşakları, Nusayriler, Hasibiler, Kilaziler, Haydariler, Arap Alevileri* (Adana: Karahan Kitabevi, 2005), 26–27, 31–34.

33 Ja'far al-Muhajir, *Al-Ta'sis li-Tarikh al-Shi'a fi Lubnan wa-Suriya* (Beirut: Dar al-Milak, 1992), 67–89.

34 Hashim 'Uthman, *Ta'rikh al-Shi'a fi Sahil Bilad al-Sham al-Shamali* (Beirut: Mu'assasat al-A'lami, 1994), 25–46; Al Ma'ruf, *Tarikh al-'Alawiyyin fi Bilad al-Sham*, 1:295–300.

being put down by the Sunni Ikhshidid governor of Egypt.[35] This revolt, while not explicitly 'Alid or Shi'i, seems to have been inspired in part by the radical Ismaili Qarmatian movement (and earned al-Mutanabbi his sobriquet "the self-proclaimed prophet") and may suggest that *ghulat* Shi'i ideology had already begun to make inroads in the coastal mountains by this time.

In 947 western Syria was divided into two zones of influence: the North under the Hamdanids who had just seized power in Aleppo, and the South under the Ikhshidids (who would soon be displaced by the Fatimids). In practice, however, the entire coastal region soon fell to the resurgent Byzantines, who occupied the formerly key Christian city of Antioch from 969 to 1084 and whose rule extended into the mountain interior through the collaboration of local Arab chiefs recruited to their cause. The Nusayri *da'wa* may well owe its early progress in the area more to the benevolence or indifference of Byzantine sovereignty than to active Hamdanid support. The *Khayr al-Sani'a* notes several *da'i*s of this era who met and presumably tried to proselytize local notables in Antioch, including Abu'l-Fath al-Baghdadi, who traveled extensively in the region (and supposedly even ministered to the "vezir of Damascus" at Antioch) around 1018–19; or Abu'l-Khayr Ahmad ibn Salama al-Hadda (d. 1065–66), who was initiated in Iraq at the age of fourteen and continued to carry on missionary work throughout Syria until his death at the age of ninety.[36] Aside from the question of such accounts' reliability, however, there is also no indication that 'Alawism gained all that many converts in the surrounding countryside of Antioch, which remained far removed from the real 'Alawi heartland emerging around Hama. One of the oldest 'Alawi shrines in the Antioch area is dedicated to the eleventh-century poet and ruler of Banyas castle in southern Syria, 'Isa ibn Muhammad al-Banyasi,[37] but there was also a *maqam* (shrine) to his honor in Banyas itself—many famous 'Alawis had *maqam*s in several different places—and the one in Antioch may have been erected only when the area was colonized by 'Alawis in the later Ottoman period.

More important than Antioch is the question of Latakia and its region, which has long been seen as the original center of 'Alawism but which had also come under renewed Byzantine rule as early as 946. According to both al-Tawil and subsequent 'Alawi writers, the community was first established at Latakia by Abu Sa'id Maymun al-Tabarani (d. 1034). Al-Tabarani, who studied with al-Jilli in Aleppo and succeeded him as head missionary in Syria, was the last definitive scholar of 'Alawism, composing the still valid 'Alawi religious

---

35 Irfan Shahid, "Tanūkh," *EI2*, 10:190–92; Regis Blachère and Charles Pellat, "Al-Mutanabbī," *EI2*, 7:769–72; Nadim Nayif Hamza, *Al-Tanukhiyyun: Ajdad al-Muwahiddin (al-Duruz) wa-Dawruhum fi Jabal Lubnan* (Beirut: Dar al-Nahar, 1984), esp. 55–66.
36 Harfush, *Khayr al-Sani'a*, 197–200, 210–15.
37 Ibid., 253.

calendar and giving the teaching its final shape. Around 1007 al-Tabarani is reported to have been in Tripoli, and toward the end of his life he settled in Latakia.[38] Yaron Friedman dismisses this account and doubts that al-Tabarani would have migrated to Latakia,[39] yet this version of events is corroborated not only in the *Khayr al-Sani'a* but also by the fact that al-Tabarani's tomb was demonstrably located in Latakia: Already described by the Damascene scholar and traveler 'Abd al-Ghani al-Nabulusi in the late seventeenth century, the shrine was renovated in 1898 before being dismantled and moved to nearby Basnada to make room for the expansion of Latakia's port in 1988.[40]

If an 'Alawi presence in the city of Latakia can thus be traced to the eleventh century after all, it is less clear if the community's establishment in the mountains above Latakia is also datable to this period. In the early eleventh century the Jabal al-Rawadif, which designated the region approximately between the Nahr al-Kabir and the city of Banyas further south on the coast, was under the control of Nasr ibn Mushraf (or Musharraf) al-Radufi, a local Arab chief who alternately allied himself with and fought against the Byzantine occupiers. While the Muslim highland population, as stated, may already have harbored Shi'i proclivities, there is no actual evidence that Nasr himself abetted the *da'wa*.[41] A thirteenth-century 'Alawi treatise, on the other hand, names three other princely families of the region that did apparently patronize the community, namely, the Banu'l-Ahmar, the Banu'l-'Arid, and the Banu Muhriz. The Banu'l-Ahmar were based in the fortress of Platanus (Qal'at Muhalaba) just north of Qardaha, before handing it over to the Byzantines in 1031. The Banu'l-'Arid were known to be a minor dynasty based in the moutains west of Homs; the Banu Muhriz were the lords of both Marqab castle on the coast near Tartus, from which the crusaders evicted them in 1117, and Qal'at al-Kahf in the Jabal al-Bahra' region above Tartus, which they held until its capture by the Nizari Ismailis in 1137–38 (see below).[42] The Banu Muhriz, according to the *Khayr al-Sani'a*, also held Qadmus castle in the eleventh century when Abu'l-Khayr al-Hadda was received there by

---

38 Al-Tawil, *Tarikh al-'Alawiyyin*, 323–24.
39 Friedman, *Nusayri-'Alawis*, 40–42; cf. Harfush, *Khayr al-Sani'a*, 269–74.
40 'Abd al-Ghani al-Nabulusi (d. 1731), *Al-Haqiqa wa'l-Mujaz fi Rihlat Bilad al-Sham wa-Misr wa'l-Hijaz*, ed. Riyad 'Abd al-Hamid Murad (Damascus: Dar al-Ma'rifa, 1989), 187; see also Yasir Sari, *Safahat min Tarikh al-Ladhiqiyya* (Damascus: Wizarat al-Thaqafa, 1992), 199; Ghayad Ilyas Bitar, *Al-Ladhiqiyya 'ibra'l-Zaman: Min 'Usur ma qabla'l-Tarikh ila 'am 1963* (Damascus: Dar al-Majd, 2001), 2:148, 293–95.
41 See Bianquis, *Damas et la Syrie*, 480–82.
42 'Ali ibn Muhammad Ibn al-Athir al-Jazari (d. 1233), *Al-Kamil fi'l-Tarikh*, ed. Muhammad Yusuf al-Daqqaq (Beirut: Dar al-Kutub al-'Ilmiyya), 9:55–56; Al-Tawil, *Tarikh al-'Alawiyyin*, 331–33; Paul Deschamps, *Les châteaux croisés en Terre Sainte*, vol. 3: *La défense du Comté de Tripoli et de la Principauté d'Antioche* (Paris: Paul Geuthner, 1973), 335, 339; Bianquis, *Damas et la Syrie*, 482; Friedman, *Nusayri-'Alawis*, 48.

FIGURE 1.2. Ba'rin, with ruins of old village in foreground

Emir 'Abdallah ibn Ja'far ibn Muhriz.[43] A poem composed by another scholar on the occasion of a religious festival around the same time also praises the Muhriz dynasty, while Emir Nasih al-Dawlah Jaysh ibn Muhammad ibn Muhriz (d. 1105–06) is claimed as an important 'Alawi scholar in his own right.[44]

While Byzantine/local Arab rule may thus have provided a congenial context for the diffusion of 'Alawism, there is nothing to suggest that the community grew out from the coastal mountains near Latakia as it has appeared in retrospect. From Aleppo, as Bruno Paoli has shown, the movement first spread to nearby inland towns such as Sarmin, Salamya, Hama, and Homs,[45] and it appears to be from the latter two that it was first disseminated in the villages on the eastern piedmont of the Syrian coastal range, rather than from Latakia on the coast. A broad survey of the *Khayr al-Sani'a* suggests that the community was originally concentrated in the relatively low-lying villages just west of Hama (Ba'rin, Dayr Shama'il, Dayr Mama, etc.), in the Wadi al-'Uyun valley, and in the highlands around Tartus and Safita, and only began to have a noteworthy presence in the North around Jabala and then Latakia starting in the Mamluk period. Of the thirty-four

43 Harfush, *Khayr al-Sani'a*, 214.
44 Ibid., 277–80, 285–92.
45 Paoli, "La diffusion," 31–32, 34.

The Nusayris in Medieval Syria * 29

medieval scholars and other 'Alawi personalities whose place of residence and/ or interment we have been able to identify positively, nine lived in what is today the Syrian *muhafaza* (province) of Hama, one in Homs, twenty-two in Tartus, and only two in Latakia. From the fourteenth to the sixteenth century, on the other hand, at least twenty-six hailed from the province of Latakia, compared with twenty-eight for Tartus, Hama, and Homs combined.[46] In modern literature it has become commonplace to speak of the entire region as the "'Alawi mountains." In fact the Syrian coastal range, much like the Lebanese range of which it is an extension, is made up of multiple, often very steeply cut ridges and valleys, stretching over 120 km from the Nahr al-Kabir in the North to the 'Akkar plain in the South. In premodern times, when access and communication across its different sectors were even more difficult and tenuous than today, the region was not uniformly identified with the 'Alawi or Nusayri sect but was known by more limited, partially overlapping, and now largely forgotten local names such as Qusayr, Jabal al-Rawadif, Jabal al-Akrad, Jabal Sahyun, Jabal Summaq, Jabal al-Bahra', and Jabal al-Lukkam.[47] The northernmost part of the range near Latakia, furthermore, is conspicuously devoid of older religious shrines such as those that mark the landscape further south between Hama and Tartus. The conversion of a large part of the mountain population to 'Alawism was likely an extremely long, drawn-out process, one that the *Khayr al-Sani'a* suggests began at the southeastern extremity and progressed northward and inward only over the course of several centuries.

Beyond Hama and Homs, the most important zone of early 'Alawi extension was further south along the Syrian coast and coastal interior, where other midsize towns played a key role in relaying what had essentially been an urban intellectual movement into the rural hinterland. A key 'Alawi center in the eleventh century, for example, seems to have been Tyre (Sur) in today's South Lebanon. One of al-Jilli's disciples, Muhammad al-Mashat "al-Suri," is reported to have made several converts there before being killed and buried in a sepulcher near Ascalon.[48] Al-Khabbaz al-Suri (literally, the baker from Tyre) was a celebrated poet who died in Tyre in 1034–35; the indefatigable Abu'l-Khayr al-Hadda visited Tyre as well as Sayda and met with several *ikhwan* (spiritual brothers) there during his travels.[49] Another native of Tyre, 'Ali al-Hasan Hayyaj al-Suri, became a leading 'Alawi theologian of the time and apparently even tutored 'Ismat al-Dawla (d. 1058–59), a scion of the Fatimid dynasty in Egypt whom the *Khayr al-Sani'a* also claims as an 'Alawi.[50]

46 Harfush, *Khayr al-Sani'a*, 312–658 and 659–944, respectively.
47 Ibrahim 'Umayri, *Silsilat al-Jibal al-Sahiliyya: Qissat al-Tarikh al-Ghamid wa'l-Hadarat al-Mansiyya* (Damascus: al-Aqsa, 1995), 17–24; Bitar, *Al-Ladhiqiyya 'ibra'l-Zaman*, 171–78.
48 Harfush, *Khayr al-Sani'a*, 178.
49 Ibid., 207–8, 210.
50 Ibid., 243, 266–68.

The other major 'Alawi center in this region was Tiberias in what is now northern Israel. Both Abu'l-Khayr al-Hadda and Abu'l-Fath al-Baghdadi included the town in their itineraries and met with several scholars named in the *Khayr al-Sani'a*.[51] Most important, of course, Tiberias was the home of al-Jilli's disciple and successor, Abu Sa'id Maymun al-Tabarani. Born in 961–62 or 967–68, Tabarani memorized the Qur'an early in his life and acquired a following while still in Tiberias, but he also came into conflict with members the Ishaqiyya sect (apparently once smacking their leader Abu Dhuhayba Isma'il ibn Khallad of Baalbek across the head with a chair after a dispute in a tailor shop). He went to study with al-Jilli in Aleppo, as indicated, and eventually took his mission to Latakia where he died in 1034 (or 1035–36).[52] 'Alawism clearly also took hold in the countryside around Tiberias, notably in Banyas in what is now the Israeli-occupied Golan Heights (not to be confused with Banyas on the Syrian coast near Tartus), where the previously cited 'Isa ibn Muhammad al-Banyasi (d. after 1029) was in possession of the local citadel. The uncle of the *Khayr al-Sani'a*'s author visited al-Banyasi's *maqam* there in the late nineteenth or early twentieth century and reported that it was supported by a large *waqf* (religious bequest) that also included a mosque and a hammam. Al-Banyasi left numerous descendants, and many of the Khayyatin tribe (see below) traced their ancestry to him.[53] The 'Alawi presence in the Golan-Tiberias area is the only one outside of northern Syria to have survived down to modern times. The German traveler Ulrich Jasper Seetzen reported visiting three Nusayri villages in the vicinity of Banyas in 1806, 'Antit ('Ayn Fit), Za'ura, and 'Ayn Ghajar, whose population practiced farming and did not have any places of worship other than perhaps a shrine near 'Ayn Ghajar.[54] John Lewis Burckhardt also noted several Nusayri villages further northeast along the flank of Mt. Hermon (Jabal al-Shaykh) near Burqush in 1810.[55] The town of Ghajar, situated just to the northwest of Banyas on the Hasbani River, is still 'Alawi-inhabited today. Seized by Israel from Syria in 1967, it was for all practical purposes integrated into Israel's occupation zone in southern Lebanon in 1982, then fenced off after Israel's withdrawal from most of Lebanon in 2000, and it now remains, along with its 'Alawi population, under direct Israeli control.[56]

---

51 Ibid., 200, 212.
52 Ibid., 179, 269–74; al-Tawil, *Tarikh al-'Alawiyyin*, 263–64.
53 Harfush, *Khayr al-Sani'a*, 253–56.
54 Ulrich Jasper Seetzen (d. 1811), *Reisen durch Syrien, Palästina, die Tranjordan-Länder, Arabia Petraea und Unter-Aegypten*, ed. Friedrich Kruse (Berlin: G. Reimer, 1854–1859), 1:325–26, 4:154–55.
55 John Lewis Burckhardt (d. 1817), *Travels in Syria and the Holy Land* (London: John Murray, 1822), 50.
56 Asher Kaufman, "'Let Sleeping Dogs Lie:' On Ghajar and Other Anomalies in the Syria-Lebanon-Israel Tri-Border Region," *Middle East Journal* 63 (2009): 539–60.

What accounts for the gap between the two compact zones of 'Alawi settlement (or rather conversion) in the Latakia-Tartus mountains in the North and the Golan–Mt. Hermon region in the South? Tripoli, Sayda, and Tyre, after all, had significant Shi'i populations and served as centers of the Nusayri-Khasibi *da'wa* in the eleventh century. Tripoli especially was governed beginning around 1070 by the Banu 'Ammar, a family of Twelver Shi'i *qadis* who were at times affiliated with the Fatimids and at times recognized the 'Abbasid caliphs. The 'Ammarids are said to have built a magnificent library at Tripoli and are seen as having presided over a golden age of Shi'ism in the area before the crusader conquest; the local district name Zanniyya (or Danniye in local dialect) probably alludes to the 'Alid esotericism of the medieval population there.[57] The rural hinterland of these cities, however, over time became identified exclusively with the Twelver Shi'is (a group often referred to in Lebanese historiography as the Matawila or Métoualis). In particular, the rugged, isolated mountains behind Sayda and Tyre known as Jabal 'Amil gained a reputation as one of the foremost centers of Imami theology and legal thought in the later Middle Ages, with numerous 'Amili scholars migrating to Iran in the sixteenth century to establish Twelver Shi'ism as the Safavid state religion. In Tripoli, the highlands as far south as Beirut were inhabited by Matawila pastoralists and would be held as a tax fief by the Twelver Shi'i Hamada clan through much of the Ottoman period; further inland, the Bekaa Valley was ruled over by emirs of the Twelver Shi'i Harfush family, while towns such as Baalbek and Karak Nuh remained important local centers of Imami learning.[58]

What is noteworthy about these historical areas of 'Alawi and Imami implantation is that they are almost perfectly contiguous without overlapping. The main area of 'Alawi population in Syria extends as far south as the plain of 'Akkar and the northernmost limit of Mt. Lebanon, where it directly adjoins the area formerly controlled by the Hamadas and other Shi'i tribes, while in the South the 'Alawi villages around Banyas and Mt. Hermon lie just adjacent to the area traditionally regarded as Jabal 'Amil. Perhaps as a result of this complementarity, there are also no documented instances, unlike the case with the 'Alawis' Ismaili and Druze neighbors, of contact, let alone friction, between 'Alawi and Imami groups. Khasibi, like other *ghulat* proponents, dismissed ordinary Twelver Shi'is as "falling short" (*muqassirin*) in their devotion to the Imams, but he never directly attacked the Syrian Shi'a or its leaders. It thus seems a real possibility that 'Alawis and Imamis initially constituted a single, indistinguishable confessional bloc, born of the same

---

57 'Uthman, *Tarikh al-Shi'a*, 47–80; Yahya Qasim Farhat, *Al-Shi'a fi Tarabulus: Min al-Fath al-'Arabi ila'l-Fath al-'Uthmani* (Beirut: Dar al-Malak, 1999).

58 Werner Ende, "Mutawālī," *EI2*, 7:780–81; Stefan Winter, *The Shiites of Lebanon under Ottoman Rule, 1516–1788* (Cambridge: Cambridge University Press, 2010).

Twelve-Imam Shi'i *da'wa* (with both gnostic and nongnostic elements), and crystallized into distinct sectarian groups only with the development of a more literate, legalist Imami Shi'ism, especially in Jabal 'Amil and the Bekaa, in the later medieval period. That the Lebanese Shi'i scholar Muhammad ibn Makki, whose execution in Damascus in 1384 and subsequent consecration as "al-Shahid al-Awwal" ("the first martyr") would mark a key step in the construction of a Twelver Shi'i sectarian identity, was suspected of adhering to "Nusayri" doctrines and practices (chiefly the consumption of wine) and of associating with Nusayris in Tripoli may be indicative of the fact that some contemporaries continued to conflate Imami and 'Alawi Shi'ism.[59] After the decline of Shi'i dynastic rule in Syria and the fall of Aleppo to the Zangids in 1144, Jabal 'Amil would emerge as the principle intellectual and cultural pole of a Shi'ism increasingly defined by its scholasticism, self-containment, and family ties to the shrine cities of Iraq. Until that time it is likely that, just as Nusayrism did not represent an actual departure from the wider Shi'i mission in the medieval period, there was no practical distinction between early 'Alawi and Imami communities in rural western Syria.

BETWEEN THE ISMAILIS AND THE CRUSADERS

If the 'Alawis' relationship with the Imami community in Syria was one of synergy, that with the various currents of Ismaili Shi'ism was considerably more problematic. The Ismaili *da'wa*, as already indicated, was the most active Islamic mission in the early medieval period and as such would have been the Nusayris' main competitor in the region. Ismailism had begun to spread in Syria since around the middle of the tenth century, when the *da'wa* was headquartered in the city of Salamya near Hama, but we have no evidence of its influence in the coastal highlands before the Fatimid conquest. Even then, Ismaili thought first seems to have been disseminated in the area in the form of Druzism, an initiatory sect (similar in its relationship to Ismailism as 'Alawism is to Twelver Shi'ism) deifying the Fatimid caliph al-Hakim bi-Amri'llah and whose own *da'wa* was launched among the disenfranchised poor of Egypt and the Syrian hinterland beginning in 1017.[60] The earliest known exposé of the 'Alawi faith is actually a polemical treatise penned by the chief Druze missionary Hamza ibn 'Ali (d. after 1021), in which he rips their "heretical" beliefs but also sows the accusation that they practice incest

---

59 Ibn Hajar al-'Asqalani (d. 1449), *Inba' al-Ghumr bi-Anba' al-'Umr* (Damascus: Maktabat al-Dirasat al-Islamiyya, 1979), 1:228.
60 Salim Hasan Hashi, *Al-Khazana al-Tarikhiyya fi'l-Isma'iliyyin wa'l-Duruz* (Beirut: Lahad Khatir, 1985); Farhad Daftary, *The Ismā'īlīs: Their History and Doctrines* (Cambridge: Cambridge University Press, 1990), 195–200.

and other sexual abominations, an accusation that was then taken over eagerly and uncritically by later polemicists. The Druze and ʿAlawis in fact shared many similar doctrines and initiatory practices, both referred to themselves as al-Muwahhidun (i.e., true believers in the unity of God), and both targeted the same rural population in Syria, so that this treatise may well reflect the functional rivalry the two groups had entered into in the region in the early eleventh century.[61]

The Ismaili mission per se seems to have made itself felt in western Syria only in the following century and resulted from a propaganda effort directed from Iran rather than from Fatimid Egypt. This new impulse was the result of the schism of the Ismaili sect after the death of the Fatimid caliph al-Mustansir in 1094, whereby the "Nizari" branch under the leadership of its chief *daʿi* Hasan-i Sabbah (d. 1124) founded a confederation of principalities centered on the mountain redoubt of Alamut in northern Iran that was militantly opposed to the Saljuq dynasty ruling the region and strove to establish a second center in the coastal interior of Syria to better pursue its religious and political activism among the local Muslim populations. Among the first Nizari Ismaili missionaries of importance in Syria was Bahram al-Asadabadi, who came from Iran and began to attract notice in Aleppo and Damascus in 1126, "moving about from place to place, followed by the most ignorant masses and foolish commoners, stupid peasant rabble having neither reason nor religion," before the Burid *atabeg* (prince) of Damascus, wishing both to contain Bahram's influence and perhaps to win him as an ally in his own struggle against the local Sunni establishment, gave him the castle of Banyas in the Golan as a base of operations.[62] Banyas had up to that point probably still been in ʿAlawi hands, but over the next years Bahram undertook to renovate the citadel, sent out further *daʿi*s to convert the local population, and brought several other strongholds in the region under his control. In 1128 he entered the Wadi al-Taym, the upper valley of the Hasbani River to the west of Mt. Hermon—which the Syrian-Kurdish chronicler Ibn al-Athir indicates was shared by Nusayris and Druze at the time—in order to fight the local emir, but he was himself killed in the engagement.[63] Thereafter

---

61 Antoine Silvestre de Sacy (d. 1838), *Exposé de la religion des druzes, tiré des livres religieux de cette secte* (Paris: Imprimerie Royale, 1838), 2:518–21, 559–86. See also Bar-Asher and Kofsky, *Nusayrī-ʿAlawī Religion*, 153–61; Friedman, *Nusayrī-ʿAlawīs*, 43–44.

62 Hamza ibn Asad Ibn al-Qalanisi (d. 1160), *Tarikh Dimashq 460–555*, ed. Suhayl Zakkar (Damascus: Dar Hassan, 1983), 342; see also Daftary, *Ismāʿīlīs*, 374–76; Jean-Michel Mouton, *Damas et sa principauté sous les Saljoukides et les Bourides 1076–1154* (Cairo: Institut Français d'Archéologie Orientale, 1994), 130–33; Taysir Khalaf, *Al-Julan fī Masadir al-Tarikh al-ʿArabi: Hawliyat wa-Tarajim* (Damascus: Dar Kanʿan, 2005), 25–26.

63 Ibn al-Qalanisi, *Tarikh Dimashq*, 351–53; ʿAli ibn Muhammad Ibn al-Athir al-Jazari (d. 1233), *Al-Kamil fiʾl-Tarikh*, ed. Muhammad Yusuf al-Daqqaq (Beirut: Dar al-Kutub al-ʿIlmiyya), 9:235–36, 250–51.

the Ismailis were persecuted in Damascus and driven out of Banyas but succeeded in ensconcing themselves in the northern coastal mountains instead. In 1132–33 they purchased the castle of Qadmus, and in 1136–37 the inaccessible mountain redoubt of al-Kahf near Tartus; in 1140–41 they seized the castle of Masyaf, which would serve as their principal center, and over the next years they took eight more fortresses (al-Khawabi, al-'Ulayqa, al-Munayqa, al-Rassafa, Abu Qubays, Platanus, Marqab, and Sahyun), which became known as the *qila' al-da'wa* or "castles of the *da'wa*."[64] These of course lay in close proximity to the 'Alawi villages of the region.

There are unfortunately few reliable sources on the nature of 'Alawi-Ismaili relations at this time. Qadmus castle is reported to have been purchased by the Ismailis from the Arab chieftain Sayf al-Mulk Ibn 'Amrun, which suggests that it would not have been in 'Alawi hands anymore at that point; Ibn 'Amrun himself, however, had apparently recovered Qadmus from the Franks with the help of the local 'Alawi population only the year before.[65] The tomb of Qadmus's former emir, the 'Alawi-friendly 'Abdallah ibn Muhriz, was venerated by both Ismaili and 'Alawi visitors before falling into neglect in modern times.[66] What seems clear is that the 'Alawi community came under increasing pressure with the arrival of Rashid al-Din Sinan (d. 1193), the new chief *da'i* in Syria (known in Western sources as the "old man of the mountain"), under whose leadership the Nizari Ismailis would emerge as one of the key forces involved in the crusader wars. The *Khayr al-Sani'a* claims that Ahmad al-Khorasani, who was one of al-Jilli's spiritual "sons" (and must therefore have lived in the first half of the eleventh century), incurred Rashid al-Din's wrath and was forced to flee to Egypt after converting a group of Khorasanian Ismailis to the 'Alawi *madhhab*; the fact that Rashid al-Din himself was born in Basra in 1133 and came to Syria around 1162 suggests, of course, that this biographical note is anachronistic and was probably redacted in the light of later tensions.[67] An Ismaili legend from the twelfth century, for its part, affirms that "the Nusayris are known to be enemies of lord Rashid al-Din"; on the other hand, the same source also indicates that many 'Alawis rallied to Rashid al-Din's cause against the crusaders, with an entire 'Alawi clan joining his forces at one point at Masyad (Masyaf) castle.[68]

---

64 Muhammad Abu Talib al-Dimashqi (d. 1327), *Nukhbat al-Dahr fi 'Aja'ib al-Barr wa'l-Bahr*, ed. August Mehren (Leipzig: Harrassowitz, 1923), 208; Daftary, *Ismā'īlīs*, 377; 'Uthman, *Tarikh al-Shi'a*, 81–84.

65 Daftary, *Ismā'īlīs*, 377.

66 Harfush, *Khayr al-Sani'a*, 214.

67 Ibid., 177; Farhad Daftary, "Rāshid al-Dīn Sinān," *EI2*, 8:442–43; Nasseh Ahmad Mirza, *Syrian Ismailism: The Ever Living Line of the Imamate* (Surrey, UK: Curzon, 1997), 24.

68 Stanislas Guyard, "Un grand maître des Assassins au temps de Saladin," *Journal Asiatique* series 7, 9 (1877): 435, 445–48, 480, 486–88; Dussaud, *Histoire et religion*, 23.

Like the 'Alawis, Rashid al-Din's own alliance policy was dictated by strategic rather than doctrinal considerations. Fiercely opposed by the Sunni Zangid dynasty of Aleppo, Rashid al-Din initially maintained good relations with the Frankish lords present on the coast and in the coastal mountains, but he allied himself with the Zangids when both he and they came under threat by the new strongman of Egypt and southern Syria, Salah al-Din ("Saladin") al-Ayyubi, in 1171. After the demise of the Zangids in 1174, Ismaili *fida'is* (self-sacrificing fighters) twice attempted to assassinate Salah al-Din, but they finally entered into a tactical alliance and together turned their sights on the crusaders. The 'Alawis, meanwhile, had their own reasons for seeking to expel the Frankish invaders. During the First Crusade the armies of Raymond de Saint-Gilles had marched from Ma'arrat al-Nu'man into the mountains near Masyaf, "where they killed a large number of the people known as Nusayris." These 'Alawis, *gens effera et maliciosa et Christianis infesta*, as they are later characterized, then attempted to block the crusader advance on Tripoli but were crushed.[69] Many 'Alawi communities would subsequently have fallen under Frankish rule in the coastal areas or become tributary to crusader warlords. The only historical account we have in this regard is a report from the archbishop of Tyre, reproduced in the Ottoman-period Maronite chronicle *Tarikh al-Azmina*, which claims that some sixty thousand Nusayris from the castles and villages around Tartus converted to Christianity in 1173 and were thereby exempted by order of King Amalric of Jerusalem from paying their previous tribute of two thousand *dirham*s to the Order of Knights Templar. Outraged, the Knights murdered Abu 'Abdallah, the messenger who had transmitted the royal letters to the Nusayri shaykhs in the mountains of Tripoli; King Amalric, however, had the killer arrested, and he died soon thereafter in prison.[70]

The Ayyubids, of course, reconquered Jerusalem in 1187 and were able to capture much of the coastal interior the following year. The Ismailis were expelled from several of their castles and, while they continued to maneuver diplomatically between the Franks and the Ayyubids in the region, never played as important a role again in the thirteenth century as they had under Rashid al-Din. From what little evidence we have, it would nonetheless seem that the 'Alawis' situation remained difficult. Al-Tawil reports that the famous poet Shaykh Hasan of Kafrun, a village near Mashtal Hilu which may have remained under crusader control, sent a stirring plea for help to his coreligionists in Egypt in 1203–04 to deliver the 'Alawis from the Franks,[71]

---

69 Bar Hebräus and Burchard de Mont-Sion, cited in Dussaud, *Histoire et religion*, 21–22.
70 Istfan Duwayhi (d. 1704), *Tarikh al-Azmina 1095–1699*, ed. Fardinan Tawtal al-Yasu'i (Beirut: Catholic Press, 1951), 73; see also Hashim 'Uthman, *Tarikh al-'Alawiyyin: Waqa'i wa-Ahdath* (Beirut: Mu'assasat al-A'la li'l-Matbu'at, 1997), 31–32.
71 Al-Tawil, *Tarikh al-'Alawiyyin*, 357.

FIGURE 1.3. Shrine of Shaykh Hasan, Kafrun (renovated in 1983)

but this account is tellingly not corroborated in the *Khayr al-Sani'a* nor by a text displayed at Shaykh Hasan's *maqam* in Kafrun (which in any event appears to be based on the same sources as the *Khayr al-Sani'a*).[72] Perhaps more important, various 'Alawi traditions relate that the community came under further pressure from both the Ismailis and the Kurds in the following years, leading them to seek outside military aid. Al-Tawil suggests that these "Kurds" were themselves recent refugees in the region fleeing turmoil further east,[73] but it may also be possible to identify them simply with the Ayyubid dynasty's Kurdish forces. Where the 'Alawi tradition is in agreement is that these troubles heralded the intervention of Emir Makzun al-Sinjari, a poet, religious scholar, and statesman from northern Iraq who would unite and radically transform the 'Alawi community in the thirteenth century.

MAKZUN AL-SINJARI

Abu'l-Layth Hasan ibn Yusuf al-Makzun al-Sinjari (d. 1240) stands as perhaps the most prominent individual in 'Alawi history. Remembered above all as a mystical poet, Makzun also left several religious treatises that were extensively commented on in the 'Alawi literature and that marked another key

72 Harfush, *Khayr al-Sani'a*, 386; on later miracles worked by Shaykh Hasan, see also Hasan, *A'lam*, 3:29–31.
73 Al-Tawil, *Tarikh al-'Alawiyyin*, 358.

FIGURE 1.4. Abu Qubays castle

step in the formulation of 'Alawi doctrine. Most important for our purposes, however, Makzun led or accompanied a new movement of immigration into the western highlands which enabled the 'Alawi community to stand up to its local challengers but also divided 'Alawi society along tribal lines that are still seen as pertinent today. Much of Makzun's oeuvre is extant and has been investigated by modern scholars. Among his most significant innovations in 'Alawi thought are his criticism of excessively monist Sufism, his apparent rejection of *taqiyya* (dissimulation), and his embrace of jihad as a duty for each believer,[74] suggesting that his overall contribution be seen as that of "secularizing" 'Alawi society and incorporating it more clearly as a sectarian community.

As a historical personage Makzun al-Sinjari remains somewhat enigmatic. Born around 1188 or 1193 in the Jabal Sinjar in what is today the northern border region between Syria and Iraq, Makzun is widely believed to have been the scion of a local dynasty of emirs who came to western Syria with a vast army to save the beleaguered 'Alawi population. He is mentioned in one non-'Alawi medieval source, the biographical dictionary of 'Abd al-Razzak ibn

---

[74] Harfush, *Khayr al-Sani'a*," 387–412; As'ad Ahmad 'Ali, *Ma'rifat Allah wa'l-Makzun al-Sinjari* (1972; Damascus: Dar al-Su'al, 1990); Paul Nwyia, "Makzun al-Sinjari, poète mystique alaouite," *Studia Islamica* 40 (1974): 87–113; Friedman, *Nusayrī-'Alawīs*, 51–56.

Ahmad Ibn al-Fuwati (d. 1323), a philologist and director of the Mustansiriyya library in Baghdad who had lived in Azerbaijan and may have had firsthand knowledge of the Jabal Sinjar. The only known manuscript of this text is heavily damaged but does reveal that the author may have had a personal connection with Makzun and saw him as a scholar and poet rather than as a political or military leader.[75] Hamid Hasan, whose 1972 study using both published sources and unpublished 'Alawi manuscripts constitutes the first critical biography of Makzun, points out that his family was not among the Saljuq or Ayyubid governors in the region and may simply have been local notables; on the other hand, another source claims that Makzun married the daughter of the Ayyubid "king" of Aleppo prior to settling in the coastal highlands.[76] According to the 'Alawi accounts, the most complete of which is that attributed to a certain Ahmad al-Qadi, it was the people of Banyas and the Latakia region who first sent messengers to Makzun asking for help around 1213–14; following a massacre of 'Alawis at Sahyun castle, Makzun arrived with a force of some twenty-five thousand fighters but was initially defeated by the Ismailis and Kurds and returned to the Sinjar. After things did not improve for the 'Alawis, he came back a second time in 1223, taking control of Abu Qubays castle just to the west of Hama and making it his base, while his son seized the ancient 'Alawi village of Ba'rin nearby.[77] Abu Qubays' link with the al-Makzun family is still in evidence today, the village's two main shrines being dedicated to putative descendants of the emir, Shaykh Musa Rabti ibn Muhammad ibn Kawkab and Shaykh Yusuf ibn Kawkab.[78] Makzun himself died either in Tal'afar (near Mosul) while returning to the Jabal Sinjar in 1240 or in Damascus; he is thought to be buried in the Kafr Susa district of Damascus.

Makzun is regarded as having been well-versed in Imami Shi'i thought, but it is not certain whether he was in fact of the Nusayri-Khasibi school before coming to Syria. As already suggested, however, the rural population of the Sinjar had certainly been exposed to *ghulat* Shi'ism, and the influx of Sinjari soldier-immigrants who accompanied Makzun and quickly assimilated into the 'Alawi community in the western highlands may have been the campaign's most important long-term consequence. Several sources indicate that this

75 'Abd al-Razzak ibn Ahmad Ibn al-Fuwati, *Majma' al-Adab fi Mu'jam al-Alqab*, ed. Muhammad al-Kazim (Tehran: Danishmendan-e Islami, 1995), 1:152 (no. 130); see also Franz Rosenthal, "Ibn al-Fuwati," *EI2*, 3:769–70.

76 Hamid Hasan, *Al-Makzun al-Sinjari bayna'l-Imara wa'l-Sha'r wa'l-Tasawwuf wa'l-Falsafa* (Damascus: Dar Majallat al-Thaqafa, 1972), 1:58–76; see also 'Ali, *Ma'rifat Allah*, 2:325–28.

77 See Yunus Hasan Ramadan, manuscript cited in 'Ali, *Ma'rifat Allah*, 2:337–49; al-Tawil, *Tarikh al-'Alawiyyin*, 359–66; Mahmud al-Salih, *Al-Naba' al-Yaqin 'an al-'Alawiyyin* (Beirut: Mu'assasat al-Balagh, 1961), 150–52.

78 Harfush, *Khayr al-Sani'a*, 473–75; further information provided by Abu Amjad Ibrahim Isma'il, Abu Qubays.

FIGURE 1.5. Entrance to the shrine of Shaykh Musa al-Rabti, Abu Qubays

wave of immigration might already have begun beforehand, coming either from the Sinjar and cities of the interior such as ʿAna, Aleppo, and Kilis or from ʿAlawi-inhabited coastal areas such as Adana and Mersin in Cilicia, which were laboring under crusader occupation.[79] In any event, several of the main tribal groupings with which ʿAlawis would later claim affiliation, including the Haddadiyya, the Matawira, the Muhalaba, the Numaylatiyya, and the Banu ʿAli, are commonly believed to be the descendants of Makzun's troops and their families.[80]

There is perhaps a problem in trying to trace a large portion of the ʿAlawi population back to certain tribes associated with Makzun al-Sinjari, inasmuch as their names and supposed affiliations never actually figure in the sources of the time or in the biographical traditions compiled by Harfush and others and likely gained currency only in the later Ottoman period (see chapter 4). The least one can say, however, is that the arrival of Makzun and

---

79 Yusuf Ramadan, Ahmad al-Qadi, and others cited in ʿAli, *Maʿrifat Allah*, 2:341; al-Tawil, *Tarikh al-ʿAlawiyyin*, 357.

80 Al-Tawil, *Tarikh al-ʿAlawiyyin*, 361; see also Lyde, *Asian Mystery*, 50–54; ʿAli ʿAziz al-Ibrahim, *Al-ʿAlawiyyun bayna al-Ghuluw wa'l-Falsafa wa'l-Tasawwuf wa'l-Tashayyuʿ* (Beirut: Muʾassasat al-Aʿlami, 1995), 12–27.

his forces marked a watershed in 'Alawi history not simply by enabling the sect to survive in an increasingly hostile environment but, in the process, by redefining the boundaries of the group as such. While Makzun himself may have left his mark more as an intellectual than as a military commander, the very fact of his leadership in this time of crisis helped unify and consolidate 'Alawi society in a way it had never been before. If 'Alawism had previously been a question of subscribing to a particular set of esoteric Shi'i beliefs, either personally or mediated through the poets and village shaykhs of the rural hinterland, it now became understood more in terms of belonging to a particular clan, following a particular emir, resisting particular Frankish and orthodox Muslim enemies, and defending a particular collective. Where 'Alawism had once been a religious ideal or calling open to anyone, by the early thirteenth century it was becoming the outward, secular identity of an increasingly circumscribed, self-conscious political community.

CONCLUSION: THE BIRTH OF A MINORITY

The pressures brought to bear on the 'Alawi community by the crusader, Ismaili, and Ayyubid threat in the twelfth century and Makzun al-Sinjari's response effectively spelled the end of the Nusayri-Khasibi *da'wa*. This call or mission had begun as an initiatory sect in ninth-century Baghdad, as a mystical elite in the Shi'i imams' entourage whose esoteric, partially antinomian reading of Islam tapped into a deeper tradition of speculative theology and gnosis at a time when neither Shi'ism nor Sunnism had yet been codified into their respective orthodoxies. The antimainstream character of Nusayri and other strands of *ghulat* thought, however, not only appealed to an urban intellectual class but also served to focus and express the social grievances of recently and perhaps still incompletely Islamized rural populaces—the *mawali* of southern Iraq, the tribesmen of Azerbaijan and the Sinjar, the newly settled bedouin of the upper Euphrates and Aleppo—for whom metempsychosis, saint worship, and millenarian expectation were already familiar, rational themes. As such the 'Alawi message was by no means unusual or marginal but an integral part of Islam's vast and multifaceted movement of expansion, conquest, and mission across the Middle East and North Africa in the ninth and tenth centuries.

In Syria the 'Alawi *da'wa* was actively supported by the Shi'i Hamdanid dynasty of Aleppo and was quickly able to establish a foothold in nearby towns. Perhaps more important, however, was the de facto religio-political vacuum, a general atmosphere of receptiveness toward unorthodox and *ghulat* ideas among the peasant population and at least of tolerance on the part of its secular lords, in much of the Syrian interior at this time. In the remote, inaccessible coastal highlands, where neither Byzantine, Hamdanid, nor Fatimid sovereignty had any real traction, 'Alawism could spread under the benign eye of local tribal chieftains such as the Tanukhis and the Banu Muhriz, themselves only vaguely Muslim and indifferent to the scholastic, sectarian debates taking place in Cairo or Baghdad. This epic age of freedom and possibility, however, necessarily ended with the crusades, when the coastal highlands were transformed from a societal backwater into a physical and ideological battleground, contested by the imperial armies of Latin Christendom, the militant Ismaili order of *fida'i*s, and finally the Zangids and Ayyubids as agents of a resurgent Sunnism. Under pressure fiscally and militarily, the 'Alawis pulled together under whatever leadership they could, supporting the Ismaili grand master when necessary and then submitting to the new authority of Makzun al-Sinjari, in order to protect their community against the outside world. The 'Alawis emerged from the twelfth century as something they had not been before but that would define them for the rest of history, as a "minority."

As such the 'Alawis are again perhaps not so much an exception as a typical illustration of the general evolution of society in the medieval Middle East: they were not especially "heterodox" before 'Abbasid and Buyid religious scholars established the standards of orthodoxy; they were not overly "sectarian" before being confronted by their Druze, Ismaili, Imami, and finally Sunni counterparts; and they were not particularly "tribal" before being forced to organize militarily as such in the twelfth century. The very fact that the Nusayris or 'Alawis hardly figure in any chronicles of the time suggests they were not yet perceived as something noteworthy, as a heretical or tribal "Other," within wider Muslim society. Henceforth, however, their constitution and self-perception as a confessionally defined, compact community ultimately reflects the growing importance of the state and state authority in later medieval Islam—an element which, in the guise of Mamluk and Ottoman rule, would continue to have a major impact on their situation in Syria well into the modern period.

* 2 *
BEYOND THE MOUNTAIN REFUGE
'ALAWISM AND THE SUNNI STATE
(THIRTEENTH–FIFTEENTH CENTURIES)

The practical end of the Shi'i *da'wa*, the arrival of Makzun al-Sinjari and his tribesmen in the early thirteenth century, and the integration of the coastal highlands into the Ayyubid and then the Mamluk empires mark the transition of 'Alawism from a universal religious calling to a closed confessional community. Hardly distinguishable from other religious movements in the past, it is in the literature and bureaucracy of the resurgent, centralized state that the "Nusayris" are first identified as a distinct societal group and written into the historical record. Not surprisingly, the written traces of a group henceforth defined by its divergence from the new norms of orthodox Sunnism are overwhelmingly negative, the term "Nusayri" essentially being equated by the scribes and scholars of Damascus with rebellion, dissoluteness, and tax liability. As a result, modern historians drawing on these sources have largely seen the 'Alawis' relationship with the later medieval state as one of essential and necessary conflict, of violence, injustice, and unreflected, unremitting, and undifferentiated "persecution."

The persecution paradigm informs one of the most tenacious clichés of 'Alawi history, that of the "mountain refuge." This view, often presented as an unequivocal geographic fact, holds that the inaccessible coastal highlands of Syria and Lebanon have served since the dawn of time as a haven for minority sects fleeing religious oppression in the cities and plains of the interior. As Kamal Salibi argued in his masterful critique of Lebanese historiography, however, this view is simply not borne out by the available evidence: neither did the Druze, Ismaili, Shi'i, or 'Alawi populations come to the region in order to escape actual persecution elsewhere, nor was the Islamic state really that unable to establish its dominance over the mountains.[1] The 'Alawis became concentrated in the coastal highlands (a region frequently if imprecisely

---

1 Kamal Salibi, *A House of Many Mansions: The History of Lebanon Reconsidered* (Berkeley: University of California Press, 1988), 133–50.

referred to in the literature as the "Ansariyya" range, from the local dialectical pronunciation of "al-Nusayriyya") in the late medieval period, not because they had to flee there as refugees but because the Ayyubids and Mamluks were successfully institutionalizing Sunnism everywhere else—for the most part building mosques, endowing madrasas, and fostering Sunni *fiqh* (jurisprudence), rather than chasing down minor rural heresies. The 'Alawis, as put perhaps most elegantly by the late Patrick Seale, were essentially "a remnant of the Shi'i upsurge which had swept Islam a thousand years before: they were islands left by a tide which had receded."[2]

This chapter addresses what can in effect be seen as the consolidation of the 'Alawi community in its newfound "compact" form. The receding tide of Shi'ism, it will argue, did not expose the 'Alawis to a Sunni or Mamluk backlash but on the contrary permitted the community to cement both its religious leadership and identity and its position vis-à-vis the state. On the local level, as will be shown in the first section, the thirteenth century was witness to an intense debate over the limits of 'Alawi orthodoxy, a debate that helped give the doctrine its final form and established the *'ulama* as the community's uncontested religious authority but in doing so also removed religion from the sphere of everyday life. The subsequent sections will again draw on the *Khayr al-Sani'a* as well as a wide range of medieval literature to explore the relationship between the 'Alawi community and the Mamluk state beyond the trope of enmity and persecution. Like the Ismailis, the 'Alawis can be shown to have been well integrated in the Mamluk administration in northwestern Syria, actively benefiting from both state institutions and the sympathy of individual authorities. One of the few documented instances of sectarian violence, a tax-cum-millenarian revolt in the district of Jabala in 1318, has only in retrospect and on the basis of a nearly hegemonic Muslim religious historiography come to be seen as typical of the 'Alawis' fate under Mamluk rule; in particular, this chapter warns against adopting Ibn Taymiyya's incendiary fatwas or any other purely normative texts as an actual measure of the 'Alawi experience. From biographical anecdotes and theological disputations to Mamluk chancery manuals and Ottoman tax registers, sufficient evidence exists to show that the 'Alawi mountain was anything but closed off from the world around it.

THE DEFEAT OF THE ISHAQIS AND THE HULULI-THAMINA CONTROVERSY

Among the 'Alawis' chief rivals in northwestern Syria, as already noted, were the Ishaqis, a rival *ghulat* Shi'i sect whose early development in the Shi'i circles

---

[2] Patrick Seale, *Asad of Syria: The Struggle for the Middle East* (Berkeley: University of California Press, 1988), 8.

of Baghdad and whose *da'wa* in many ways paralleled those of 'Alawism. Like Ibn Nusayr, their eponymous founder Ishaq ibn Muhammad al-Nakha'i had considered himself the one true "gateway" (*bab*) to the Imams, and in the tenth and eleventh centuries his disciples competed for the hearts and minds of the same lower-class urban and rural populations in Syria and elsewhere as the Nusayri-Khasibi missionaries.[3] An entry in the *Khayr al-Sani'a* suggests that there was still a substantive Ishaqi community in Basra, living in conflict with other *ghulat* and Mansur al-Hallaj-inspired groups in the Euphrates delta region, as late as the thirteenth century.[4] Regarding Syria, we have already referred to the violent confrontation between the 'Alawi leader Abu Sa'id al-Tabarani and the chief Ishaqi missionary, Abu Dhuhayba Isma'il ibn Khallad of Baalbek, around the turn of the eleventh century, when both sects were based mainly in Aleppo. Around the time when Tabarani left Aleppo to take up residence in Latakia, Abu Dhuhayba also appears to have moved to the coast, first to Jabala and then to Latakia too. Al-Tawil writes that there was actually no fundamental religious dispute between them, only that Tabarani was known for his piety and asceticism while Abu Dhuhayba was seen as rich and corrupt. Abu Dhuhayba began to harass the fledgling 'Alawi community until he was hunted down and killed by the emir of the Banu Hilal, an 'Alawi-affiliated tribe from the Orontes region; his putative tomb on the coast near Latakia (known as Qabr Shaykh Qar'ush) remained an object of loathing among local 'Alawis down into modern times.[5] The negative image of Abu Dhuhayba may well be a literary trope (inspired, among other things, by his cognomen, "the guy with a small fortune in gold," and the popular attribution of the otherwise obscure Shaykh Qar'ush tomb), but the 'Alawis' aversion to the Ishaqi leader appears to be religiously underpinned as well: in the *Majmu' al-A'yad*, the authoritative calendar of 'Alawi ritual compiled by Tabarani in the eleventh century, there is an explicit call to curse Abu Dhuhayba.[6]

Did the Ishaqis continue to pose a concrete challenge to the 'Alawi community in Syria in the later Middle Ages? Eliminating them may have been a primary objective of Makzun al-Sinjari: following his conquest of the highlands west of Hama in 1223, Makzun is said to have convened a theological debate with the Ishaqis, after which he executed their leaders and had all their books burned.[7] The conflict with Ishaqism is also evoked in one

---

3 See Heinz Halm, "Das Buch der Schatten: Die Mufaddal-Tradition der Gulat und die Ursprünge des Nusairiertums (I)," *Der Islam* 55 (1978): 237, 242–53.

4 Harfush, *Khayr al-Sani'a*, 610–11 (see also below).

5 Al-Tawil, *Tarikh al-'Alawiyyin*, 262–64, 324.

6 Strothmann, *Festkalender der Nusairier*, 222; see also Edward Salisbury, "The Book of Sulaimân's First Ripe Fruit, Disclosing the Mysteries of the Nusairian Religion," *Journal of the American Oriental Society* 8 (1866): 239–40; Friedman, *Nusayrī-'Alawīs*, 43, 295.

7 'Ali, *Ma'rifat Allah*, 2:346; al-Tawil, *Tarikh al-'Alawiyyin*, 262.

of the best-known and most studied 'Alawi treatises of the medieval period, the *Munazara* ("Disputation") of Shaykh Yusuf ibn al-'Ajuz al-Nashshabi of Aleppo. Dating from the second half of the thirteenth century, the *Munazara* relates the author's voyage to the region of Homs and Hama and his confrontation of a number of local shaykhs whom he deems to have a corrupted understanding of 'Alawism. The main targets of Nashshabi's criticism are the heirs of Abu Dhuhayba and Ishaqi thought, which he qualifies as *hululiyya* or the belief in the separation of 'Ali from the divine *ma'na* and his physical incarnation in the Imams. Nashshabi's trip culminated in a bitter theological debate with a certain Shaykh Rabi'a of Suwayda and his followers at Asfin village in the hills northwest of Homs, which apparently lasted for several days and came to an end only through a trick on the spiteful Rabi'a's part: learning that the local Ayyubid governor happened to be in town, Rabi'a put out word that Nashshabi was attracting a throng of people who were more devoted to him than to the governor, serving wine and hosting Nashshabi without the governor even being invited. When the governor, apparently intrigued, sent for Nashshabi, Rabi'a's men warned the latter to pack his books and flee because the governor "was out to get him." Nashshabi and his party thereupon went into hiding in the surrounding villages rather than continue the disputation.[8]

Yaron Friedman, noting that the *Munazara* makes no mention whatsoever of Makzun al-Sinjari and his presumed elimination of the Ishaqis (and that the governor apparently in question, Zayn al-Din Qaraja al-Salahi, died in 1207), proposes that the text be more properly dated to the late twelfth or early thirteenth century. However, the reference to a connection with the famous Ayyubid governor may again be a literary trope more than conclusive evidence of the treatise's historical context, and the suggestion that a later copyist simply misstated the date given for Nashshabi's trip by one *hijri* century (in which case it would have fallen, somewhat improbably, in November/December 1189, or barely a year after the region's reconquest by Salah al-Din) is at best speculative.[9] More circumspectly, Meir Bar-Asher and Aryeh Kofsky have cautioned that Nashshabi may have characterized the "heterodox" views espoused by Rabi'a and others as Ishaqism only for polemical purposes, and that they do not really prove the continuing existence of the Ishaqi sect at the time; the *Munazara* would primarily reflect an "internal Nusayri dispute" over the nature of 'Ali and, more broadly, "the religious and theological ferment that existed in the first centuries of the consolidation of the Nusayri religion."[10]

---

8 Yusuf ibn al-'Ajuz al-Nashshabi al-Halabi, *Munazara*, Bibliothèque Nationale, Paris (Richelieu): Ms. Arabe 1450, fol. 111a–112b.

9 Friedman, *Nusayrī-'Alawīs*, 48–50.

10 Bar-Asher and Kofsky, *Nusayrī-'Alawī Religion*, 13.

The *Khayr al-Sani'a* provides some important details on "al-Raddad al-Halabi" (the Aleppine refuter)—as Nashshabi is more widely known in the 'Alawi tradition—that allow the *Munazara* to be dated with a higher degree of certainty. The version of the treatise consulted by Harfush apparently indicates that the author was born in 1225–26 and held his final dispute in Asfin in July 1267, or well after the disappearance of the actual Ishaqis in Syria, while additional biographical sources give his date of death as 1284–85.[11] Perhaps more important, the various narrative strands that have gone into the *Khayr al-Sani'a* support the impression of an overall period of heightened religious strain and controversy from the late twelfth through the thirteenth century. One may argue, however, that this was not simply the "ferment" of an immature religion but rather an essential struggle over the definitions of orthodoxy, deviance, and ultimately authority, which accompanied the transformation of the 'Alawiyya into a sectarian community in this time. The detection and repression of *hululi* belief in all its forms, whether as an identifiably Ishaqi teaching or as a more vernacular version of the incarnationist ideas that are inherent in all *ghulat* Shi'ism, were a key part of this process.

If confronting the actual Ishaqi sect may have played a role in securing Makzun's leadership after his conquest, it appears the community was rife with many other conflicts that did not leave as much of an imprint in later theological writing but are nonetheless evoked in the *Khayr al-Sani'a*. Harfush refers, for instance, to Mahmud al-Sufi, a supposed pupil of the famous Abu'l-Fath al-Baghdadi, who around 1164 penned a "Treatise of Guidance and Counsel." In this treatise he among other things berated "the obstinate ones" involved in an otherwise obscure argument over the attributes of the *ism* (the outward manifestation of the divine), and in which both sides had begun to treat the other as liars and heretics.[12] Another contemporary scholar, Khalifa ibn 'Abdallah al-Tanukhi (d. 1184–85), also seems to have been troubled by a decline of orthodox standards and particularly by the rise of debased, popular beliefs among ordinary 'Alawis:

> In our day and age people have appeared who have embraced illegal innovations [*bida'*] and forgone piety.... There are those who make Khasibi the *bab* of the Almighty, those who believe the sun is the ultimate *ma'na* (divine essence) and lord of the scriptures (*rabb al-mathani*), and those who say that whoever is powerful and can perform miracles ... is the best of the believers, and these people make their religion a mockery and a joke, destroying the faith and poisoning the faithful.[13]

11 Harfush, *Khayr al-Sani'a*, 628.
12 Ibid., 275–77.
13 Ibid., 294.

The 'Alawi intellectuals' discomfiture with popular or folk theology is also brought to the fore in the *Munazara*. Nashshabi recounts that he and an unnamed teacher set out to various villages in the Hama-Homs area, the Jabal al-Manasif hills just to the west of Homs and the coastlands, and found the "people of the mountain" especially to have deviated from the true path laid out by Khasibi. Their view of religion had essentially become materialistic, with some even claiming that God lives among them since he is merely an incarnation of the divine and a medium of expression, and the *ma'na* cannot express itself except through speech, which is a human attribute.[14] Nashshabi in particular accuses the Hatimiyya or "followers of Hatim" of believing 'Ali to be a created, corporeal manifestation of God, ascribing them "*hululi*" ideas not unlike those once attributed to the Ishaqis. This seems contradictory, however, since "Shaykh Hatim" himself is referred to favorably in the *Munazara*,[15] and indeed because he is remembered in the 'Alawi tradition as the very paragon of orthodoxy. According to the *Khayr al-Sani'a*, Hatim al-Tubani—better known as al-Judayli—was born in the Banyas (Syria) region around 1180. He was soon recognized as a gifted poet (writing, among other things, of his apparent time in Frankish captivity) but found acclaim above all for his treatise refuting Sinan Qazhal, disciple of Saraj al-Din, whom he met and debated at Homs around 1218–19. The *Risalat al-Tajrid*, since considered a classic in the field, among other things condemns Sinan for claiming that the eyes, ears, nostrils, and mouth represented various prophets—a standard article of *hululi* belief according to Judayli.[16]

Like the enmity with the Ishaqis, Judayli's efforts again have to be seen in the broader context of the struggle against incarnationist elements or influences in 'Alawism. The *Tajrid*, for example, makes direct reference to several other contemporary scholars' treatises attacking Sinan's master Saraj al-Din, someone who appears to have traveled around Iraq disseminating *hululi* teachings and acquired a following in Baghdad and 'Ana in the late twelfth century. The most prominent of these (mainly Iraqi) orthodox 'Alawi scholars, Safi al-Din 'Abd al-Mu'min al-Fariqi, produced a paragraph-by-paragraph rebuttal of a propaganda tract written by Saraj al-Din after meeting with a group of his disciples in 'Ana and sent a copy of this rebuttal to Judayli in Syria around 1201, which the latter drew on in his famous refutation of Sinan.[17] Another important treatise from the time attributes incarnationist beliefs to the "heretics" (*mulhida*) without explicitly mentioning Saraj al-Din or any particular group.[18]

14 Nashshabi, *Munazara*, fol. 69a.
15 Ibid., fol. 112b, see also Bar-Asher and Kofsky, *Nusayri-'Alawi Religion*, 16.
16 Harfush, *Khayr al-Sani'a*, 369–71; see also Harfush, *Al-Maghmurun*, 229–30; Hasan, *A'lam*, 1:38–41.
17 Harfush, *Khayr al-Sani'a*, 193–96, 293, 308–10, 420–21, 425–36, 605–6.
18 Ibid., 312–16.

Judayli's *Tajrid* came out in 1223–24—perhaps not coincidentally the same year as Makzun al-Sinjari's conquest of the 'Alawi highlands in Syria and defeat of the local Ishaqis. This, however, did not mark the end of the *hululi* problem. Around 1236 another Iraqi scholar with whom Judayli was in contact, Mansur ibn Sa'id, wrote of the formation of a new sect called the Ahl al-Thamina, after an esoteric text, the *Kitab al-Thamina* ("Book of Eight"), which someone had found in Aleppo, had read and not properly understood, and had then begun preaching to fools and simpletons back in Baghdad. One of the two main followers of this new teaching, Shaddad, sought to propagate it around Basra and especially among the local Ishaqi population, which must still have been fairly substantial at that time. He was rebuffed by the Ishaqis, tried to ingratiate himself with an 'Alawi or *ghulat* current particularly devoted to Mansur al-Hallaj, and finally came to 'Ana. Here, according to the *Khayr al-Sani'a*, "this Shaddad—may God *not* have mercy on him—continued to corrupt the weak of understanding" until the community responded and apparently had him killed surreptitiously in the nearby hill country. Hasan al-Jubayli, the other leading Thamina apostle in the region, for his part continued to "pervert the minds of those who have none."[19]

There is nothing in Mansur ibn Sa'id's account that ties the Thamina directly with *hululi* ideas, although its appeal to the Ishaqis of lower Iraq already suggests a possible link. An explicit connection, however, is made in the context of Syria, where Thamina propagandists were also known to have been active. 'Ali ibn Baqrat of Hama, most notably, is remembered as one of several people who fought the Ahl al-Thamina in the mid-thirteenth "so that their *da'wa* did not penetrate in Hama as it had in Homs." To this end, according to the *Khayr al-Sani'a*, he used the writings of both Judayli and Makzun "against the Thamina *madhhab*," an indication that here at least the Thamina was assimilated to the *hululi* influences that had been the actual objects of Judayli's and Makzun's campaigns.[20] While there are no more references to the "Thamina" movement in the available literature after the conflict with 'Ali ibn Baqrat at Hama, the notion that it had some impact in the Homs region is probably not unrelated to the fact that this is precisely the area targeted by Nashshabi's visitations a few years later.

In this context, it is somewhat surprising that Judayli's own followers, the "Hatimiyya" (as they are called in the *Munazara*; the term does not appear elsewhere), would come to be associated with *hululi* belief themselves. A possible explanation is provided by the copyist of Harfush's *Khayr al-Sani'a* manuscript, Ibrahim Ahmad Harfush, who states in a marginal note that Hatim al-Judayli (d. 1252–53) is not the same person as Hatim al-Tubani,

---

19 Ibid., 609–12.
20 Ibid., 439–40; see also Harfush, *Al-Maghmurun*, 173; Hasan, *Al-Makzun al-Sinjari*, 1:78–80.

but this seems specious and is not supported by any other source.[21] Perhaps a more promising line of inquiry would concern the social milieu in which this 'Alawi "inquisition" of the thirteenth century progressed. The *Munazara*, for instance, refers to several minor notables in Asfin and elsewhere, who, while initially backing Shaykh Rabi'a, were won over to the truth of Nashshabi's reasoning and therefore ultimately won praise in the 'Alawi tradition: the village elder al-Mu'allim ("teacher") Abu Muhammad Jibrin (d. 1270–71), the headman (*al-ra'is*) Salim Nasr al-'Usayda, Shaykh 'Abd Allah of Jaris, and others.[22] The most important of Nashshabi's local allies was perhaps Shaykh Jami', the imam of al-Murrayih village (near the fortress of Qulay'a), who had already made a name for himself "disputing the authors of corrupt articles" and who now lent his support to Nashshabi's crusade.[23] On the other hand, Jami''s pupil al-Mu'allim Musa ibn Ayyub, who succeeded Jami' upon his death in 1266, was and remains a good deal more controversial: some note that he was Rabi'a's teacher and the probable source of his debased ideas, while others recall that Nashshabi himself showed him indulgence after rebuking him in a long and intense theological debate.[24]

The picture that emerges from this series of disputations between the late twelfth and the late thirteenth centuries is ultimately less one of a clash of well-defined dogmas than a concerted effort by a small intellectual elite to impose a uniform, literary authority on the whole 'Alawi community. In its initial impulse at least this movement was urban-based: 'Ali Baqrat concerned himself with Hama and Homs; Nashshabi had been recruited and financed by wealthy members of the community in Aleppo; 'Ali al-Suwayri (d. 1313–14), the last major advocate and chronicler of this "inquisition," continued to cite the *'ulama* of Aleppo, Baghdad, and 'Ana as references for Khasibi-'Alawi orthodoxy.[25] These scholars' adversaries (not enemies) were *hululi*s in the widest sense, village elders or just ordinary believers among whom the complex doctrine of 'Ali's *ma'na*-divinity was watered down into a more tangible, objective belief in the incarnation of God in the earthly 'Ali, the Twelve Imams, and other charismatic figures. This natural tendency to simplify and humanize the rather esoteric teachings of *ghulat* Shi'ism may already have found expression in the original Ishaqi sect but also in lesser-known, essentially local groups such as Abu Dhuhayba's disciples, the Thamina at Homs, and even among the popular following of leading clerics such as Hatim al-Judayli and Yusuf al-Nashshabi. The fact is that 'Alawism remained a secret initiatory faith, one whose religious mysteries were not accessible, let

---

21 Harfush, *Khayr al-Sani'a*, 369–70, 385. The biography of Tubani given in al-Tawil, *Tarikh al-'Alawiyyin*, 376–79, appears too fanciful to be of use.

22 Nashshabi, *Munazara*, fol. 70a; Harfush, *Khayr al-Sani'a*, 417, 418, 437, 631.

23 Nashshabi, *Munazara*, fol. 69b–70b; Harfush, *Khayr al-Sani'a*, 413–16.

24 Harfush, *Khayr al-Sani'a*, 468–72, 574–79, 631–44.

25 Ibid., 565–85, 613–17.

alone comprehensible, to everyone who, by the thirteenth century, had come to be included in the wider 'Alawi social community. The efforts by Makzun, the Aleppine clergy, and certain particularly literate mountain-based shaykhs to impose (or construct) an orthodox standard signify the consolidation of a uniform religious authority over the community but also its bifurcation into distinct classes of elect and nonelect believers, of actual 'Alawi *'ulama*, and of adepts of popular ritual and saint veneration—a division that continues to mark the community down to the present day.

At first glance, it might seem surprising that such a process would occur at virtually the same moment the community was constituting itself in sectarian terms in the face of pressure from outside forces such as the crusaders, the Ayyubids, and the Ismailis. But in fact this bears many similarities to the rise of the Cathar sect in northern Italy and southern France in almost exactly the same period, where persecution by Catholic officials was accompanied by an ever sharper internal delineation of Cathar orthodoxy.[26] It is a bit unfortunate that 'Alawism has never been included in the long-standing historical debate about the potential links between Catharism and Bogomilism, two Mediterranean "heresies" with whom it shared a common origin in Manichean thought and an initial dissemination in or from Byzantine lands. More instructive for our purposes, in any case, is the sociological similarity between their leaderships: inasmuch as both the Bogomil/Cathar and 'Alawi belief systems are radically dualist (in the sense of subscribing to a twin cosmogony of good and evil that is much more pronounced than in mainstream Christianity and Islam), they not only inherently repudiate the created universe (and especially the organized church and/or the secular authorities of the ever more intrusive medieval state) but at the same time also exert relatively little pressure on the individual believer to live up to the extremely rigorous, world-renouncing moral standards of the initiated or "consoled" *parfait*. Even while establishing the norms of correct 'Alawi belief and securing their own clerical authority, the shaykhs immortalized in the *Khayr al-Sani'a* were not, any more than Pierre Clergue or Guillaume Bélibaste of Montaillou, presiding over a society in which religion and theology were expected to be foremost in ordinary people's concerns.[27]

In conclusion, the defeat of the Ishaqis and the fight against all things *hululi* between the late twelfth and the late thirteenth centuries has to be regarded in the context of the 'Alawi community's sectarian consolidation. Previous writers have taken the *Munazara* and other controversy literature as proof of 'Alawism's initial vigor, and the absence of such texts in the

---

26 See R. I. Moore, *The Origins of European Dissent*, 2nd ed. (Oxford: Blackwell, 1985), esp. 178–81, 190; Malcolm Lambert, *The Cathars* (Oxford: Blackwell, 1998), esp. 22–37, 157–65.

27 Emmanuel Le Roy Ladurie, *Montaillou, village occitan de 1294 à 1324*, 2nd ed. (Paris: Gallimard, 1982).

later medieval and Ottoman periods as a sign of intellectual decline, an explanation which of course dovetails with the long-held general narrative of Muslim or Arab decline in the postcaliphal age. At least as far as the 'Alawi community is concerned, however, it can be argued that the internal "inquisition" of the thirteenth century ushered in a period of ideological and social stability, of expansion toward the North, political autonomy, and ultimately even recognition by Sunni state officials. In establishing their own religious authority and removing theological speculation from the realm of everyday 'Alawi life, the legacy of newly "orthodox" scholars such as Judayli, Nashshabi, and Suwayri is again above all one of bounding and secularizing 'Alawi society.

RELATIONS WITH THE STATE AUTHORITIES AND THE ISMAILIS

If the end of the Crusades and Makzun al-Sinjari's advent opened the way for an important internal reorganization of the 'Alawi community, we have considerably less information about its relations with neighboring communities or Sunni state officialdom during this time. There are hardly any references to the 'Alawis or Nusayris at all in the Ayyubid or Mamluk chronicles of the twelfth to thirteenth centuries, despite the obvious importance of the coastal highlands between Salah al-Din's conquest in 1188 and the Mamluk sultan Qalawun's seizure of the last remaining Frankish strongholds there in the 1290s. The 'Alawi sources, for their part, give the impression that the Sunni authorities' attitude toward the community ranged from indifferent to cordial. We have already referred to the Ayyubid/Mamluk governor Qaraja, who was supposedly contacted by the deviant 'Alawi shaykh Rabi'a to scare off his rival, al-Nashshabi. Aside from the problem of this account's dating and reliability, it interestingly does not evince any hostility on the governor's part toward the 'Alawis per se. Another Ayyubid or Mamluk governor, known only as Emir al-Mawsili, is even said to have become a friend to the 'Alawis. Appointed to the province of Tripoli in 1276–77, he caused great consternation upon arrival when a detractor informed him that the "Nusayris" were Shi'i heretics (*rawafid*) who neither read the Qur'an, performed ablutions, nor prayed toward Mecca. Al-Mawsili, though outraged upon learning this, concealed his anger and summoned the Nusayris' leaders and *'ulama*. They were too frightened to appear, however, and prepared to flee, with the exception of Musallam ibn 'Abdallah of al-Bayda' village near Hama, who went to meet the emir, "sacrificing himself for his brethren and defending his faith and confession." After a lengthy legal discussion and cross-examination by a *qadi* (judge), mainly over the question of whether it was permissible to perform ritual prayers over the dead, al-Mawsili came to realize that Musallam was right, and that his people were in fact the best of all Muslims.

He sent Musallam back in honor and munificence and even forgave the 'Alawi community part of its *kharaj* (agricultural land) taxes.[28]

The already cited Shaykh Hasan al-Ajrud of Latakia, for his part, is reported to have traveled to Cairo on behalf of a group of 'Alawi peasants around 1336 and successfully petitioned the sultan to abolish a number of oppressive measures (*mazalim*) weighing on them.[29] Still other stories tell of the 'Alawis' friendly contacts with the Ayyubid rulers of Hama; of Tamerlane's vezir Muhammad al-Qarani consulting the previously mentioned Shaykh Musa al-Rabti in Abu Qubays village on religious matters, and of the "*ta'ifat al-Khasibiyya's*" support for the Mamluk sultan Barsbay for his reconquering Cyprus (in 1425) from the Franks, whose constant ravages had forced many 'Alawis from Latakia and Jabala to flee the coastal regions and take refuge in Aleppo.[30] In the *Tarikh al-'Alawiyyin*, the Circassian Mamluks as a whole are in fact presented as 'Alawis.[31] That the historical veracity of such accounts is doubtful is, for our purposes, immaterial; what is important is that the 'Alawi tradition, as passed down in the stories of individual poets and scholars and as exemplified today in the *Khayr al-Sani'a*, recalls several prominent Sunni figures with distinct pro-'Alawi sympathies but contains no trace whatsoever of the persecution, sectarian violence, and other forms of religious hostility that are commonly thought to have defined the 'Alawis' lot under medieval Sunni rule. The collective memory of constant oppression and sheltering in the mountains is clearly the product of a later era.

In any event, many 'Alawis' most immediate superiors in the mountains would have been local Ismaili emirs rather than the more distant Ayyubid and later Mamluk state officials. The Ismailis' own political situation during this time has been the subject of some speculation but may offer some useful analogies to that of their 'Alawi subjects and neighbors. According to Friedman, for example, the Nizari Ismailis were "liquidated" by the Mamluks, the Mamluks' policy toward both them and the Nusayris being "extreme in many aspects" and part of "the general process of Muslim radicalization in the late medieval period."[32] In fact the Mamluks' policy toward the Ismailis, as historians such as Abdul-Aziz Khowaiter, Farhad Daftary, and Charles Melville have convincingly shown, was anything but extreme. After losing Masyaf and three other fortresses to the Mongols in 1260, the Syrian Nizaris

---

28 Harfush, *Khayr al-Sani'a*, 597–99.

29 Abu Musa and Shaykh Musa, eds., *Majmu' al-Ahadith*, 8:166; al-Tawil, *Tarikh al-'Alawiyyin*, 379–80. This anecdote, however, is clearly anachronistic since it refers to the sultan as being al-Ashraf Barsbay and may have to be brought into connection with the 'Alawis' general approval of the latter (see following note).

30 Harfush, *Khayr al-Sani'a*, 301–3, 473–75, 500, 711, 904–5.

31 Al-Tawil, *Tarikh al-'Alawiyyin*, 401. This is already disputed by 'Abd al-Rahman al-Khayyir in his introduction to *Tarikh al-'Alawiyyin*, 46.

32 Friedman, *Nusayri-'Alawis*, 62, 223.

actively collaborated with the rising Mamluk leader and founder of the Qipchak sultanate, Baybars, helping him drive out the invaders later the same year and recovering most of their former possessions. Thereafter the Nizaris maintained good ties with Baybars and were granted the same fiefs and territorial privileges they had already enjoyed under the Ayyubids, though at the price of becoming ever more politically divided among themselves and co-opted by the Mamluk authorities. By 1270 the Nizaris had begun to pay a yearly tribute to Baybars, who in turn now appointed and dismissed their leaders.[33] Their last remaining castles were brought under Mamluk supervision in 1273, but unlike the Mongols in Iran, the Mamluks accommodated the Nizari Ismailis and never attempted to exterminate them. On the contrary, well into the fourteenth century the Mamluks repeatedly relied on Nizari spies and *fida'i*s to assassinate high-ranking enemies, especially Mamluk army defectors who had gone over to the Mongol Ilkhanids in Iran. Over a hundred members of the Syrian community are thought to have perished on these extremely dangerous missions to Iran, in return for which they were permitted to retain effective control over Masyaf, Qadmus, and other *da'wa* castles.[34]

Much as the Mamluk authorities tolerated and indeed integrated the Nizari Ismailis into the local administration in western Syria, it appears the politically unobtrusive 'Alawi community also did not suffer any particular vexations. According to the *Khayr al-Sani'a*, there was even at least one 'Alawi, Sa'd ibn Dabal, who served as *muqaddam* (foreman) in Baybars's *fida'i* forces.[35] Al-Tawil, for his part, claims the 'Alawis (viz. Twelver Shi'is in general) and Ismailis worked toward a reconciliation at Safita in 1291 but were not able to come to an agreement despite the best of intentions.[36] While such accounts are difficult to substantiate historically, the few biographical references to direct 'Alawi-Ismaili ties we have in this period do suggest a relationship of sectarian accommodation and even symbiosis rather than essential conflict. Shaykh Salman of Funaytiq village just northwest of Qadmus, for example, one of the leading 'Alawi poets of his age and famous for his verse predicting the coming of the antichrist and other apocalyptic events, was reportedly forced to quit his home by the local Ismailis but then settled in nearby al-Hatiriyya, itself a dependency of Qadmus.[37] Another shaykh buried in al-Hatiriyya, Mahmud al-Qusayr,

---

33 Abdul-Aziz Khowaiter, *Baibars the First: His Endeavours and Achievements* (London: Green Mountain Press, 1978), 118–26; Daftary, *Ismā'īlīs*, 430–34; Mirza, *Syrian Ismailism*, 57–67.

34 Charles Melville, "'Sometimes by the Sword, Sometimes by the Dagger': The Role of the Isma'ilis in Mamluk-Mongol Relations in the 8th/14th Century," in *Medieval Isma'ili History and Thought*, ed. Farhad Daftary (Cambridge: Cambridge University Press, 1996), 247–63.

35 Harfush, *Khayr al-Sani'a*, 541–43.

36 Al-Tawil, *Tarikh al-'Alawiyyin*, 365; see also Halm, "Buch der Schatten," 263–65.

37 Harfush, *Khayr al-Sani'a*, 548–58.

FIGURE 2.1. Qadmus

is thought to be descended from the Adra'i emirs of Masyaf and may thus have been of mixed 'Alawi-Ismaili origin.[38] The famous shrine of Shaykh 'Afif al-Din in Masyaf, which was sought out by people of all confessions to resolve minor ownership disputes, was apparently built by the local Ismaili emir after the shaykh appeared to him in a dream and promised to heal him of sickness. The shrine's *waqf* (pious foundation) was administered by Ismailis until 1863–64, when the last trustee died and the *shar'iyya* court of Hama transferred control of the foundation to the shaykh's 'Alawi descendants.[39] Similarly, the *maqam* of the fourteenth-century 'Alawi scholar Ibrahim al-'Idda ibn Musa in al-Harif, which today remains one of the best-preserved older shrines in the highlands west of Hama, was supported by *waqf* moneys from the once predominantly Ismaili-owned village.[40] And finally, the fifteenth-century shrine of Shaykh Ibrahim at al-'Aliyya near Qadmus is said to have been endowed by the Ismaili emir Tamir, after he had pitched his tent directly in front of it but then saw the shaykh in a dream and reconsidered. The site was revered by both 'Alawis and Ismailis; in modern times, the *Khayr al-Sani'a*'s author reports from personal experience, wheat from every threshing floor of the Ismaili-owned village continued to be set aside each year to be distributed there as charity.[41]

38 Ibid., 593–95.
39 Ibid., 656–58.
40 Ibid., 672–74.
41 Ibid., 813–14.

FIGURE 2.2. Cenotaph of Shaykh Mahmud al-Qusayr, al-Hatiriyya (renovated in 2009)

IBN TAYMIYYA AND THE POLITICS OF PERSECUTION

Perhaps nothing has contributed to the image of the 'Alawis' persecution under Sunni rule so much as the fatwas of the Damascene jurist and theologian Ahmad ibn Taymiyya (d. 1328). Guiding luminary of the Hanbali school of law (*madhhab*) and key inspirer of Wahhabism and other fundamentalist reform movements, Ibn Taymiyya can certainly be regarded today as one of the most influential scholars in the history of Islam.[42] While his "*profession de foi*" and critique of rational thought hold pride of place in his literary oeuvre, Ibn Taymiyya is equally known for his lifelong struggle against Sufi mystics and popular religion as well as his sustained attacks on "*rafidism*" or Shi'ism. His fatwa (legal opinion) or treatise[43] condemning the Nusayris in

---

42 Henri Laoust, *Essai sur les doctrines sociales et politiques de Takī-d-Dīn Ahmad b. Taimīya* (Cairo: Institut français d'archéologie orientale, 1939); Ferhat Koca, "İbn Teymiyye, Takıyyüddin," *Türkiye Diyanet Vakfı İslam Ansiklopedisi* (Istanbul: İSAM, 1999), 20:391–405.

43 Ahmad Ibn Taymiyya, *Majmu' Fatawa Shaykh al-Islam Ahmad ibn Taymiyya*, ed. 'Abd al-Rahman ibn Muhammad ibn Qasim al-'Asimi (Riyad: n.p., 1961–66), 35:149–60; Ahmad ibn 'Abd al-Wahhab al-Nuwayri (d. 1333), *Nihayat al-Arab fi Funun al-Adab*, ed. Muhammad 'Alawi Shaltut (Cairo: Dar al-Kutub al-Misriyya, 1998), 32:262–74.

FIGURE 2.3. Shrine of Shaykh Ibrahim al-'Idda, al-Harif (2011)

particular as "more godless than the Jews, Christians, and many polytheists" was indeed cited by members of the Syrian Muslim Brotherhood to justify guerrilla attacks on 'Alawi government figures in the 1980s; its obvious political ramifications have made it a primary object of modern scholarly investigation, the most recent example of which again considers that such rulings were followed by the "large majority" of Muslims and can therefore be said to have "shaped the history of the Nusayris."[44]

From their historical context, however, it appears that Ibn Taymiyya's views on the 'Alawis were largely unrelated to contemporary events or had little direct impact. The fatwa, which exists in several different versions, declares that the 'Alawis are heretics, that it is a religious duty to combat them, and that the shedding of their blood and the seizure of their property is permissible. As Yaron Friedman has rightly argued, however, Ibn Taymiyya

---

44 Stanislas Guyard, "Le fetwa d'Ibn Taimiyyah sur les Nosairis," *Journal Asiatique* 18 (1871): 158–98; Laoust, *Essai*, 94, 108, 111, 124–25, 201, 366–67; Michel Mazzaoui, *The Origins of the Safawids: Šī'ism, Sufism and the Gulat* (Wiesbaden: Franz Steiner, 1972), 34–36; Gregor Voss, *'Alawīya oder Nusairīya: Schiitische Machtelite und sunnitische Opposition in der Syrischen Arabischen Republik* (Hamburg: n.p., 1987), 71–83; Yaron Friedman, "Ibn Taymiyya's *Fatāwa* against the Nusayrī-'Alawī Sect," *Der Islam* 82 (2005): 349–63; Friedman, *Nusayrī-'Alawīs*, 62–63, 188–99, 299–309; Yvette Talhamy, "The *Fatwa*s and the Nusayri/Alawis of Syria," *Middle East Studies* 46 (2010): 175–91, esp. 175, 181.

seems to have been distinctly uninformed about 'Alawism: while the lengthy original request for a fatwa (submitted by a certain Ahmad ibn Mari al-Shafi'i) displays a certain knowledge of its esoteric beliefs, hierarchy of saints, and ritual use of wine as well as a concern about interacting socially with members of the sect, in his response Ibn Taymiyya adds almost nothing concrete in their regard and evidently also conflates the 'Alawis with the Ismailis "and other kinds of Qarmatians." A second version of the fatwa in turn assimilates the 'Alawis to the Druze and was likely an emendation added by a Baalbek-based disciple of Ibn Taymiyya.[45] Aside from a third version of the fatwa, which was prompted by the 'Alawi revolt of 1318 (see below), it is unclear when and in what context the original ruling was produced. In response to the (apparently sincere) question of whether 'Alawi fighters could be relied on to help defend the frontiers and port cities of Islamdom against Frankish crusaders, Ibn Taymiyya accuses them of outright complicity with the Franks and even the Mongols. This is essentially the same accusation he also used to legitimize the Mamluks' punitive campaigns against the Shi'i populations of the Kisrawan highlands near Beirut in 1300 and 1305, which might appear to indicate that his fatwa on the 'Alawis was given in support of a wider Mamluk policy against heterodox Muslim sects. As Henri Laoust already pointed out, however, the fatwa has no bearing on the campaigns and likely dates from a later time.[46]

More important for our purposes, the Kisrawan campaigns and Ibn Taymiyya's involvement should not be seen as indicative of a Mamluk "policy" on sectarian groups per se. Modern historians of Lebanon, Ahmed Beydoun has shown, have often used the conflicting accounts of whether it was the Maronites, Druze, or Shi'a who were the principal victims to stake a particular community's claim to a historical Lebanese identity.[47] The Hama-based chronicler Abu'l-Fida' (d. 1331) states unequivocally that the campaign in 1305 targeted "the Nusayris and esoteric Shi'is [*al-zaninin*]" and that many of these were killed or captured; the Damascene religious scholar al-Birzali (d. 1338) likewise speaks of "the party of error, the Rawafid and Nusayris."[48]

45 Friedman, *Nusayrī-'Alawīs*, 188–93.

46 Henri Laoust, "Remarques sur les expéditions du Kasrawan sous les premiers Mamluks," *Bulletin du Musée de Beyrouth* 4 (1940): 93–115; see also Kamal Salibi, "Mount Lebanon under the Mamluks," in *Quest for Understanding: Arabic and Islamic Studies in Memory of Malcolm Kerr*, ed. Samir Seikaly et al. (Beirut: American University in Beirut, 1991), 15–32; Albrecht Fuess, *Verbranntes Ufer: Auswirkungn mamlukischer Seepolitik of Beirut und die syro-palästinensische Küste (1250–1517)* (Leiden: Brill, 2001), 146–50, 330–32.

47 Ahmed Beydoun, *Identité confessionnelle et temps social chez les historiens libanais* (Beirut: Université Libanaise, 1984), 77–157.

48 'Imad al-Din Isma'il Abu'l-Fida', *Al-Mukhtasar fi Akhbar al-Bashar* (Cairo: al-Matba'a al-Husayniyya al-Misriyya, 1968), 4:52; repeated in 'Umar Ibn al-Wardi (d. 1348), *Tarikh* (Najaf: al-Matba'a al-Haydariyya, 1969), 2:363; Qasim ibn Muhammad al-Birzali, *Al-Muqtafa 'ala Kitab al-Rawdatayn*, ed. 'Umar 'Abd al-Salam al-Tadmuri (Sayda': al-Maktaba al-'Asriyya, 2006), 3:292–3. Al-Zaninin could also simply refer to the (Shi'i) inhabitants of the Zanniyya district above Tripoli.

This can again be considered in light of the question whether there was already a precise distinction between the 'Alawis and Twelver (Imami) Shi'is at the time. From a letter Ibn Taymiyya wrote Sultan al-Nasir Muhammad in Cairo in 1305, and in which he seems at pains to justify the carnage that resulted in the annihilation of a large part of the Kisrawan population, it is clear that he himself believed the victims to be not 'Alawis but Imami Shi'is, whose false doctrines he enumerates and whose books he asserts were seized during the campaign.[49] Aside from the fact that the alleged discovery of incriminating books is a cliché found in many such accounts of the persecution of heretics, Ibn Taymiyya here again assimilates the 'Alawis to the "Ismailis, Hakimis, and Batinis," raising the question whether he knew precisely who was being targeted or simply used the campaigns to propagate his own agenda against Shi'ism.

A close look at the contemporary chronicle sources suggests that the Mamluks were not in fact motivated by religion in their attack on the Kisrawan. A first campaign in 1292 seems to have targeted Christian villages that were accused of abetting the crusaders; the second followed on the Mongols' occupation of Damascus from January to April 1300, when the (largely Hanbali-inhabited) suburb of al-Salihiyya was sacked and fleeing Mamluk soldiers were subsequently robbed by the inhabitants of the Kisrawan. Ibn Taymiyya, who had been actively involved in the defense of the city and the ransoming of Muslim prisoners, threw his support behind the governor of Damascus, Aqqush al-Afram, in his plan to recoup the seized weapons, but the expedition was actually led by the Druze Buhturid emirs, scions of the Tanukhi dynasty mentioned earlier. The Buhturids were assigned *iqta'* fiefs in the area as well as a rank in the Mamluk *halqa* (provincial auxiliary) corps, and the events of 1305 were in turn precipitated by a tax revolt of the Kisrawanis, many of whom would have been Shi'is and/or 'Alawis, and possibly even Druze themselves, against these, their equally heterodox overlords.[50] Prior to the military assault, moreover, Aqqush al-Afram had made a point of sending a Twelver Shi'i notable of Damascus, the *naqib al-ashraf* Muhammad ibn 'Adnan al-Husayni, to the Kisrawan in an attempt to mediate in good faith between the two sides; after the campaign, according to the Druze Buhturid chronicler Salih ibn Yahya (d. 1436), the Mamluk authorities "evicted those

---

49 Muhammad ibn Ahmad ibn Qudama al-Maqdisi (d. 1343), *Al-'Uqud al-Durriyya min Manaqib Shaykh al-Islam Ahmad ibn Taymiyya*, ed. Muhammad Hamid al-Fiqi (Beirut: Dar al-Kutub al-'Ilmiyya, 1975), 182–94.

50 'Imad al-Din Ibn Kathir (d. 1373), *Al-Bidaya wa'l-Nihaya fi'l-Tarikh*, ed. Ahmad Abu Mulhim et al. (Beirut: Dar al-Kutub al-'Ilmiyya, 1985), 14:14; Li Guo, ed., *Early Mamluk Syrian Historiography: Al-Yunini's Dhayl Mir'at al-Zaman* (Leiden: Brill, 1998), 1:171, 2:130–31; Salih Ibn Yahya, *Tarikh Bayrut*, ed. Francis Hours and Kamal Salibi (Beirut: Dar al-Mashriq, 1969), 24–28; see also Kamal Salibi, "The Buhturids of the Garb: Mediaeval Lords of Beirut and of Southern Lebanon," *Arabica* 8 (1961): 74–97; Hamza, *Tanukhiyyun*, 125–32.

[Shi'is/'Alawis] who had remained in the Kisrawan mountains and killed a number of their notables, [but] gave quarter to those who settled elsewhere."[51]

The moralist prejudices of Ibn Taymiyya and his supporters ultimately did not coincide with the actual day-to-day concerns of the Mamluk administration in Damascus. If one compares the reasons given by the leading chroniclers of the day for the campaigns, it becomes clear that those who cite the Kisrawanis' political sedition were members of the military and bureaucratic establishment, while those who cite their foul religious beliefs were mainly piety-minded *'ulama*.[52] (The Mamluk commander Aqqush al-Afram, incidentally, later defected to Iran and ended his career as the governor of Hamadan for the Shi'i Ilkhanid monarch Öljeitü.[53]) To suggest that Ibn Taymiyya's positions on the 'Alawis and Shi'ism were reflective of a general Mamluk "policy" or accorded with the views of the great majority of Muslims is also to obscure his rather marginal standing within contemporary Mamluk society. The previously cited chronicler Abu'l-Fida', for example, mentions in the same breath that Ibn Taymiyya legitimized and accompanied the 1305 campaign (against the "Nusayris and esoteric Shi'is") and was immediately afterward summoned to Cairo, arrested and put on trial for anthropomorphism (*tajsim*).[54] Ibn Taymiyya's notorious insistence on taking God's physical attributes literally was of course one of his key bones of contention with Shi'ism, the threat of which he may ultimately have played up in an effort to impose his extremist Hanbali views against his more moderate Shafi'i opponents. The Mamluk authorities were ambivalent about (or disinterested in) Ibn Taymiyya's doctrines as such but certainly did condemn him for contradicting the consensus of the established *'ulama*, disquieting the minds of the common believers with his inflammatory fatwas, and causing civil upheaval.[55] Beginning in 1305 he was jailed on six separate occasions, in both Cairo and Damascus, for a sum total of more than six years; his fatwas on the 'Alawis may well have been composed while in prison. Ibn Taymiyya was by all accounts an exceptional scholar but also a profoundly polarizing figure in Mamluk society. Already in the fourteenth century historians began to ask whether he did not in fact "have a screw loose";[56] at the very least, Ibn

---

51 Ibn Yahya, *Tarikh Bayrut*, 27; Muhsin al-Amin (d. 1952), *A'yan al-Shi'a*, 2nd ed. (Beirut: Dar al-Ta'arif, 1996), 6:157; discussed in more detail in Stefan Winter, "Shams al-Din Muhammad ibn Makki 'al-Shahid al-Awwal' (d. 1384) and the Shi'ah of Syria," *Mamluk Studies Review* 3 (1999): 150–54.

52 See Donald Little, *An Introduction to Mamluk Historiography* (Wiesbaden: Steiner, 1970).

53 Melville, "Sometimes by the Sword," 249–50.

54 Abu'l-Fida', *Mukhtasar*, 4:52; Ibn al-Wardi, *Tarikh*, 2:363.

55 Donald Little, "The Historical and Historiographical Significance of the Detention of Ibn Taymiyya," *International Journal of Middle East Studies* 4 (1973): 311–27.

56 Donald Little, "Did Ibn Taymiyya Have a Screw Loose?," *Studia Islamica* 41 (1975): 93–111.

Taymiyya cannot remotely be considered to have been representative of the Mamluk or later medieval Sunni mainstream.

The importance that Ibn Taymiyya and his views on 'Alawism have been accorded in modern times underlines the pressing need to investigate the reception history of his thought in the medieval and Ottoman periods. Aside from a handful of Hanbali disciples, he does not seem to have been much commented on by Arab scholars before the rise of Wahhabism in the eighteenth century.[57] Several of his works are listed in Katib Çelebi's (d. 1657) bibliographical lexicon *Kashf al-Zunun*, but he is virtually never cited in Ottoman letters.[58] The Sufi mystic 'Abd al-Rahman al-Bistami of Bursa (d. 1454) appears to have referenced an earlier treatise by Ibn Taymiyya in his condemnation of the Hurufi sect; among the leaders of the fundamentalist Kadizadeli movement in Istanbul under Mehmed IV, the Syrian-born Üstüvani Mehmed Efendi alone might be considered to have been a follower of the Ibn Taymiyya "school."[59] Beyond that it is likely that Ibn Taymiyya's rejection of the great sufi master Ibn al-'Arabi made him anathema to Ottoman scholars, even to such leading critics of Sufism as Birgivi Mehmed (d. 1573), who never cited him.[60] Several sixteenth-century Ottoman fatwas that legitimized warfare against Safavid Iran do bear certain similarities to Ibn Taymiyya's texts; the anonymous and undated polemical treatise *Risale der Redd-i Revafiz* reproduces a number of historical rulings against the Shi'a, including those of Ahmad ibn Hanbal, but again does not mention Ibn Taymiyya himself.[61] While Ibn Taymiyya was thus not entirely unknown to Ottoman scholars, it has to be noted that neither his rulings on Shi'ism nor those on 'Alawism found any echo in the late medieval through early modern period.

THE UPRISING OF 1318

The most important instance of state-sanctioned violence against the 'Alawis in the medieval period was the suppression of a local uprising in the Jabala region in early 1318. The event is covered in a vast panoply of sources and

---

57 Laoust, *Essai*, 500–505; Koca, "İbn Teymiyye," 20:393–94.

58 See Isma'il Basha al-Baghdadi (d. 1920), *Hadiyat al-'Arifin: Asma' al-Mu'allifin wa-Athar al-Musannifin min Kashf al-Zunun* (Istanbul: Wakalat al-Ma'arif, 1951), 1:105–7.

59 Denis Gril, "Ésotérisme contre hérésie: 'Abd al-Rahmân al-Bistâmî, un représentant de la science des lettres à Bursa dans la première moitié du XVe siècle" in *Syncrétismes et hérésies dans l'Orient seldjoukide et ottoman (XIVe-XVIIIe siècle): Actes du Colloque du Collège de France, octobre 2001*, ed. Gilles Veinstein (Paris: Peeters, 2005), 192; Ahmet Yaşar Ocak, *Osmanlı Toplumunda Zındıklar ve Mülhidler (15.–17. Yüzyıllar)* (Istanbul: Tarih Vakfı, 1998), 112.

60 Emrullah Yüksel, "Birgivî," in *Türkiye Diyanet Vakfı İslam Ansiklopedisi* (Istanbul: İSAM, 1992), 6:191–4.

61 Süleymaniye Kütüphanesi, Istanbul: Ms. I. Serez 1451, fol. 14b–15b, 21b–27b; cf. Winter, *Shiites of Lebanon*, 15–16, 21–22.

has often been taken as proof of the Mamluks' supposed intolerance toward religious heterodoxy,[62] while fewer have argued that the revolt was motivated first and foremost by economic reasons.[63] What is clear is that the revolt began in the immediate aftermath of a cadastral survey of the province of Tripoli, which had both fiscal and religious implications for the 'Alawi population. Between 1313 and 1325 the Mamluk state authorities carried out a whole series of such surveys (*rawk*) with the aim of reorganizing the local administration, maximizing sources of revenue, and consolidating their hold over the Syrian coastal interior, where the threat of renewed crusader and Mongol incursions had only recently been banished. The stipulations resulting from the 1317 *rawk* for Tripoli, which were recorded by the Mamluk chancery secretary al-Nuwayri (d. 1333) and later copied by Qalqashandi and al-Maqrizi,[64] actually provided for a significant reduction in the taxes and administrative abuses weighing on the local peasant population. In addition to abolishing various supplementary charges and bondships (*daman*) for the use of pastures, threshing floors, salt, irrigation canals, and so forth, a sultanic rescript dated December 1317 also ordered the closing of all prisons besides that in Tripoli city and eliminated the local governors' privileges in the fortresses of Sahyun, Platanus, and al-Kahf. According to Urbain Vermeulen, all these measures were in line with Sultan al-Nasir Muhammad's attempts to curtail the power of the Syrian Mamluk emirs, who had amassed too many autonomous resources and were thereby threatening his own authority; the sultan, he concludes, was probably so "moderate" toward the Nusayris as they had become "a kind of ally" in his struggle to consolidate control over the provinces.[65]

Nevertheless, the rescript does contain elements that were prejudicial to the 'Alawi sect as such and that likely explain the eruption of the revolt only a few weeks after its promulgation. Noting that "there are villages in the remote districts of this province whose inhabitants are known as Nusayris, where Islam has neither entered their hearts nor penetrated their minds, and who neither exercise its rituals nor raise up minarets, but rather break its laws and ignore that which is right and wrong," the rescript vows to "put

---

62 Henri Laoust, *Les schismes dans l'islam: Introduction à une étude de la religion musulmane* (Paris: Payot, 1965), 258–59; Moosa, *Extremist Shiites*, 272–73; and especially Sato Tsugitaka, *State and Rural Society in Medieval Islam* (Leiden: Brill, 1997), 162–76.

63 Urbain Vermeulen, "Some Remarks on a Rescript of an-Nasir Muhammad b. Qala'un on the Abolition of Taxes and the Nusayris (Mamlaka of Tripoli 717/1317)," *Orientalia Lovaniensia Periodica* 1 (1970): 195–201. See also Fuess, *Verbranntes Ufer*, 151–52, 334–35; Friedman, *Nusayri-'Alawis*, 57–63.

64 Nuwayri, *Nihayat al-'Arab*, 32:257–62; Shihab al-Din Ahmad al-Qalqashandi (d. 1418), *Subh al-A'sha fi Sina'at al-Insha'* (Cairo: Al-Mu'assasa al-Misriyya al-'Amma, 1964), 13:30–35; Taqi al-Din Ahmad al-Maqrizi (d. 1442), *Kitab al-Suluk li-Ma'rifat Duwal al-Muluk* (Cairo: Lajnat al-Ta'lif wa'l-Tarjama wa'l-Nashr, 1971), 2:935–52.

65 Vermeulen, "Some Remarks," 201.

them back on the straight path, both doctrinally and practically (*aslan wa-far'an*)." Consequently the Nusayris were ordered to build a mosque in every village and to set aside plots of land both for the mosques themselves and to finance their upkeep; these lands would be demarcated by a special deputy of the governor of Tripoli and registered in the provincial property records (*al-diwan al-ma'mur*) so that neither the inhabitants nor any Mamluk feudal lords could oppose themselves to the order. At the same time, the Nusayris were prohibited from pursuing with the *khitab*, the traditional "engagement" ceremony by which young men were initiated into the faith.[66] The uprising that began in February 1318 in Platanus (one of the districts specifically targeted by the rescript) seems to have been a direct reaction against both the sectarian and the economic constraints placed on the local 'Alawi community, when a man claiming to be the Twelfth Imam declared the 'Alawis' sovereignty over the lands they farmed and then led his followers in an attack on the coastal city of Jabala before being overwhelmed by Mamluk state forces. As in most such millenarian revolts, the religious and worldly motivations here no doubt overlapped and were mutually reinforcing.

What is less certain is what the revolt's suppression says of the wider relationship between the Mamluk authorities and the 'Alawi community during this time. In relating the events of the revolt, leading Mamluk-era historians such as Ibn Kathir and al-Maqrizi have dwelt on the religious deviance of the 'Alawis, thereby contributing to the notion that it typified a generalized state of Sunni vs. heterodox conflict. It should be said, however, that the sectarian interpretation is above all the product of later, mainly Cairo-based *'ulama* scholars, whose accounts must be traced back to their original sources rather than collated as equally valid historical testimonies. The most comprehensive description of the revolt is doubtless that provided by Nuwayri, in which at least three separate narrative strands can be detected. Nuwayri had previously served as military inspector in the province of Tripoli and evidently still disposed of independent sources of information in the region. This is suggested in another instance by his unique report (later copied by Maqrizi) of a certain Sharaf, the headman (*ra'is*) of Salaghno (or Salafto) village in the Sahyun district, in whom the local Nusayris apparently believed God had been incarnated and who claimed to be able to heal the sick. The anecdote, which Nuwayri heard from "someone trustworthy" and which he recounts with some obvious bemusement but no polemical intent, in itself acknowledges the pressure exerted on the local 'Alawi community by the Mamluk state: a man had supposedly come to Sharaf asking him to cure his ailing father and, when the father died under great pain after all, told Sharaf he would not worship him until he brought his father back to life. Sharaf thereupon told the man to pray using the words "Verily, if the state is

---

66 Nuwayri, *Nihayat al-Arab*, 32:261–62; Qalqashandi, *Subh al-A'sha*, 13:35; Maqrizi, *Suluk*, 2:941.

tyrannical and does not open this door, this will force us to resurrect all the dead who want to return to life!" Sharaf, according to the same source cited by Nuwayri, was also known in the area for being high-minded and generous toward the weak and all those who sought his help.[67]

Perhaps drawing again on his personal sources, Nuwayri provides a detailed account of the 1318 revolt's origins in a village he identifies as Qirtya'us "in the district of Jabala." According to Abu'l-Fida' of Hama, who had an intimate knowledge of the region (and who is claimed to have been a friend of the 'Alawis in the *Tarikh al-'Alawiyyin*) but who himself only gives a summary account of the revolt, it began more precisely in the "mountains of Platanus."[68] This would corroborate Nuwayri's information, especially if the otherwise obscure "Qirtya'us" can be identified with the present-day town of Qardaha near Platanus castle in the highlands above Jabala. Nuwayri recounts how a man from the area claimed he had been tilling his fields when a white bird appeared, pecked a hole in his side, took out his soul, and replaced it with that of Muhammad ibn Hasan, the awaited Mahdi and Twelfth Imam of the Shi'a. The man managed to attract some five thousand followers whom he ordered to worship him and whom he permitted to drink wine and abandon prayers, drawing them in with what appears in Nuwayri's rendition to have been a naive confidence game:

> He set up a red banner and had a beardless youth hold a burning candle by day, claiming that the youth was Ibrahim ibn Adham, his brother Miqdad ibn Aswad al-Kindi, his father Salman al-Farisi, and someone else [the archangel] Gabriel. He would tell the latter, "Go to him and say something that sounds as if it is the glorious Creator [speaking]," who he claimed was 'Ali ibn Abu Talib, and the so-called Gabriel would leave him, disappear for a moment, and then return and say, "It's you I saw!"[69]

For his description of the attack on Jabala, on the other hand, Nuwayri draws entirely on a report which has been preserved in its most complete form by the Damascene religious scholar al-Birzali. According to Birzali, whose account is the only one with some limited eyewitness features, news of the revolt arrived in Damascus in early 1318, whereupon the *qadi*s and jurists of the city were convened in the Great Mosque to give their thoughts on the matter. Later on, Birzali recounts, he read an official report (*mahzar*) of the revolt that had been certified by the *qadi* of Jabala, which he then abridges:

67 Nuwayri, *Nihayat al-Arab*, 32:256–57; Maqrizi, *Suluk*, 2:936–37.
68 Abu'l-Fida', *Mukhtasar*, 4:83; al-Tawil, *Tarikh al-'Alawiyyin*, 376–79.
69 Nuwayri, *Nihayat al-Arab*, 32:275.

After Friday prayers on Friday 22 Dhu'l-Hijja 717 [24 February 1318] the godless, insolent Nusayris, more than 3,000 in number, appeared in the city of Jabala. Leading them was an individual who at times claimed that he was Muhammad ibn Hasan the Mahdi in the name of God, at times that he was 'Ali ibn Abi Talib the creator of heaven and earth, and at other times that he was Muhammad ibn 'Abdallah; that the country was his country, that the kingdom of Islam was his kingdom, that the Muslims were infidels and the Nusayris had the truth, and that sultan al-Malik al-Nasir, the head of state, had died eight days ago. This individual brainwashed a number of Nusayri chiefs and appointed each person a commander of 1,000 or governor of one of the castles belonging to the Muslim state, and he distributed the fiefs of the emirs and the provincial auxiliary corps among them.

The said faction split into three columns before the city of Jabala. One of them came from the southeast and was met by the Muslims' troops, who broke them and killed 124 of their number, with only a few Muslims killed. This column was defeated, while of the Muslims, Jamal al-Din, the commander of the army at Jabala, was injured. The second column came from the south of Jabala near the coast. The third came from the northeast of Jabala, overwhelmed the Muslims, and defeated them. They assaulted Jabala, stole property, carried off children, ravished women, and killed a number of Muslims in town, crying, "There is no God but 'Ali, no *hijab* but Muhammad, and no *bab* but Salman, and cursing Abu Bakr and 'Umar (may God be pleased with them). The old men, children, and women remaining among the Muslims wailed, "Oh Islam, oh sultan, oh emirs!" But there was no one to help them save God most high, whom they began to beseech and implore.

What happened that day was immense. The said leader gathered the property taken and divided it up among his headmen at the village called Busaysil, and told them that the Muslims no longer had any renown, reputation, or state, and that if he had been in ten selves with only a stick but neither a sword nor a lance he would have defeated the Muslims and killed them. He proclaimed the Nusayri religion and announced throughout the country that the tithe would be shared by them and no one else, and ordered his companions to destroy the mosques and turn them into wine shops. The Nusayris seized a number of Muslims in Jabala and wanted to kill them. They told them to bear witness to Muhammad ibn Hasan, to say "There is no God but 'Ali," and to prostrate themselves to Muhammad ibn al-Hasan the Mahdi, "for he is your god who takes your life or gives it." Those who said it were spared and their possessions saved, and he gave them safe passage.

On that day, prior to their entry into Jabala, they had raided Zuq Sulayman al-Turkman as well as Zuq Turkman on the side of Aleppo, carrying off goods, children, and women. The fiercest among all these was a faction called the Baladis ["locals"], which included the aforementioned individual, and a faction of Jaranis [from the Jaranana highlands southeast of Jabala], who were all from al-Marqab town, al-'Ulayqa, and al-Munayqa. On the evening of that day, Emir Badr al-Din al-Taji, the commander of the army at Latakia, arrived in order to protect Jabala. Had it not been for his presence and that of his army, these people were determined to enter Jabala a second time, as their leader was gathering his horses and men at a village called al-Surayfa on the outskirts of Jabala.

Concluding the *mahzar*, Birzali adds: "Their leader was killed soon afterward and so their affair dwindled and vanished, God spare us from evil, defeat and destroy them. This was immense insolence on their part, a lack of brains and extreme stupidity."[70] In his shorter summary, on the other hand, Nuwayri provides details that were apparently not known to Birzali or included in the *mahzar*, namely, as regards the arrival, a few days later, of a group of Mamluk emirs and a thousand cavalry troops from Tripoli. Hearing that the self-proclaimed Mahdi had told his followers they needed "neither sword nor weapon" but only reeds to fend off their enemies, the Mamluk knights fell upon them in a village near Jabala and killed six hundred rebels and their leader after a one-hour battle. The surviving rebels sued for and were granted safety, "and went back to where they came from to carry on their farming."[71]

We may therefore infer four separate narrative strands or sources of information on the revolt thus far: (1) local knowledge on the origins of the revolt as provided directly to Nuwayri, analogue, if not directly linked, to that of Abu'l-Fida'; (2) the *mahzar* from Jabala, reproduced in its fullest form by Birzali and used by Nuwayri either directly (though with less detail) or through Birzali's abridgement; (3) Birzali's brief testimony of receiving news of the revolt and reading the *mahzar* in Damascus; and (4) Nuwayri's information, not supplied by Birzali, on the defeat and annihilation of the rebels. One might speculate that a possible source for this last information was the Damascene scholar Muhammad ibn Ibrahim al-Jazari (d. 1338), a close friend and collaborator of Birzali frequently cited by Nuwayri, the fragment of whose chronicle covering precisely these years, however, unfortunately

---

70 Birzali, *Muqtafa*, 4:298–99.
71 Nuwayri, *Nihayat al-Arab*, 32:276.

appears to be lost.[72] What is striking is that none of these narrative elements is particularly concerned with the rebels' heterodox beliefs, and that they are relatively free of pious invocations and religious polemics even when describing the rebels' overtly sectarian attacks on the Sunni inhabitants of Jabala. The Mamluk authorities' attitude, at any rate, appears to be summed up by Nuwayri's observation that the remaining 'Alawis were spared and simply returned home after the suppression of the revolt.

All subsequent Mamluk-era histories, many of which one regularly sees cited in modern studies as primary sources on the revolt ('Umari, Dhahabi, Ibn al-Wardi, Yafi'i, etc.), in fact copied from one or a combination of Birzali's, Nuwayri's, and Abu'l-Fida's accounts. The only partial exceptions to this are the somewhat obscure Coptic historian Mufaddal ibn Abi'l-Fada'il (d. after 1358), who relates from an unknown source that the Mahdi's severed head was paraded around the Jabala area in triumph after his death,[73] and the famous Moroccan traveler Ibn Battuta (d. after 1368). Ibn Battuta visited Jabala in 1326 and repeats much of what is already known from Birzali and Nuwayri, but he adds some details that again emphasize the profane side of the rebellion. According to this account, the self-proclaimed Mahdi had given his followers olive leaves to show as if they were title deeds or orders for taking possession of the fiefs he had bestowed on them, but they were repeatedly beaten up or imprisoned when they tried to do so. The Mahdi then prepared the attack on Jabala (where Ibn Battuta puts the number of rebels killed at an improbably high twenty thousand). The sultan sent orders by pigeon post to put them all to the sword but was finally convinced by the local Mamluk commander that the 'Alawis were needed to work the Muslims' fields. The results of the 1317 cadastral survey and subsequent revolt, in any event, do not appear to have been very far-reaching. According to the stories Ibn Battuta heard in Jabala (he never actually visited the mountains), the mosques the 'Alawis had been forced to build in their villages stood far from the houses and were never used or only served as stables. If a stranger passing through a village would stop to give the call to prayer, the people would shout back, "Stop braying! You'll get your fodder!"[74]

---

72 Little, *Introduction*, 24, 53–57; 'Umar 'Abd al-Salam al-Tadmuri, ed., introduction to Muhammad ibn Ibrahim al-Jazari, *Hawadith al-Zaman wa-Anba'ihi wa-Wafayat al-Akabir wa'l-A'yan min Abna'ihi* (Beirut: al-Maktaba al-'Asriyya, 1998), 2:29–32. On al-Jazari's possible pro-Shi'i sympathies, see Ulrich Haarmann, *Quellenstudien zur frühen Mamlukenzeit* (Freiburg: D. Robischon, 1969), 22, 141–42.

73 Samira Kortantamer, ed., *Ägypten und Syrien zwischen 1317 und 1341 in der Chronik des Mufaddal b. Abi l-Fada'il* (Freiburg: Klaus Schwarz, 1973), 453.

74 Muhammad ibn 'Abdallah (Ibn Battuta), *Rihlat Ibn Battuta: al-Tuhfat al-Nizar fi Ghara'ib al-Amsar wa-'Aja'ib al-Asfar*, ed. 'Abd al-Hadi al-Tazi (Ribat: Akadimiyyat al-Mamlaka al-Maghribiyya, 1997), 291–92.

Later historians then concentrated increasingly on the doctrinal aspect of the revolt. Already Nuwayri, who includes Ibn Taymiyya's fatwa in his discussion of the 1317 sultanic rescript on the 'Alawis, toward the end of his account begins to refer to the rebel leader with the religiously charged term *khariji*. The hardline conservative Damascene scholar Ibn Kathir (d. 1373), himself a fervent disciple of Ibn Taymiyya and author of the perhaps best-known chronicle of medieval Syrian history, augments his rendition of Birzali's otherwise sober account with invectives against the "misguided" Nusayris, their "false messiah" and his followers, "God rebuke them all," then finishes with a Qur'anic verse to support his conclusion that their leader will surely be the first to suffer the tortures of hell on judgment day.[75] And Maqrizi (d. 1442), doubtless the most influential historian of the entire Mamluk period, abridges Nuwayri's account to focus almost exclusively on the Mahdi's millenarian claims and then uses the incident a few pages later as a peg for his own polemical exposé of the 'Alawis' contrary beliefs and practices.[76] As Donald Little indicates, however, many of the authors relating current affairs in Syria were of course religious scholars, "whose professional interests emerged in their writings."[77] These can and should be weighed against the more neutral depictions of 'Alawism in secular Mamluk-era literature. In addition to the older, more impartial accounts, for example, the already-cited chief chancery secretary al-Qalqashandi (d. 1418) demonstrates a veritable anthropological interest in the 'Alawi community and its folklore, situating them within a balanced, object-oriented review of all the different Shi'i sects living under Mamluk rule that is completely free of the religious valuation of his *'ulama* colleagues.[78] The 1318 revolt at Jabala, in short, unquestionably marked a profound crisis in the relationship between the 'Alawis of the region and the Mamluk state authorities; its reinterpretation first and foremost as a religious conflict, however, is simply a construct of later, piety-minded historiography.

MAMLUK FISCAL POLICIES TOWARD THE 'ALAWIS

The choice by many modern writers to privilege Ibn Taymiyya and Maqrizi over Birzali and Qalqashandi, to consistently emphasize essential doctrinal difference over sociopolitical context, in this and many other episodes relating to confessional minorities in the Middle East, is not anodyne. There is of course no doubt that the Mamluk sultanate, in extending its rule over Egypt and Syria and building one of the earliest bureaucratic states in the region,

---

75 Ibn Kathir, *al-Bidaya wa'l-Nihaya*, 14:83–84.
76 Maqrizi, *Suluk*, 2:174–75, 178.
77 Little, *Introduction*, 46, 95.
78 Qalqashandi, *Subh al-A'sha*, 2:169; 33:226–27, 249–51.

instituted certain legal and administrative measures that were not in the long term beneficial to heterodox sects or other peripheral societal groups. The official recognition of four schools of Sunni Muslim jurisprudence (*madhhab*), the promulgation of an edict against Twelver Shi'is in Beirut and Sayda in 1363, and the conversion of the Zaydi sharifs of Mecca to Sunnism in the second half of the fourteenth century are all illustrative of the Mamluk state's attempt to establish its ideological as well as political dominion over the rest of society. And in the medieval chronicles we do find a number of glaring examples of the persecution of individual mystics, free-thinkers, and *rafidi* sectarians, which have subsequently been taken as self-evident proof of overarching religious radicalization, of a veritable "inquisition," or of the systematic oppression of non-Sunni populations in the empire. The very richness of these literary sources, however, should not blind us to the fact that whatever cases of religious coercion that did occur can virtually always be explained by precise, local circumstances rather than simply be assumed to have been part of a diffuse, timeless matrix of Muslim intolerance. Besides the Mamluks' pragmatic attitude toward the Ismaili community already referred to, a number of historians have shown that the conformist pressures put on the Zaydis and Twelver Shi'is were motivated above all by geopolitical concerns and did not issue in campaigns of persecution, that the trials of individual Shi'i and other scholars for heresy resulted from tensions and rivalries among local judicial authorities rather than from a general policy of religious discrimination, and so on.[79]

As regards the 'Alawis' situation under later Mamluk rule, we have only incidental references in the contemporary literature, which again give little indication of an official state policy toward them. The Damascene chronicler Ibn Qadi Shuhba (d. 1448) refers briefly to an uprising or dispute involving the (presumably Druze and Twelver Shi'i) populations of the Bekaa and Wadi al-Taym in the summer of 1344; the Mamluk commander Shihab al-Din ibn Subh was sent out against them after books which had been seized from them supposedly demonstrated their "*zandaqa* and Nusayrism."[80] Inasmuch as it is unclear if there actually were 'Alawis living in the region, and that these would not have had much connection with *zandaqa* thought (somewhat of a catch-all term for heresy in the 'Abbasid period), it is again possible that

---

79 Urbain Vermeulen, "The Rescript against the Shi'ites and Rafidites of Beirut, Saida and District (764 AH/1363 AD)," *Orientalia Lovaniensia Periodica* 4 (1973): 169–75; Richard Mortel, "Zaydi Shi'ism and the Hasanid Sharifs of Mecca," *International Journal of Middle East Studies* 19 (1987): 455–72; Mortel, "The Husaynid Amirate of Medina during the Mamluk Period," *Studia Islamica* 80 (1994): 97–123; Winter, "Shi'ah of Syria," 167–79; Anne Broadbridge, "Apostasy Trials in Eight/Fourteenth Century Egypt and Syria: A Case Study," in *History and Historiography of Post-Mongol Central Asia and the Middle East: Studies in Honor of John E. Woods*, ed. Judith Pfeiffer and Sholeh Quinn (Wiesbaden: Harrassowitz, 2006), 363–82.

80 Ahmad ibn Muhammad Ibn Qadi Shuhba, *Tarikh* (Damascus: IFÉAD, 1997), 1:410.

the reported seizure of such books was a trope deployed to legitimize and dramatize a police operation against an only vaguely identified rural populace. Similarly, the Egyptian scholar Ibn Hajar al-'Asqalani (d. 1449) describes the famous Shi'i theologian Muhammad ibn Makki martyred in 1384 as well as the latter's friend supposedly beheaded in Tripoli around the same time as "Nusayris" who declared licit the consumption of wine "and other such abominations"; at least in the case of Ibn Makki, however, this accusation is demonstrably false.[81] A brief reference in the *Khayr al-Sani'a* places violence that ostensibly occurred in the Safita region in the fourteenth century in the reign of the Ayyubid sultan al-'Adil (d. 1218) and is thus anachronistic; another reference to a skirmish in a village near Aleppo in 1388–90 in which two recently immigrated sons of an 'Alawi shaykh were killed does not mention the involvement of state authorities and is at any rate not verifiable.[82]

The institution that perhaps best exemplifies the Mamluk state's "policy" toward the 'Alawis is a unique but little-regarded capitation tax which was imposed on male members of the community. The *dirhemü'r-rical* (*dirham al-rijal*) or "*dirhem* (piaster) on men" is known to us from the Ottoman tax censuses referred to as the Tahrir Defterleri and will be extensively dealt with in the following chapter. Much like the Mamluk *rawk*s, Ottoman *tahrir*s represented one of the state's most important acts of sovereignty in newly acquired areas, and they epitomize the development of the empire's bureaucratic apparatus in the early modern period. In actual fact, however, Ottoman administrative law (*kanun*) was largely based on precedent, incorporating local customary practice (*'urf/örf*) wherever possible and systematically invoking "ancient law" (*kanun-ı kadim*) as its primary source of legislation, including when this older law predated the Ottoman or even the original Muslim conquest. Though rarely noticed by Mamlukist historians, the earliest Ottoman *tahrir*s and the provincial law codes (*kanun-name*) that accompany them thus constitute one of our foremost sources on late Mamluk-era administration in Syria.

The *dirhem* is first noted in Tahrir Defteri (TD) 68, a tax census compiled for the *sancak* (military province) of Tripoli in 925/1519 or shortly after the Ottoman conquest. The *kanun-name* appended to this census stipulates that the *dirhem* continue to be levied on those villages where it had always been collected "in the past" (*kadimü'l-eyyamdan*) but does not explicitly refer to the 'Alawis or Nusayris.[83] It is in later *kanun-name*s that the tax is specifically linked to the community:

---

81 'Asqalani, *Inba' al-Ghumr*, 1:228; Winter, "Shi'ah of Syria," 176–77.
82 Harfush, *Khayr al-Sani'a*, 910.
83 Başbakanlık Ottoman Archives (BOA), Istanbul: Tahrir Defteri (TD) 68:5–6, transliterated in Ahmet Akgündüz, ed., *Osmanlı Kanunnâmeleri ve Hukukî Tahlilleri*, 9 vols. (Istanbul: FEY Vakfı/Osmanlı Araştırmaları Vakfı, 1990–96), 3:499–501.

In the villages of [Tripoli] *sancak* there is a people known as Nusayris who neither fast nor pray nor submit to any of the Islamic *şeriat*. In the old register [*defter*], a part of this sect [*taife*] was assessed a tax called the "*dirhem* on men," in the amount of one each, and it was collected each year in accordance with the *defter*. Some of them were not assessed in the *defter* and they were not levied. Presently ... an appeal was made to the noblest throne, and it is my command that it be collected from all of them. Thus on the basis of ancient custom, a *dirhem* on men of 12 *para* [copper coins] each from married men, and six each from boys who can work and earn independently, is to be registered in the new *defter*.[84]

As a result, some authors have likened the *dirhemü'r-rical* to the *jizya/cizye*, the per-capita tax assessed on Christian and Jewish (and all non-Muslim) populations under shari'a law.[85] However, if the Mamluks levied the *dirhem* only on parts of the 'Alawi community (which may have been difficult to assess otherwise), it is not certain that it was initially construed as a sectarian tax; similar terms, such as *resm-i ricaliye* or *'adet-i ricaliye*, for example, were used to describe dues on individual tribal groups in the region rather than on entire religious communities.[86] Other measures that did target Shi'is specifically, on the other hand, were eliminated by the new Ottoman regime: the 1519 Tripoli *kanun-name*, for example, announces the abolition of the *sarha* or *serce*, which had until then been collected from the *evlad-ı akil*, the leaders of the local Ismaili community, as this tax had only been instituted by the Mamluk sultan Qansuh al-Ghawri and had apparently led to much oppression and the ruin of numerous villages in the area.[87] A 1526 *kanun-name* for Hama and Homs, for its part, stipulates that four *osmani* (gold coins) be collected at Hama from "Rafızis" (i.e., Twelver Shi'is) traveling from the Damascus region to the shrine of 'Ali at Najaf in Iraq; this tax too disappears from later *defters*, presumably once Iraq had also been added to the empire.[88] In other words, neither the Mamluks nor the Ottomans seem to have followed a policy of sectarian fiscal discrimination per se, as suggested by the expansion of some Shi'i-specific taxes and the elimination of others. As Margaret Venzke has rightly argued, the Ottomans' objective in adapting and modifying Mamluk taxes in Syria was not ideological but aimed to centralize and consolidate the

---

84 TD 1107:9, transliterated in Akgündüz, *Osmanlı Kanunnâmeleri*, 7:83.
85 Robert Mantran and Jean Sauvaget, *Règlements fiscaux ottomans: les provinces syriennes* (Beirut: Institut français de Damas, 1951), 76–77; see also Jean Sauvaget, "Décrets Mamelouks de Syrie (III)," *Bulletin d'études orientales* 12 (1947–48): 48–49.
86 Bernard Lewis, "Ottoman Land Tenure and Taxation in Syria," *Studia Islamica* 50 (1979): 121.
87 TD 68:5–6, transliterated in Akgündüz, *Osmanlı Kanunnâmeleri*, 3:499–501. The *sarha* was later reinstituted.
88 Akgündüz, *Osmanlı Kanunnâmeleri*, 6:671.

provincial administration.[89] To this end, and despite the constant rhetoric in support of "ancient tradition" and against "illegal [religious] innovation" (*bidatlar*) that permeates the Tahrir registers, the Ottomans did not hesitate to broaden and institutionalize a tax specific to the 'Alawis, which, in consequence, denotes an official recognition, by both the Mamluk and Ottoman state, of the community as such.

CONCLUSION: THE PERSECUTION SYNDROME

The picture that the situation of 'Alawis under Muslim state rule presents is a complex one. If, given the evidence, it is simply not accurate to characterize Mamluk policy vis-à-vis the 'Alawis (or any other such group) as one of extremism or radicalization, it would be equally wrong to idealize the 'Alawi mountain as a sort of northern Syrian Ruritania marked by peace and blissful coexistence with the authorities and other sects. The discussion of religious minorities today all too often revolves around the binary opposites of persecution and toleration; in fact both are modern anachronisms that have no equivalent in the political discourse of the medieval period. The practical constraints on Mamluk state power in the rural hinterland meant that there could be no question of forcing the native population to adhere to a particular literature-based ideology; that their leaders had to be co-opted to some degree to ensure a modicum of security and tax revenue in the region; and that the 'Alawis were ultimately not that different, from an administrative point of view, from other sectarian, tribal, or economically defined "factions" (*ta'ifa*). Nor, on the other hand, could a state that claimed religious legitimacy explicitly sanction a heterodox deviation from this religion. When used in the medieval texts, the term "Nusayri" (which, as has been pointed out, was never used by the 'Alawis themselves) was always essentializing and discriminatory, deployed to justify certain communal obligations, state punitive action, or simple, self-serving moral reprobation.

The inherent limitations of our written sources for this period underline the importance of not imposing an exclusive master narrative along the lines of "persecution" or "mountain refuge" on the history of 'Alawis under Sunni Muslim rule. Beyond the obvious autarchy of any rural population inhabiting the inaccessible hinterland and the inevitable weaknesses of the premodern state, the 'Alawis also did not all share one single, uniform situation under Mamluk or Ottoman sovereignty: communal violence with the Ismailis in one district did not preclude neighborliness and cooperation in another; a tax revolt in

---

89 Margaret Venzke, "Syria's Land-Taxation in the Ottoman 'Classical Age' Broadly Considered," in *V. Milletlerarası Türkiye Sosyal ve İktisat Tarihi Kongresi: Tebliğler*, ed. Marmara Universitesi Türkiyat Araştırma ve Uygulama Merkezi (Ankara: Türk Tarih Kurumu, 1990), 428–29.

Jabala did not detract from cordial relations with government representatives at Hama; and most of all, the well-publicized diatribes of individual *'ulama* cannot be equated with a universal Sunni position toward the sect.

Yet this is exactly what has been done today, to the point that engaged observers of the civil conflict in Syria have spoken of a veritable "Ibn Taymiyya syndrome" or deep-seated fear among the 'Alawis that "the" Sunnis "have always" hated the community and wished its elimination as per such fatwas.[90] This fear is of course not irrational: Islamist militants in Syria in the 1980s appear to have invoked Ibn Taymiyya as their guiding authority (a fact most eagerly publicized by the regime itself); more recently, statements on Sunni jihadist websites or by leading antiregime scholars like Yusuf al-Qaradawi do indeed make unattributed but precise textual reference to Ibn Taymiyya's rulings when they proclaim that 'Alawis are "greater infidels than the Christians and Jews and do greater harm to Islam."[91] The media, as well as some modern-day specialists of Islam, have not hesitated in cherry-picking the so-called historic roots of "the" Sunni-Shi'i or Sunni-'Alawi sectarian divide, relating any incidence of violence in the Middle East today back to a single, ongoing conflict which supposedly "began" in the seventh century and continued unabatedly throughout the Middle Ages and the Ottoman period, thus reinforcing the notion that all politics in the region are somehow always based on religion. To do so, however, is to overemphasize the perspective of piety-minded narrative historiography, to overstate the importance of religion in actual Mamluk and Ottoman statecraft, and to overlook the complex internal evolution of the 'Alawi sectarian community as well as the mundanity and ambivalence of its rapport with the state authorities.

---

90 Bahar Kimyongür, *Syriana: La conquête continue* (Brussels: Investig'Action, 2011), 75.

91 Olivier Carré and Michel Seurat, eds., *Les Frères musulmans: Égypte et Syrie (1928–1982)* (Paris: Gallimard, 1983), 151–53; "Middle East Media Research Institute" (www.memrijtmm.org); "Syrian Rockets Hit Hezbollah Stronghold in Lebanon, Influential Cleric Fans Sectarian Flames," *Washington Post*, 1 June 2013.

* 3 *

SURVEY AND PUNISH

THE 'ALAWIS' INTEGRATION INTO THE

OTTOMAN EMPIRE

(1516–1645)

If the Mamluks have generally received bad press regarding their purported Islamic radicalism and bad treatment of minorities, it is even truer of the Ottomans. Part of the reason is modern nationalist historians' refusal to consider the Ottoman period as anything other than one of tyranny and decline, as a narrative backdrop to the struggles of emerging nationhood in the Balkans and the Arab world just before and after World War I. Another part of the reason, however, is also conventional orientalist scholarship's disdain for Ottoman literature and theology, which is largely seen as stagnant and inferior to the (Greek-inspired) high scholasticism of the medieval period and thus not worthy of study in its relationship to other religious or sectarian traditions. As a result, the leading presentations of 'Alawi history by the likes of René Dussaud and Jacques Weulersse hardly mention the pre-nineteenth-century Ottoman Empire with so much as a word, while Yaron Friedman's recent monograph jumps straight from the community's religious evolution and supposed oppression by the Mamluks to its political identity in modern times, because "there are no reliable sources concerning the situation of the Nusayris between the fifteenth and nineteenth centuries."[1]

The purpose of this chapter is to prove the exact opposite and show that there exists a wealth of very credible sources regarding the 'Alawis' social, administrative, and political situation beginning in the early sixteenth century and ultimately extending throughout the Ottoman period. The first two parts examine the Ottoman conquest of northwestern Syria and suggest that while the traditional accounts of an 'Alawi massacre at Aleppo appear to be unfounded, early tax censuses show the coastal mountain region to have been

---

1 Dussaud, *Histoire et religion*, 31; Weulersse, *Pays des Alaouites*, 110–13; Friedman, *Nusayrī-'Alawīs*, 199.

in a state of rebellion against the Ottomans until around the middle of the sixteenth century. These same Tahrir censuses are then used in the following sections to provide a detailed list of villages inhabited by 'Alawis and assessed the *dirhemü'r-rical* tax in the provinces of Homs, Tripoli, and Jabala. While indicating the extent of the 'Alawi community's integration into the regular structures of Ottoman administration, these censuses also make clear to what extent the Ottoman state was willing to accommodate and conciliate a population it knew full well to be heretical in order to maximize its tax revenues in the region. The final section examines the executive administration of the 'Alawi heartland, more specifically in the province (*sancak*) of Jabala, on the basis of Ottoman imperial orders sent from Istanbul to the local authorities. These documents are evocative of the northward shift of the 'Alawi community's center as well as the growing importance of the northwestern Syrian coastal region in the sixteenth century, and they deal with numerous cases of rebellion and brigandage by the local 'Alawi population, more specifically the Kelbi tribe. Remarkably, however, these sources also make clear that the 'Alawis' religious identity per se was never an issue for the Ottoman authorities. Starting in the early seventeenth century there is a marked decrease in the official documentation available for the region; by this time, however, the 'Alawi community had been fully integrated into the administrative system of the northwestern Syrian provinces, and the 'Alawis were as much subjects of the Ottoman Empire as any other rural hinterland population.

THE OTTOMAN CONQUEST

The Ottomans' defeat of the Mamluks and conquest of Syria and Egypt in 1516–17 marked the end of a conflict which had pitted the two empires against each other for many years. In 1485 the Ottomans had tried but failed to establish their hegemony over the frontier marches separating the two states; over the next decades the Ottomans observed with increasing misgivings, and sometimes sought to remedy, the Mamluks' inability to defend the Red Sea and western Indian Ocean against the encroachment of the Portuguese. In the end, however, the reasons for the Ottoman campaign against the Mamluks had, at least on the surface, much to do with religion: confronted by a massive, ongoing revolt in Anatolia of the "Kızılbaş," Turkmen tribes who subscribed to various forms of *ghulat* Shi'ism and revered the young "shah" Isma'il of the Safavid sufi order as a living incarnation of the divine, the Ottoman sultan Selim set out in 1514 to smash the nascent Shi'i Safavid state at Çaldıran on the border with Iran. In essence the Kızılbaş revolt had been against the ever-increasing presence and dominance of the central Ottoman state over the rural Anatolian population, but its adoption of militant Shi'i doctrines and the foundation of a Shi'i counterstate in Iran constituted an ideological challenge that would fundamentally transform the Ottoman sultanate's perception of itself in the sixteenth century and lead it to cast itself as a champion of religious orthodoxy for the first time. With the defeat and elimination of the Mamluks, the Ottomans assumed the all-important title of protector of the Holy Places (Mecca and Medina); later on it would be claimed that the caliphate had been transferred to the Ottoman sultans as well. During the campaign itself Selim spent an inordinate amount of time at Damascus in order to oversee the reconstruction of the tomb of Muhyi al-Din Ibn al-'Arabi (d. 1240), the guiding luminary of Turkish Sufism and "patron saint" of the Ottoman state, while in Egypt he had the Safavid shahs cursed from the pulpit and the last Mamluk sultans denounced as Shi'i sympathizers.[2]

It is perhaps for these reasons that the Ottomans are often believed to have targeted the 'Alawis during the conquest of Syria in the same way they had pursued the Anatolian Kızılbaş. Al-Tawil, most notably, claims that "millions" of 'Alawis (i.e., Shi'is) were eliminated throughout Anatolia, Syria, and Egypt: in Syria, knowing that the Sunnis of Aleppo and Damascus harbored evil designs against the sects, Sultan Selim solicited fatwas from the local *'ulama*, in particular from an otherwise unattested "Shaykh Nuh al-Hanafi al-Dimashqi," which permitted the shedding of their blood as well as their enslavement. Selim then proceeded to massacre the 'Alawis, forcing them to flee into the mountains where the remnants of the community barely managed to survive in poverty and obscurity until the modern age.[3] The notion that the 'Alawi population was actively driven out of Aleppo in 1516 is repeated by other Syrian authors who state that fanatical mobs killed forty thousand or more of them in the city, burned down their houses, and plundered their belongings.[4] Yunus Tümkaya, while admitting that this is not corroborated in any chronicles of the period and that al-Tawil's account was composed under the sign of Arab nationalism at the beginning of the twentieth century, nonetheless confirms that the "Aleppo massacre" (*Halep katliamı*) constitutes a key episode in the community's sectarian identity, its memory having been passed down from generation to generation and remaining vivid among the 'Alawis of northwestern Syria and Hatay down to the present day.[5]

2 Winter, *Shiites of Lebanon*, 13–14, 36.
3 Al-Tawil, *Tarikh al-'Alawiyyin*, 445–46. The text of the purported fatwa is examined in Talhamy, "The *Fatwas*," 181–82.
4 Al-Salih, *Al-Naba' al-Yaqin*, 161–62; al-Musa, *Al-Imam 'Ali wa'l-'Alawiyyin*, 172–74. In another version it was the Imami population of Aleppo that was targeted; see Nasrallah, *Halab wa'l-Tashayyu'*, 152–61.
5 Muhammad Khunda, *Tarikh al-'Alawiyyin wa-Ansabihim* (Beirut: Dar al-Mahajja al-Bayda', 2004), 178–81; Yunus Tümkaya, *Farklılığa Rağmen Bir Olmak: Nusayri Alevi Dünyasında Bir Gezi* (Istanbul: Can Yayınları, 2004), 167–75; see also Mahmut Reyhani, *Gölgesiz Işıklar*, vol. 2: *Tarihte Aleviler* (Istanbul: Can Yayınları, 1995), 74–82.

From a historical perspective, there are obviously several problems with the "Aleppo massacre." Al-Tawil's story, for one, is colored by his extremely favorable impression of the Circassian Mamluks, who (as indicated above) he believes were Shi'is themselves and therefore sided with the Safavids in what was in essence a war of religion against Selim. In reality, however, the Mamluks' relations with the Safavids were never all that good. As early as 1502 the Mamluks imprisoned the leader of a pro-Kızılbaş revolt who had fled to Aleppo from Karaman in central Anatolia, prompting the threat of an attack on the city by Shah Isma'il himself. A few years later, in 1507, Isma'il sent an embassy to Cairo demanding the provinces of Adana and Tarsus, which were ruled by vassals of the Mamluks, be ceded to him. Shortly thereafter a Safavid force marched through Mamluk territory on its way back from a campaign against the Ottomans in Anatolia; "Sultan Qansuh al-Ghawri took the precaution of sending an expedition to Syria, but his soldiers avoided engaging the Kızılbaş who moved unhampered to Iran."[6] When Shah Isma'il began to initiate secret contacts with the Ottoman sultan Bayezid's rebel son Şahinşah in 1510, his messages were intercepted and their content divulged to Bayezid by the Mamluk governor of Aleppo, Khayir Beğ. Later that same year Isma'il seized an opportunity to demonstrate his defiance of both Bayezid and Qansuh al-Ghawri by sending them the skulls and stuffed heads of Sunni Uzbek khans recently slain in battle in Afghanistan, and he demanded that the Mamluks allow him to provide a honorary covering for the *ka'ba* in Mecca during the annual pilgrimage.[7] Even when war with the aggressive new sultan Selim became imminent and Qansuh al-Ghawri undertook secret, last-ditch talks with Isma'il in 1516, these were betrayed to the Ottomans by a Mamluk double-agent.[8] Considering that Khayir Beğ immediately abandoned the Mamluk side at the battle of Marj Dabiq in August 1516, thus enabling the Ottomans to seize Aleppo without a fight, and then continued to serve Selim for several more years as governor in Egypt, it seems probable that he and other leading Mamluk commanders in northern Syria had never been that adverse to Selim's policies or even to an Ottoman takeover in the region.

There is ultimately little to support the notion that the Mamluks' defeat at Marj Dabiq gave way to a massacre of 'Alawis or other groups in Aleppo, where the Ottomans were welcomed by the local population a few days after the battle. It is in fact rather doubtful that the city still housed much of any Shi'i population at this time after having been converted back to Sunnism by the Zangid dynasty in the twelfth century, the presence of some Shi'i-leaning

---

6 Adel Allouche, *The Origins and Development of the Ottoman-Safavid Conflict (906–962/1500–1555)* (Berlin: Klaus Schwarz, 1983), 81–82, 84.

7 Ibid., 91, 93.

8 Ibid., 125–26.

notables such as the Zuhrawi family of sharifs and several (Imami) Shi'i villages in the countryside notwithstanding. Neither the Arabic nor the Ottoman chronicles give any indication of sectarian violence during the conquest, even though the latter readily claim high numbers of Kızılbaş victims during Selim's other campaigns. The figure of forty thousand such victims in particular is a literary trope encountered in several contemporary Ottoman histories,[9] and which simply appears to have been transposed into the Syrian context by later authors. While the struggle against Shi'i Iran and the Ottomans' new role as defenders of Muslim orthodoxy were key reasons behind Selim's war with the Mamluks, by all indications this did not herald a change in the relationship between the state authorities and confessional minorities per se in Syria during or after the conquest.

THE 'ALAWI REBELLION

However, if the conquest of Aleppo was not marked by violence against the 'Alawis, this is less certain for the coastal highlands where the community was actually concentrated. After Homs and Hama, the city of Tripoli also appears to have been taken peacefully, but there is virtually nothing in the chronicles regarding the Ottomans' further progress in northwestern Syria. It is thus all the more significant that Ottoman documents offer some sparse but critical evidence of an 'Alawi rebellion in the mountains at the beginning of the Ottoman occupation that in some ways corroborates but also sheds a different light on the standard accounts of state oppression in this time. The Tahrir Defterleri, as mentioned at the end of the previous chapter, record tax surveys which were carried out in different parts of the empire and which often provide detailed information about agricultural productivity and other revenues in a given province; it is a subject of debate among Ottomanists to what extent these constitute comprehensive statistical material or can be used for demographic and social analyses.[10] What is less discussed is the fact that the early *tahrir*s especially sometimes also contain brief marginal notes on a village's or district's incorporation into the administrative system and can thus serve as a source on certain microhistorical events that are otherwise unaccounted for in the narrative literature.

While the Ottoman administration generally avoided acknowledging sectarian differences within the Muslim population, the maintenance of the Mamluk-era *dirhemü'r-rical* ("piaster on men") tax on 'Alawis discussed

---

9 Hanna Sohrweide, "Der Sieg der Safaviden in Persien und seine Rückwirkung auf die Schiiten Anatoliens im 16. Jahrhundert," *Der Islam* 41 (1965): 162.

10 See Metin Coşgel, "Ottoman Tax Registers (*Tahrir Defterleri*)," *Historical Methods* 37 (2004): 87–100.

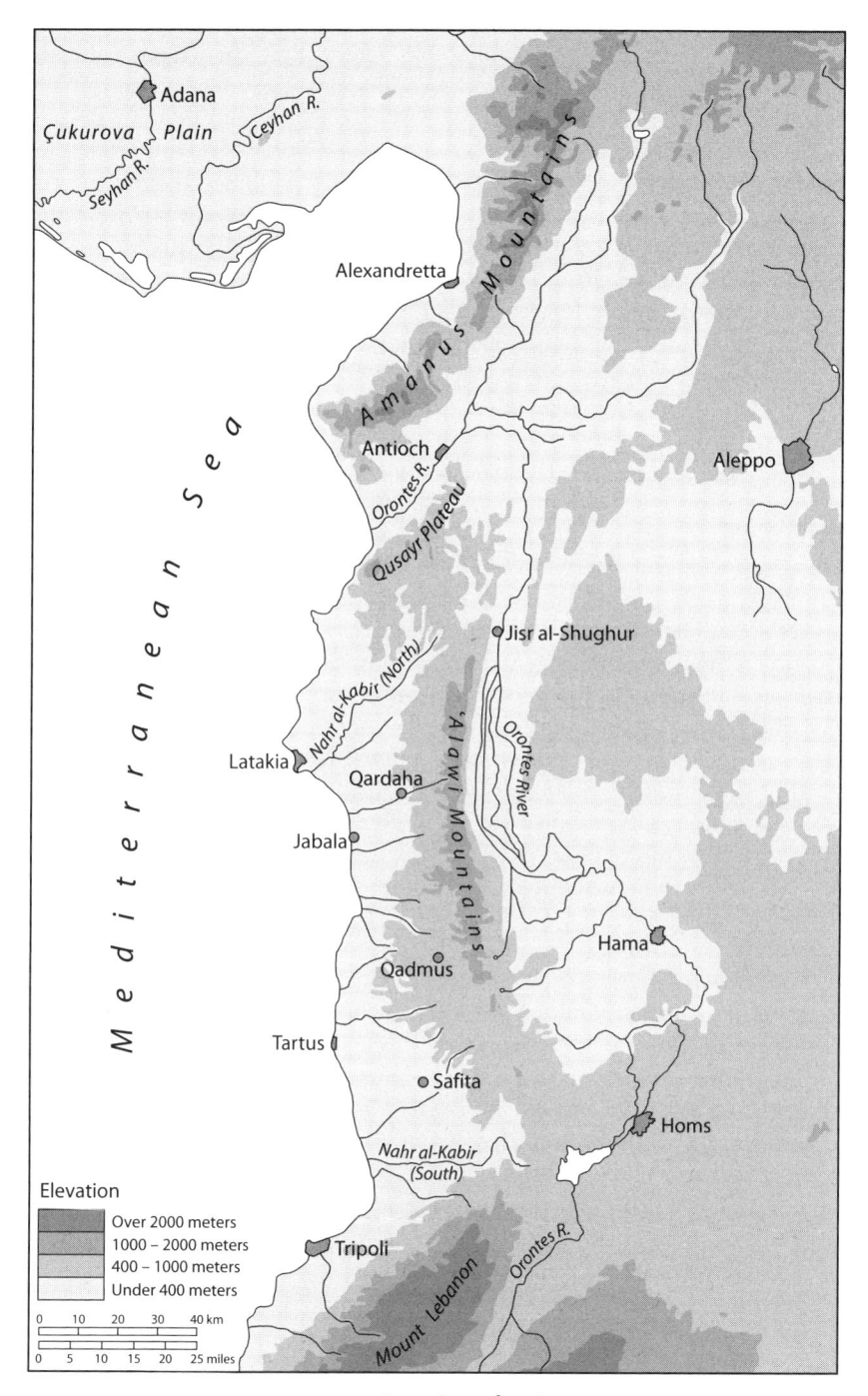

MAP 1. Overview of region

above ensured that villages inhabited by 'Alawis were clearly identifiable in the Tahrir registers. As indicated, the earliest of these tax censuses for the province (*sancak* or *liva*) of Tripoli, TD 68, was carried out in 1519. Of the twenty-six tax districts (*nahiye*) included in the province at this time, fourteen comprised villages or towns with an 'Alawi population that was assessed the *dirhem*: Antartus, Jabala, Kahf, Khawabi, Latakia, Marqab, Mi'ar, Munayqa, Platanus, Qadmus, Qulay'a, Safita, Sahyun, and 'Ulayqa. The distribution and progression of *dirhem* charges will be examined in the next section; what is of concern here is that the register explicitly notes a number of villages in the one district of Jabala (Cebele) to have been in an endemic state of rebellion since the Mamluk period. The marginal comments in this regard appear to be making direct reference to the 1318 uprising in Platanus and to Ibn Taymiyya's condemnation of the 'Alawis as "even worse" than Christians and Jews and confirm that the Ottomans regarded locally produced fatwas, rather than their own, as the legal basis for attacking the 'Alawis as heretics. What is particularly noteworthy, however, is that while the Ottomans did apparently engage an 'Alawi resistance during or shortly after the conquest, this did not cause the 'Alawis to flee from the Aleppo region and into the mountains but rather the other way around. In the (no longer extant) village of Istafalin, for example, "the houses and places have been burned down" and the "entirety of the *ghulat* Rafizi Nusayri rebels are now in Hama, the Aleppo region, and elsewhere." Other villages, according to the register,

> are situated in the mountain fastnesses, and their people are *ghulat* Rafizis and Nusayris who are perhaps even more misguided and recalcitrant than the unbelievers. They are always rebelling against God's commands and the Sultan's laws in one way or another and have been in constant revolt and sedition since the time of the Circassians. The scholars of Damascus and Egypt attested their *zandaqa*, heresy, and apostasy and deemed it permissible to kill, plunder, and enslave them in order to wipe them out. After fatwas in this regard were found in the region, these evildoers were destroyed and their villages and hamlets ruined, and in the first days of the campaign of justice the town of Platanus was laid waste and burned down. Then they came again and still did not submit in this matter. After this faction was attacked, in accordance with an imperial order, many individuals were killed and a great victory was fought. Of this faction, however, six to seven hundred returned and most are in fact alive and frequent the region of Aleppo with their folk and family. They are to be given the possibility of coming to settle and develop areas that are conducive to submission outside their region of origin.[11]

11 TD 68:316.

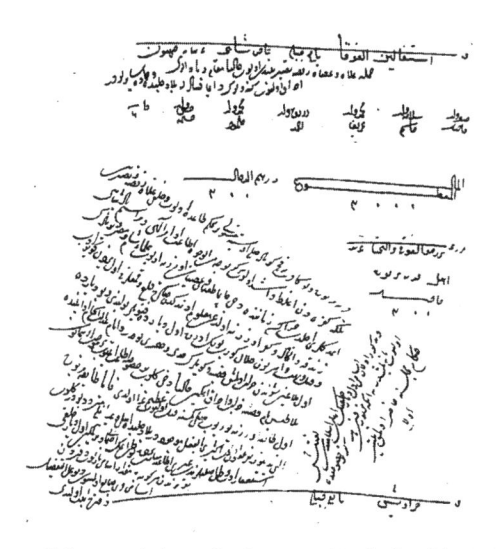

FIGURE 3.1. Detail from Tahrir Defteri 68:316 (Başbakanlık Archives, Istanbul)

In other words, while facing down the resistance in the mountains the Ottomans were clearly not interested in persecuting the 'Alawis per se but on the contrary wished more than anything to settle them where they could more easily be controlled and taxed. A close look at the area concerned suggests that this rebellion was a very localized affair and did not affect other districts. The villages that can be identified positively today—'Amuda, Bakarrama, Bassin, Halbakko, Hillat 'Ara, Mutawwar, Qurn Hulya, and Rayhanat Mutawwar—are all concentrated in a mountainous zone 16 to 22 km due east of Jabala at altitudes between 580 and 1000 m, which was likely very difficult for the state to submit: 'Amuda occupies an impenetrable position overlooking the Farshat River and the Banu-Qahtan citadel; Halbakko, at 1000 m altitude, was originally built as a forest outpost by villagers from Bayt Yashut further down the ridge; Hillat 'Ara nearby extends along a steep precipice above the valley of the same name; Qurn Hulya, situated on a rocky ledge between two ravines, is among the last villages before the Jabal al-Sha'ra, the highest portion of the Syrian coastal range. The neighboring Platanus district, on the other hand, which was at the heart of the Mamluk-era revolt, is accounted for a few pages later in the register and was evidently not involved this time around.[12]

12 TD 68:316–20. Villages located using the map *Muhafazat al-Ladhiqiyya* (Aleppo: Khara'it al-Naddaf, 2001); village name transliterations established in part using the French mandate-era gazetteer *Répertoire alphabétique des villages et hameaux* (Latakia, [1924]); additional geographical information from Mustafa Talas, ed., *Al-Mu'jam al-Jughrafi li'l-Qutr al-'Arabi al-Suri* (Damascus: Al-Mu'assasa al-'Amma li'l-Masahat, 1992).

Survey and Punish * 81

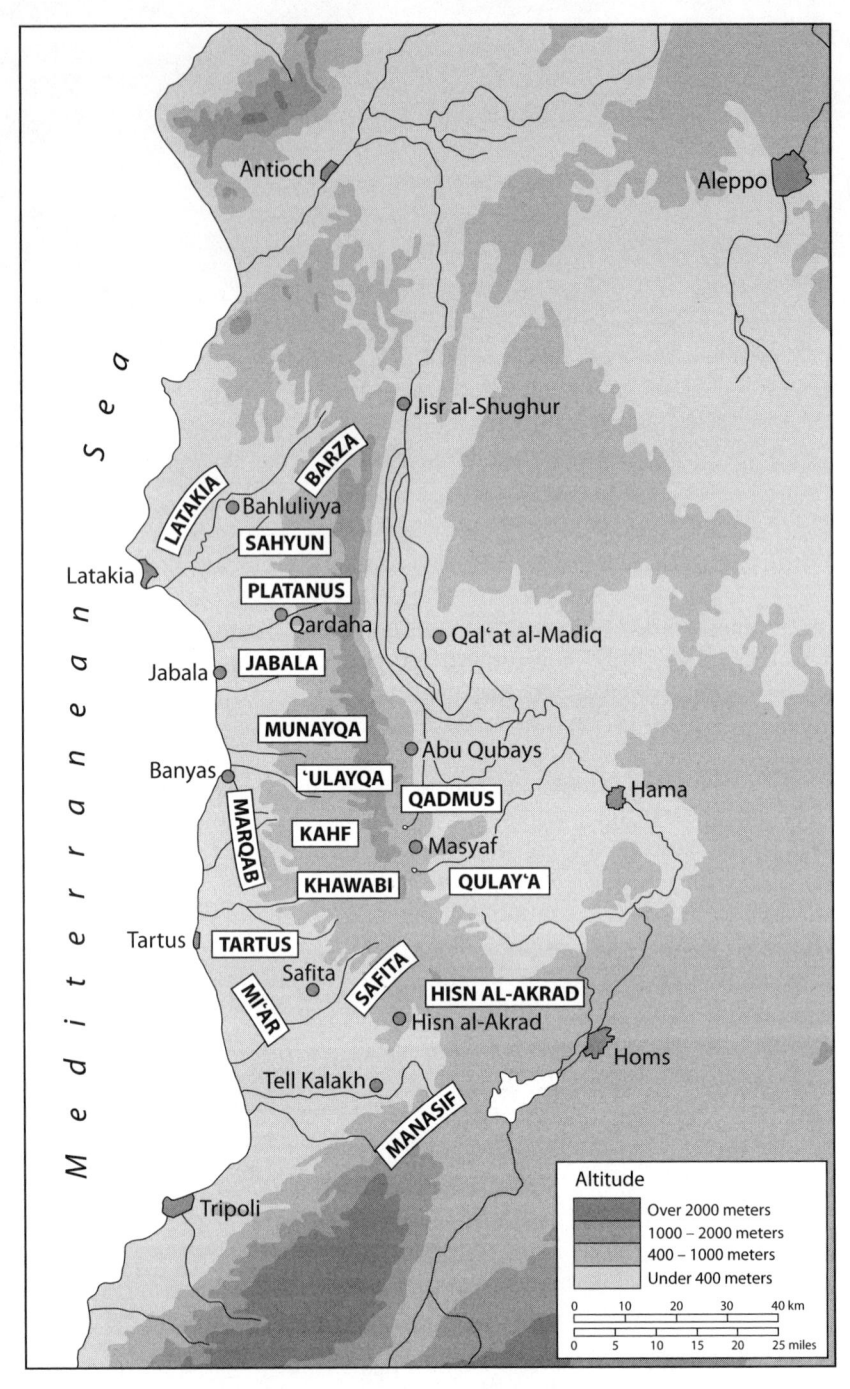

MAP 2. 'Alawi-populated tax districts (collection of *dirhemü'r-rical*)

82 * *Chapter Three*

Despite the pejorative terms employed, TD 68 also shows how the Ottomans were intent on pursuing a differential policy vis-à-vis the highland population rather than combatting the 'Alawis as a whole. The rebel villages are indicated by a variety of similar labels such as "Nusayri rebels; not in obedience," "*ghulat* Rafizis; [religious] ingrates who are never compliant and constantly sowing corruption, being stubborn, and ruining the country," or "of the group of disobedient Nusayri rebels," whereby the difference in wording appears to be above all a stylistic choice. More interestingly, a number of villages are noted as being "of the Nusayri Kelbi rebels" or in the hands of "the constantly refractory group of Kelbiyyin rebels," marking the first time in our sources that 'Alawis are identified by a tribal rather than an exclusively sectarian name. For twelve of the rebel villages, the *defter* provides no figures whatsoever; for five others, on the other hand, it lists the total amount of *dirhem* and *maktu* (regular lump-sum agricultural tax) dues and provides the names of the heads of household, suggesting that here at least the fisc could assess, if not actually collect, taxes. 'Arqub, though located in the revolt area, is expressly noted as being "in submission," while Janaro (not identified) is said to be "at times in rebellion, at times in submission" and is thus assigned as a benefice to an Ottoman *timariot* (cavalryman; tax lord). Moreover, the Ottoman authorities seem to have genuinely hoped to redevelop the region or were willing to negotiate and make compromises in order to maximize their revenues. Several lower-lying 'Alawi villages such as Qatarba (Qutriyya) are noted to have suffered damage from the rebellion so that no taxes could be expected; Nuzin's population had apparently fled to neighboring villages, where their dues were now to be collected; in Qurn Hulya as well as Darawish (not identified) the authorities hoped to bring the population back into submission and the village back under cultivation (*der mamur*); in other villages the troublemakers were to be registered (but apparently not otherwise prosecuted); and in the above-mentioned Janaro, where the authorities have forgone the *dirhem* but where the village is assessed a fixed *maktu* tax, it is explicitly noted that the population "has accepted [to pay] this amount of money."[13]

THE *DIRHEMÜ'R-RICAL* AND THE TAX DISTRICTS OF THE COASTAL HIGHLANDS

This section draws on TD 68 and subsequent Tahrir surveys to provide a broad overview of the 'Alawi-inhabited tax districts (*nahiye*) of northwestern Syria from the time of the Ottoman conquest to the mid- to late seventeenth century. Villages where the Ottoman authorities knew or believed an 'Alawi

13 TD 68:315–21, 329, 332, 334.

population to be present were assessed the special *dirhemü'r-rical* tax, making the 'Alawis the only Muslim sectarian group in the region whose geographic distribution can be precisely traced in the Ottoman registers. (No such distinction is made for the Shi'i or Druze populations in Lebanon, for example.) Moreover, the progression of *dirhem* charges between 1519 and 1645–46 (or 1680 for two 'Alawi-inhabited *nahiye*s in the province of Homs), the last years for which we have *tahrir* records mentioning the tax, give some general indication of the growth and regional spread of the community.

The Tahrir Defterleri have long been used by sociodemographic historians such as Ömer Lutfi Barkan, Justin McCarthy, and 'Issam Khalifa to calculate the population, confessional makeup, agricultural production, taxation level, and other economic indicators of a given town or district. The *dirhem* charge would appear to lend itself ideally to such an exercise in that it was imposed on the 'Alawis on a per capita basis: in 1547–48, as already mentioned, 12 copper *para* were to be collected from every head of household and 6 from each nondependent unmarried man (equivalent to 36 and 18 silver *akça*, respectively); in a *tahrir* from 1571–72 the rate is given as 24 and 12 *akça*, respectively; and by 1645–46 it has risen to 50 *akça* for both married and unmarried men.[14] Several reasons, however, prevent us from using *dirhem* figures as a precise measure of the local 'Alawi population. For one, the *dirhem* is not accounted for in the all tax surveys or is included in a particular register for one 'Alawi village but not for another. Tahrir censuses frequently concerned only one type of income beneficiary, such as the sultanic crown reserve (*hass-ı şahi* or *hass-ı hümayun*), the provincial governor (*hass-ı mirmiran*), or a pious foundation (*vakıf*), so that the omission of *dirhem* charges in one register may simply mean they were earmarked for another recipient, not that the village no longer had an 'Alawi population.[15] In our case, the earliest *tahrir*s frequently emphasize that the *dirhem* is to be reserved for the *hass-ı şahi* rather than given in fief to an Ottoman officer; on several pages the *dirhem* charge appears to have been added on in the margins of the original text, as if it had come to the attention of the authorities and had been included in the census only as an afterthought. Second, in many instances the *dirhem* is not indicated individually but in combination with the regular *maktu* or *dimos* land tax, which generally makes up far more of the peasants' total charges but which is assessed on agricultural production rather than on a per capita basis. Moreover, the *dirhem* figures themselves are frequently not divisible by the corresponding tax rate of 36, 24, or 12 *akça* per person; are rounded

14 Akgündüz, *Osmanlı Kanunnâmeleri*, 7:83, 792; BOA: Maliyeden Müdevver (MAD) 842:210.
15 See also Heath Lowry, "The Ottoman Tahrîr Defterleri as a Source for Social and Economic History: Pitfalls and Limitations," in *Studies in Defterology: Ottoman Society in the Fifteenth and Sixteenth Centuries* (Istanbul: Isis Press, 1992), 3–18; Margaret Venzke, "The Ottoman Tahrir Defterleri and Agricultural Productivity: The Case for Northern Syria," *Osmanlı Araştırmaları* 17 (1997): 1–13.

to the nearest hundred or even thousand; are carried over from one *defter* to the next without change for several decades; or show sudden leaps that are unlikely to have correlated to an actual growth in population. Much as with other Ottoman taxes that were collected on a per-household basis (*cizye*, *avarız*, *sürsat*, etc.), the figures given for the *dirhemü'r-rical* were not precise statistics but rather a fiscal and administrative ideal, one that reflected the government's valuation of the 'Alawi community's revenue potential and was thus constantly subject to adjustment, contestation, and renegotiation. The Tahrir registers are nevertheless valuable in that they enable us to trace with some degree of certainty where the rural 'Alawi population was established in the sixteenth and seventeenth centuries and how the region was organized administratively. Tables 1a–1f list all the villages of a given *nahiye* where the *dirhem* was collected at some time between 1519 and 1645–46 (or 1680). Where possible the exact amount in *akça* is given; "yes" indicates that the *dirhem* was assessed but that it was combined with other taxes and its precise amount is therefore unknown. A dash (–) indicates that the village in question appears in the *defter* but was not assessed the *dirhem* that particular year, which can mean that there were indeed no 'Alawis resident at the time; that the authorities were not aware of them; or that their dues were collected and/or registered elsewhere. Of all the villages listed, approximately half have been identified and located, allowing us to provide a rough sketch map of some of the more important *nahiye*s. These districts did not have exact borders but were defined by the villages whose revenues were designated to a particular beneficiary; later, as will be shown in the following chapter, they were farmed out to private tax collectors (*mültezim*). Individual villages could therefore change affiliation or in some instances be shared between two different tax districts; they are indicated as dots connected to a particular jurisdiction rather than as part of an integrated territory. This section marks one of the first attempts to reconstruct the Ottoman *nahiye*s of northwestern Syria, and in the scope of the present study only those villages that were assessed the *dirhem* in the *sancak*s of Tripoli, Jabala, and Homs have been considered. (The *dirhem* does not appear to have been collected in the provinces of Hama, 'Ana, or Safad, all of which still had an 'Alawi population at the time.) The *tahrir*s used here constitute a representative rather than an exhaustive sample of all the fiscal registers available, and no attempt has been made to calculate the *dirhem* as a percentage of overall production and revenue; a more global examination of the region's geography, economy, and administration along the lines of Göyünç and Hütteroth's pioneering work on the Mesopotamian borderlands[16] must be left for future studies.

---

16 Nejat Göyünç and Wolf-Dieter Hütteroth, *Land an der Grenze: Osmanische Verwaltung im heutigen türkisch-syrisch-irakischen Grenzgebiet im 16. Jahrhundert* (Istanbul: Eren, 1997).

HISN AL-AKRAD, MANASIF (SANCAK OF HOMS): While the great majority of the 'Alawi population was concentrated in the province of Tripoli at the beginning of the Ottoman period, two 'Alawi-inhabited *nahiye*s at the southern extremity of the Syrian coastal highlands that appear in the Tripoli census of 1519 and 1524–25 were subsequently included in the *sancak* of Homs. Hisn al-Akrad, centered around the crusader-era fortress of the same name (the "Crac des Chevaliers" in Western sources), was an average-size district of some thirty-five to forty permanent villages, not including the numerous taxable farm plots (*mezraa*) that were not inhabited year round nor the district's sizable Arab, Kurdish, and Turkman tribal population. Of these villages, four situated in close proximity to one another in the foothills northwest of Homs paid *dirhem* taxes at various junctures between 1519 and 1570–71. No *dirhem* charges are indicated in the final census for the province from 1680, and in the eighteenth century the tax farm on the Hisn al-Akrad district was actually negotiated at the *shari'yya* court of Tripoli rather than in Homs. Manasif, again an average-size *nahiye* of some forty to forty-five small villages not counting *mezraa*s, takes its name from the Jabal Manasif highlands west of Homs (the site of Nashshabi's visitations in the thirteenth century; see chapter 2). Unlike other tax districts, Manasif does not appear to have had a specific center; the largest town attached to it was Hermel in the northern Bekaa valley, which by the early eighteenth century had become a *chasse gardée* of the Hamada and later the Shihabi tax lord dynasties of Lebanon. Several villages, all situated due west of Homs, were still assessed the *dirhem* in the 1680 census, most notably the important local center of Shin, at an exceptionally high 12,800 *akça*.

SAFITA, ANTARTUS, MI'AR, QULAY'A: Safita was by far the largest tax district in the southern 'Alawi mountains, with upward of fifty inhabited, in part very substantial villages. Centered on the crusader-era fortress-church of Safita, the majority of the district's population was probably Christian, and only eighteen villages were assessed the *dirhem* at one time or another between 1519 and 1645–46. Beginning in the later seventeenth century it would nevertheless be given as an *iltizam* (tax farm) to one of the most powerful 'Alawi families in Syria's history, the Shamsin clan (see following chapter). Interestingly, in two 'Alawi-inhabited villages it is noted that "all illegally introduced charges" (*cemi'-i aklam-ı bid'at*) have been abolished;[17] in the case of Ubin, which would later become one of the principal bases of the Barakat clan, these charges expressly include the *dirhemü'r-rical*, which is consequently never assessed. In another village the *dirhem* is abolished in the 1524–25 register because the population had become partially dispersed.[18] Mi'ar, on the other hand, was a very small tax district comprising only a handful of villages, while the coastal city of Antartus (Tartus) had a similarly small number of hinterland

17 TD 68:241, 243.
18 TD 1017:274.

Table 1a. Hisn al-Akrad and Manasif, *dirhemü'r-rical* assessments, in *akça*

Year	1519	1524–25	1551–52	1570–71	1680
Source	TD 68	TD 1017	TD 281	TD 502	MAD 9833

Hisn al-Akrad

Hadya al-Tahta			624	792	
Hasur (al-Sifli wa'l-Fawqa)		—	480	600	
Muqlus			236	96	
Na'ra	434	424			—

Manasif

'Awd Jubayl, a.k.a. 'Ayn Jubayl	—	—	2,544	2,052	
Balabil	—	—	yes	1,428	3,400
Basta	186	186			
Bilqisa			504	1,356	
Hil	186	286		732	
Khirbat al-Hammam	—	—		yes	yes
Khirbat al-Qabu	248	247			
Tanuna	186	187	252	288	
Qawaliyya		186			
Qiqaniyya (-i Tahta)	186	186	672	288	
Shin	—	—	yes	2,500	12,800
Tarin		—	1968	2500	

villages attached to it. Both *nahiye*s are in fact described as dependencies of Safita (*tabi-i Safita*) in the 1645–46 register MAD 842. Yahmur, the only village in Mi'ar to have paid the *dirhem* at one point in the sixteenth century, is noted in this last register to have lain abandoned for many years so that new farmers had recently come to settle on its lands.[19] Qulay'a, also considered a dependency of Safita (and occasionally called Qulay'at, possibly for the town

19 MAD 842:204.

Survey and Punish ∗ 87

FIGURE 3.2. View of Safita (published in *Harper's New Monthly Magazine* 45 [1872])

of that name in the Wadi al-'Uyun), was a minor *nahiye* in the mountains due west of Hama. At 730 m altitude, Qulay'a was actually one of the very few ex-crusader or Ismaili sites in the southern coastal range where the castle (*qal'a*) itself was occupied by an 'Alawi population in the seventeenth century. The marked increase in *dirhem*-paying villages in the 1645–46 register suggests there may indeed have been an influx of 'Alawis into the area by this time.

KAHF, KHAWABI, QADMUS: After 1547–48 the *sancak* of Tripoli was split in two and all the *nahiye*s north of the Khawabi (Baluta) River and Wadi al-'Uyun (Khawabi, Kahf, Qadmus, Marqab, Munayqa, 'Ulayqa, Jabala, Platanus, Latakia, Sahyun, and Barza) were constituted as the *sancak* of Jabala (Cebele). The southern part of this new *sancak* included most of the classical Ismaili *da'wa* castles, most notably Kahf and Qadmus, which, along with Masyaf in the province of Hama, were the only districts that remained under the control of Ismaili lords throughout much of the Ottoman period. The great majority of the local population was nevertheless 'Alawi. Kahf, one of the largest districts in the region, comprised at least forty villages, three quarters of which were assessed the *dirhem*; in Khawabi, a minor district centered on Khawabi castle in the coastal foothills northeast of Tartus,[20] approximately

20 This and other castles in the region are described in Ross Burns, *Monuments of Syria: An Historical Guide* (London: I. B. Tauris, 1999).

Table 1b. Safita, Antartus, Mi'ar, Qulay'a

Year	1519	1524–25	1547–48	1571–72	1645–46
Source	TD 68, TD 421	TD 1017	TD 1107	TD 513	MAD 842

Safita

Abbula			—	—	1,600
Baham'ash (?)	744	*dirhem* abolished	—	—	
Basalluh	—	—	—	—	7,000
Bashmaz	—	372	276		3,400
Bramana	—	—	560		
Harb Raffa (?)	—	—	—	—	6,400
Janniye, Junayna (?)	248	yes		—	
Jarwiyya	496	yes	—		3,000
Judaydat Jam'ash	—	—	—	—	2,000
Kafr Mahrak		200		—	
Khamsiqin					800
Khirbat al-'Amud	186	186	192	168	6,000
Khuraybat al-Qasbiyya	—	—	—	—	4,000
Lukaym	186	—	—	—	
Majdalun al-Bustan	—	—	—	—	4,600
Mandara	434	434	434	yes	20,000
Masmayya				572	
Sarijis	248				
Shamar	372			—	
Sindiyanat Baham'ash		132	130	—	
Siristan	—	—	—	—	3,000

Survey and Punish ∗ 89

Takhli	496	500	1,008	—	7,000
Tarkab	310	310	—	—	3,900
Tishur	—	—	318	342	
Tuffaha	372	372	456	—	2,800
Tulay'a	—	—	—	—	5,000
Ubin	*dirhem abolished*	—	—		10,000
Zuwaytuna		—	—		600

Antartus

Dayr (Duwayr) al-Nu'man, a.k.a. Dayr al-Kabir	—	—	—	—	2,400
Judayta	310	—	—	—	—

Mi'ar

Yahmur		200	—	—	—

Qulay'a

Anshir	120	120	168		
'Ayn al-Tina					1,000
'Aynu					600
Bamna	—		—	—	2,400
Basarsar	—				1,600
Bat'alus	—		—	—	2,000
Dayruna					800
Huwayzi					800
Kafr Jawaya	120	—	—	—	2,400
Qulay'a	—		—	—	5,000
Samuqa	248	248	468	—	1,000
Saraghis					600

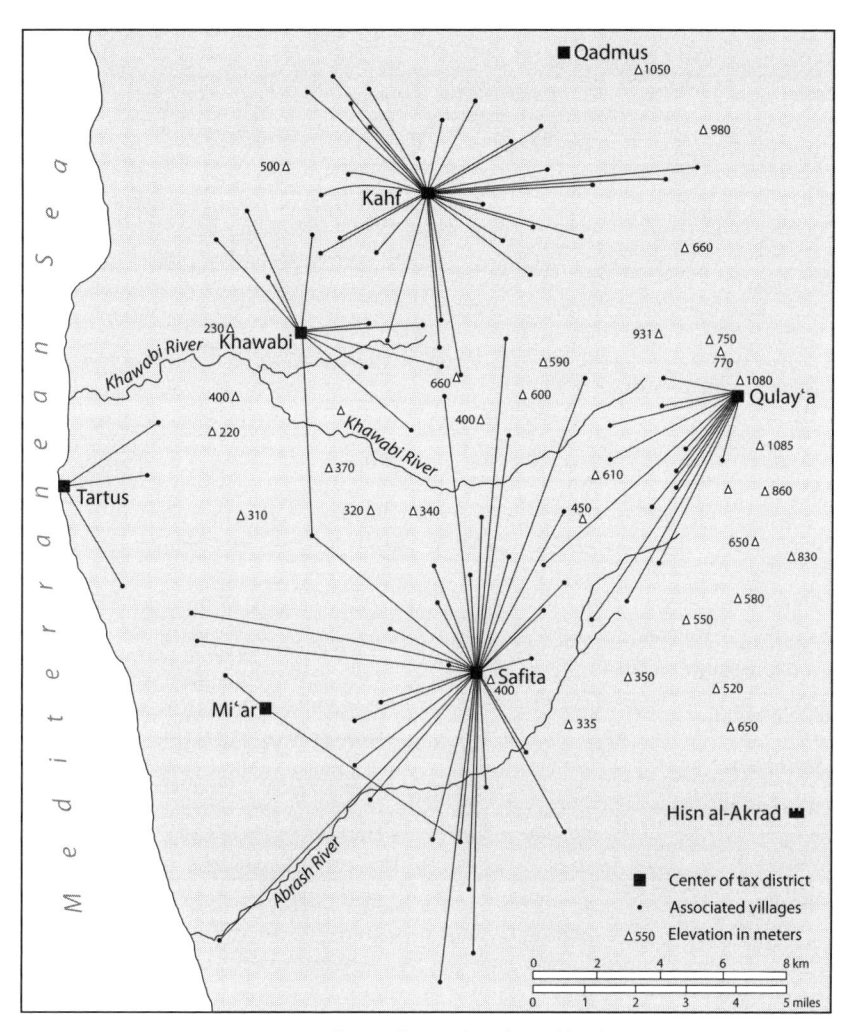

MAP 3. Safita and associated tax districts

half were assessed, and in Qadmus, almost every village aside from the fortress of Qadmus itself was 'Alawi-inhabited. In all three cases there appears to be a clear progression, reservations about the statistical quality of the Tahrir data aside, in total *dirhem* revenues and numbers of villages assessed.

MARQAB, MUNAYQA, 'ULAYQA: Marqab was an average-size district of thirty-five to forty villages including the crusader-era fortress and neighboring village of the same name. It was, however, fairly atypical in that it did not extend very far into the hinterland but rather stretched in a narrow band along the coast, from around Qutaylibiyya north of Banyas to the Khawabi River (now also known as the Husayn River) just north of

Survey and Punish * 91

Table 1c. Kahf, Khawabi, and Qadmus

Year	1519	1524–25	1547–48	1645–46
Source	TD 68	TD 1017	TD 1107	MAD 602

Kahf

'Amudi	—	310	324	3000
'Arya (?)		yes		
'Asliyya			yes	
'Ayn ('Uyun) al-Jawz, 'Uyun	310	310	340	1,200
Ba'adra	186	140	300	2,200
Bab Shahin (?)	228	284	600	
Bala'adar	186	186	48	
Bamlakha	496	496	yes	2,400
Barmana al-Gharbiyya			204	1400
Bashama'a	186			
Bayt Dara			yes	
Bazrad (?)	124		108	
Buraysin			744	1,600
Burdi	248	240	348	3,000
Dababiyya (?)	186			—
Danbiyya		124	372	—
Duwayr al-Qamsiyya	124	124	216	
Hammam	372	372	1080	4,200
Istafliyya (=Safliyya?)	62	62	984	
Jamasa	311	311	864	3,400
Jufiyya	124	124		
Juwayta	62	60	276	—
Kafr Laha (?)				3,000
Kafriyya	186	186	yes	—

Kanisa	228	248	1,212	
Karim	196	198	384	—
Khirbat al-Jubab	186	150	408	2,800
Latun	93	100	324	1,400
Mujaydal		146	180	2,400
Muqabla	(to Qadmus)	(to Qadmus)	48	
Murayqib	186	186	396	1,600
Namriyya	124		yes	400
Na'mu	124			
Na'nu	124	124	228	200
Niha al-Sharqiyya	248	248	312	4,000
Qamsiyya	310	310	672	
Qulay'at			312	600
Quziyya (?)	—	—	120	
Safliyya				5,400
Sarijis	186			
Sarijis al-Gharbi			144	
Sarijis al-Qibliyya		—	180	1,800
Sindiyana			yes	
Suran al-Gharbi			108	
Suran al-Sharqi	248	248	216	
Taba'at (?)	186			
Wanisa (?)	124			
Wardiyya			196	2,600
Zurayqa	186	186	240	

Khawabi

'Adhraya (?)			96	
Baghamlikh	—	—	312	2,400
Bahnin	—	—	yes	6,200

Baq'u			—	5,400
Bathaniyya	200	350	96	
Dayrani			144	
Duwayr al-Jumayz			288	
Hanafiyya	250	250	816	3,600
Kawkab	—	—	196	
Khalamma (?)			252	
Tayshur	318	318		
Ziratha (?)	—	100		

Qadmus

'Arid			192	
Baryaha	124	124	48	400
Buraybdan	174	124	240	1,200
Funaydiq	620	620	1,020	3,800
Hatiriyya		500	yes	800
Hattaniyya	210		120	2,200
Isqabla	620	620	792	
Jufin			48	
Kahf Shuja'	620	620	1,092	2,600
Khirbat Makkar	124	124	yes	—
Khuraybat al-Hamra'	62	62	300	
Maqaramda	372	372	yes	
Marashti	248	250	392	1,600
Muqabla	(to Kahf)	62	(to Kahf)	
Mushayrifa al-Sharqiyya	188	186	456	
Nafisa			24	
Qanniya			1,512	1,400
Qawiyya (?)	62	62		
Qudaymisa	186	186	984	1,800

Ra'i Batn (?)			72	
Ra's Qibli (?)				6,000
Ram Huzayr	248	248	552	1,400
Sab'anith (?)	62		264	
Salma (?)	124	124		
Sha'ra	500	500	yes	2,600
Tanakha	186	186	yes	
Tilla	124	124	yes	1,200

Tartus. It is thus noteworthy that the *nahiye* nevertheless comprised a majority of 'Alawi-inhabited villages, many of which, such as Bayda', Qarqafta, and the important regional center of Qutaylibiyya itself, lay immediately above the coastal plain at altitudes of only 140–180 meters. This of course contradicts the notion that the entire 'Alawi community was relegated to the mountains in the Ottoman period and suggests that numerous 'Alawis also participated in the more typically coastal rural economy of the region (bean and citrus tree growing, fishing, etc.). Munayqa and 'Ulayqa were smaller-size *nahiyes* again centered on former *da'wa* castles, Munayqa at 600 m in the hills northeast of the coastal city of Banyas (which no longer had an 'Alawi population itself at this point), and 'Ulayqa in the higher mountains west of Hama, where several villages were also assessed the *sarha* tax and are thus likely to have still had an Ismaili population. In the 1519 census the famous 'Alawi village of Abu Qubays (site of Makzun al-Sinjari's immigration in the thirteenth century) appears to have been included in the district of 'Ulayqa; it was, however, not assessed the *dirhem* and was then attached to the province of Hama in later censuses.

JABALA, PLATANUS: The *nahiyes* of Jabala and Platanus undoubtedly formed the heartland of the 'Alawi community in the Ottoman period. Jabala comprised up to eighty different villages, the great majority of which were assessed the *dirhemü'r-rical*. Seventeen of these villages were noted to be in a state of rebellion at the beginning of the Ottoman presence in Syria, as elucidated above. What is particularly interesting for our purposes here, however, is the evolution of the region in the following censuses. In 1524–25 most of these villages were still in a state of rebellion and a few more had even joined them, including Bashraghi, where no *dirhem* had been assessed at all in 1519, and Bashamman, which had previously paid 300 *akça*. Some villages, on the other hand, had now apparently been brought under control. For Humayn (not identified) it is explicitly noted that "the said village was in rebellion in the past, but because the region has now been registered and

Table 1d. Marqab, Munayqa, and 'Ulayqa

Year	1519	1524–25	1547–48	1645–46
Source	TD 68, TD 421	TD 1017	TD 1107	MAD 602

Marqab

'Abba	248	248	374	
'Anayniza				1,400
'Anaza			yes	1,400
'Annan (?)		248		
Anrin (?)	248			
Arin (?)			yes	
'Arqub	186	186	yes	
Balmana			696	3,400
Balutiyya			yes	
Bamalka			420	
Bayda'	494	494	—	
Bulawza	492	496	312	
Darta	124	120	yes	2,800
Dayr, Dayr (al-) Marqab	496	496	660	2,400
Gharrat (?)	—		240	
Husayn	372	372	564	
Jalita		186	yes	
Jazillu (?)	310	310	720	
Ka'biyya	186	186	912	3,200
Kafrun	372	372	yes	100
Khirbat (Khuraybat) al-Asad	62	62	504	7,200
Khuzayriyya (?)	434		516	1,200
Kurdiyya			72	
Latun	500	500	420	3,000
Ma'budiyya			1020	
Mazari'	186	186		
Mushayrifa			553	1,400

Muzayri'a, a.k.a. 'Amruniyya			306	1,000
Qamsu	93	92	yes	1,600
Qarqafta	500	500	1,488	
Qutaylbiyya			(Munayqa)	2,600
Salluriyya			72	
Shana (?)		124	168	
Talin		124	168	
Taraq	248	248	228	800
Tiru	yes	744	1280	5,000
Ubin	496	510		3,400
'Uqaybiyya				2,400
'Usayba			384	
Zamad (?)	620	630	576	
Zimrin			yes	1,600
Zuba	248	248	156	

Munayqa

'Ayn Sina (?)	186	186	312	1,600
Ba'abda	186	186	1,320	yes
Banayizla (?)			348	
Banzala (?)	124	186		1,400
Barmana			96	
Basmalikh	62		96	1,000
Bastwar	148	248	252	3,600
Batruna (?)		186	504	1,200
Bayt 'Ana	incl. in Bastwar	— (*mezraa*)	72	
Bila			48	
Dali (*mezraa*)				1,000
al-Duwayr al-Gharbi	62			
al-Duwayr al-Sharqi	112			
Fuwayrsat			1,188	yes
Istabluna	154	124	72	
Kimo (?)			48	

Qutaylbiyya			1,296	(to Marqab)
Salamiyya	258	258	672	1,800
Sur'ayn (?)	62	186		
Tall 'Uwayri al-Fawqa	124	—	48	
Tall 'Uwayri al-Sufla	124	150	300	1,000
Udayyish (?)				yes
Zawiyya (al-Fawqa)	124	124	228	800

'Ulayqa

'Anazat (al-Dibs)	310	310	960	3,600
Bab al-Nur			48	—
Baduqa	248	248	384	yes
Balghunis	—	—	756	
Balusin			yes	
Basarmun	186	186	516	yes
Basbasa	—	146	300	—
Bu'ayd (?)	yes			
Duwayr al-Fawqa	—	—	72	1,200
Ghansala	124	124	504	
Haddada	189	186	516	2,600
Kawka'i	—	— (*mezraa*)	264	400
Khirbat al-Suhul	62			
Khirbat al-Tawahin	426	496	120	
Khirbat Nuwaytin (?)			120	
Latun	62	62	216	1,800
Marrana	124	124	300	800
Masyaf			96	—
Nahl al-Gharbi	248	248	622	2,400
Nahl al-Jurd			212	—
Na'mu	62	62	504	
Qal'at al-Baqali (?)		62	432	
Ram Tarza	124	124	168	3,000
Shafiruh	124	—	240	
Siddin	100	100	192	2,000
'Ulayqa	—	—	—	3,200

is in submission, it has been entered in the new imperial register." Similarly, the people of Mutawwar, which "had been in rebellion and not paid a single grain" since the first census, had now agreed to pay a given amount "after the *padişah* (sultan) had stimulated their obedience."[21] Bassin, Halbakko, Hillat 'Ara, and Qurn Hulya, for their part, are no longer listed as rebellious and are assessed regular taxes, though not the *dirhem*. In several instances there seems to be a clear intent on the part of the state to sustain and redevelop the area: the villages of Bashamman, Bashraghi, Upper and Lower Mirdasiyya, and Zaghrano are all indicated to have "been given to a *sipahi* [cavalry officer] to populate and make flourish [*mamur etmek üzere*]"; the people of Amyanus, which is described as "ruined on account of all the oppression," are forgiven a large part of their agricultural taxes to entice them to bring their lands back under cultivation; and Rusiyya, which had previously been assessed 4,000 *akça* in regular taxes and 400 (or 800) in *dirhem* dues but was abandoned because the population was incapable of paying such an amount, was now given as a tax farm at a much lower rate (and no *dirhem*) in order to attract them back.[22]

What is then particularly significant is how these same villages were assessed twenty-three years later, in 1547–48. Virtually every village is now assessed the *dirhem* but also explicitly noted to "belong to [*min*; *tabi-i*] the Kelbiyyin," that is, the Kelbi (Kalbi) tribe of the northern coastal highlands whose name has almost completely replaced the sectarian term "Nusayri" in Ottoman documents by this time. Today the Kelbis are frequently cited as one of the four principal 'Alawi tribal groupings in Syria, but, as already stated, they are never mentioned as such in medieval sources: the Kelbis were not one of the tribes associated with Makzun al-Sinjari, and in the *Khayr al-Sani'a* the term appears only a few times, referring specifically in one instance to the coastal region southeast of Latakia (Sahil al-Kalbiyya).[23] This is not to suggest that the Kelbi tribe did not exist as a group before (indeed the term may originally have invoked a link with the classical Kelbi bedouin confederation) but that it played no special role within 'Alawi society before it was discovered and consecrated as the dominant local faction by the Ottoman administration in the sixteenth century. To judge by the same census registers, the Ottomans pursued a similar strategy in Lebanon (and presumably elsewhere) when entire groups of villages in the mountain hinterland were left under the fiscal authority of the villagers themselves or in the hands of local Druze or Shi'i tribal tax collectorships.[24] In Jabala several other villages that had not been involved in the revolt at the beginning of the century were also included in the Kelbis' domain by 1547–48, most notably 'Arqub, Bakarrama, Bal'alin,

21 TD 1017:386, 399.
22 TD 1017:385, 387, 396.
23 Harfush, *Khayr al-Sani'a*, 680, 851, 856.
24 Winter, *Shiites of Lebanon*, 64–68.

Dulaybat, Hasnayn (Hisn Yashut), as well as Balat in the neighboring district of Platanus, all of which lay at altitudes between 500 and 840 m and may not have been easy for an Ottoman *sipahi* and his forces to hold.

Platanus was a more average-size *nahiye* of about forty villages and, as indicated before, does not seem to have participated in the original revolt against the Ottomans. Two highland villages (one of which is assessed the *dirhem*, the other not) are actually described later, in the 1547–48 register, as being in a state of rebellion, but this is likely to have been a very local tax revolt rather than part of a larger movement that had ended elsewhere. Compared with other districts, Platanus comprised an unusually high number of villages which either changed affiliation, occur in only one or two censuses, or can no longer be identified and located today, suggesting a relatively high degree of population movement and unsettledness. Qirtyawus, for example, the focal point of the 1318 uprising, appears in the earliest of the Ottoman censuses but not thereafter. In Istamo, defter MAD 602 relates that ten or more peasants had simply quit their lands and moved into the "Kelbi mountains" so that it had not been possible to register their names, but they were expected to return and therefore still had to be assessed.[25] Only one village, as already indicated, is noted to belong to the Kelbi tribe; numerous *mezraa*s, on the other hand, are listed in 1547–48 as being under the authority of the local population, and no less than twelve villages in the Qardaha area are assigned to (*tabi-i*) a certain "Ibn Muhannad." All but one of these villages were assessed the *dirhem*, and it seems likely that Ibn Muhannad, who is not described as an official *sipahi* or as holding a *timar* military fief, was among the Ottomans' first local notable (*ayan*) intermediaries in the region. Interestingly, virtually all his villages were separated from Platanus and attached to the district of Jabala by the time of the final census in 1645–46.

LATAKIA, SAHYUN, BARZA: The tax district of Latakia was fairly small, initially comprising only about twenty villages in addition to the modest port city of Latakia itself. Beginning with the 1547–48 census the formerly separate *nahiye* of Wadi Qandil, a narrow, rugged coastal strip halfway between Latakia and Ra's al-Basit that was inhabited mainly by Arab and Turkmen tribes, was incorporated into Latakia. (It is this area to which Turkish and Turkish-oriented media began referring in 2012 as the "Jabal al-Turkman" or "Türkmen Dağı," a name not indicated in any historical source.) Only one of the Wadi Qandil villages, Iraqanata (unidentified), was assessed the *dirhem* at that point. All the other 'Alawi villages in the Latakia district, however, also lay at low altitude in close proximity to the coast or in the lower Nahr al-Kabir valley, most of them only a few kilometers northeast of the city, with which they were no doubt closely linked economically. Sahyun, on the other hand, with its eighty villages, was, along with Jabala, one of the two great mountain *nahiye*s in the

---

25 MAD 602:41.

Table 1e. Jabala and Platanus

Year	1519	1524–25	1547–48	1645–46
Source	TD 68, TD 421	TD 1017	TD 1107	MAD 602

Jabala

Abu Mirdas		62	—	
'Adiyya		—	300	
'Ammariyya	310	310	372	yes
Amsit	(Platanus)	(Platanus)	(Platanus)	1,200
'Amuda	in rebellion	in rebellion	144 (Kelbiyyin)	
Amyanus		yes	180	
'Aramta			468	yes
'Arqub	250	250	384 (Kelbiyyin)	1,800
Asyan(i) al-Jarraniyya		—	624	12,400
Bahurta (?)	—	124	132	yes
Bakarrama	—	186	288 (Kelbiyyin)	
Bala'alin ('Arus al-Jabal)	200		72 (Kelbiyyin)	
Bani 'Isa	yes	620	696	3,200
Basaqnara (?)			216	
Basawtar	465	—	—	
Basbana (?)	in rebellion	in rebellion		
Bashakuh	yes	454	276	—
Bashamman	300	in rebellion	540 (Kelbiyyin)	
Bashraghi	—	in rebellion	468	800
Basindiyana		248	336	800
Bassin	200; in rebellion	—	288 (Kelbiyyin)	
Batara			660	—

Survey and Punish ∗ 101

Bijiftana		150	228	—
Bila	248	248	636	yes
Binjaro	620	620	1800	8000
Bulaytanus	yes	496	768	—
Buray'in		—	1,600	1,800
Busaysin	700	700	1356	
Dayr Maryam	494	496	648	
Dayr Mina	yes	yes	1,880 (Kelbiyyin)	
Dayr Yuhanna		310	272	
Dayrutan		310	504	
Dulaybat			72 (Kelbiyyin)	
Duwaydariyya				yes
Duwayr Andriya	—	—	1,308	
Duwayr Atna	—	—	1,396 (Kelbiyyin)	
Duwayr Bila	250	250	314	
Duwayr Jarraniyya			168	yes
Ghanariyya (?)	—	—	660	
Halbakko	in rebellion	—	300 (Kelbiyyin)	
Hammam	—	—	1,056	2,000
Harmana (Jarmata?)	in rebellion	in rebellion		
Hasnayn	500	500	636 (Kelbiyyin)	800
Haymala	yes			
Hikmiyya	496	—	492	yes
Hillat 'Ara	in rebellion	—	468 (Kelbiyyin)	
Hubal (?)	yes; in rebellion			

Humayn (?)	in rebellion	rebellion ended	72 (Kelbiyyin)	
Husayniyya			72	—
Istafalin (?)	200; in rebellion		360 (Kelbiyyin)	
Istagho (?)			48	
Istamna		62	(Platanus)	abandoned
Istino (?)			84	
Jan(y)aro	part. in rebellion	in rebellion		
Kafara	248	350	yes	1,400
Kafr Dibl	490	490	1584	
Kafr Zubayn		—	yes	
Kalbu	496	496	600	1,000
Khuraybat al-Hiyak	200	240	240	
Ma'adiyya	310	310	564	yes
Malukh			(Platanus)	1,000
Marniyo			(Platanus)	1,600
Mazra'at al-'Araj (?)				6,200
Mirdasiyya al-Fawqa wa'l-Tahta (Mirdasiyyatayn)	in rebellion	in rebellion; (?)	960 (Kelbiyyin)	
Mutawwar	in rebellion	in rebellion	1,284 (Kelbiyyin)	2,400
Nananta	in rebellion	60	336 (Kelbiyyin)	800
Nani		in rebellion		1,000
Nani Jaranana	—	—	yes	
Naqashiyya al-Shamaliyya	110	310	348	
Nuzaydiyya	496		156	
Nuzayn	310; in rebellion	310		

Survey and Punish * 103

Qalamun	(Platanus)	(Platanus)	(Platanus)	5,200
Qammin	620	620	456	
Qamyas	—	—	948	—
Qardaha	620	950	1,632	3,400
Qarfiko (?)			108	—
Qatarbiyya	—	122	420	—
Qirtyawus	250			
Qissabin	400 or 416	416	732	
Qubaysiyya	492		132	
Qulay'at			—(Kelbiyyin)	
Qurn Hulya	500; in rebellion	—	480 (Kelbiyyin)	4,600
Qurnbadiyya (?)	434	yes	384	
Ra's Raja	yes	yes	714	6,600
Rama	in rebellion	—	612 (Kelbiyyin)	400
Rayhan Jaranana		in rebellion		
Rayhan(a)	in rebellion	in rebellion	—(Kelbiyyin)	400
Rusiyya	400	suspended	648	—
Sakniyya	620	620	1,632	—
Salamiyya	yes	yes	1,200	yes
Sallurin	600	620	1,476	yes
Sanjala	620	1,000	yes	
Sharashir	—		252	
Tall Aris	—	—	540	5,400
Tall Ibn Mas'ud	—	—	1,872	6,000?
Tana (?)	in rebellion	in rebellion	192 (Kelbiyyin)	
'Urbayn (?)	110	124	96	—
Wulaydiyya (?)				yes
Zaghrano (?)		in rebellion		1,400

| Zarinhiyya (?) | 124 | yes | 96 | |
| Zino | | | (Platanus) | 800 |

Platanus

Albina (?)			96	
Amsit	150	depopulated	120?	(to Jabala)
ʿAyn Jandal	248	248		
Baʿabdus		310	192	
Bakhdarmo al-Fawqa			876	1,400
Balat(a)			— (Kelbiyun)	7,000
Bantul (?)			84	
Baqanna	162	yes		
Baqliyun				4,000
Barta	186	—	288	3,200
Basarramo, Basarrama	186	186	636	1,400
Basut			— (in rebellion)	
Bataʿala	248	250		
Busaymihan (?)			660	1,800
Butayma			120	
Buwayba (?)	300	310	744	
Dabbash				4,200
Dayr Afriqo	—	yes		
Dayr Ibrahim	312	310	492	—
Dayr Qamma (?)	310	310	540	3,200
Dulayʿa (?)	186	186	252	
Farzala			120	
Ghalasto	*dirhem* abolished	—	2,100	
Hassaniyya	200	—		
Humaym, Humaymim	300	300	1,032	
Huwayzat Bilghano (?)	1,600			
Isqafin (?)			yes	

Istamna		(Jabala)	720	(Jabala)
Istamo		—	1,272	yes
Kafr Bun (?)		248	840 (in rebellion)	
Khirbat (Khuraybat) Bata'ala	186	186	672	yes
Khirbat al-Shaykh		120	120	
Ludayna				1,500
Luwaydiqiyya	124	124		600
Maksiriyat (?)	248	yes	324	
Malukh			360	(to Jabala)
Marniyo			168	(to Jabala)
Naquru	496	300	600	yes
Qalamun	90	90	600	(to Jabala)
Qalluriyya	248	yes	1,368	5,800
Qatliyya (?)		186	216	
Quhaydina (?)			6,408	
Ra's Kalmakho	310	310	368	1,400
Sahaya			1,980	800
Sakino			1,512	2,000
Tabarja		372	540	1,400
Ubiyya (?)				1,800
Zino			120	(Jabala)

northern part of Tripoli or Jabala province. Centered on what was perhaps the most prodigious of all Crusader castles (Saône in Western sources), the district was dominated by Sunni Kurds for much of the Ottoman period,[26] and only about a quarter of its villages were inhabited by 'Alawis. Likewise, the small district of Barza at the extreme northeastern end of the Syrian coastal range was dominated by local Kurdish groups (see following chapter), with only two villages being assessed the *dirhem* in the 1547–48 census.

While much still remains to be done with the Ottoman Tahrir registers regarding the economic and administrative history of the whole region, already

---

26 See Stefan Winter, "Les Kurdes de Syrie dans les archives ottomanes," *Études Kurdes* 10 (2009): 132–34.

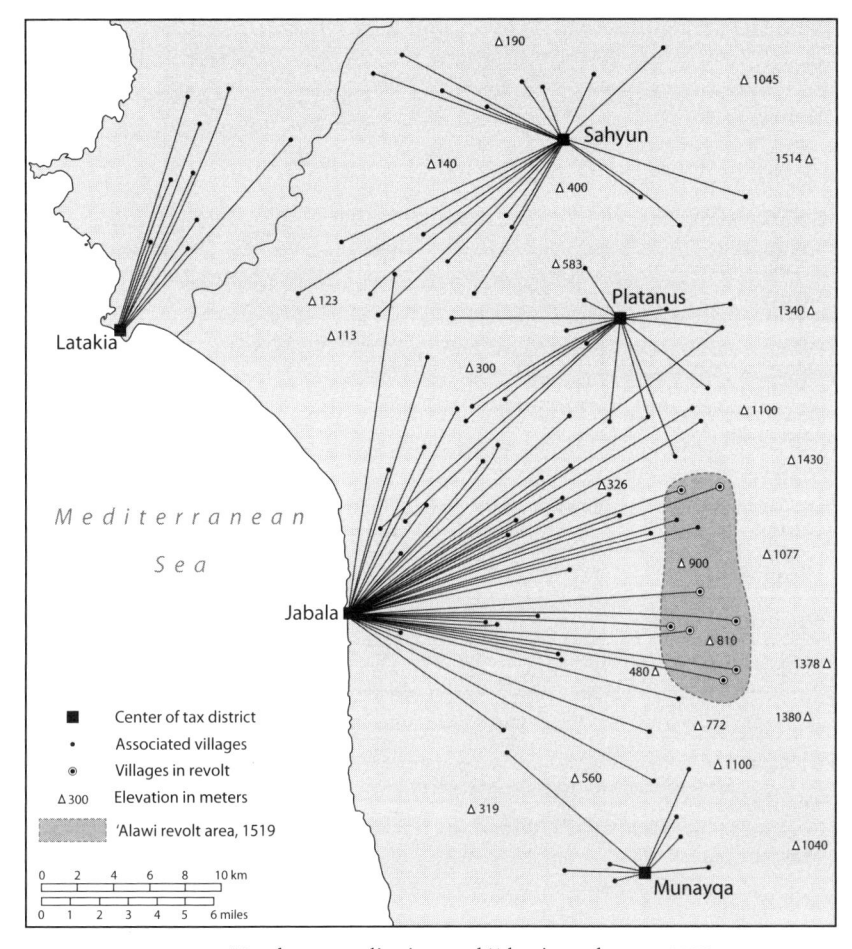

MAP 4. Northern tax districts and 'Alawi revolt area, 1519

this first survey of villages that were assessed the *dirhemü'r-rical* provides some insight into the 'Alawi population's distribution in both the mountains and coastal areas of western Syria in the sixteenth and seventeenth centuries, its settlement of new villages and its spread particularly in the northernmost *nahiye*s of Tripoli province. Perhaps most important, however, these records evoke a regular, institutionalized rapport between the Ottoman state and local society beyond the polemics of religious differentiation. Even though the Ottomans did maintain a specifically sectarian tax as part their overall fiscal policy and encountered resistance on the part of specific 'Alawi communities, they can also be seen to have adapted to local circumstances, abolishing the *dirhem* in some villages that had been ruined, reducing other taxes, mandating either *timar* fief-holders or tax farmers to redevelop other 'Alawi areas, and

Survey and Punish * 107

Table 1f. Latakia (Lazkiye), Sahyun, and Barza (Berze)

Year	1519	1524–25	1547–48	1645–46
Source	TD 68, TD 421	TD 1017	TD 1107	MAD 602

Latakia

Abniq (?)		496	344	
Afrito (?)	124	124	1,512	
Anqun (?)			1,200	
Bisnada				2,600
Damsarkho			2,304	10,000
Farqlu (?)	248	yes	504	
Fattiro	186	186		
Ghamiriyya	372		1,540	
Iraqanata (?)			348	
Jandariyya			yes	
Jinnata			yes	
Kirsana			264	
Maghrit			yes	2,200
Makarmiyya (?)		496	564	3,000
Mihnala (?)			348	
Mushayrifa	496	496	1,368	
Qadumo	372	372	816	
Qammudata (?)		—	yes	
Qanjara			1,176	
Qatarbiyya		248		
Sanbalo (?)	620	620	yes	
Sarbaniyya			384	
Shuqayriyya			156	
Sinjuwan				yes
Squbin	496	496	1,332	2,600

Tarjano	620	620	1,860	
Zahiriyya	228	350		

Sahyun

'Annaqiya			yes	2,400
Arayto (?)	682	682	768	—
'Arus			yes	
Asinar (?)			204	
'Ayn al-Tina	496	496	492	3,200
Ba'amaran	272	372		
Babanna	620	620	yes	—
Bahluliyya	620	620	588	4,000
Balanyo			324	—
Baluta			240	
Baqaraha	—		208	
Bashimmana		372	432	1,800
Batarnas		186	264	
Binlaz (?)			276	
Bughit			636	1,000
Busa (?)			368	
Dayr Mamma				1,400
Difa			yes	4,000
Dudaniyya			84	
Duwayr Ansir (?)			144	1,400
Duwayr Karim (al-Kurm)			980	1,200
Fadra	372	372	324	
Fidyu	744		1,656	
Habbath	62		84	
Hubayt				1,600

Survey and Punish * 109

Jankin (Çenkin)	310	310	408	
Jinjaniyya				yes
Kafariyya			96	
Karkik	248	248	432	
Kart	248	208		
Kasimin (?)			228	
Khuraybat Ubin			888	
Kimin			240	5,000
Manbisa			276	
Manjila	yes		634	
Mardido			204	
Masalla	448	248	432	—
Mashqita			1,176	
Mazra'at Hamq	500	500	1,320	3,400
Mazra'at 'Ayn al-Tina			624	
Midan		yes	408	
Milyo			240	
Munissi (?)				2,000
Mushayrifa (al-Matn)	494	496	552	—
Mushayrifa al-Tahta				1,400
Muzayra'a			1956	
Quraymani	496	496	756	
Raqiq	186	yes	216	
Rastin			3,800	2,000
Sarna			864	
Sharifa	744	500	yes	
Shiballo		yes	336	
Shufan (*mezraa*)				yes
Siliflu (?)			540	

Talla			324	
Tarbiniyyat al-Hilwa			408	
Tarbiniyyat al-Marta			756	
Ubin			204	
Yasnus		—	444	1,400
Zidaro			216	

Barza

Furayki			176	
Mazzin	—	—	528	

conceding certain responsibilities to the Kelbi tribe or to local leaders such as Ibn Muhannad as state intermediaries. What these sources cannot tell us, of course, is how heavily the entire system weighed on the 'Alawi peasantry. Modern historians have usually asserted that the taxation of the 'Alawis was oppressive and discriminatory,[27] but this is essentially the same claim made today of the Christian, Arab, Balkan, Greek, Kurdish, and almost every other subject nation of the former Ottoman Empire. Objectively the 'Alawis' taxes are indeed likely to have been as high as they could bear—since this was of course the whole purpose of the early modern bureaucracy's monumental effort to survey, settle, fine-tune, and police the revenue-producing agrarian population. In this the 'Alawis were not treated any differently from other subjects. The very extent to which the 'Alawis were surveyed, monitored, and accounted for in the Tahrir registers ultimately shows how completely integrated they were in the Ottoman state administration.

THE PROVINCE OF JABALA UNDER OTTOMAN RULE

The attention the Ottomans devoted to the development and taxation particularly of the northern part of the *sancak* of Tripoli, the creation of the separate *sancak* of Jabala, and finally the creation of a new *eyalet* (regional province) around Tripoli that incorporated the *sancak*s of Tripoli, Jabala, Hama, and Homs in 1579 all point to the growing importance of the region in the sixteenth century. Part of the reason for this growing importance may simply have been demographic. Chapter 1 referred to the fact that the 'Alawi community was originally established in the piedmont west of Hama in the

---

27 Cf. Dick Douwes, *The Ottomans in Syria: A History of Justice and Oppression* (London: I. B. Tauris, 2000), 142–43.

medieval period and only gradually expanded northward. That its epicenter had essentially shifted to the hinterland of Jabala by the Ottoman period is also suggested by the *Khayr al-Sani'a*, which beginning in the late fifteenth century lists a large number of leading shaykhs as natives or residents of the Jaranana, a local toponym that is obscure today but used to designate the medium-altitude mountains around Hammam al-Qarahala, Basawtar, and Nani approximately 18–20 km southeast of Jabala.[28] Since the 'Alawis would already have constituted the largest sectarian group in the coastal highlands by this time, this expansion alone may have been a leading factor in the Jabala region's growth. It is at any rate probably no coincidence that the 1519 rebellion against the Ottomans was concentrated in an area immediately adjoining the Jaranana to the north.

A bigger part of the reason, however, would have been the Ottomans' interest in consolidating their hold over the strategically situated northwestern Syrian coastlands. The Mamluks' policy toward the coastal region had been one of neglect and scorched earth, razing maritime fortresses and rebuilding cities such as Tripoli several kilometers inland to prevent them from falling into the hands of renewed crusader ventures.[29] The Ottomans, in contrast, not only had endeavored from the very beginning to become a Mediterranean sea power but also began to depend on the region in the sixteenth century to transport war material and recruit tribal levies for the empire's military campaigns to the east. Jabala first appears to be mentioned as a separate *sancak* in 1564, when it was under the authority of Habib Bey, son of Canpolad Bey, the head of the Kurdish tribal province of Kilis (Liva-ı Ekrad) in the *eyalet* of Aleppo. That the governorship of Jabala was essentially treated as a family appanage of the Canpolads up to this point is suggested by an imperial order from 1572, when both were notified that Habib was to command a company of archers (*kavas*) that had been provisioned with funds from Kilis.[30]

The conquest of Cyprus in 1571, however, likely marked a turning point in Jabala's history. Since the conquest of Egypt earlier in the century, this province's vast revenues, the importance of its foodstuffs in Istanbul's markets and Cairo's standing as the second city of the empire had made controlling the eastern Mediterranean a vital concern of Ottoman naval force and diplomacy; the invasion of Rhodes from Marmaris and the expulsion of the Knights of St. John to Sicily as well as the establishment of a new fleet at Alexandria all served the same purpose. Venetian-held Cyprus, lying just 120 km

---

28 Harfush, *Khayr al-Sani'a*, 667–721, 682, 717–23, 724–26, 728, 788–92, 819–20, 823–27, 831–32, 847–49, 887–89.

29 Fuess, *Verbranntes Ufer*.

30 BOA: Mühimme Defteri (MD) 6:181; 12:579. On the Canpolad dynasty, see also Şenol Çelik, "XVI. Yüzyılda Hanedan Kurucu Bir Osmanlı Sancakbeyi: Canbulad Bey," *Türk Kültürü İncelemeleri Dergisi* 7 (2002): 1–34; on the Liva-ı Ekrad, see Winter, "Kurdes de Syrie," 135–39.

offshore from Jabala (and visible on a clear day), was the key to securing the entire region. After the end of the war in 1571, the Ottomans therefore moved quickly to repopulate and build up the island, leaving thousands of janissaries, cannoneers, and unmarried volunteers from the expeditionary forces behind to garrison its towns and fortresses, then deporting or attracting numerous new settlers from Anatolia over the next years.[31] This policy appears to have carried over to Jabala as well, where a noticeably high number of veterans of the Cyprus campaign can be seen to have been awarded *timar* benefices for good service (*ziyade yoldaşlık*) beginning in the winter of 1570–71.[32] Perhaps another sign of Jabala's newfound importance and wealth during this time is the fact that the *beylerbeyis* (super-governors) of Damascus and Aleppo now also fought over whose jurisdiction the *sancak* should be placed under.[33] In 1579, however, Jabala was incorporated into the new *eyalet* of Tripoli and then generally granted to a member of the Shu'ayb, 'Assaf, or Sayfa families of notables, so that by the early seventeenth century the province had largely become tributary once again to more parochial, northern Lebanese feudal politics.[34]

Even if the hinterland of Jabala had been by and large brought under submission by 1547–48, dealing with the 'Alawis seems to have remained at all times a primary concern of the local Ottoman authorities. In May 1560, for example, the *bey* (*sancak*-level governor) of Tripoli was informed of a certain "Süleyman" who was "residing among the constantly rebellious Kelbi faction in the Jabala district, even instigating and leading them when they sow corruption and attack caravans on the roads. The insurgents then give him what they steal and he brings it to either Tripoli, Jabala, or Antioch, takes the money, and goes back to them."[35] The *bey* does not seem to have been able to take sufficient action, however (and it is not clear whether Süleyman himself was 'Alawi), for only a few months later the Sublime Porte turned to the *beylerbeyi* of Damascus after the *kadı* (judge) and "all the Muslims of Jabala" had complained in Aleppo that the Kelbi and "Zayadin" faction was now also attacking villages in the district, "plundering and stealing property and goats or sheep, ruining the villagers," and thus "preventing the collection of state (*miri*) taxes."[36] Toward the end of the year the governor of Damascus wrote back to the Sublime Porte saying that the *alaybeyi* (*timariot* regiment

---

31 Ronald Jennings, *Christians and Muslims in Ottoman Cyprus and the Mediterranean World, 1571–1640* (New York: New York University Press, 1993), 214–39.

32 MD 42:367, 375, 381, 387, 389, 400, 404, 405, 436, 456, 459.

33 MD 19:72; MD 26:30, 93.

34 MD 36:314; MD 39:20; MD 46:118, 197; MD 53:237; MD 54:195. On the Shu'aybs and Jabala under the Sayfas, see also Abdul-Rahim Abu-Husayn, *Provincial Leaderships in Syria, 1575–1650* (Beirut: American University of Beirut, 1985), 13–14, 38, 41, 54.

35 MD 3:352.

36 MD 3:467.

commander) of Jabala and Latakia (likely the highest military authority in the region at the time) had succeeded in quelling the Kelbis' insurgency, "securing the roads and capturing many of them," and recommended him for a generous promotion.[37]

Aside from the Kelbis' own tendency to revolt, their utilization by powerful local figures seems to have been a recurrent problem. In early January 1565 the *beylerbeyi* of Aleppo was notified that a former low-level troop commander (*çeribaşı*) who had been awarded a *timar* benefice in Jabala was now residing in Latakia with numerous sons and followers, "close to the evildoing Kelbi faction."

> And since these are devoid of leaders, the aforementioned Hacci Kasim is leading and governing them himself, committing evil and malice and joining and associating with several ill-fortuned individuals of the Kelbi faction, constantly bringing them to his side and seducing and misguiding them. He sends them to attack and kill the people he hates, and they bring the money and other effects they steal back to [him].

According to the order, Hacci Kasim had had two *sipahi*s (cavalrymen) in Latakia assassinated and robbed in this way, then instigated an attack on the village of Muzayra'a (presumably in the Sahyun district) in which five men from Latakia and one villager were killed. An investigation had previously been ordered against Hacci Kasim and his sons, but the *kadı* of Latakia was dismissed before it could be carried out and the imperial rescript to this effect had then apparently been ripped out of the court register and replaced by a blank page. And finally Hacci Kasim had even demolished the government fortress at Latakia, stealing the lumber and stone to build his own palace, surrounding himself with powerful tribal elements and drawing a huge number of "thugs and scoundrels" to his side in order to form a sort of "Celali" (provincial rebel) coalition.[38]

What is conspicuous in all these cases is the Ottomans' failure to condemn the Kelbis or any other 'Alawis on the basis of their religion. On account of the *dirhemü'r-rical* assessments, the central bureaucracy had precise knowledge of the sectarian affiliation of the villages and tribal groups in the region but generally chose not to take issue with it even when castigating 'Alawis for concrete acts such as tax rebellion and brigandage. In November 1573, for instance, the *bey* of Jabala received an order explicitly reminding him that "the majority of the *sancak*'s subjects are of the Nusayri, Zaydi [*sic*; probably a reference to the previously cited Zayadin tribe], and Kelbi faction." This

---

37 MD 4:162. The Zayadin or Zayadiyya are considered to be a division of the Kelbis; see Munir al-Sharif, *Al-'Alawiyyun: Man-hum wa-Ayna-hum?* ([Damascus:] Al-Maktaba al-Kubra, 1946), 73.
38 MD 6:276.

in itself was not the issue, however: while his predecessor had succeeded in keeping them "under control" so that they had "renounced their stubbornness and corruption," the current *bey* was not proving as capable, allowing a certain Muhammad ibn Ghazzal to divert moneys from the imperial crown reserve lands (*hass-ı hümayun*) and thus preventing the requisite taxes from being collected. Here again, the main culprit was a local ringleader ('Alawi or otherwise) perceived to be exploiting common 'Alawis; the 'Alawis or Nusayris themselves are not subject to recrimination.[39]

Similarly, in September 1581 the *bey* of Jabala was instructed "to not tarry and delay, [but to] protect and defend your *sancak* ... and join and support the governor of Tripoli with the fiefholders and *sipahi*s of the *sancak*" in order to "get your hands on and punish (*haklarından gelinmek*) the Kelbi faction and the villainous thug named Ba'd who are sowing evil and corruption in the area."[40] And only a month later the *beylerbeyi* of Tripoli was informed that all the civil officials of Jabala, Latakia, and Qadmus had petitioned the Sublime Porte, stating that "our region lies between the seawater on one side and the high mountains inhabited by the Arab tribal brigands known as the Kelbis who are famous for their evil, corruption and maliciousness on the other"; this time the inhabitants were in desperate need of help from the government after "infidel" (European Christian) pirates had attacked two merchant vessels and taken numerous Muslim hostages at Ra's Basit.[41] That the 'Alawis themselves were not censured in such instances is perhaps all the more surprising in light of how the Mühimme registers show another Shi'i minority, the above-mentioned Anatolian Kızılbaş, to have been subject to a campaign of outright religious persecution on the part of the Ottoman state in exactly the same period.[42] Unlike the Kızılbaş, however, the 'Alawis were never thought to be acting in concert with an external enemy or challenging the imperial religious order; they were to be perceived and dealt with primarily as a social problem.

The most serious incidents involving 'Alawis appear to have occurred in the following years, perhaps a sign of the increasing instability and disorganization of Ottoman provincial government toward the end of the sixteenth century. In May 1582 the governor of Tripoli received an order concerning a Kelbi revolt in which several of Muhammad ibn Mansur's (presumably the *bey* of Jabala's) men had been killed. "With their oppression and transgression growing day by day, a force had been sent straight to Qadmus," the order continues, so that a number of 'Alawi *mukaddem*s (headmen) as well as the Twelver Shi'i emir of Baalbek, 'Ali ibn Harfush, with whom they interestingly

39 MD 23:117.
40 MD 46:117.
41 MD 46:164.
42 Colin Imber, "The Persecution of the Ottoman Shiites according to the Mühimme Defterleri, 1565–1585," *Der Islam* 56 (1979): 245–73.

seem to have been collaborating in this instance, sued for peace. However, "Mansur-oğlı (Ibn Mansur) had taken such fright" and "the people of the Hisn al-Akrad district had been so agitated by the brigands that most of them had fled," so that additional support had been requested from the *beylerbeyi* of Damascus. Yet once again, the 'Alawis are not even the main object of the order: the region had now been invested by so many provincial forces, including the governor of Aleppo's deputy as well as the powerful Druze tax farmer Ibn Ma'n, that these had begun "using this pretext" (i.e., of the Kelbis' insubordination) to oppress the local population with "excessive and illegal" demands for tax arrears and other payments and had to be dealt with.[43] Finally around January 1583, the *kadı* of Latakia wrote the Sublime Porte a long letter about the Kelbis' depredations, accusing them of constantly cutting roads and attacking travelers, robbing the Yeni İl Turkmen who had come to winter in the area, fighting with local government troops and generally making the region unsafe all the way to Jisr al-Shughur on the border with Aleppo province. A huge delegation of more than five hundred people had already gone to Tripoli to submit a petition stating that "For two years now the above-mentioned faction has seized control of our threshing floors, homes and gardens, so that we face great difficulty in feeding our folk and families. If they are not punished, it is certain that their harm and oppression will continue." The central state authorities were nevertheless still under the impression that such crises could be resolved through good administration. Rather than impose a collective punishment or denounce the 'Alawis per se, the Sublime Porte ordered the governor of Tripoli to

> get your hands on those individuals who have harmed and oppressed the people of the region and travelers, have them or the bondsmen (*kefil*) of those who are absent, and generally everyone who must be found by law, brought to court together with their adversaries and examined at the same time according to law, and have those cases where less than fifteen years have elapsed be heard and investigated through the local judges and in the presence of their adversaries, in complete respect of and attention to the requirements of established law [*şer'-i kadim*].[44]

CONCLUSION: FROM REBELS TO *REAYA*

The provincial law codes (*kanun-name*), tax censuses (*tahrir*), and executive orders (*mühimme*) provide a normative picture of Ottoman administration that can have corresponded only in part to the reality on the ground in

---

43 MD 47:109, 163. On 'Ali Harfush see also Abu-Husayn, *Provincial Leaderships*, 130–33; Winter, *Shiites of Lebanon*, 45–49.

44 MD 48:268.

northwestern Syria. The *dirhemü'r-rical* tax, which the Ottomans inherited from their Mamluk predecessors and which enables us to identify villages that were inhabited by 'Alawis in the sixteenth century, neither was uniformly assessed nor offers evidence in itself that the community was discriminated against. Tax surveys, which were carried out irregularly and only in view of certain taxation categories, are likely to have left out numerous nonassessable villages or population groups, before being abandoned entirely in the later seventeenth century. *Mühimme* decrees were generally issued by the Sublime Porte in response to petitions by well-informed local observers or Ottoman men-on-the-spot and thereby reflect the interests and concerns of local politics as much as the more distant imperial gaze. These sources are nevertheless invaluable, as this chapter has have tried to show, in that they bespeak a regular, institutional, perhaps imperfect but normalized rapport between the "state" and one of the most prominent rural populations of the region. As in any early modern society, this rapport was not free of violence and rebellion, but more than the 'Alawis' contumacy the Ottomans were concerned with their lack of leadership, their exploitation by more powerful figures, and of course their capacity for paying taxes. The temporary remission of some charges in order to revive abandoned 'Alawi villages, the rights conceded to individuals such as Ibn Muhannad, and the recognition of the Kelbis as a dominant local faction, while not necessarily corresponding to our modern notions of tolerance, at the very least call into question the idea that the 'Alawi experience of Ottoman rule was fundamentally determined by injustice and oppression.

Most of all, these sources undermine the claim that the Ottomans persecuted the 'Alawis on account of their religion or were in any way concerned by their confessional identity. This is all the more noteworthy in a time when the Ottomans were constantly engaged in war with the Kızılbaş and Safavid Iran, were routinely denouncing domestic Twelver Shi'is as "*rafizi*" heretics, and had already begun, to judge from these same documents, to label provincial rebels in the area as "Celalis," a term alluding to earlier Kızılbaş revolts but that would in fact come to define the entirely secular rebellions against Ottoman government throughout Anatolia and northern Syria around the turn of the seventeenth century. The Ottoman state's two-sidedness vis-à-vis the 'Alawis is well summarized in our final executive order from this period. The order mainly concerns the Homs region rather than Jabala and is noteworthy because it is one of the few documents that does address the 'Alawis' "heretical" Shi'i identity and objectionable mores but ultimately comes back to temporal law and fiscal benefit as the linchpin of provincial government policy. In February 1584 the Sublime Porte wrote the provincial secretariat of Tripoli, acknowledging:

> You have submitted a petition stating that the mountains of Tripoli are mainly inhabited by the Nusayri faction, who are *rafizi*s and are constantly bringing wine [*hamr*] to sell and trade, and that it is most

advantageous in every respect for the state purse [*miri*] if these sorts of people are assessed the wine tax [*bac-ı hamr*] and pay the stamp tax [*resm-i damga*] and weighing taxes [*resm-i mizan*] in the province of Homs and all the other places specified. I have therefore decreed that—so long as this causes no harm to other tax farms—the new imperial *defter* shall record that Nusayris bringing loads of wine from the outside to sell be assessed, as per ancient custom, the wine tax, weighing taxes, and the stamp tax in the province of Homs and other places indicated.[45]

Like elsewhere in the empire, the inflationary crises, janissary uprisings, and Celali revolts of the late sixteenth–early seventeenth century would mark a broader retreat of Ottoman state power in the Syrian periphery and bring about a sharp decrease in provincial diplomatic correspondence, so that we have next to no further official documentation regarding 'Alawis until late in the seventeenth century. By that time the nature of Ottoman provincial government, and the nature of the historical sources available, had changed significantly. And like other rural populations elsewhere in the empire, 'Alawis would be among the first to benefit from these changes: if the first century of Ottoman rule had been characterized by a monumental—and in large part successful—effort to insert the entire highland population as *reaya* (subjects) into the imperial administrative framework, the decentralizing reforms of the seventeenth and eighteenth centuries would see the rise of a new 'Alawi notable class (*ayan*) in the region that would be commissioned to dominate local society on the Ottoman state's behalf.

45 MD 52:210.

* 4 *
THE AGE OF AUTONOMY
'ALAWI NOTABLES AS OTTOMAN TAX FARMERS
(1667–1808)

An important qualitative change takes place in the written record of 'Alawi history in the late seventeenth century, as it begins to take 'Alawi secular figures into account for the first time. If in previous centuries the only names committed to historical memory were from the 'Alawi religious and literary tradition, with even the likes of Makzun al-Sinjari not unequivocally identifiable as a political actor, the growing exposure of the 'Alawi community to the Ottoman state and its bureaucracy has bequeathed us a rich archive of negotiation, contestation, and co-optation that can serve as the basis for a new prosopography of the 'Alawis in the early modern period—and thereby contribute further to revising the cliché of their perpetual disaffection from wider society.

In part this change is directly linked to the types of sources available. While the Ottoman fiscal surveys and executive orders examined in the previous chapters generally dealt with the 'Alawis, when they were even recognized as such, on an anonymous and impersonal level, the extensive documentary holdings of the local *shar'iyya* (*şeriye*; law) courts in Tripoli and to a lesser extent Antioch and Hama can be used to trace the careers of individual 'Alawis as government tax farmers (sing. *mültezim*), as well as other interactions with neighbors and state authorities or within the community over the course of the eighteenth century. Court records have of course always constituted a mainstay of Ottoman social history, in that they preserve the lived experiences of ordinary subjects, women, slaves, non-Muslims, and other reputedly voiceless minorities. A common misconception today holds that 'Alawis, being regarded as heretics, were excluded from the Ottoman court system. In practice, however, the courts—which did not distinguish between religious (*shari'a*), administrative (*kanun*), and traditional (*örf*) sources of jurisprudence and should therefore not be cast as "Islamic" tribunals—virtually never acknowledged inter-Muslim sectarian differences and freely accommodated non-Sunni subjects even when their confessional identity was known from other contexts. The Tripoli court registers, in particular, which have been used only rarely in the writing of Syrian provincial history, as well as other Ottoman tax records, can thus provide us with a valuable glimpse into the economic circumstances, family composition, and political connections of an entire class of 'Alawi protagonists who were characterized by their social, rather than their religious, status.

The profusion of tax collection contracts and other fiscal records from the eighteenth century, however, is itself reflective of the larger transformation of Ottoman government and administration in this period. If much of the agricultural revenue from northwestern Syria and other parts of the empire had originally been assigned as *timar* military fiefs to Ottoman cavalry soldiers, the growing necessity and cost of maintaining a standing infantry army, inflation, deficitary trade, population pressure, and a series of provincial governor rebellions (possibly linked to an ecological phenomenon referred to as the "little ice age," though this remains conjectural) ultimately led to a decentralization of authority in the seventeenth century by which provincial government office was assigned for extended periods of time to local or localized Ottoman notable families to exploit on behalf of the state. Though already in use in parts of Syria before the reform, the practice of *iltizam* tax farming (as well as the *malikane* lifetime tax farm, introduced in 1695 but never widely applied in Syria) thereby concretized not only the emergence of provincial governor dynasties such as the 'Azms (Azmzades) in Hama and Damascus but also the appearance of numerous rural *ayan* (notable) households as state intermediaries. The leeway or autonomy these families enjoyed in the exercise of their government commissions, often in multiple tax districts, in turn ensured their ascendancy over local society. Sometimes portrayed in modern national historiographies as resilient to Ottoman imperial authority, 'Alawi and other *ayan* of the Syrian coastal interior were in fact its very incarnation in the eighteenth century.

This chapter follows the rise to power of the Shamsins, the Bayt al-Shillif, and associated 'Alawi families as Ottoman tax concessionaries. It seeks to show that their position of local autonomy, rather than having evolved out of some domestic or "tribal" leadership structure, resulted from this shift of paradigm in Ottoman provincial administration as well as from a very favorable economic context, in particular the development of commercial tobacco farming in the northern highlands around Latakia. If the eighteenth century witnessed the emergence of a veritable Ottoman-'Alawi landed gentry, however, it also saw increasing social disparities lead to large-scale emigration away from the highlands toward the coastal and inland plains as well as toward the Hatay district of what is today southern Turkey. The relative autonomy enjoyed by the 'Alawi notability in the eighteenth century would therefore have a lasting impact not only on the community's internal structure but also on its overall relationship to wider Syrian (and Anatolian) society. Once again the 'Alawi experience was not so much an anomaly within Middle Eastern history as the result of long-term economic and administrative processes shared in by the rest of the region and therefore has to be understood within the larger matrices of Ottoman society and governance in the early modern period.

ʿALAWI TRIBALISM, TRIBALIZATION, AND GENTRY

Upon their initial contact, as we have seen, the Ottomans dealt with the ʿAlawis on a village-by-village basis, and it is only in some parts of the Jabala district that the Kelbis were identified in government sources as the overarching faction or population (*taife*). By the later eighteenth century, however, this appears to have changed. While Ottoman tax registers have by this time fallen out of usage, Western travel reports and consular correspondence now describe ʿAlawi society as fundamentally divided into tribes and sects.[1] In part this may be ascribed to the hubris of contemporary European travelers, who unlike their more open-minded predecessors had increasingly begun to imagine and represent foreign societies in evolutionist terms and categories of cultural superiority and inferiority by the eighteenth century.[2] The divisions themselves, on the other hand, are substantiated by numerous local accounts and seen as pertinent by many ʿAlawis and other Syrians down to the present day.

The first critical discussion of the ʿAlawis' tribal organization comes from the already-cited Anglican reverend Samuel Lyde, who ran a mission at Bahamra in the mountains above Jabala between 1854 and 1860. According to Lyde, the ʿAlawis were split into two main "sects," the Shamsis ("sun-worshippers") and the Qamaris ("moon-worshippers"), whereby he soberly minimizes the religious significance of the denominations and describes them rather as tribal groupings. What sets Lyde's account apart from others is its historicization of this division: thus the generally more pious or observant Shamsis would have constituted the oldest inhabitants of the coastal range and comprised such groups as the Muhalaba, the Banu ʿAli (originally Kurdish converts to ʿAlawism), the Diryus, and the Qaratala, while the more aggressive and refractory Qamaris were those tribes that migrated from the Sinjar in the thirteenth century or later, driving out numerous clans of the Shamsis with whom they henceforth lived in enmity. The main representatives of the Qamaris were the Kelbis, the dominant tribe of Lyde's own district, who "it is certain ... within the last few hundred years have come over from the east of the mountains, and opened a road for themselves to the sea; conquering the Beni Ali to the south ... and the Muhailby people to the north."[3] Al-Tawil's account of

---

1 See, e.g., Volney, *Travels through Egypt and Syria*, 2:208; Burckhardt, *Travels in Syria*, 156.
2 Jürgen Osterhammel, *Die Entzauberung Asiens: Europa und die asiatischen Reiche im 18. Jahrhundert* (Munich: C. H. Beck, 1998).
3 Lyde, *Asian Mystery*, 50–54.

'Alawi tribal divisions, though not always reliable and indeed contradicted in several points of historical detail, also corroborates the long-standing conflict between the Banu 'Ali-Muhalaba bloc and the Kelbis.[4] Local tradition holds that Ahmad ibn Makhluf was the first Kelbi chief to establish himself on the western side of the mountain, building numerous *maqam*s in the area, and that it was his grandsons who founded the leading Kelbi lineages Hassun, 'Ali, Jirkis (or Çerkes), and Ahmad. While the Kelbis were never considered to be very prestigious in the past, it is clear that affiliation with these clans became a major determinant of Syrian politics in the republican era, and especially under the regime of the Kelbis' most famous scion, Hafiz al-Asad.[5]

For our purposes here, the comparatively recent emergence of the Kelbis, and of the 'Alawi tribal system in general, of course raises the question to what degree this was a result of Ottoman policies in the early modern period. If the medieval sources take no account of supposed 'Alawi tribalism, it appears likely that the Ottomans' concern with the Kelbis and others beginning in the mid-sixteenth century reflected not a mere recognition but rather a conscious privileging of tribes as the primary unit of social organization in the area. Whereas Middle East historiography, not least of which the traditional accounts of many tribes themselves, has usually assumed tribalism to have been the universal, natural prestate mode of social being among rural and pastoral peoples, anthropologists have for many years now argued that tribes only form through contact with a more complex political structure, that is, a state: whether through warfare against an imperial power, deportation and resettlement, or the selection and appointment of certain individuals to tax and police an autochthonous population, tribes would therefore always be derivative, "secondary," or "colonial" products of the state.[6] Al-Tawil affirms as much regarding the 'Alawis, claiming that indigenous society was never divided into tribes until forced to do so in the face of constant Ottoman aggression.[7] In his more radical critique, however, David Sneath has dismissed the entire idea of an organic, tribal "segmentary society" as "total fiction" and argued that "the organization of commoners into groups under named heads is more likely to have been an administrative act than the result of some indigenous kinship structure," thus attacking the entire

---

4 Al-Tawil, *Tarikh al-'Alawiyyin*, 412–46.

5 Hanna Batatu, *Syria's Peasantry, the Descendants of Its Lesser Rural Notables, and Their Politics* (Princeton, NJ: Princeton University Press, 1999), 142, 194, 217–25.

6 Morton Fried, *The Notion of Tribe* (Menlo Park, CA: Cummings, 1975), 100; Richard Tapper, "Anthropologists, Historians and Tribespeople on Tribe and State Formation in the Middle East," in *Tribes and State Formation in the Middle East*, ed. Philip Khoury and Joseph Kostiner (Berkeley: University of California Press, 1990), 48–73; Neil Whitehead, "Tribes Make States and States Make Tribes: Warfare and the Creation of Colonial Tribes and States in Northeastern South America," in *War in the Tribal Zone: Expanding States and Indigenous Warfare*, ed. N. Whitehead and R. Brian Ferguson (Santa Fe, NM: School of American Research, 1992), 127–50.

7 Al-Tawil, *Tarikh al-'Alawiyyin*, 407–8.

concept of "tribalization" as such. According to Sneath, the concentration of wealth even in pastoral societies always produced stratified rural "aristocracies," central to whose effective rule over local society was not an essential ethnic or sectarian affinity but rather the "processes and institutions of descent and the inheritance of status and political office."[8]

The possibilities for capital accumulation and social differentiation were of course not the same in the Syrian coastal mountains as among the Inner Asian nomad societies studied by Sneath, so that it may be more useful to conceive of the 'Alawi leaders and other "lesser rural notables" (to use Hanna Batatu's apt expression) who were co-opted by the Ottomans as a local gentry rather than a full-blown aristocracy. Political office was no less important to their social status, however. Already in Mamluk times, numerous village or sectarian elders, including Christians, Druze, Twelver Shi'is, and 'Alawis, were designated as *muqaddam* (headman) and given responsibility for collecting tribute and otherwise representing their communities; after the Ottoman conquest some of the more powerful *muqaddam*s in the region, such as the Shi'i Harfushes and the Druze Ma'nids, were formally assigned a provincial *sancak* governorship and could henceforth claim the prestigious title of *bey* or "emir." Like their predecessors, the Ottomans found that conciliating provincial strongmen (sometimes even granting them a rank within the state military hierarchy) was often the best method of extending government control over the otherwise inaccessible rural hinterland. What was new in the sixteenth century was the rise of *iltizam* tax farming. If state office had previously been tied to military service, the rapid monetization of the Ottoman and eastern Mediterranean economy and the central government's growing need for cash revenues meant that the authorities increasingly sought to "farm out" or subcontract the collection of taxes in many provinces to local or locally rooted urban notables, financiers, or rural community leaders. The Syrian coastal range was one of the areas where tax farming was instituted the earliest, with Ottoman-consecrated "tribal" leaders such as the Ma'nids and later the Shihabis holding tax concessions on such a large scale that they constituted "veritable forms of governance."[9] Though on a smaller scale, the awarding

---

8 David Sneath, *The Headless State: Aristocratic Orders, Kinship Society, and Misrepresentations of Nomadic Inner Asia* (New York: Columbia University Press, 2007), esp. 5, 20, 43, 47, 52, 59, 189. See also Pierre Bonte and Édouard Conte, "La tribu arabe: approches anthropologiques et orientalistes," in *Al-Ansâb, La quête des origines: Anthropologie historique de la société arabe tribale*, ed. P. Bonte et al. (Paris: Maison des sciences de l'homme, 1991), 24–28.

9 Cf. Ariel Salzmann, *Toqueville in the Ottoman Empire: Rival Paths to the Modern State* (Leiden: Brill, 2004), 21; Fadil Bayat, *Dirasat fi Tarikh al-'Arab fi'l-'Ahd al-'Uthmani: Ru'ya Jadida fi Daw' al-Watha'iq wa'l-Masadir al-'Uthmaniyya* (Tripoli, Libya: Dar al-Madar al-Islami, 2003), 150–52; Winter, *Shiites of Lebanon*, 40–43, 77–79. On the process of monetization and the emergence of provincial strongmen in Syria, see also Baki Tezcan, *The Second Ottoman Empire: Political and Social Transformation in the Early Modern World* (Cambridge: Cambridge University Press, 2010), 141–45.

of state *iltizam* farms in several key districts of the more northerly coastal mountains (where, as already indicated, Ottoman soldier-fiefholders played a bigger role than in what would eventually become Lebanon) underpinned the emergence, beginning in the seventeenth century, of an 'Alawi "landed" gentry or lesser rural notable class. As with other such populations throughout the region, 'Alawi patrilineage was "not the original building block of a clan society" but rather a regulating technique applied by the state; their leaders, mansions, clans, and parties were "not based on the elaboration of a local system of kinship" but were rather "country extensions of the imperial military and administrative establishment."[10]

THE SHAMSINS AND THE *MUKATAA* OF SAFITA

The most prominent and apparently longest-serving of the 'Alawi tax-farming gentry were the Shamsins (Shiblis) of Safita. Safita, as indicated in chapter 3, was the principal *nahiye* in the southern part of the Syrian coastal range, encompassing around forty villages with the districts of Mi'ar, Tartus, and Qulay'a sometimes added as appanages, and about a third of their combined villages were assessed the *dirhemü'r-rical* tax in the sixteenth and first half of the seventeenth centuries. Before their demise around 1640, the town of Safita was generally held by the Sayfa lords of northern Lebanon, its citadel playing a frequent role in their wars against the Druze Ma'nid emirs.[11] Thereafter the region is never mentioned in the chronicles of the period. Because Safita was located in the *sancak* of Tripoli, however, a number of its *iltizam* contracts and related documents have been preserved in the *shar'iyya* court records of Tripoli city, affording us a unique view into the historic role of the Shamsin family as local *mültezim*s and their relationship with the Ottoman state.

The earliest extant Tripoli court records date from 1666 (1077 *hijri*), and the oldest *iltizam* contract available for Safita was written out at the start of the next solar-fiscal year, in March 1667. According to this contract, the *mukataa* (tax concession) for the district of Safita was "sold" (*füruht*) to the two brothers Muhammad and Zaydan ibn Shamsin for one full year for 15,000 silver *guruş*. The charges they were to collect in the district included summer and winter moneys (*mal-i şitvi ve sayfi*); the *harac* (agricultural tax) on fruit trees and *maktu* on the number of acres (*feddan*) under the plow; taxes on falcons, bees, buffalo, and wage labor; festival and accession dues (*idiye ve kudumiye*); silk and flour mill taxes; *kışlak* (wintering dues) on Turkmen and Arab nomads; bridal taxes,

---

10 Michael Meeker, *A Nation of Empire: The Ottoman Legacy of Turkish Modernity* (Berkeley: University of California Press, 1997), 32; Sneath, *Headless State*, 189–91.

11 Duwayhi, *Tarikh al-Azmina*, 321–22, 332; Abu-Husayn, *Provincial Leaderships*, 43, 48, 51, 54–55, 110.

the *jizya* (*cizye*) poll-tax on Christians and church charges; as well as other "customary" dues—though there is interestingly no separate mention of the *dirhemü'r-rical*, which was perhaps no longer universally current by this time. In any event, all these taxes, most of which had never been itemized in the Tahrir registers, accrued to the provincial governor's reserve (*havass-ı mirmiran*) and were now assessed on the district in a single yearly lump-sum payment, rather than on individual villages or communities.[12]

Three quarters of the total amount were to be remitted to the *divan* (government) treasury of Tripoli during the "silk season" (late summer), an indication of what doubtless constituted Safita's economic mainstay, while the remainder was to be paid three months before the end of the fiscal year, that is, in December, after the autumn harvest. More important for our purposes, however, are the contract's stipulations concerning the Shamsin family itself. The two brothers, who are consistently addressed in honorific terms ("paragon of the most eminent"; "may [God] make their power be eternal"), are explicitly noted to have "sought and solicited" the tax farm, perhaps suggesting that it was not attributed to them automatically but that they had to compete for it and, in all likelihood, demonstrate their ability to discharge it beforehand. They are then exhorted to make the district flourish, to not harm or oppress the people and not let anyone else interfere in their functions. Most notably, each of the two was obliged to place one of his sons and/or women as a "hostage" (*rehn*) with the Tripoli authorities until such time as the *iltizam* was paid in full. In a second document, in which the brothers pledged to "mutually uphold and guarantee" (*müteahhid ve mütekeffil*) the contract, it is indicated that they indeed sent Muhammad's two sons and their mothers, and Zaydan's son and his wife and mother, to live together "under the Paşa's care" in Tripoli.[13] This was pretty much a standard clause in all the province's tax-farm contracts of the time, but which in the case of more powerful families occasionally led to impromptu escapes or even to armed attacks on the citadel of Tripoli in order to liberate their hostages.[14] In the case of more docile gentry such as the Shamsins, this obligation at least enabled members of the family to live for extended periods of time, and perhaps gather valuable experience, at court in the provincial capital.

The degree of the Shamsins' sociopolitical standing in the region is also shown by a violent incident that had apparently taken place the year before. In May 1667 a court hearing was held in Tripoli regarding a group of Hazur Turkmen who had been settled in the district and were ostensibly providing *derbend* ("mountain pass," i.e., high-road security) services, but who had recently attacked and robbed a commercial caravan near Safita. Upon being called to

12 Qasr Nawfal, Tripoli: Tripoli Shar'iyya Court Records [TShCR] 1:107.
13 Ibid. 1:5.
14 Winter, *Shiites of Lebanon*, 79, 87; Winter, "Kurdes de Syrie," 131.

account, their leaders responded that it had in reality been Abdülaziz, the tribe's former *kethüda* (captain), who had committed the crime in association with a certain Muhammad ibn Kassar "and the Nusayri *muqaddam* Hamad," testimony which was corroborated by eyewitnesses from Safita.[15] Further evidence, however, suggests that this was not merely about brigandage. According to sworn depositions given a few days later, the same three had the previous year gathered a number of followers and besieged Muhammad ibn Shamsin's mansion (*saray*) in Safita, killing several of his acolytes. In one of the depositions, a group of notables from the 'Akkar district in northern Lebanon stated that the Turkmen and their 'Alawi allies were always coming at night to steal their animals; in this case, they had also stolen one and a half *kantar* (approximately 180 pounds) of silk as well as animals and other goods that had been collected from the villagers in taxes and were being stored in the Shamsins' *saray*, before setting fire to the building itself. Abdülaziz, unlike Muhammad Kassar and the *muqaddam* Hamad, presented himself in court and denied all the charges.[16] While we do not know how the case was finally resolved, it appears that these incidents together may have been more of a concerted attack on the Shamsins' authority, prestige, and financial basis than simple lawlessness on the part of Abdülaziz and his 'Alawi supporters.

The evidence regarding the Safita tax farm over the next decades is somewhat fragmentary. Not all revenues in the district were always necessarily included in the concession. In 1668, for example, the Sublime Porte awarded the son of a deceased Ottoman officer and the commander of a local army unit parts of a *zeamet* (military benefice) of 32,000 *akça* (approx. 267 *guruş*) which the officer had previously held on Sudayda and other villages.[17] The overall *iltizam* for the district was awarded that same year not to the Shamsins but to the powerful Hamada family of northern Lebanon, marking the furthest-ever extent of the latter's tax-farming enterprise. The value of the contract was reduced to 14,000 *guruş* in this instance, possibly because the Hamadas were already operating multiple tax concessions in the region, including the lucrative 'Akkar.[18] We next hear of the Safita *iltizam* in the spring of 1686, when it was reconfirmed (*ikrar*) as being in the shared possession (*ber vech-i iştirak*) of a certain Murad Bey and *muqaddam* Muhammad ibn Ahmad. By this time its value had risen to 19,000 *guruş* and included several new or newly designated charges such as a cash exchange tax (*sarafiye*) and grazing dues (*otlak akçası*). A second version of the contract issued only a few weeks later (which lists a different set of charges) refers to the *muqaddam* and Derviş

---

15 TShCR 1:17.
16 TShCR 1:18–19.
17 TShCR 2/1:74.
18 TShCR 2/1:60–61.

Bey instead of Murad Bey.[19] Either way, however, these documents point to a functional partnership between an Ottoman military officeholder and a local 'Alawi notable in the business of farming Safita's taxes.

If the Shamsin family seems to have been somewhat eclipsed in the later part of the seventeenth century, it would return to dominate Safita throughout the eighteenth. The earliest evidence we have in this regard dates from December 1721, when the Sublime Porte informed the *qadi* of Tripoli that "the shaykh of the Safita *mukataa*, Shibli, has fled" (reneging his fiscal obligations) and taken refuge in the ('Alawi) villages in the foothills west of Hama. Since the local population there was "neither his friends nor his bondsmen," however, they were not to be extorted for the amounts still owed for Safita.[20] Shibli's family nonetheless still retained control of the tax farm. Only two years later, in April 1724, Shaykh Darwish (Derviş) "ibn Shibli Shamsin" submitted a claim at the trial of the famous northern Syrian feudal lord Rustum Agha (to be examined in the next section) to demand moneys which the latter's deputy had apparently collected but failed to remit for the previous year's *iltizam* on Safita.[21] In 1729 we see the same Darwish ibn Shibli engaged in a complex partnership for five-sixths of the *iltizam* (one-sixth was held by Abu Qasim al-Shibli, who may have been a relative too) for a total of 27,000 *guruş*; Darwish's partner in this instance was a Christian from Kafrun village (near Mashta'l-Hilu), while a bondship (*kefalet*) for the fulfillment of their contract was provided by Isma'il ibn al-Za'nabi, an Ismaili emir from Qadmus.[22] A decade later, in 1738, Darwish joined up with his sister's son Mulham ibn Husayn Shamsin for the full tax farm (33,050 *guruş*), sending off two of his cousins to Tripoli as "security" (*istisak*). Two further contracts made out to Darwish and Mulham and again guaranteed by the former's cousins, one for 1,500 *guruş* and one for 2,500 *guruş*, likely covered payments in arrears from the previous years.[23] The smaller *nahiye*s of Mi'ar and Qulay'a, which some Tahrir censuses described as dependencies of Safita, are not the object of distinct *iltizam* contracts in the Tripoli court registers and were probably included in the larger Safita concession.

The financial details of the Shamsins' tax contracts changed little over the next years and need not detain us here.[24] What these documents allow us to appreciate, on the other hand, is the increasing implication of the extended Shamsin clan as well as of the local population in their regional tax farming operation. In March 1740, for example, Darwish partnered with his brother

19 TShCR 3:69, 173, 191.
20 MD 130:249.
21 TShCR 4/2:67.
22 TShCR 5:18.
23 TShCR 7:6–7, 106.

24 Copies of at least some of the Shamsins' *iltizam* contracts in this period were forwarded to Istanbul and are preserved in the Başbakanlık Archives' Başmuhasebe Kalemi/Trablus-Şam Mukataası (head accountancy/Tripoli tax farm) collection [D.BŞM.TŞH] 11:61, 13:52.

'Ali ibn Shibli Shamsin, but their contract was countersigned this time by a dozen different family members, including two other brothers and a nephew, the village shaykhs of fifteen, mostly non-'Alawi villages under their control, and three 'Alawi *muqaddam*s. This provision too had parallels in other parts of the Syro-Lebanese coastal range, where beginning in the mid-eighteenth century the local village elders were increasingly expected to underwrite their tax farmer's engagement and share his liability.[25] For some reason this particular contract was rewritten a few months later with 'Ali Shibli now appearing as coguarantor and Mulham Husayn resuming his role as Darwish's partner, and with a more formal bondship provided by two local *agha*s or low-level military officers. Among the coguarantors of the revised contract we also find Mulham's father Husayn Shamsin, suggesting that a more collective, corporate responsibility for the Safita farm's discharge was starting to extend to the Shibli line's in-laws as well.[26] In subsequent contracts, Mulham in turn sent two of his sons, several nephews, and a maternal cousin, Muhammad ibn Idris Raslan, to live under official supervision until the *iltizam* was paid; starting in 1746 these hostages were usually made to reside in the citadel of Arwad Island, just off the coast at Tartus, rather than in Tripoli, so as to be closer to their family.[27]

If the Shamsins were thus able to establish their dominance over the southern 'Alawi mountains, their reign was not without its troubles. The Sublime Porte repeatedly complained that Nusayris as well as other bandits and heretics were making the roads between Hama, Homs, and Damascus unsafe and threatening the pilgrimage traffic; in one especially problematic year it specifically commissioned the *bey* of Hama to go and investigate "those boors and scoundrels ... who are bent on brigandage from the borders of Ma'arrat al-Nu'man all the way to the far borders of Hama, Homs, and Hisn al-Akrad" and to "strike them and teach them a lesson," though without using this as a pretext to oppress the poor and the innocent of the region.[28] Pillage and violence also hit closer to home, for example, when Husayn ibn 'Umar of the Sha'ra-based Dandashli clan, who already had a fearsome reputation for his depredations in the 'Akkar district, attacked several Safita villages in 1732, carrying off livestock and prompting an official complaint by the local population to the authorities.[29] In a particularly colorful case from 1724, a certain Yusuf ibn Fakhr al-Din of the Safita district was brought to court in Tripoli

and confirmed of his own free will that his father is of the Nusayri faction, that he was in the service of Abu Fayyad, the *dabit* [tax collector]

25 Winter, *Shiites of Lebanon*, 162–64.
26 TShCR 7:257, 326.
27 TShCR 8:100, 328–29; TShCR 9:94.
28 MD 112:155; MD 147:124a.
29 TShCR 6:108–10.

of the ['Alawi] village of Tuffah[a], and that "I advised him [Abu Fayyad] of the problem in taking the watermelons from a watermelon patch which he had sold to the stranger named *hajj* Ibrahim ibn 'Abdallah, and that he ordered me to kill him [Ibrahim]. So I went to him, choked him, and took a large stone in my hand and struck him under the ear, causing blood to flow. Then I left him there to die. He lingered on for about forty days, then died from the injury and the suffocation." This admission was a condition for demanding talion (*qisas*). As the victim has no executor or representative, the honorable judge . . . has ruled that it is the governor of the aforesaid province who has the right of talion, so it is up to his deputy (present here at court) . . . whether to forgive or to demand talion from the aforesaid, and this is essential for prohibiting vice and preventing others from committing similar acts.[30]

This case is of course interesting because the defendant's confessional identity is taken to note, but finally does not seem to have played a role in his conviction (with the sentence at any rate left to the political authority's discretion). Another time, in 1732, 'Alawi identity was implicitly a factor in a dispute over taxes, when a local *muqaddam*, "the eminent peer" Dargham ibn Qansuh, accused Yusuf ibn 'Ali al-Turkmani of not having contributed to the payment of the *miri* in the district of Safita. Put to question, Yusuf responded that he was the son of (the famous scholar) 'Ali al-Turkmani, that he was born in Tripoli, that he did not owe taxes in the district, and that "he is Sunni, whereas the community and people of Safita are Nusayri, and he is innocent (*bari*) of them." Yusuf's testimony was corroborated by viable witnesses, and the *muqaddam*'s claim was turned down.[31]

A similar dispute over tax jurisdictions concerned the Shamsins more directly in 1743, when an agent for the "people of Tartus" came to court complaining that the Shamsins had taken over and begun planting on a piece of land adjoining Safita that an order from the governor confirmed belonged to Tartus. A hearing was held in the presence of Darwish Shibli and Mulham Husayn in which the piece of land, which stretched all the way down to the sea, was precisely delimited and where the *dabit* of Tartus, Mustafa Agha, argued that the *kışlak* collected there from the Arab and Turkman tribes and other dues had always gone to his *nahiye*. Darwish and Mulham denied this claim but were again contradicted by witnesses and were thus ordered to cease and desist in their exploitation of the land.[32] As in the previous case, it is possible to surmise that Darwish and Mulham's confessional identity put them at a disadvantage vis-à-vis the Muslim *agha* of Tartus and his witnesses,

30 TShCR 4/2:60.
31 TShCR 6:125.
32 TShCR 8:4–5.

but this is not made explicit in the court proceeding. Formally at least the Shamsins as well as various 'Alawi *muqaddam*s and other figures, the registers suggest, were admitted to the Sunni Hanafi court in Tripoli, addressed in respectful terms, and treated on an equal footing.

In reality the Shamsins' greatest problem in these years appears to have been their growing indebtedness. In 1749, most notably, Darwish and Mulham contracted for part of the Safita *iltizam* for 24,050 *guruş* but already had arrears from previous years and other late payments that amounted by now to an additional 20,143 *guruş*.[33] Late the following year, in October 1750, an extraordinary court session was held in Tripoli to register the Shamsins' as well as other districts' debts, those of Darwish and Mulham by now totaling over 35,000 *guruş*. Their hostages, perhaps not coincidentally, were now also made to live once again in Tripoli rather than on Arwad.[34] Beginning around the same time, as will be seen further on in this chapter, the Safita *iltizam* was divided into several sections that were awarded to other 'Alawi families more or less closely associated with the Shamsins. All this is not to signify that the Shamsins or the Shiblis had necessarily fallen from the Ottoman authorities' graces: debt, legal vulnerability, and stoking rivalry with other tax entrepreneurs were primary means for the early modern state to keep the gentry dependent and loyal. It does suggest, however, that the entire district—its leading families and the peasant population—would be subject to increasing fiscal and political pressures in the course of the second half of the century.

THE BAYT AL-SHILLIF

The history of the northern *mukataa*s of the Syrian coastal range is considerably more obscure than that of Safita. Tax-farm contracts for the *sancak* of Jabala would have been registered at the court of Jabala, but these records are not known to have been preserved. Virtually the only references to the region in this period occur in Ottoman executive orders regarding tax arrears and brigandage or in the occasional Western travel accounts, but these are incidental and provide little indication of an established notable class, the distribution of fiscal offices, or other aspects of local society. In late 1691, for example, the Sublime Porte warned the *beylerbeyi* of Tripoli that a number of Nusayri *muqaddam*s in the mountains of Jabala, including Mursin (?) ibn (al-)Makhnuq, Sulayman ibn Mahfuz, Muhammad ibn Shillif, and Shahin ibn Salhab, were banding together with Turkmans from the neighboring Sahyun and Bayezid districts, sowing corruption and causing tax shortfalls, and should

---

33 TShCR 10:163, 246.
34 TShCR 11:36, 70–71.

be either killed or deported.[35] A few years later the English chaplain Henry Maundrell, traveling from Aleppo to Latakia in the winter of 1697, reported spending a miserable couple of days in the Nahr al-Kabir valley northeast of Latakia: In Bahluliyya—actually one of the leading 'Alawi villages in the area—he was ungraciously put up the first night by the Turkish-speaking *agha*, while on the second, the inhabitants of nearby Shalfutiyya, who he noted "hate and renounce [the orthodox caliphs] Omar and Abu Beker" but "make very much and good wine, and are great drinkers," refused to let him and his rain-soaked company take shelter in the local *maqam*.[36]

Fortunately, however, the history of one of the area's leading 'Alawi families, the Bayt al-Shillif, comes to light through its entanglement with the most powerful feudal lords of the northwestern Syrian hinterland in the eighteenth century, the Rustum Aghas. The Rustum Aghas' own history has remained largely unexplored, even though their radius of influence at times rivaled that of the famous Shihabi emirate in Lebanon—the reasons being not only that there are fewer chronicle sources for the northern region and that the documentary evidence is widely dispersed among the archives of Istanbul, Ankara, Antioch, Aleppo, and Tripoli but probably also that they were Kurds. They first appear to be mentioned in 1695, when Hasan ibn Rustum became the beneficiary of a *malikane*, the new lifetime tax concession instituted in the Ottoman Empire that year, which gave him quasi-proprietary rights to much of the Qusayr and Bayir districts in the mountains of Aleppo province immediately north of Bahluliyya.[37] This seems to have placed the Rustum Aghas in competition with other local actors including the Shillifs, who, as we have seen, were implicated in brigandage in the area as early as 1691. Ottoman chancery orders conserved in the annex (*zeyl*) series of the Mühimme registers refer to a violent incident in 1698–99, in which

> Muhammad ibn Shillif of the Nusayri faction, his relatives and followers, together with Sulayman of Bahluliyya and his sons Muhammad and Hassun's gangs, the captains of the Bayir district, and Mustafa of the Şexan Kurds, joined up with several thousand of their Nusayri cohorts and attacked Hasan ibn Rustum while he was out traveling between Jabala, Latakia, and Jisr al-Shughur minding his own affairs, killing several of his men, and cutting down 124,000 mulberry trees and burning the tobacco and other crops on his farms outside of Latakia.

---

35 MD 102:61.

36 Henry Maundrell (d. 1701), *A Journey from Aleppo to Jerusalem, at Easter A.D. 1697* (Boston: Samuel Simpkins, 1836), 11–21.

37 See Fayiz Qawsara, *Al-Rahhala fi Muhafazat Idlib: Itlaqa Tarikhiyya* (Aleppo: Matba'at al-Sharq, 1985–88), 2:152–54; Stefan Winter, "Les Kurdes du Nord-Ouest syrien et l'Etat ottoman, 1690–1750," in *Sociétés rurales ottomanes*, ed. Mohammad Afifi et al. (Cairo: IFAO, 2005), 252–57.

FIGURE 4.1. Tobacco fields near Salma (2001)

Here the 'Alawis had actually been acting once again on behalf of more powerful interests, namely, of a certain Berber Mustafa and other "spiteful" enemies of Hasan Rustum in Latakia, who were then condemned on the basis of a fatwa issued by the *şeyhülislam* in Istanbul to compensate him for the damage incurred.[38] According to a list of Tripoli *mukataa* arrears from 1709–10, Muhammad ibn Shillif was only one of several lesser rural notables to hold a tax concession in the mountains of Latakia in this period.[39] But it is nevertheless he who seems to have emerged as the Rustum Aghas' principle rival—as witnessed among other things by the fact that they endeavored to have him killed a few years later, around 1714. This follows from the proceedings of a vast murder and embezzlement trial held for Hasan Rustum's eldest son Rustum in 1724, which occupy the better part of an entire volume of Tripoli court records. The immediate cause of this indictment was the unjustified killing some years before of a local peasant boy, a crime for which Rustum was then indeed executed. In the course of the weeklong trial, however, numerous other charges were brought against him, which in themselves speak to the extent of his family's hegemony in the region. In one deposition, thirty-five different *mültezim*s attested that "Rustum Agha of Latakia, known as the son of Hasan the Kurd," had "illegally and oppressively" been seizing state taxes and *cizye* dues from them for the past decade. The list of afflicted areas includes entire *mukataa*s such as Khawabi, Marqab, Qadmus,

38 BOA: Mühimme Zeyli Defteri [MZ] 12:173, 175.
39 MAD 4455:41.

and Kahf as well as the 'Alawi districts of Qardaha, Bani 'Ali, Bahluliyya, and the Cebel-i Kelbiyun Dağı (Kelbi mountains)—tax districts which had replaced or superseded Jabala, Platanus, and Sahyun by this time—but also individual 'Alawi-inhabited villages such as Bayt Yashut, Istamo, and Tabarja, which had apparently been divided off into smaller subfarms and which all suffered to some degree from the Rustum Aghas' interference.[40]

In addition to this collective suit, Rustum ibn Hasan Rustum Agha was also charged with purloining money from or mistreating a number of individuals in the region. We have already referred to Shaykh Darwish Shamsin writing the court in 1724 to seek the restitution of dues that an adjunct of Rustum's had collected but then failed to remit for an area as far away as Safita in the southern 'Alawi mountains. Closer to home, Rustum was accused of extortion by several different villagers, including from the 'Alawi hamlet of Husayniyya in the district of Jabala.[41] And finally, "*muqaddam* 'Ali son of *muqaddam* Muhammad, known as Şillif-oğlı [Ibn Shillif] of Kimin village in the district of Latakia," sent the court a petition stating that "ten years ago, the said Rustum invited my father Muhammad ibn Ahmad to his *saray* as a guest. At a given moment he dropped a rope around his neck, pulling one end while his cousin Musa pulled on the other, causing him to scream and killing him by strangulation." Asked to corroborate 'Ali Shillif's claim, three "righteous men from among the Muslims of Latakia" thereupon went before the judge to confirm that they had witnessed the murder firsthand. On the basis of this evidence, the court examined another affidavit from the Bayt al-Shillif the following day, in which the family attested that after their father's murder, "Rustum Agha came to our village with 78 *levend* mercenaries and stole x quantity of possessions from our house" (150 head of buffalo, horses, and cows), for which they now sought and were awarded damages.[42] The court record itself provides some interesting insights into the Shillif family's composition. Muhammad's ancestry is traced back two generations, suggesting that they were already well-rooted in the area before leaving their mark in the historical documentation. The court recognized eighteen individual family members as his legal heirs: four wives, seven adult sons and one minor-age son, and six adult daughters. One of his wives is noted to be the daughter of an "emir Shahin." While the name Shahin was fairly common, there were very few notables in the region who could lay claim to the emir title; to deduce from an unrelated inheritance case involving the Ismaili emirs of Qadmus, this Shahin is likely to have been the brother of the same Emir Isma'il who was mentioned above as a guarantor of the Shamsins' tax-farming concession.[43]

40 TShCR 4/2:68.
41 TShCR 4/2:61, 63–65; see also MD 131:469.
42 TShCR 4/2:61–62.
43 TShCR 4/1:26.

Three of Muhammad Shillif's adult sons are identified as *muqaddam*s, suggesting a not inconsiderable degree of control over the local village population in the district of Latakia. While his eldest son Ahmad is named as the estate's executor (*vasi*), both the initiative for the lawsuit and, as events would show, real authority within the family devolved upon his second son, 'Ali. Most of all, of course, the very fact of their recourse to the Ottoman court in Tripoli, the backing they received from the Sunni witnesses of Latakia, and the judgment rendered in their favor against the (Sunni) Rustum Aghas all indicate to what degree the Bayt al-Shillif was entrenched and accepted within provincial notable society in northwest Syria at the time.

With the Rustum Aghas temporarily out of the way, the Shillifs wasted little time in asserting themselves as the region's new dominant faction. In 1730 the governor of Tripoli received an urgent order warning him that

> one of the *mukaddem*s of the Jabala tax farms, the Nusayri known as Şillif-oğlı Ali, acting in accordance with the malice and evil that are in his heart and that are typical of his kind, wished to get his hands on all the *mukataa*s of that district. He turned and deviated from the path of submission and went and followed the road of banditry and rebellion, and has not ceased to constantly oppress and afflict the poor commoners who are not of his whim. Thus last year, while you, the governor, had departed for the *cerde* [relief command of the annual pilgrimage], he seized on the occasion to carry out his infamous designs and gathered 1,000 musketeers from among the Nusayri vermin, came straight to Latakia, and took out the tax-farm contracts he sought from your district deputy under force and duress and at an exorbitant discount. Moreover, he then failed and refused to pay the moneys that were asked of him for the tax farms which had been sold to others with his *kefalet* [guarantee].... With the degree of his disobedience and rebellion increasing every day, he has now ensconced himself with his gang of brigands in the Kelbi mountains, on the borders of the said district.[44]

With his controlling interest in a number of tax concessions, 'Ali Shillif appears to have been able to extend his influence beyond Kimin and the narrow hinterland of Latakia. Ironically, the first to profit from the general breakdown of government order in the area were the Rustum Aghas, who after having retreated to the Kurdish village of Salma in the northern Sahyun district, were now accused of fomenting a new revolt, together with the Musan tribe, at the same time as the Shillifs. While the 'Alawis and Kurds were not necessarily acting in concert, the governor of Aleppo received strict instructions to seize and detain members of either group who might attempt

44 MD 136:83.

to flee to his province.[45] Perhaps most important, 'Ali Shillif is portrayed in the same orders as having the support of Hamad al-'Abbas, the powerful leader of the Mawali bedouin confederation whom the Ottomans had named governor of the desert *sancak*s of Dayr al-Zor/Rahba and Salamya but who himself represented the greatest single challenge to Ottoman authority in the Syrian interior at the time. If, as indicated by Norman Lewis, the Mawali had in fact undertaken a large-scale move westward in this period, it is not unlikely that their growing presence in the mountains was made possible in part by this alliance with the leading local 'Alawi gentry.[46]

In any event, the Shillifs appear to have been able to consolidate their position throughout the region. An anecdote in the 'Alawi biographical dictionary *Khayr al-Sani'a* recounts that 'Ali Shillif—whatever family ties may have bound him to the Ismaili emirs—once plundered the town of Qadmus (in 1631–32).[47] Though misdated or anachronistic, the story does show that his exploits were important enough to find a place within the wider 'Alawi oral tradition. More concretely, in the winter of 1733 the governor of Tripoli received an order informing him that the rebels who had been repressed in Latakia a few years before had now regrouped and were again threatening the peace and stability of the area.[48] The Shillifs are not explicitly named here, but only a few months later the governor received a new order specifically regarding the depredations of the "Nusayri brigands" Ahmad and Hassun ibn Shillif of Kimin and Muzayra'a villages, evidently the sons of 'Ali (who is no longer mentioned and may have been dead by this point). According to this order, the leading religious notables of Latakia had sent a petition stating that the Shillifs—long known for their highway robbery, thievery, and shedding of Muslim blood—had recently "gathered together the Nusayris with some of the local Christians and raised the flag of rebellion, attacking villages in the surrounding *mukataa*s, stealing and pilfering the inhabitants' goods and property, torching their homes and houses, and killing a number of people." The *mütesellim* (deputy governor) of Latakia had been sent out against them, but they had absconded to the Hama region and were now "living in 'Annab, 'Ayn al-Kurum, and other villages of their nation and coreligionists, with whom they pursue their evil and corruption in unity and understanding, ensconcing themselves ... in these villages and extending the hand of oppression to other districts."[49]

---

45 MD 136:84–85.
46 See Norman Lewis, "Taïbe and El Kowm, 1600–1980," *Cahiers de l'Euphrate* 5–6 (1991): 72; Stefan Winter, "Aufstieg und Niedergang des osmanischen Wüstenemirats (1536–1741): Die Mawali-Beduinen zwischen Tribalisierung und Nomadenaristokratie," *Saeculum* 63 (2013): 259.
47 Harfush, *Khayr al-Sani'a*, 910; see also Khunda, *Tarikh al-'Alawiyyin*, 205–6.
48 MD 139:55.
49 MD 139:191.

The governors of Latakia, Hama, and Homs were to be mobilized to "get their hands on and punish" (that is, execute) the troublemakers, but we have no indication how the case finally ended. Not surprisingly, the family nonetheless continued to hold on to their tax farms back in the Latakia region. Ottoman finance orders for the province of Damascus (Şam-ı Şerif Ahkam Defterleri) in April/May 1750 record a *mültezim* from Latakia by the name of Hafiz ibn Shillif who had been engaged for many years in the local silk trade;[50] a complaint lodged by the overseer of imperial pious foundations and registered in the same records indicates that a Mahfuz ibn Shillif and several (apparently Turkish) partners were operating a joint *iltizam* on some 'Alawi and non-'Alawi villages in the Jabala and Platanus districts in the 1750s: "owing to the scarcity of land in the area," a number of villagers had begun encroaching on that of their neighbors, leading Mahfuz and his partners to demand ever higher taxes (including *dirhemü'r-rical* charges) from these villages. Because this occasioned a shortfall in the *vakıf* income of the famous Sultan Ibrahim Edhem shrine in Jabala, however, the Sublime Porte had to issue orders prohibiting all taxation beyond that stipulated in the classical Tahrir registers.[51] In 1758 the governor of Tripoli was told to get his hands on the "brigand named Şillif-oğlı *mukaddem* Mahfuz" after the notables of Latakia complained that he and his ilk were constantly oppressing villagers and travelers; only two years later, however, he is once more listed as tax farmer of Muzayra'a and Jabal 'Ali (in the Sahyun area).[52] The Rustum Aghas reemerged as the dominant feudal faction in the northern coastal highlands toward the end of the eighteenth century, but the Shillifs seem to have continued to play a lead role at least among the local 'Alawi population well into modern times. In the nineteenth century, when the *sancak* of Jabala was reorganized and divided into twenty new *nahiye*s, "Bayt al-Shillif" would be the name of the second biggest district of the whole province, centered around the family fief of Kimin in the mountains due east of Latakia.[53]

THE RISE OF LATAKIA

The increasing prominence of 'Alawi gentry such as the Shillifs and Shamsins in our sources is also linked to a wider phenomenon that has thus far received very little scholarly attention: the sudden development of Latakia in the eighteenth century. In the early decades of Ottoman rule Latakia was a provincial backwater, home to a few Muslim scholars who had migrated there from

---

50 BOA: Şam-ı Şerif Ahkam Defterleri [ŞŞAD] 1:222.
51 Ibid. 2:5–6, 22.
52 MD 160:73; TShCR 15:303.
53 See Martin Hartmann, "Das Liwa el-Ladkije und die Nahije Urdu," *Zeitschrift des Deutschen Palästinavereins* 14 (1891): 161–64, 216–18.

Aleppo and site of one imperial religious foundation but otherwise with little commercial or economic significance. After the foundation of the *eyalet* of Tripoli in 1579, Latakia seems to have come under the influence of the powerful Lebanese Druze leader Fakhr al-Din Ma'n for a few years but was more generally governed by a *mütesellim* (deputy governor) appointed from Tripoli.[54] It was under the Ibn al-Matraji (Mataracı-oğlı) dynasty that the city witnessed a rebirth beginning in the late seventeenth century. The origins of this family are uncertain but likely go back to Mataracı ("campaign gourd carrier") Ali, an Ottoman janissary officer who died in Latakia around 1666 and whose heirs continued to live there afterward.[55] In 1694 Arslan Mehmed Mataracı-oğlı was named *vali* of Tripoli after his friend and predecessor Ali Paşa was promoted to grand vezir with a specific mandate to put down an uprising of Twelver Shi'is in the northern Lebanese mountains. Religiously educated but with no prior experience in office, Arslan soon acquired a reputation for "keeping the locals under control" and appointed his brother Kaplan to rule Latakia.[56] Arslan and Kaplan were later both named governor of Sayda and pilgrimage commander of Damascus but continued to hold Latakia as somewhat of a family fief. In 1719 Kaplan's son Mehmed Bey was accused of "oppressing the poor, embezzling money, preventing the *ezan* [call to prayer] from being given in the mosques, seizing tobacco stores, and confiscating supplies from the people of the surrounding districts by force in order to make them follow him"; after a joint petition by the city's religious notables and the villagers (most of whom would have been 'Alawi), a detachment was sent from Tripoli to arrest Mehmed but encountered fierce resistance upon attempting to storm his *saray*.[57] A few years later, in 1723, a local *seyyid* was still trying to recover moneys owed his late father by "Kaplan-zade Mehmed Paşa [*sic*]."[58]

In any event, in a manuscript history of Latakia begun in 1873, Ilyas Salih (d. 1885) credits the Mataracıs with having restored a number of the city's ancient buildings and remaking it into the center of the *liwa'* (*sancak*) of Jabala. Around the same time, according to Salih, numerous Armenians and other Christians from the surrounding region also returned to settle in Latakia after it became the seat of an unsuccessful rival claimant to the Greek Orthodox patriarchate and its ecclesiastic province was expanded to include Jisr al-Shughur and Suwaydiyya (near Antioch) in 1683. Following lengthy negotiations with both the Ottoman imperial authorities and the local Muslim community, no less than five churches were renovated or reconstructed in Latakia beginning

---

54 Hashim 'Uthman, *Tarikh al-Ladhiqiyya 637m–1946m* (Damascus: Wizarat al-Thaqafa, 1996), 53–59; Bitar, *Al-Ladhiqiyya 'ibra'l-Zaman*, 1:198–203, 21:269–70.
55 BOA: Şikayet Defteri [ŞD] 4:149.
56 Mehmed Süreyya (d. 1909), *Sicill-i Osmanî*, ed. Nuri Akbayar and Seyit Ali Kahraman (Istanbul: Türkiye Ekonomik ve Toplumsal Tarih Vakfı, 1996), 324, 867; Winter, *Shiites of Lebanon*, 107–8, 125, 127.
57 MD 127:360.
58 ŞD 99:220.

in 1722.⁵⁹ The city's growing importance is perhaps most clearly reflected in France's consular correspondence of the time. As early as 1728, French officials in Tripoli noted that trade (mainly in tobacco, cotton, and silk) as well as "caravanning" (that is, local shipping by French vessels) could be greatly expanded around Latakia if a diplomatic mission were established there, barring which the town would remain an "outlaw port" and France's merchants at the mercy of freebooters, pirates, and disloyal English competition. Over the next decades, the benefits of protecting French commercial captains and missionaries in Latakia take up an ever greater portion of the dispatches sent to the Marine Ministry in Paris, until a *résident* (consular manager) was finally appointed to set up office in the city in 1788.⁶⁰ Even more important, the French consuls at Tripoli reported with misgivings that the governor was spending more and more of the year at Latakia, often several months at a time, so that by the mid-eighteenth century Latakia had become the de facto cocapital of the *eyalet*. In 1756, for example, Sadeddin Paşa (of the famous 'Azm or Azmzade dynasty of Syrian governors) went straight from his previous posting in Egypt to Latakia and spent so many weeks there that a very indignant French consul finally had to make the long trip north himself to attend to the nation's business.⁶¹ The degree of the 'Azms' personal attachment to Latakia is also suggested by the number of pious works which at least three different members of the family founded in the city while serving as governors of Tripoli in the eighteenth and early nineteenth centuries.⁶²

Several long-term factors help explain the emergence of Latakia as a regional center in this time. Earlier chapters have alluded to the Ottomans' growing interest in the eastern Mediterranean and the 'Alawi community's slow northward shift; this chapter has already referred to the emigration of Christians from rural areas and their increasing urbanization in the Ottoman period (a phenomenon observable in other cities such as Aleppo as well).⁶³ Politically, the rise of the southern Lebanese Shihabi emirs in the eighteenth century and the extension of their hegemony over the rural tax farms of all northern Lebanon by 1763 effectively undercut Ottoman sovereignty in the area and contributed, along with the relative decline of silk and the transfer

---

59 Ilyas Salih, "Athar al-Hiqab fi Ladhiqiyyat al-'Arab" (private manuscript, Syria, 1952), 1:87–90. I express my gratitude to Jamal Barout for providing me with a copy of this manuscript.

60 Archives Nationales, Paris: Affaires Étrangères, série BI (Consulat de Tripoli) [AE/BI] 1116 fol. 56–57b, 221b; AE/BI 1117 fol. 157a, passim, 241a, 272a–b, 324a ff., 365b–366a; AE/BI 1119 fol. 50a, 62a, 72a ff., 96b, 232a, 245a, 256a–257b, 283a–85b, 301a–304b; AE/BI 1120 fol. 66a, 207a–210b, 290a–b; AE/BI 1123 fol. 114b–123a, 206b–207a, 210a ff.; AE/BI 1124 fol. 1a–19b, 46a–51a, 103a ff., 194b–195a, 262a–b.

61 AE/BI 1115 fol. 103a; AE/BI 1116 fol. 444a, 467b; AE/BI 1118 fol. 318a; AE/BI 1119 fol. 15a, 50a–b, 145a, 149a, 197a–198a, 214a, 221a, 231a–232a, 241a, 263a, 269b; AE/BI 1120 fol. 244a, 276a.

62 Süreyya, *Sicill-i Osmanî*, 1230–31, 1416, 1546.

63 See Bruce Masters, *Christians and Jews in the Ottoman Arab World* (Cambridge: Cambridge University Press, 2001), 55–60.

of much of Aleppo's export trade to Alexandretta, to relegating Tripoli as an administrative and commercial hub. The principal reason for Latakia's ascent, however, was economic. To wit, American tobacco leaf was first imported into the Ottoman Empire in the early seventeenth century and quickly proved popular among upper- and middle-class society throughout Syria and the wider region. Despite recurring, half-hearted attempts to ban it on account of its noxious and addictive qualities, it began to be cultivated on a large scale in coastal and highland areas such as Latakia and became subject to taxation in the 1690s.[64] The role played by tobacco in the city's rising fortunes is clearly evidenced in the court records and Ahkam (finance decree) registers of the mid-eighteenth century. In 1761, 6,700 *dönüm* (approximately 620 hectares) of land were planted with tobacco in the Tripoli-Jabala-Latakia region, for the most part in the vicinity of Latakia. Under the "new tobacco regime" (*nizam-ı cedid*) instituted at that time, both a tobacco cultivation tax (*resm-i dönüm-i duhan*) and a lucrative export duty collected at Latakia were assigned to Istanbul's tobacco customs superintendent (*İstanbul duhan gümrüği emini*).[65] This appears to have occasioned rivalry and conflict with the local authorities, however, for the *mütesellim* of Latakia was accused at one point of unlawfully boarding merchant vessels coming from Damietta and of seizing bundles of tobacco and money for his own benefit.[66] In the 1780s the head of the tobacco merchants in the harbor district (*Lazkiyetü'l-Arab iskelesinde duhan tüccarının başı* or *şeyh-i tüccar*) was one of the most important officials in the city, reporting directly to the customs superintendent in Istanbul.[67] The dues collected at Latakia at this time actually constituted the bulk of all Ottoman tobacco revenues, so that by 1793 an independent customs superintendent was finally appointed to take office in Latakia itself (*Lazkiye duhan gümrüği emini*).[68]

The development of the tobacco trade at Latakia of course had major implications for the rural population of the surrounding region, essentially by dictating what crops would be produced and how they would be marketed. The very genesis of Latakia's signature "Abu Riha" tobacco is linked by popular tradition to the 'Alawis: according to an account given by Ilyas Salih and repeated in all later histories, the local variant of tobacco acquired its strong taste and name ("the aromatic") after an 'Alawi rebellion in 1744 prevented the peasants from bringing their crop to town that autumn, so that

---

64 Rhoads Murphey, "Tobacco Cultivation in Northern Syria and Conditions of Its Marketing and Distribution in the Late Eighteenth Century," *Turcica* 17 (1985): 205–26; James Grehan, *Everyday Life and Consumer Culture in 18th-Century Damascus* (Seattle: University of Washington Press, 2007), 146–55; Sam White, *The Climate of Rebellion in the Early Modern Ottoman Empire* (Cambridge: Cambridge University Press, 2011), 285–86.
65 TShCR 16:53, 117.
66 TShCR 17:140–2; ŞŞAD 2:261.
67 ŞŞAD 3:147; ŞŞAD 4:89, 165.
68 TShCR 24/1:77; TShCR 27:275–76.

it remained hung up drying in the smoky indoors of their mountain shacks for the entire winter. The following spring, the now darker and more intensely flavored leaf proved even more popular with the merchants from Damietta than before.[69] While this may be a bit of a local myth, documents preserved in the Tripoli court records indeed confirm an important fiscal peculiarity of Latakia's fire-cured tobacco: unlike more conventional cash crops, including silk, that were taxed in the autumn, Abu Riha was to be weighed and assessed "fifteen days before the feast of Khidr (*ruz-ı Hızır*)," that is, in April.[70]

If tobacco cultivation doubtless employed a growing number of 'Alawi peasants and may help explain the community's expansion in the northern districts of Latakia, it also produced an increasing concentration of wealth, as described by David Sneath, that was likely the very basis for the emergence of a local gentry in the region. Whereas traditional subsistence farming was organized on an individual family basis and taxes collected by a simple *muqaddam*, often in kind, the introduction of a new, export-oriented cash crop that could furthermore only be sold a full year after planting required an unprecedented level of investment and coordination by a new class of rural entrepreneurs such as the Rustum Aghas and the Shillifs. The increasing social stratification and the economic pressure brought to bear on the highland peasantry as a result are perhaps best illustrated by the appearance of two new figures in Latakia's landscape, the *murabahacı* (usurer) and the *hiwat* (field guard). Ottoman officials themselves began to raise the problem of usury in the second half of the eighteenth century, for example, after the people of Kafr Dibl and other 'Alawi villages in the Jabala area petitioned the Sublime Porte for relief from their creditors, Christian moneylenders from nearby Qardaha and Muhalaba, in 1759. The Sublime Porte initially ordered their debts to be certified in court and paid in full but issued more stringent instructions to protect the peasants after the local overseer of the Ibrahim Edhem *vakıf* foundation to which the villages were attached wrote to Istanbul a second time, depicting the moneylenders as usurers who "out of pure greed" were constantly demanding additional payments and keeping the peasants in a state of poverty. (Only a few months later, however, the same overseer wrote again, this time accusing the villagers of having in turn failed to remit their taxes to him for the past years).[71] In another instance, the 'Alawi and Christian inhabitants of Karkid, Mushayrifa, and other villages near Bahluliyya in the Sahyun district petitioned together to denounce a group of Muslim *murabahacı*s who were demanding exorbitant payments; here again

---

69 Salih, "Athar al-Hiqab," 1:92–93; see also Gabriel Saadé, "Lattaquié au dix-huitième siècle," in *Orient et Lumières: Actes du Colloque de Lattaquié (Syrie)* (Grenoble: Recherches et Travaux, 1987), 3–9; Haydar Na'isa, *Suwar Rifiyya min al-Ladhiqiyya* (Damascus: Wizarat al-Thaqafa, 1994), 112–18.

70 TShCR 24/1:76.

71 ŞSAD 2:133, 137, 158.

the Sublime Porte ordered that the sums owed be paid "in installments" so long as the interest demanded "did not constitute legal usury."[72] The *hiwat*, on the other hand, is known to us not from Ottoman archival sources but from the 'Alawi oral tradition. Occasionally also referred to as a *natur* (rural warden) or *khudarji* ("planter"), the *hiwat* was the village expert on produce farming. It thus became his job to manage crop rotation and fallowing; protect fields from goats, theft, and other damage; settle disputes with more traditional peasants and herders; look after communal resources such as forests; and host visiting government officials. Sometimes considered the "second man" of the village, the *hiwat*, as recalled by local historian Haydar Na'isa, was in fact largely a creation of the *agha*s and large landowners of this period, whose economic interests he was ultimately there to safeguard.[73]

The situation of the 'Alawis vis-à-vis the rise of the tobacco industry was therefore complex but by no means unique: the introduction of commercial agriculture in economically marginal areas, the cycle of increasing indebtedness and vulnerability of peasant families, and the overuse of land and breakdown of traditional rural institutions have indeed been described as an early crisis of modernization on a worldwide scale.[74] There is still an infinite amount to be learned in our sources about Latakia's commercial evolution and increasing grip on the coastal mountain interior in the eighteenth century, a region and topic often neglected in the study of both Ottoman and Syrian history. Already this brief survey of financial and court documents suggests, however, that tobacco probably provides a much better framework for understanding the long-term constraints and prospects of the 'Alawi community in the area than any minority or persecution paradigm.

POPULATION PRESSURE AND MIGRATION TOWARD ANTIOCH

The wide-reaching changes wrought on the economy of northwestern Syria in the eighteenth century produced increasing competition and friction among the coastal highland population and were likely key to the emergence of new local leaderships and centers of power in this time. The scarcity of land, it will be recalled, is already invoked in contemporary Ottoman documents as a cause of strife between villagers in the region—a view later echoed in the account of al-Tawil, who writes that "the 'Alawis fought not only with the Turks but also each other, because the land was

---

72 ŞŞAD 3:93.

73 Na'isa, *Suwar Rifiyya*, 57–62.

74 Jürgen Osterhammel, *Die Verwandlung der Welt: Eine Geschichte des 19. Jahrhunderts* (Munich: C. H. Beck, 2009), 309–10.

confined and the inhabitants many."[75] Lebanese social historian Antoine Abdel Nour, for his part, dismissing the idea that the coastal mountains constituted a sectarian "refuge," indicates that the 'Alawi-inhabited zones "suffered from chronic overpopulation" in the eighteenth century and witnessed a steady stream of emigration toward the plains of Latakia, Hama, Homs, and elsewhere.[76]

This expansion may indeed help explain a growing number of conflicts in areas not previously identified with 'Alawi unrest. In 1743, for example, Ottoman finance orders note that several gardens and mulberry orchards located around Bahluliyya, the incomes from which had formerly been farmed to an imperial sword-bearer (*silahdar*) whose father had served as governor in the province, were illegally seized by a groupd of unnamed usurpers; two years later, a gang of 150 "Nusayri" villagers in the same area reportedly attacked and killed a government tax collector who had been sent there from Latakia, savagely mutilating his body.[77] Around the same time, in November 1744, the Mühimme registers tell of a major incursion by upward of three thousand men against the coastal town of Marqab and twenty-seven villages in which numerous houses were torched and animals or other property taken. The perpetrators, though not explicitly identified by their sect, hailed from the 'Alawi villages in the foothills west of Hama (Dayr Mama, 'Annab, 'Ayn al-Kurum, and others) and are furthermore accused of having broken into the mosque of Marqab and burned copies of the Qur'an they found there.[78] The Sublime Porte ordered the governor of Tripoli to mount a campaign to capture the evildoers and retrieve the stolen goods but then wrote again a few months later to complain that the governor's deputy had in turn overstepped his bounds and gathered thousands of villagers from Marqab to ravish the countryside all the way to Madiq castle (overlooking the Ghab marshlands northwest of Hama) in retaliation. (Given the date, this may well have been the campaign that gave rise to the myth of the invention of Abu Riha tobacco.) The people of both districts, the order concludes again without reference to confessional affiliations, were to be protected against such excesses.[79] Only in an official report and request for indemnification sent to Istanbul the following summer is the original attack on Marqab attributed to the "Kelbis."[80] In the spring of 1759 the Damascus finance orders describe another raid by two hundred Nusayris from 'Annab,

---

75 Al-Tawil, *Tarikh al-'Alawiyyin*, 420.
76 Antoine Abdel Nour (d. 1982), *Introduction à l'histoire urbaine de la Syrie ottomane (XVIe–XVIIIe siècle)* (Beirut: Librairie Orientale, 1982), 77–78.
77 ŞŞAD 1:51, 91.
78 MD 151:129–30.
79 MD 151:287.
80 ŞŞAD 1:115.

led by the habitual brigand *muqaddam* Ja'far, on Madiq castle itself, in which hundreds of oxen and buffalo were stolen.[81]

The increasing unsettledness and insecurity in the region is seemingly reflected in the growing importance of "tribal" affiliations. The Kelbis, as seen in chapter 3, were the first such group among the 'Alawis to be recognized by the state authorities, and only since the mid- or later sixteenth century. By the mid-eighteenth century, however, the names of not only individual families such as the Shillifs but entire kinship groups had become more and more associated with political and administrative divisions. According to al-Tawil, for example, the Muhalaba and Banu 'Ali, traditionally reckoned to be among the oldest of all 'Alawi clanships, joined together in the "Haddadin" confederation to resist the Kelbis after the latter had managed to impose their hegemony with the connivance of an Ottoman governor in the eighteenth century. Clearly outmatched, the Banu 'Ali then sought the help of 'Uthman Khayr-Bey, the head of the powerful "Matawira" tribe, and continued to confront the Kelbis well into the nineteenth century.[82] While these accounts cannot be corroborated from other sources, the fact that the ancient castle of Platanus in the mountains just north of Qardaha, which was still used to stockpile government grain and rice provisions in the early seventeenth century,[83] had by now come to be called "Muhalaba" (or "Qal'at al-Muhalaba") and begins to figure as such in Ottoman tax records, is significant. In 1754 we find that an *iltizam* for half of the "Muhalaba district" was made out to "one of the *muqaddam*s of [the] Muhalaba" and registered in the court of Tripoli; in 1760 a list of *mukataa* arrears for the province of Tripoli (cited above) shows the "Muhalaba tax farm" as being in the hands of a Kan'an 'Asaq (?), with his son and nephew serving as security hostages.[84] The *mukataa* for Qardaha/Cebel-i Kelbiyun was by this time held by the Khayr-Bey family and in 1760 specifically by Barakat 'Ali Khayr-Bey—likely the Matawira chief 'Uthman Khayr-Bey's ancestor; the Banu 'Ali, for their part, beginning in the eighteenth century constituted their own tax farm, either under their name or in conjunction with the "Semt Qibli" (southern district), centered around the traditional Banu 'Ali family fief of 'Ayn al-Shaqaq (just south of Qardaha).[85] In 1780, according to documents preserved at the Turkish *vakıf* directorate in Ankara, the overseer (*nazir*) of imperial pious foundations complained that villages belonging to the Sultan Ibrahim Edhem *waqf* in Jabala were being ruined by local officials as well as by the "Kelbis and Nusayris of the environs";

---

81 ŞŞAD 2:117, 124.
82 Al-Tawil, *Tarikh al-'Alawiyyin*, 420–28.; al-Ibrahim, *Al-'Alawiyyun bayna'l-Ghuluw wa'l-Falsafa*, 24–26.
83 MZ 9:6, 49, 50, 94, 144, 151, 166.
84 TShCR 14:212; TShCR 15:303–4.
85 TShCR 4:68; TShCR 15:303. For detailed descriptions of the Qardaha, Banu 'Ali, and Semt Qibli *nahiye*s in the nineteenth century, see Hartmann, "Das Liwa el-Ladkije," 223–30.

FIGURE 4.2. Qal'at al-Muhalaba (ancient Platanus)

a year later he noted that the leaders of the Kelbis and Banu 'Ali were in fact substituting themselves as superintendents (*mütevelli*) of the foundation and unrightfully dividing the village incomes among themselves.[86]

It thus appears that the economic displacements of the eighteenth century both reinforced the role of parochial leaderships in the high mountains and encouraged emigration toward the coastal and interior plains, where 'Alawi peasants would increasingly find work as day laborers on large, Muslim-owned commercial estates. Perhaps most significantly, it is from this period that we also have the first documentary evidence of 'Alawi migration toward Antioch or what is today the Hatay in south-central Turkey. There is no indication of the presence of an 'Alawi community, 'Alawi notables, or the collection of *dirhemü'r-rical* dues in the district, which constituted a *sancak* or *muhassıllık* (tax collectorship) of the province of Aleppo, prior to the eighteenth century. A single entry in the city's *şeriye* court records, which are extant from the beginning of the century onward, refers to an individual who was accused of breaking and entering in the village of Mushraqiyya (now Mızraklı) near Suwaydiyya (at the mouth of the Orontes) in 1735 as being Nusayri (and

---

86 Vakıflar Genel Müdürlüğü, Ankara [VGM]: Register 339:167; 354:11.

therefore deserving the death penalty, one of the only instances ever where 'Alawi identity is explicitly made a factor in a court case).[87] In January 1745, on the other hand, the imperial finance registers for Aleppo (Halep Ahkam Defterleri) record that a small group of "Nusayri subjects" (*reayaları*) "referred to as 'farmers'" (*fellah tabir olunur*) had come to settle in the Suwaydiyya area eight years earlier: they had formerly paid their taxes but were now gathering in ever greater numbers and had taken to stealing animals and other property, leading the other peasants of the area to quit the land. In accordance with a complaint made by a local official, the 'Alawis were thus to be "removed and resettled" back to the district of Latakia from where they had come in the first place.[88]

Other documents from this time corroborate the movement of 'Alawis from the Latakia region toward the coastal plain of Suwaydiyya (Samandağ). In June 1753, for example, the *kadı* and *voivode* (district governor) of Antioch received word that the inhabitants of the Bayir district in the mountains north of Latakia had dispersed due to too much oppression and taken up residence in Suwaydiyya and Kışlak but were to be returned to their original homeland.[89] Similarly, a Mühimme decree from February 1756 recounts in some detail how 'Alawis began to colonize the area. Several years before, according to the decree, a certain Shaykh Ibrahim "of the Nusayri faction" and his brothers Nu'man and Qasim Mu'ayrati (?) had come from Latakia to the *mezraa* (uninhabited farm plot) of Mağaracık (on the coast just north of Suwaydiyya) "to settle and build houses, turning the said *mezraa* into a village." Consequently, however, they and their followers had entered into conflict with the locals, "cutting and destroying their mulberry trees, burning down their silk barns, and shedding innocent blood." The authorities were clearly at a loss over how to deal with the issue. The 'Alawis refused to heed an order referring the dispute to court (*mürafaa-ı şer*), and when an imperial *çavuş* (sergeant), the *voivode* of Antioch and the local janissary commander caught nineteen of them to send them into arbitration "willingly or unwillingly," Shaykh Ibrahim encircled the company at Zeytuniye village and liberated his followers by force. The authorities then tried snatching 'Alawis whenever one of them ventured into town but would essentially "wink at their crimes" and let them off with a warning to mind their own affairs. The 'Alawis apparently did not heed these warnings, however, and returned to their old ways, attacking innocent villagers and stealing livestock, so that the entire population in the area scattered and dispersed or would not go

---

87 İslam Araştırmaları Merkezi, Istanbul (Üsküdar): Antakya Şeriye Sicilleri Defteri [AŞSD] 2:5–6. On brigandage in the Antioch district in the eighteenth century, see also Mustafa Öztürk, "XVIII. Yüzyılda Antakya ve Çevresinde Eşkiyalık Olayları," *Belleten* 54 (1990): 963–93.
88 BOA: Halep Ahkam Defteri [HAD] 1:114.
89 AŞSD 5:45.

out anymore to tend to their gardens. The governor of Aleppo province (the famous Ragıb Mehmed Paşa) and the *kadı* of Antioch were therefore instructed to get to the bottom of and investigate the reasons for the Nusayris' rebellion, raze the houses they had built in Mağaracık, and restore order in the area, though as always without using this as a pretext to harm those not directly implicated in acts of brigandage.[90]

Other sources also attest to the northward migration of 'Alawis in the eighteenth century. By al-Tawil's account, the first 'Alawis' to "return" to the sect's ancestral home in the Antioch region were the brothers Ibrahim, Muslim, Ma'ruf, and 'Ali, who came from Rama and Siyano to settle near Suwaydiyya in the early 1700s—possibly an echo in the oral tradition of the same Shaykh Ibrahim and brothers referred to above. Al-Tawil's own ancestors supposedly came to Antioch in their entourage before moving on and settling in Adana in 1785–86.[91] Many 'Alawis, especially from the Muhalaba, are thought to have continued further north into Cilicia. The oldest *maqam*s in the Adana-Tarsus region, which are often named for classical 'Alawi saints back in Syria, date from the end of the century.[92] An Ottoman *vakıf* for the shrine of the prophet Khidr on the beach at Suwaydiyya, meanwhile, is first attested in 1817; it of course remains the focal point of 'Alawi piety in the Hatay down to the present day.[93]

Interestingly, in 1819 a group identifying itself as the Arab "peasantry" (*fellahin*; a common self-designation of the 'Alawis) of Tarsus and Adana complained that in addition to their regular dues, they had recently begun to be assessed a "*jizya*-like" head tax known as the *sarik akçası* (turban charge), despite the fact that "they are Sunnis, go on pilgrimage, adhere to the holy law," and so forth. The Sublime Porte, noting that the Arab immigrant population had first been subjected to taxes in the region in 1779, prohibited the local authorities from imposing any new, discriminatory charges.[94]

THE TOWNSHIPS (*HILLA*S) OF SAFITA AND THE BARAKAT AND RASLAN FAMILIES

The district of Safita, which under the Shamsin family remained the center of 'Alawi feudal power in the coastal mountain region, also seems to have witnessed significant economic and structural changes in the second half of the eighteenth century. These changes must be inferred from the tax-farm (*iltizam*) contracts preserved in the Tripoli court records, virtually the only

90 MD 157:285–86.
91 Al-Tawil, *Tarikh al-'Alawiyyin*, 437, 538–39.
92 Procházka-Eisl and Procházka, *Plain of Saints and Prophets*, 51–52.
93 AŞSD 14:193; see also VGM 284:188.
94 BOA: Cevdet Maliye 11/461.

written historical source dealing with the southern 'Alawi highlands in this period. We have already seen that the Shamsins' tax concessions were involving an ever greater number of family members including in-laws, and that the family as a whole had amassed considerable debts by 1750. Around the same time a new administrative unit was introduced in the Safita contracts that does not appear to have been applied in any other part of Syria, the *hilla* (literally an "encampment" or "hamlet") as an official subdivision or township of the larger *nahiye*. Between 1751 and the reincorporation of a single tax farm under Saqr ibn Mahfuz al-Shibli's care in 1782, these *hilla*s served as the basis for the rise a new 'Alawi elite in the region.

The *nahiye* of Safita is already described as being composed of four *hilla*s in 1749, but it is only in the following years that some of them were removed from the Shamsins' purview and officially assigned to other leading families of the district. The oldest and most established of these families were the Barakats. Elia Giacinto di Santa Maria, an Italian Carmelite monk who left a unique account of his missionary efforts among the 'Alawis in the early eighteenth century, reports being well received by a "Mahamad Baracat," head of the "Melike" family and shaykh of Ubin village near Safita, during his visit there in 1711.[95] A local *maqam* dedicated to the famous medieval scholar al-Nashshabi is said to have been furnished with a dome by an Ibrahim Muhammad Barakat.[96] The Barakats first appear in the court documentation in 1740, when Hasan ibn Muhammad Barakat as well as Musa Barakat joined a long list of local village shaykhs to underwrite the Shamsins' tax concession on Safita as guarantors.[97] In March 1749 Hasan Barakat himself had an *iltizam* contract for the collection of unspecified taxes in the district (in addition to debts he apparently already owed on a previous contract) and as such had to send his son Ahmad to Tripoli as a security hostage;[98] the following year, when Ahmad went to Tripoli a second time to replace a different son serving as hostage, their father is described for the first time as the tax farmer "of one of the *hilla*s of Safita."[99] All subsequent contracts then refer to his concession specifically as the "*hilla* of Ubin."

It is not clear from the documents what other lands this township encompassed. The price of the Ubin part-*iltizam* was 9,000 silver *guruş* per annum, which represented just over a quarter of Safita's total worth of 33,050 *guruş*.

---

95 Bernard Heyberger, "Peuples 'sans loi, sans foi, ni prêtre': druzes et nusayrîs de Syrie découverts par les missionaires catholiques (XVIIe–XVIIIe siècles)," in *L'islam des marges: Mission chrétienne et espaces périphériques du monde musulman XVIe-XXe siècles*, ed. B. Heyberger and Rémy Madinier (Paris: Karthala, 2011), 53–54, 60, 66.
96 Harfush, *Khayr al-Sani'a*, 655.
97 TShCR 7:257, 326.
98 TShCR 10:163, 164.
99 TShCR 11:54.

FIGURE 4.3. *Iltizam* contract for Ubin, 1778
(Shar'iyya Court Registers, Qasr Nawfal, Tripoli)

The dispositions in Hasan Barakat's contracts were all fairly standard, with at least eight different sons, nephews, and cousins going as security hostages to Tripoli or Arwad between 1751 and his final contract in 1757.[100] What is perhaps more noteworthy is the increasing attention devoted to the Barakats' (as well as the other families') debts. Already in October 1750 Hasan Barakat was made to appear (along with numerous other *mukataaci*s from the region) at an extraordinary court session at the government *diwan* in Tripoli to acknowledge his payment arrears of more than 8000 *guruş*.[101] Over the next years, the validation of debt takes up an ever greater portion of the annual *iltizam* renewal contract or is the subject of a separate deposition signed in court at the same time as the contract. In many cases these debts were simply moneys outstanding from a previous assignment, for example, when Hasan Barakat confirmed in April 1756 that he still owed a grand total of 13,000 *guruş* for the years 1753, 1754, and 1755 in addition to his newest contract

100 TShCR 12:43, 147; TShCR 14:113–16, 250, 256.
101 TShCR 11:70–71.

of that year.¹⁰² In other instances, however, what is labeled as debt (*bi-tariq al-dayn*) is actually a series of extra charges that do not seem to have been part of the legal terms (*tamassuk shar'i*) of the original *iltizam* but that are nevertheless added onto the amount to be remitted to the governor at the end of the year. These special charges, which in a given year were assigned not only to the Barakats but to the other tax concessionaries of the district as well, were perhaps akin to the "irregular" dues that provincial Ottoman government agents and their retainers often collected from local populations for their own benefit, and in this case they included such obscure items as a "retinue expenditure" (*kapu harcı*), a "horse apparel price" (*at paha'l-ilbas?*), "four fodder provisions" (*arba'a zakhayir*), and a "conventional surcharge" (*damm mu'tad*).¹⁰³ If this reading is correct, then the contributions being demanded of the *hilla* tax farmers under the rubric of "debt" may in essence have been a legal means for the governors of Tripoli to raise the return from what had become one of the province's most lucrative *mukataa*s in the second half of the eighteenth century beyond its original, nominal value.

The other new family awarded a township-level tax farm in this period was the Raslans. Like the Barakats, the Raslans were local notables already closely associated with the Shamsins. Their patronymic ancestor, Raslan ibn 'Alan, is said to have been a leader of the Zayadiyya branch of the Kelbis.¹⁰⁴ The Shamsins' 1740 *iltizam* for Safita was underwritten among others by a *muqaddam* Sulayman ibn Raslan, who was incidentally also a paternal cousin of the Barakats.¹⁰⁵ In 1743 one of the security hostages Mulham Husayn Shamsin sent to live in Tripoli was Muhammad ibn Idris Raslan, a maternal cousin of his.¹⁰⁶ In 1751 Mulham Husayn and Darwish Shibli were awarded the tax farm for all four *hilla*s of Safita, described in this instance as "the three *hilla*s of the Bayt [family] Shamsin and the *hilla* of the Bayt Raslan"; the following year Mulham ibn Sulayman Raslan received the latter in his own right.¹⁰⁷ In all the time the *hilla* was farmed to the Raslans, it was named only for the family (rather than a village or area), and it remained relatively small in value: 8,500 *guruş* in 1752 and 5,000 *guruş* when it was given to Ahmad ibn Hasan Dib and *muqaddam* Darwish ibn Sulayman Raslan in 1757.¹⁰⁸

---

102 TShCR 14:114–15, 117, 253.
103 TShCR 10:164; TShCR 12:43, 147; TShCR 14:250; TShCR 15:52; cf. Qasim al-Samad, "Nizam al-Iltizam fi Wilayat Tarabulus fi'l-Qarn 18 min khilal Watha'iq Sijillat Mahkamatiha al-Shar'iyya," in *Al-Mu'tamar al-Awwal li-Tarikh Wilayat Tarabulus ibana al-Hiqba al-'Uthmaniyya 1516–1918* (Tripoli: Lebanese University, 1995), 81.
104 Sharif, *'Alawiyyun*, 73.
105 TShCR 7:257, 326.
106 TShCR 8:100.
107 TShCR 12:42–43, 153.
108 TShCR 15:66.

The Shamsins' own *hilla*s, as indicated, were initially named for the family as well. The *hilla* nevertheless appears to have been conceived of territorially and not just as a fiscal parcel assigned to specific notable families. In 1752, when the Shamsins seem to have been temporarily relieved of their functions, a "*hilla* of Darwish" (presumably still named for Darwish Shibli Shamsin) was defined as comprising the villages Tayshur, Khirbat Malik, Majdalun, Dahbash, Bayt Maqsud, and Basuram (in the coastal foothills west of Safita) and farmed to the local shaykhs.[109] After Darwish Shibli and his long-standing partner Mulham Husayn were reappointed in 1756, their farm was referred to as the "*hilla* of Tayshur and Hammin" (the latter being a somewhat larger village in the mountains northwest of Safita) or, alternately, as the "*hilla* of Tayshur and the *hilla* of Hammin," at a combined worth of 15,000 *guruş*, the largest of the entire district. In 1757 it was formally split and assigned to Darwish, Mulham, and his brother 'Ali Husayn al-Shibli as two distinct *hilla*s, at 3,500 and 13,500 *guruş*, respectively.[110] The last *hilla*, centered around al-Mandara village just 1 km down from Safita to the west, was also reckoned at 3,500 *guruş*. It was assigned in 1756 and 1757 to Shamsin ibn Muhammad, who had previously partnered with Darwish Shibli and Mulham Husayn to farm three *hilla*s attributed to the Shamsins collectively in 1753–54 (and running up a huge debt in the process).[111] He and his son Mustafa ibn Shamsin, who served as his security hostage for al-Mandara, likely represented a lesser branch of the extended Shamsin family.

Apart from binding a greater number of local notables to the collection of revenues, it is not certain what the Ottoman authorities hoped to achieve by dividing Safita into subdistricts. If the *iltizam* contracts of this period appear to have been primarily concerned with the management and maintenance of debt, the *mukataacı*s are also constantly solicited to see to the development and peace of their district, to protect the roads and wayfarers, and to assure the prosperity of the *reaya* (subjects). In 1756 special additional orders were issued to both Hasan Barakat and Shamsin Muhammad for the "securement" (*ta'min*) of Ubin and al-Mandara in which they were instructed, among other things, to "safeguard the residents living there" and not "suffer or connive to allow anyone to sojourn in the *hilla* and its surroundings who might cause the slightest damage or disruption or opposition," suggesting the provincial government in Tripoli specifically looked toward the local leaderships to address problems of unsettledness in these townships, much as it did in the 'Akkar and Sha'ra districts of far northern Lebanon, where similar orders were sent.[112]

109   TShCR 12:292–93.
110   TShCR 14:254, 257–58; TShCR 15:30, 44–45.
111   TShCR 14:108, 247, 252–53, 255, 256; TShCR 15:90–91.
112   TShCR 14:254, 255–56.

At the same time, the provincial authorities were likely not eager to create all too powerful local dynasties and therefore frequently rotated the assignments. In 1757, for example, we see a separate tax farm for the collection of "bureau" (*aqlam*) charges in Safita given to Husayn ibn Yusuf in partnership with a local *agha*; in 1758 Darwish and Shamsin appear on a list of *mültezim*s accused of not having paid their taxes and indeed of having kicked out government agents (*mübaşirler*) sent to their district to collect.[113] In 1763 the combined *hilla*s of Safita were atypically awarded to a joint partnership of Hasan Barakat and five *muqaddam*s from the Raslan family.[114] Thereafter, however, the central (Shibli) branch of the Shamsin family seems to have reacquired a near-monopoly on the district. Over the next decade the *iltizam* for all of Safita is consistently given to Mahfuz ibn Darwish al-Shibli, surprisingly at the now lower price of 25,000 *guruş*, so that the very term *hilla* begins to fall from usage and the farm is usually referred to again as a single *mukataa*.[115] We last hear of the concept starting in 1775, when Mustafa Shamsin and Muhammad Muhsin of the secondary Shamsin lineage again acquired the "four ordinary townships" of Safita, while As'ad ibn Hasan Barakat, after a nearly twenty-year hiatus (and presumably after his father Hasan's passing) was reappointed to the family *hilla* in 1776 and 1778. In the first instance, interestingly, the farm is actually referred to as the "*hilla* of the Bayt Malikh" (the family name mentioned by Giacinto di Santa Maria in 1711), before being called again for Ubin in 1778.[116] In 1778 the *hilla* of the Bayt Raslan was also awarded one last time to *muqaddam* Sulayman ibn Muhammad Raslan, while Muhammad Muhsin and Mahfuz al-Shibli took contracts on the *hilla*s of Hammin and Tayshur, respectively, with Mahfuz nevertheless providing a financial guarantee (*kefalet*) for his relative.[117] Almost immediately, however, the court in Tripoli accused Mahfuz of "unfaithfulness in the exercise of his *iltizam*, excessive lying, delaying the payment of the required charges, and insecurity of the roadways due to his failure to defend and protect them" and transferred his share of the district back to Mustafa and 'Ali Shamsin.[118] Yet this was not to have long-lasting consequences. Muhammad Muhsin and Mustafa Shamsin were again awarded partial contracts in 1780; in March 1782 'Ali Shamsin was initially awarded a quarter of the Safita farm, but five days later this contract was crossed out in the register and the entire district assigned to Mahfuz and his son Saqr Mahfuz al-Shibli.[119] Henceforth Saqr

113 TShCR 15:31; MD 160:73.
114 TShCR 17:175.
115 TShCR 18/1:80; TShCR 18/2:38, 59–60; TShCR 20/2:28–29; TShCR 20/3:139; TShCR 21:33, 137; TShCR 22/1:34; TShCR 22/2:257.
116 TShCR 22/3:173–74; TShCR 23:21.
117 TShCR 23:6, 21.
118 TShCR 23:32.
119 TShCR 24/1:26–27; TShCR 24/2:105–6.

would emerge as the sole master of Safita and the southern 'Alawi mountains, his rise marking the end of the independent *hilla* period.

The Raslans would remain one of the key 'Alawi notable families of the region, taking the lead among other things in the war against the Ismailis in the early nineteenth century (see below). They are evoked incidentally in the Tripoli court registers as a dominant faction in Safita as late as 1847.[120] The Barakats, for their part, do not appear to have left any further trace in the documentation of the period. It is the hamlet of Zuq Barakat, site of the best-known feudal mansion in the Safita district, that still recalls to their importance today.

SAQR IBN MAHFUZ

Saqr ibn Mahfuz al-Shibli Shamsin was arguably the most prominent figure in 'Alawi history between the death of Makzun al-Sinjari in the thirteenth century and the rise of Hafiz al-Asad between 1966 and 1970. His career, which spanned six decades before his death at age eighty in 1813,[121] marks the high point of 'Alawi feudal autonomy under Ottoman rule. The struggle he and other 'Alawi local notables would increasingly face in the nineteenth century with regard to the encroachment of the modern state will be dealt with in the following chapter; here, his growing hegemony over Safita and the entire southern half of the Syrian coastal range as well as his ties with the Lebanese Shihabi emirs can be used to illustrate the unprecedented social dominance of an 'Alawi landed gentry at the turn of the modern era.

The Shamsins, as shown before, had been the paramount *mukataacı* family of Safita since the second half of the seventeenth century. Beginning in the mid-eighteenth century, they may have further cemented their position by investing, much like the leading families of Latakia, in commercial tobacco production. This is suggested by a business deal registered at the court of Tripoli in July 1765, in which Mahfuz ibn Darwish and other members of the family renewed an agreement they had already had for several years with a local merchant to set the price per bushel at which the entire crop of both coastal (*sahili*) and highland (*jurdi*) types of tobacco from the district of Safita would be sold later in the season.[122] In addition to taxes and tobacco, the Shamsins also seem to have been involved in the raising and selling of horses.[123] Saqr Mahfuz first appears in the court records in 1756 and 1757, when he was sent to reside in Tripoli, even though still underage,

---

120 TShCR 33:263.
121 Ministère des Affaires étrangères, Paris-La Courneuve [MAE]: Correspondance consulaire et commerciale [CCC] Tripoli 16, fol. 143a.
122 TShCR 19/1:23–24.
123 TShCR 21:191

as a security hostage for his grandfather Darwish's *iltizam* on Safita.[124] Later on he of course joined with his father Mahfuz in farming the district. What possibly precipitated his emergence as main *mültezim* and de facto head of the family was his leadership in a major conflict with the neighboring district of Tartus. The Shamsins' involvement in an acrimonious territorial dispute with Mustafa Agha of Tartus in 1743 has already been noted. In December 1780 we see Saqr Mahfuz going to court in Tripoli to represent the entire family after two of his cousins had been killed by unknown assailants in Tartus earlier that year. Under the terms of a somewhat singular peace treaty hammered out between the "Bani Shamsin" and "the people of Tartus," the former accepted payment of 5,000 *guruş* of blood money and in return absolved the latter of any further liability. Both sides agreed henceforth to work toward securing the region, with Saqr Mahfuz guaranteeing the safety of any Tartusi on Shamsin territory. By the same token Saqr also took sole control of the Safita farm, which until then had still been partially held by other extended family members.[125]

Thereafter Saqr's and his sons' rule went virtually uncontested until the Egyptian occupation of 1832. The Damascus finance registers in March 1782 record a complaint by the villagers of Junayna (Junaynat Raslan, near Draykish) concerning Saqr's father and cousin, who had purportedly gathered thirty retainers, attacked the village, burned houses, cut trees, killed or abused several inhabitants, and made off with fifty bags of money and other effects. While the governor of Tripoli received instructions to investigate and recover any stolen property, the fact that "fifty bags of money" happens to correspond to the annual worth of the Safita *iltizam* (25,000 *guruş*) indicates this may have been another case of strong-arm tax collection rather than actual brigandage.[126] Over the next two decades, to go by the available Tripoli court documents, the tax farm was in any event consistently awarded to Saqr, except in 1791, when it was nominally held by his son Darwish, and in 1793, when it was given one last time to the Muhammad Muhsin branch.[127] Throughout all these contracts, however, each incumbent's supposed "debt" remained pegged at a constant 18,820 3/4 *guruş* or was reduced (in 1801) to 11,320 3/4 *guruş* with the *iltizam*'s official value raised in corresponding measure to 32,500 *guruş*—suggesting once again that the yearly assignation of the farm by the Ottoman authorities was really little more than a formality, and the Shamsin family almost completely autonomous in its exercise.

124 TShCR 14:257; TShCR 15:30.
125 TShCR 24/2:57–58; TShCR 24/1:ii.
126 ŞŞAD 3:81.
127 TShCR 26/1:80; TShCR 26/2:74, 153; TShCR 27:223; TShCR 28:53; TShCR 29A:62, 82. See also Bassam 'Isa al-Qaht, "Al-Tarikh al-Ijtima'i wa'l-Iqtisadi li-Muqata'at Safita 1790–1832 m.: Qira'a fi Sijillat Mahkamat Tarabulus al-Shar'iyya" (graduate thesis, Lebanese University, 1997), 31–36, 66–69.

Saqr Mahfuz's reign seems overall to have been a period of relative stability. The *Khayr al-Sani'a* says little in regard to the eighteenth century, but local oral traditions as well as a number of manuscript texts (as collated in Dib 'Ali Hasan's new biographical dictionary of 'Alawi *Luminaries*) refer to numerous 'Alawi scholars hailing from or moving to the southern coastal mountains in this time. Around 1785–86, to cite only one example, the ruling "lord" of the Bayt Shamsin is specifically remembered to have intervened to settle a dispute between various local families.[128] One of the most expansive Ottoman-era shrines in the entire region, that of the "prophet" Yusuf ibn 'Abdallah, was founded at Ba'rin in 1781–82. Other shrines are said to have been constituted as *waqf*s (pious foundations) by a leading religious shaykh, Khalil al-Numayli, around the same time.[129] The chronicles of the period also give no particular indication of strife with the state authorities. In May 1787 the Greek Catholic historian Rawfa'il Karama recounts a major incursion by Mawali bedouin into the Hama region in which the shaykhs of both the Kelbi and Nusayri "countries" (*bilad*) were killed, but which does not seem to have reached the Safita district.[130] In 1795 a historian from Homs reports that the 'Alawis banded together and ravaged sixteen Turkmen villages in the area after hearing that the local *agha* had supposedly put two 'Alawi peasants under the yoke (literally) in order to plow his field.[131]

Perhaps the most noteworthy aspect of Saqr's reign was his burgeoning relationship with the Shihabi emirate of Lebanon. The history of the 'Alawis in what was fast becoming a separate polity within Ottoman Syria during this time has itself received very little attention. Local accounts refer vaguely to Nusayris in the northern Lebanese district of Zanniyya in the late Middle Ages, but these are not noted in the Ottoman Tahrir censuses.[132] The Damascus provincial finance registers from the mid-eighteenth century record a few isolated cases of brigandage involving 'Alawis in Baalbek or the *kaza* (judicial district) of Tripoli, but otherwise the community does not appear to have attracted much notice.[133] In 1770 the French consul at Tripoli reported briefly on a campaign to evict some local *muqaddam*s who had been delaying the payment of taxes; only the year before, however, the governor himself had

---

128 Hasan, *A'lam min al-Madhhab al-Ja'fari*, 1:102–3; see also al-Musa, *Al-Imam 'Ali wa'l-'Alawiyyin*, 181–93.

129 Georges Jabbour, "Safita et son environnement au XIXe siècle," in *Histoire économique et sociale de l'Empire Ottoman et de la Turquie (1326–1960)*, ed. Daniel Panzac (Paris: Peeters, 1995), 608–9; Khunda, *Tarikh*, 146–48.

130 Rawfa'il ibn Yusuf Karama (d. 1800), *Hawadith Lubnan wa-Suriya: min sanat 1745 ila sanat 1800*, ed. Basilus Qattan (n.p., Jarrus Pars, n.d.), 102.

131 Munir al-Khuri 'Isa As'ad, *Tarikh Hims: Min Zuhur al-Islam hatta Yawmina Hadha Sana 622–1977* (Homs: Matraniyya Hims al-Urthudhuksiyya, 1984), 2:363.

132 See 'Isa Iskandar al-Ma'luf (d. 1956), *Diwani al-Qatuf fi Tarikh Bani al-Ma'luf* (1908; new ed. Damascus: Dar Hawran, 2003), 204.

133 ŞŞAD 1:128; ŞŞAD 2:64, 131.

FIGURE 4.4. Shrine of Nabi Yusuf ibn 'Abdallah, Ba'rin

tried recruiting 'Alawi peasant fighters from the surrounding countryside in an ill-fated effort to force Yusuf al-Shihabi to pay additional surcharges on the tax districts he had recently taken over in the province.[134]

The extension of the Shihabis' control over most of northern Lebanon in 1763, on the other hand, brought the emirate into direct contact with the 'Akkar and Safita districts, by virtue of which the Shamsins were then drawn ever more into Lebanese feudal politics. This is at any rate the impression that arises from the family history of Haydar Ahmad al-Shihabi, which, starting in the later eighteenth century, emerges as a key narrative source for the entire region. According to H. A. al-Shihabi, Saqr Mahfuz was called on to play a role in the emirate's internecine conflicts and struggles with the Ottoman provincial authorities on at least two occasions: In 1784, Saqr received emir Yusuf al-Shihabi as he was fleeing from his brothers and the famously sanguinary governor of Sayda, Cezzar Ahmed Paşa, in a *fitna* (civil war) over the tax districts of southern Lebanon, permitting him and his entourage to enter Safita and putting them up in a village near Tartus until the dispute was resolved.[135] Similarly, in January 1800 Saqr and his sons played host to Emir Hasan al-Shihabi and let his troops camp in the southern part of the district for several days while they were on flight from Cezzar and the paramount

---

134 AE/BI 1121 fol. 21b, 44a; Winter, *Shiites of Lebanon*, 169–70.
135 Haydar Ahmad al-Shihabi (d. 1835), *Lubnan fi 'Ahd al-Umara' al-Shihabiyyin*, ed. Asad Rustum and Fu'ad al-Bustani (Beirut: Lebanese University, 1969), 137–39.

emir Bashir al-Shihabi. In this instance, the Shamsins furthermore agreed to supply their guests with fodder and other provisions at the express written request of Azmzade Abdullah Paşa—the governor of Damascus and Cezzar's long-standing rival in the region.[136]

Bashir al-Shihabi would exact his revenge on the Shamsins in later years, notably when he provided Cezzar's successor in Tripoli (Berber Mustafa Agha) with the necessary forces to ravage the Safita district in 1807, after Saqr's tax payments had fallen into arrears (and Abdullah Paşa, not coincidentally, had just been dismissed from the governorship of Damascus);[137] or, more important, when he joined Ibrahim Paşa and backed the Egyptian invasion in 1832 (to be examined in the next chapter). By continually implicating Saqr and his sons in their ceaseless battle for power in and over Lebanon, however, the Shihabis effectively also ensured that "the" 'Alawis would always be regarded as the ally of one provincial authority or another and thus an unavoidable regional partner of the Ottoman state as such. The splendid isolation that had allowed for the emergence of an autonomous 'Alawi notable class in western Syria in the first place would simply no longer be operative in the nineteenth century.

THE WAR WITH THE ISMAILIS

The 'Alawis' conquest of Masyaf and other Ismaili castles in 1808 can be seen as the culmination, but thereby also as the point of inflection, of their rise in power under Ottoman rule. Because of its wider implications, the event is recounted in numerous sources of the time. According to H. A. al-Shihabi and others, the governor of Damascus, Genç (or Kanj) Yusuf Paşa, led a force of four to five thousand men into the mountains in June 1808 after the Raslans had killed the Ismaili emir Mustafa al-Yazidi, taken over Masyaf and adjoining villages, and oppressed and violated the local Ismaili population. While the Raslans and their followers held out in Masyaf for three months, the government forces quickly gained the upper hand, using artillery to raze several 'Alawi villages and fortresses, laying waste to the entire countryside, and taking a huge amount of plunder before Saqr Mahfuz was able to pay off Genç Yusuf to "take pity" and let the 'Alawi refugees return to their homes in safety.[138]

In terms of the 'Alawis' relationship with the Ismailis, this episode was of course of profound significance, completing the slow reversal in the

---

136 Ibid., 202–3.
137 Ibid., 501–2; CCC Tripoli 13, fol. 150b, 153a–b.
138 Shihabi, *Lubnan*, 534–35; Hasan Agha al-'Abd (d. after 1826), *Tarikh Hasan Agha al-'Abd: Hawadith Bilad al-Sham wa'l-Imbaraturiyya al-'Uthmaniyya, 1771–1826 m.*, ed. Yusuf Jumayyil Na'isa (Damascus: Dar Dimashq, 1986), 144–46; see also E. Honigman and Nikita Elisséeff, "Masyad," *EI2* (1991), 6:791.

balance of power from when the 'Alawis had been subject to the *fida'i* emirs of Qadmus and Masyaf in the later medieval period. Though it is not clear precisely which other places the 'Alawis managed to seize or hold in 1808, the fact is that most of the *qila' al-da'wa* and other formerly Ismaili-inhabited castles such as Rassafa and Bani Qahtan had passed into 'Alawi control around this time. John Lewis Burckhardt, who visited Masyaf only a short while later, reports that the Ismaili emir had actually taken in about three hundred dissident 'Alawis in 1807, giving them asylum "till one day, when the greater part of the people were at work in their fields, the Anzeyrys, at a given signal, killed the Emir and his son in the castle, and then fell upon the Ismaylys who had remained in their houses, sparing no one they could find, and plundering at the same time the whole town. On the following day the Anzeyrys were joined by great numbers of their countrymen, which proved that their pretended emigration had been a deep-laid plot."[139] Though evidently partisan, this account does gesture toward the more long-term shift in forces underlying the war. The Ismailis were subsequently permitted to return but never reestablished themselves in the area the same way as before; Ismaili historians trace the origins of the Nizari community's epochal *hijra* (emigration) to Salamya on the eastern edge of Hama province in the nineteenth century to their defeat at the hands of the 'Alawis in 1808.[140] The two sides continued to coexist and often enough to cooperate in the region but in a power ratio now clearly dominated by the latter; the collective memories of 'Alawi ascendance and Ismaili decline in the Ottoman period are said to inform sectarian tensions in Masyaf and Qadmus down to the present day.[141]

In terms of the 'Alawis' rapport with the state authorities, however, the 1808 campaign appears once again to have been a sideshow to the growing standoff between the governorships of Sayda and Damascus. Genç Yusuf Paşa's real objective was to continue on and evict Berber Mustafa Agha from Tripoli, which had for all intents and purposes ceased to exist as a separate *eyalet* since Cezzar's reign and become a dependency of Sayda. Genç Yusuf had furthermore been appointed to Damascus with the express mandate to stem the Wahhabi movement's advance into Syria and had therefore made the defense of Sunni conservatism the cornerstone of his policy to reassert Ottoman prestige and control in the region. In an extraordinary report sent in Genç Yusuf's name and preserved in the Topkapı Palace archives, apparently the only official document to make mention of the campaign, he therefore blankly accuses "that good-for-nothing" (*nemek be-haram*) Berber Mustafa of having been the one to instigate the "self-protective Nusayri bands" to revolt

---

139 Burckhardt, *Travels in Syria*, 151–54.
140 Daftary, *Isma'ilis*, 532–33.
141 Joshua Landis, "Alawi-Ismaili Confrontation in Qadmous: What Does It Mean?," 28 July 2005, http://syriacomment.com.

and wreak havoc in the Latakia and Masyaf area, adding that seven of the "sultan's castles" were then retaken by force before the campaign turned its sites on Berber Mustafa himself (though ultimately failing to dislodge him from Tripoli). Interestingly, the Ismailis are not referred to once in the report.[142]

Ultimately, neither the Ismailis nor the 'Alawis seem to have mattered much at this point to the imperial authorities. The French consul at Tripoli corroborates that the 'Alawis were indeed initially making common cause with Mustafa Berber but also insinuates that Saqr Mahfuz may have negotiated his retreat from the battle with Genç Yusuf's forces beforehand (leaving the Raslans alone to lead the resistance).[143] The paşa's victory in the end proved harder-fought than expected: the French vice-consul at Latakia speaks of the involvement of fifteen thousand government troops, and of 'Alawi women, girls, and boys being sold in Latakia's market afterward to be sent to Egypt as slaves.[144] Despite the necessary rhetoric against the "enemies of the true faith," however, it does not appear that Genç Yusuf, any more than his patron and predecessor Azmzade Abdullah, saw the 'Alawis as anything other than a political card to be played against his regional rivals. Reacting to popular expectations, he later did coerce the defeated 'Alawi rebels to feign conversion to Sunni Islam in order to ransom their captives, but as the contemporary Egyptian historian Jabarti notes, he "accepted their words at face value, pardoned them and left them in their homeland."[145]

CONCLUSION: THE ECONOMICS OF ANARCHY

The 'Alawis unquestionably enjoyed greater latitude during the long eighteenth century than in any other period of their history. If the Ottoman state had already shown little interest in their religious identity and social organization at the time of Syria's integration into the empire, the decentralization or more properly the privatization of provincial government and tax collection offices beginning in the seventeenth century brought to the fore a new class of local or localized petty gentry who henceforth dominated the rural hinterland. After the 'Alawis had, for centuries, made it into the historical record only as heretics or thieves, the very fact that the likes of the Shamsins, the Raslans, the Shillifs, or the Muhalaba now figure on a regular basis as local dignitaries and servants of the state in the legal papers of Tripoli and even Istanbul speaks to the enfranchisement of 'Alawi society under Ottoman rule.

---

142 Topkapı Palace Archives, Istanbul: E. 2465.
143 CCC Tripoli 14, fol. 36a–b, 43b, 47a–b.
144 CCC Lattaquié 1, fol. 216a, 220a, 224a.
145 'Abd al-Rahman al-Jabarti (d. 1825), *Aja'ib al-Athar fi'l-Tarajim wa'l-Akhbar*, trans. Thomas Philipp and Moshe Perlmann (Stuttgart: Franz Steiner, 1994), 4:377.

Much of the newfound success of these families was due to a favorable economic conjuncture, which saw the Syrian coastal highlands and especially the Latakia region develop into one of the empire's leading centers of commercial tobacco production. However, while agricultural expansion no doubt benefited the 'Alawi community as a whole, it also produced significant changes within 'Alawi society, consecrating certain family leaderships as quasi-landowners and government proxies, and by the same measure reducing the rest of the population to dependence on moneylending, clientelism, and political patronage. The increasing division of 'Alawi society into clans and tribes, far from reflecting a traditional, counterstate mode of organization, can be seen to have been the direct result of increasing social stratification in the eighteenth century. This situation was of course not peculiar to the 'Alawis; indeed, the concentration of wealth and power in the hands of a few, their adoption of patronyms or the designation of their followers as patronymic groups, and their inhabitance of *saray*s and castles in emulation of higher state officials were the veritable hallmarks of *ayan* (provincial notable) rule throughout the empire.[146]

The impact of this unprecedented hierarchization of 'Alawi society has all too often been disregarded in favor of essentializing communal differences. Today it has become commonplace, for example, to assert that "the" 'Alawis were so poor in Ottoman times as to sell their daughters into virtual slavery to rich Sunni bourgeois families—a claim somewhat disingenuously deployed both by antiregime polemicists to disparage 'Alawi morality in itself and by 'Alawi apologists to evoke past oppression. In reality, of course, it was precisely the economic disparities within the community that resulted in such poverty, and that ultimately determined its relationship to wider Syrian (and Turkish) society, most prominently by spurring the colonization of the Hatay district as well as labor migration toward Latakia, Hama, and Homs, where individual 'Alawis increasingly escaped their parochial bonds and came into contact with members of other classes and communities. Ironically, the very autonomy enjoyed by the 'Alawis in the eighteenth century may have hastened their integration and to some extent assimilation in the modern era.

Perhaps the most immediate and ominous consequence of this autonomy, however, was the emergence of the rural 'Alawi plutocracy as political actors in their own right. If the Ottomans had taken little issue with the 'Alawis as a group in previous centuries and occasionally even deplored the absence of an autochthonous leadership, the rise of Shibli Shamsin, 'Ali al-Shillif, or Saqr Mahfuz as lords of multiple tax districts, capable of raising large peasant armies, negotiating with the authorities in court, conspiring with the Shihabi emirs, or assisting the governor of Damascus, destined them to play an active part in the ever more contentious struggle for power in the Syrian provinces

---

146 Meeker, *Nation of Empire*, 31.

around the turn of the nineteenth century. For the most part the 'Alawis were a minor concern, less associated with European imperial interests than the local Christians and less of a menace to Ottoman law and order than the Druze or Wahhabis. The fact that through their leaders they were always seen to be in the pay of one provincial strongman or another, however, meant that the 'Alawis now began to appear, in the archival documentation as much as in the local chronicles, not as a rural populace among others but as a uniform sectarian faction (*taife/ta'ifa*) pursuing a single political goal. This did not so much trouble the imperial administration, which had long ceased to manage Syrian provincial affairs directly and whose purely fiscal interests the mountain gentry continued to serve quite well. But it is in this context of laissez-faireism, Western penetration, and generalized instability that the local Ottoman officials in Sayda, Tripoli, or Latakia began to perceive of the 'Alawis and other "tribal" *taife*s as a threat, to be henceforth categorized not as *reaya* but by their religious identity, subjected to conversion and other social disciplining efforts, or collectively redefined as enemies to the state.

* 5 *
IMPERIAL REFORM AND INTERNAL COLONIZATION
'ALAWI SOCIETY IN THE FACE OF MODERNITY
(1808–1888)

It would be a platitude to say that the Ottoman Empire underwent a great number of important changes during the nineteenth century, and that these had a significant impact on Syrian provincial society. In part the major innovations characterizing the Ottomans' "longest century" (to reprise a popular phrase encapsulating the multiplicity of new challenges confronting the empire) are predictable in that they touched and transformed virtually the entire planet during this time: increasing industrial, agricultural, and governmental efficiency; the increasing mobility of individuals, ideas, and armies; the increasing economic, political, and cultural hegemony of Europe and the United States; growing inequalities between centers and peripheries, between haves and have-nots; and nascent popular mobilization and struggles for emancipation.[1] Other challenges, however, were more specific to northwestern Syria, or to 'Alawi society in particular: France's unparalleled commercial and diplomatic offensive, and the Ottomans' concomitant loss of power, in the area; an upswing of religious identity politics and rhetoric that issued in a backlash against heterodox groups; and subsequent efforts by the imperial state, under the sign of modern Westernizing reforms, to better control, integrate, and wherever possible assimilate rural hinterland populations throughout its territory.

The object of this chapter is not to provide a total narrative of 'Alawi history in the nineteenth century, something which becomes nearly impossible as the available sources provide for an ever more complex picture of society, but to highlight the major trends in Ottoman and Syrian history affecting the 'Alawi community. The first two sections deal with the retreat of central government authority at the beginning of the century, as symbolized by the final (though not precisely datable) disappearance of the Ottoman *eyalet* of Tripoli, and the

1 Cf. Osterhammel, *Verwandlung der Welt*, 1287–1300.

heightened religious bigotry faced by the 'Alawis during the reign of Berber Mustafa Agha, the region's new provincial strongman. A brief third section highlights the role of the Latakia-based Shaykh al-Moghrabi, who is recalled even today as a leading ideologue of anti-'Alawi discrimination. The fourth section details the resurgence of more direct state control in the form of the Egyptian occupation of 1831–41, when the exactions committed by the new regime pushed the 'Alawi feudal notability to favor the weaker, more distant sovereignty of the empire. After the restoration of Ottoman rule over Syria, however, the empire itself adopted an ambitious program of reforms known as the Tanzimat, during which the 'Alawis and other sectarian minorities were drawn ever closer into the state and subjected to social disciplining measures such as military conscription and modern education, as covered in the fifth and sixth sections. Despite the multiple forms of pressure being exerted on traditional 'Alawi society in the name of civilization and progress, however, the conclusion contends that the 'Alawis nonetheless also succeeded in turning the discourses of modernity to their own advantage, actively promoting the construction of Ottoman state schools in the region and pursuing their own reformist agenda.

What characterizes the nineteenth century from a historian's perspective is the unprecedented abundance of documentation. In addition to the numerous local chronicles available for Syria from the beginning of the century, the growing interventionism of the French (and to a lesser extent the British and Russians) in the "Levant" generated a vast inventory of travel accounts and diplomatic missives that bespeak a special interest in sectarian, tribal, and other perceived social divisions. More important, however, even before the Tanzimat reforms the Ottoman state itself began to display a new concern with preserving the trace of provincial government. From the time of Mahmud II, the first veritable reformist sultan, a wealth of administrative reports sent from Syria and frequently bearing marginal comments in his hand, the Hatt-ı Hümayun collection, show the imperial authorities abreast of local events in a way not seen since the Mühimme records of the sixteenth century. Later on, the foundation of modern government ministries (sing. *nezaret*) during the Tanzimat, as well as Sultan Abdülhamid II's obsession with personally overseeing the state administration from the seclusion of his palace at Yıldız, gave rise to numerous dedicated archival series that provide for an ever tighter-meshed coverage of Syrian affairs. And while the *defter*s (register books) from previous centuries remain uncataloged and must be painstakingly searched for single references to the 'Alawis, almost all the relevant series from the nineteenth century are now accessible through simple keyword searches in the Başbakanlık Archives' computer catalog; many have been digitalized, and a selection of eighty-eight key documents on the 'Alawis has recently been published.[2] As a result not

---

2 Rıza Ayhan et al., eds., *Osmanlı Arşiv Belgelerinde Nusayrîler ve Nusayrîlik (1745–1920)* (Ankara: Gazi Üniversitesi Türk Kültürü ve Hacı Bektaş Velî Araştırma Merkezi, 2010).

only is there a much greater volume of research on the 'Alawis and similar groups in the nineteenth century, but the available documentation also allows for a completely different level of analysis of what Timothy Mitchell in this timeframe has termed the "localised ability to infiltrate, rearrange and colonise."[3]

In concentrating on the new technologies of government, there is of course a risk, inherent to many studies of the Ottoman nineteenth century, of lapsing into a teleology of the modern state's hegemony over society. What this chapter seeks to emphasize is therefore the historical continuity, but also the historical contingency, of the 'Alawi experience under nineteenth-century Ottoman rule. Neither the Egyptian, the Tanzimat, or the Hamidian authorities pursued a single, unified "policy" toward the 'Alawis per se, but much like in the past they continued to adapt to local realities in northwestern Syria and depend on the notability already in place for their ability to infiltrate, rearrange, and colonize. Despite the seeming omnipotence of unimaginable new economic and political forces beyond their control, the 'Alawis perhaps more than ever found their own voice as a community in this period and, within the revised parameters of the reformist state, largely participated in the fashioning of their own history.

THE DISAPPEARANCE OF OTTOMAN TRIPOLI

A key legacy of the reign of the provincial notables in the eighteenth century was the complete redrawing of Ottoman authority in the region most inhabited by the 'Alawis, the *eyalet* of Tripoli. As mentioned previously, the decline of Aleppo's silk export, the growth of Latakia, and the de facto sovereignty of the Shihabi emirs over most of northern Lebanon had already stripped Tripoli of much of its former economic and political importance. Toward the end of the century, furthermore, Syria's commercial and diplomatic center of gravity shifted toward the Southwest, as first Zahir al-'Umar, then Cezzar Ahmed Paşa established their cotton trading empire at Acre, turning it into the effective capital of the province of Sayda. In the context of a growing rivalry between the governors of Sayda and Damascus for regional primacy, Tripoli—which in any event had often been governed by a junior member of the 'Azm dynasty of Damascus—became a permanent object of contention between the two. In 1799, moreover, the tobacco superintendent and Christian merchant leaders in Latakia managed to get that district recognized as its own tax collectorship (*muhassıllık*) under the immediate control of Istanbul, so that Tripoli was henceforth reduced to a single *sancak*.[4] Even

---

3 Timothy Mitchell, *Colonising Egypt* (Berkeley: University of California Press, 1991), ix.
4 CCC Tripoli 15, fol. 180a–81a, 281a, 292a–b, 304b; Salih, "Athar al-Hiqab," 1:215–16; Ignace Muradgea D'Ohsson (d. 1807), *Tableau général de l'empire Ot[h]oman* (Istanbul: Isis, 2001), 7:285.

after the reconstitution of the *paşalık* in 1812, it either was ruled by a simple deputy (*mutasarrıf* or *mütesellim*) appointed from Acre or joined with the governorship of Damascus and, except for a last brief interlude in the 1820s, never again formed a proper Ottoman jurisdiction in its own right.

Into this power void stepped Berber Mustafa Agha, easily one of the most polarizing figures in Syrian-Lebanese history. Berber Mustafa (or Mustafa Agha Barbar) was a lower-class native of the Tripoli area who began his career as a local janissary attached to Cezzar Ahmed Paşa. Energetic and ruthless, he managed to impose himself as garrison commander (*agha*) and captain of the citadel in Tripoli, so that in 1801 the provincial governor of Damascus had little choice but to name him as *mütesellim* for the city. Neither the imperial authorities nor later governors of Acre/Sayda were particularly happy with his insubordinate demeanor, but ultimately they had to rely on him as a local intermediary. He seems to have had the support of a good part of the urban population, who appreciated his efforts to defend Tripoli against the excessive demands of the Ottoman governorates as well as against the tribal factions of the surrounding area.[5] The degree of his independence in the region is evoked by the French consul in April 1807, who notes that Berber "no longer observes any limits. He used to content himself with sending the feudatories of the province their letters of investiture. Now he demands that they come to Tripoli to receive them, as if he were a pasha. The shaykh of the Nusayris, the first to be summoned, came with fifty horsemen to pay him obeisance."[6]

Over the next three decades Berber Mustafa was thus the principal face of Ottoman authority for the 'Alawis. In many cases their interaction remained limited, as ever, to the business of tax farming. The Tripoli court records provide several examples of Saqr ibn Mahfuz, still respectfully qualified as "the most excellent of peers," or of his son Dandash receiving the *iltizam* on Safita from the hands of "Mustafa Ağa Berberzade, the *kaimakam* [deputy governor] of Tripoli and Latakia";[7] in one instance the French relate that Berber was irritated because Saqr had decided to pay the *miri* in tobacco instead of in cash, but the Shihabis were preventing him from doing anything about it.[8] Their relationship seems indeed to have been rather fraught. In a letter dated "1er Floréal 14" (21 April 1806), the French consul reports of Berber's "indisposition" toward the 'Alawis of Safita and of his plans to attack them using Lebanese Druze, Shi'i, and other irregular forces—a campaign finally averted by Saqr's payment

---

5 Ighnatiyus Tannus al-Khuri, *Mustafa Agha Barbar: Hakim Ayalat Tarabulus wa-Jabala wa-Ladhiqiyyat al-'Arab (1767–1834)* (Tripoli: Jarrus Bars and Dar al-Khalil, 1984), 68–71; 'Abd al-Latif Kurayyim, *Barbar Agha: Majd Tarabulus U'tiya Lahu* (Tripoli: Imbras, 2004).

6 CCC Tripoli 13, fol. 240b.

7 TShCR 29B:2–3; TShCR 45:20; TShCR 46:126.

8 CCC Tripoli 13, fol. 227b–228a.

of two hundred bags of silver.[9] Other times, Saqr tried claiming he was unable to pay the *miri* or other charges but was usually brought to reason by the appearance of Berber's Albanian mercenaries.[10] In October 1818 Dandash al-Saqr was taken to court by the overseer of the imperial Haramayn *vakıf*, who claimed that he was illegally trespassing on the lands of a village belonging to the foundation. Three months later, nevertheless, Dandash successfully sued Berber for restitution (*istirja'*) of the land, arguing that he had disposed of it since time immemorial, and convincing the judge that the witnesses who had testified against him in the first trial were not credible because of the "long-standing animosity, spite, and enmity between them."[11]

There is no question that Berber's rule witnessed an increase in conflict and outright violence with the 'Alawis.[12] If much of this strife originated in the collection of taxes, it also appears to have been systematically aggravated by the political rivalries in the region. As early as September 1803, for example, Cezzar Ahmed Paşa himself wrote to the Sublime Porte to accuse 'Abdallah Paşa al-'Azm of Damascus of allying with the "Druze, Shi'i, and Nusayri factions" in an attempt to dislodge his protégé Berber from Tripoli;[13] in 1808, as we have seen, 'Abdallah's successor Genç Yusuf invoked a similar pretext in his own war on Berber. Even in seemingly mundane disputes, regional politics were never far below the surface. In the summer of 1811 the long-serving French vice-consul at Latakia (Charles-Édouard Guys) reported that the local 'Alawis, who were far more fearsome than those of Safita, were once again refusing to pay the *miri* and had in the past thwarted more than one pasha who tried to collect it by force. Many of these 'Alawis worked the fields on the coastal plain of Latakia during the summer, and their lighting of bonfires to celebrate the end of the harvest that August was now also understood to be a show of force in support of Genç Yusuf, who they fervently hoped would be reappointed to the governorship of Damascus and Tripoli.[14] Berber therefore spent the autumn preparing a vast force of Albanian and other troops to lead to Latakia on behalf of his patron (Genç Yusuf's rival) Süleyman Paşa, the incumbent governor of Damascus, rapidly occupying the lower-lying villages of the Kelbiye (Qardaha) district, which the 'Alawis had abandoned and burned down themselves in anticipation

---

9 Ibid., fol. 147b–148a, 150b, 153a–154a, 155b. (The consul was apparently not yet aware that France's revolutionary calendar had been abolished on 1 January.)

10 Ibid. 15, fol. 247a, 254a–b; 16, fol. 108a–b.

11 TShCR 46:88, 134–35.

12 Hashim 'Uthman, *Tarikh al-'Alawiyyin. Waqa'i' wa-Ahdath* (Beirut: Mu'assasat al-A'lami, 1997), 39–47.

13 BOA: Hatt-ı Hümayun [HAT] 3784i; Stefan Winter, "The Nusayris before the Tanzimat in the Eyes of Ottoman Provincial Administrators, 1804–1834," in *From the Syrian Land to the States of Syria and Lebanon*, ed. Thomas Philipp and Christoph Schumann (Würzburg: Ergon, 2004), 100–109.

14 CCC Lattaquié 1, fol. 378a, 390a, 394a–b.

of an attack. By December, however, Berber realized he would again have to come to terms with the rebels—not only because the district *mütesellim* of Hama had deliberately failed to support the campaign but also because it seemed a real possibility that his nemesis Genç Yusuf might indeed be reappointed in Süleyman Paşa's stead.[15] This did not actually then happen, but the following year Berber was called to account by imperial officials in Istanbul, after the customs superintendent and de facto mayor of Latakia, ever jealous, in turn, of his own authority in the area, denounced Berber for having unjustly "pressured" and "extorted" the 'Alawi population![16]

The result of politically edged events such as the campaign of 1811 was what might be termed the increasing confessionalization or sectarianization of the 'Alawis' rapport with the rest of society. In reality there was no fundamental division between the 'Alawis as such and the Sunnis of Latakia. Many 'Alawis actually lived in or around Latakia—and had to fear for their lives only when their highlander cousins came and attacked Sunni villages in revenge for the arrest and torture death of two of theirs in early September. The city, for its part, was at all times dependent on the 'Alawi hinterland for its supply of export tobacco and most of its foodstuffs and suffered severe hardship throughout the autumn of 1811 and winter of 1812, not only from

FIGURE 5.1. Port of Latakia, early nineteenth century (Bibliothèque Nationale, Paris, coll. Estampes)

15 Ibid., fol. 417a–b, 428a; CCC Tripoli 15, fol. 106a, 140a, 146a.
16 CCC Tripoli 15, fol. 287a; 16, fol. 25a.

the military operations in the mountains but also from the presence of Berber's troops.[17] If the people of Latakia long knew that they could expect no taxes from the highlanders (a local official once remarked to Guys that if their arrears were calculated, they "would amount to millions"), Berber also did nothing to further communal relations when he arrived in Latakia in November 1811 "and started by making war in the prisons, putting to death the Anssariés [Nusayris] held there."[18] The Latakians' fear and loathing of the 'Alawis predictably grew as more and more of them descended from the mountains to raid villages, burn gardens, and steal horses in the surrounding plain, and even as far away as Tripoli. The 'Alawi shaykhs, according to Guys, were now "preaching hatred of all those who recognize the prophet," while Berber sought to motivate and encourage his army commanders by telling them that previous campaigns to root out the 'Alawis failed because they had not been led "by as good Muslims as they."[19]

The touchstone of these campaigns' success, and perhaps an indicator of how far communal relations had indeed become envenomed, was the number of rebel heads taken as trophies. The French vice-consul at Latakia indicates that Süleyman Paşa put a stop to the war when it disappointingly did not yield a single head, leaving Berber to negotiate a ceasefire as well as very minor, symbolic reparations with the Muhalaba, then with the Qardaha district.[20] One of the only references to the campaign in the contemporary Arabic literature also focuses on the taking of 'Alawi heads: the semiofficial biography of Süleyman Paşa, who was otherwise trying to forge himself a reputation as "the just" ("al-'Adil") in order to distinguish himself from his predecessor Cezzar Ahmed, for its part claims that Berber did send twenty-seven heads to Acre, where they were displayed at the entrance of the city for several days before being forwarded to Istanbul.[21] Cutting off and displaying the heads of fallen rebels was of course not specific to the 'Alawis but rather was used as a dissuasive measure throughout the empire. Western travelers of the time recount that the punishment usually reserved for 'Alawis was impalement, among other reasons because the 'Alawis themselves, believing the soul leaves the body through the mouth, preferred it over hanging as a method of execution.[22] Taken together, however, these sources at the very least suggest that the treatment of the 'Alawis under Berber's rule was becoming increasingly brutal and dehumanizing.

17 CCC Lattaquié 1, fol. 403a–b; 2, fol. 2b, 29b, 38b.
18 CCC Lattaquié 1, fol. 378a; CCC Tripoli 15, fol. 122a.
19 CCC Lattaquié 1, fol. 407b, 428b; 2, fol. 12a, 18a
20 CCC Lattaquié 1, fol. 430a–b; 2, fol. 12a, 29a, 38a.
21 Ibrahim al-'Awra (d. 1863), *Tarikh Wilayat Sulayman Basha al-'Adil 1804–1819*, ed. Antun Bishara Qiqanu (Beirut: Lahad Khatir, 1989), 205–6; see also Shihabi, *Lubnan*, 573; Salih, "Athar al-Hiqab," 1:105–6.
22 Burckhardt, *Travels in Syria*, 156; Lyde, *Asian Mystery*, 143; CCC Lattaquié 3, fol. 303b.

Süleyman Paşa himself makes reference to the 1811–12 campaign in a report on Berber's even bloodier, five-month assault on the 'Alawis in 1816. This renewed expedition was undertaken at the behest of the English adventuress Lady Hester Stanhope following the murder of a friend, French colonel Vincent Boutin, during a tour of the crusader castles near Marqab the year before, and where the presumed killers, quickly pinpointed as 'Alawis, had taken refuge in the high villages of the Qardaha district.[23] Süleyman's letter, addressed to the grand vezir and accompanied by the heads of thirty-eight fallen rebels, makes no actual mention of Stanhope or Boutin but rather seeks to show how law and order have finally come to reign in Latakia. Süleyman recalls that after the district was placed under his jurisdiction, in 1811, "some of the aforesaid brigands agreed to forswear their thievery and pay the *miri* on time, and committed themselves to becoming *reaya* [Ottoman subjects]." Within a year, however, new troubles had required him to send "a massive army . . . to twist some ears and teach a lesson, so that they would no longer oppress and injure Muslims and wayfarers." Now, four years later, the inhabitants of several tax farms of the Semt-i Qibli [south of Qardaha] had stocked weapons and resumed "their former brigandage and vice." Since "it was to be expected that exhibiting patience and forbearance toward their brigandage and rebellion, which these heretics commit with impudence and presumption, would cause it to spread to the other vermin of villainous thievery," he had sent out his deputy in Tripoli (that is, Berber Mustafa) against them. With the help of God, "the fire of their rebellion and conceit was quieted, and the majority of their fighters killed and crushed." A note added by Sultan Mahmud II in the top margin of the letter approves the grand vezir's suggestion to commend Süleyman Paşa for his actions, and to have the heads "rolled into the dust of admonition [*galtide-i hak-ı ibret*] in front of the Sublime Porte."[24]

Unsurprisingly, violence did not resolve the issue. Three months later, Süleyman sent another letter (along with eleven more heads), reporting that in spite of the recent operation, the 'Alawis had still not submitted and numerous additional battles had been fought against them. It was perhaps inevitable that the autumn would bring more bloodshed—Süleyman's second letter is dated 5 October 1816—after the government forces had devastated crops and gardens throughout the late summer and the 'Alawis faced a winter of starvation. It is thus noteworthy that Süleyman insists they have been "put into order" conclusively this time, and hence, "there no longer remaining any need for warfare, it

23 CCC Lattaquié 2, fol. 378a–b, 383a–b; CCC Tripoli 16, fol. 225a–226a, 270a–b; Shihabi, *Lubnan*, 630; al-Khuri, *Barbar Mustafa*, 150–56. According to Lyde, *Asian Mystery*, 195–96, the perpetrators were actually 'Arab al-Mulk bedouin who afterward sought the 'Alawis' protection, a possibility already raised by the French vice-consul at Latakia; see CCC Lattaquié 2, fol. 385a–b.

24 HAT 24372; transcription in Stefan Winter, "Les Nusayris au regard des administrateurs provinciaux ottomans d'avant les *Tanzimat*," *Chronos* 9 (2004): 234–35.

was necessary to propitiate the soldiery and return them [home]."[25] In reality, things remained far from settled in the northern reaches of the province. In 1818 Berber Mustafa had to deal somewhat uncharacteristically with a revolt by the Ismailis of Qadmus and al-Kahf, in which even Süleyman Paşa refused to lend him assistance; perhaps even more uncharacteristically, according to a report made to the Sublime Porte that July, the 'Alawis of the area had apparently put aside their old grievances and joined with the Ismailis against Berber.[26] Later the same year, the French vice-consul related that Berber was still occupying the 'Alawi districts and demanding 1,200 rather than the usual 800 *bourses* (bags of money); "he has seized all the livestock and the tobacco and cotton harvest, razed numerous villages, cut all the trees ... and reduced the unfortunate Ansariés to desperation and the most horrible misery." According to rumor, Berber was thinking of repopulating the devastated countryside with two thousand Druze families to be sent by his ally, Emir Bashir Shihabi, and of making himself completely independent; the Sublime Porte had supposedly ordered his execution, but following Süleyman Paşa's intervention he was once again left to rule the region unchallenged.[27]

Few periods, these sources therefore suggest, had as negative an impact on the 'Alawis as Berber Mustafa Agha's highhanded reign over Tripoli. It is only an irony of modern-day 'Alawi historical consciousness that the collective memory of Ottoman oppression is usually projected onto the distant sixteenth-century sultan Selim, while the much better attested, material acts of the nineteenth-century *mütesellim* are largely ignored. And although the Arabic chronicles, Ottoman provincial correspondence, and French consular reports all tend to highlight Berber's personal character and hatred of the 'Alawis, his local despotism was more than anything a consequence of the weakness of central state authority in Syria in the early decades of the century. The impression that the 'Alawis suffered disproportionately during this period is of course embellished by the very abundance and evocativeness of these sources. The fact that nothing comparable is documented before or after, however, does suggest that the oppression so often invoked in regard to the 'Alawis occurred within a tangible, historical framework rather than being timeless and diffuse.

CONVERSION AND SECTARIANIZATION

When did the Ottomans begin to conceive of the 'Alawis as a religious problem? In previous centuries, as we have seen, the state authorities invoked their confessional identity to justify certain taxes or to proscribe specific acts of

---

25 HAT 24295.
26 Al-'Awra, *Tarikh Wilayat Sulayman Basha*, 288–90; HAT 24282.
27 CCC Lattaquié 3, fol. 52a–b.

brigandage and rebellion but continued to treat with 'Alawi villages and tribes on an individual basis and employed known 'Alawi notables as local government intermediaries. 'Alawis, like other Ottoman Shi'is, were never induced to conform to an official standard of Islamic belief. The early modern state did attempt to define the limits of Sunni orthodoxy and deployed vast efforts to bring Christian and Jewish converts into the fold of Islam. Significantly, however, there was no institutional, church-like authority to impose standardized religious teachings and rites, community visitations, normalized moral codes, or other measures of *sozialdisziplinierung* (social disciplining) such as were integral, for example, to the precipitation of rival Catholic and Protestant confessions in Europe around the same time.[28] Despite superficial similarities, the various Sunni and Shi'i Muslim populations of the empire were not subject to confessionalization and sectarian differentiation before the modern era.

One possible sign that the community with its *ayan* leadership was beginning to be seen as a sectarian actor in the early nineteenth century is the French vice-consul's somewhat quixotic claim of the existence of a "Grand Cheikh" of the 'Alawis who had authority over the *muqaddam*s of the Kelbiye and Muhalaba districts and who decided over the continuation or not of hostilities against the state in 1811.[29] No such personage appears in the Ottoman or 'Alawi sources (and the vice-consul is tellingly not able to offer a name), so that this may indeed point toward a specifically European, orientalist reading of factional politics in the coastal highlands in this time. This propensity to divide the "natives" into religious tribes and nations, as Ussama Makdisi has cogently argued with respect to Mt. Lebanon, would in any event have a profound impact, as it came to form the basis for competing Ottoman and European discourses of backwardness, progress, and political reform in the region.[30]

A surer sign the Ottomans were beginning to take issue with the 'Alawis' religious group identity is the growing concern with their conversion. Already in Mamluk times, as we have seen, the state attempted to repress 'Alawism by having mosques built in the Jabala area, suggesting that their rebelliousness was seen above all as a failure or lack of opportunity to conform to orthodox religious practice rather than as an outright heresy. After the 1808 uprising, and in a context clearly marked by the surge of Wahhabism into Syria, Genç Yusuf Paşa had made the defeated 'Alawis profess Sunni Islam in order to ransom their captives but simply accepted their word so long as they gave

28 Stefan Winter, "Osmanische Sozialdisziplinierung am Beispiel der Nomadenstämme Nordsyriens im 17.–18. Jahrhundert," *Periplus: Jahrbuch für außereuropäische Geschichte* 13 (2003): 54–55; cf. Tijana Krstić, *Contested Conversions to Islam: Narratives of Religious Change in the Early Modern Ottoman Empire* (Stanford, CA: Stanford University Press, 2011); review by Marc Baer, *Journal of Islamic Studies* 23 (2012): 391–94.

29 CCC Lattaquié 1, fol. 431b; 2, fol. 29a–b.

30 Ussama Makdisi, *The Culture of Sectarianism: Community, History and Violence in Nineteenth-Century Ottoman Lebanon* (Berkeley: University of California Press, 2000), 23–25, 60, 68–69.

up their armed resistance. Then in 1816–17, under the title "The Rebels of Safita, Their Submission and Entry into Islam," Ibrahim al-'Awra (Süleyman Paşa's biographer) reports of a new campaign in which Berber Mustafa went to put down a revolt and ravage the Safita area on the governor's instructions. According to 'Awra, the 'Alawis were so badly defeated that they wrote Süleyman Paşa to beg for mercy, offering to "embrace the faith of Islam" if their *muqaddam*s Saqr and Dandash Mahfuz were released from captivity. "They also asked permission to build a mosque in order to worship and perform their prayers, and showed they wanted to become devout. Süleyman Paşa accepted their adoption of Islam and sent Berber an edict to that effect, ordering him to allow them to build a mosque and sending them *'ulama* from Tripoli to live among them and instruct them in the religion and precepts of Islam."[31]

'Awra's account is inaccurate inasmuch as the famous Shaykh Saqr had already been dead for a few years. The fact of the Shamsin family's public embrace of Sunnism, however, is substantiated by an extraordinary document preserved in the *shar'iyya* court records of Tripoli, which provides some of the only written testimony ever of an intra-Islamic "conversion" in Ottoman history. Interestingly the document never actually states which faith the Shamsins were renouncing, as if naming it would have lent it the same fundamental legitimacy as, say, Christianity or Judaism. It is nevertheless unique in that it addresses not only the 'Alawis' outward, legalistic behavior but also their inward, spiritual beliefs: thus on 10 March 1817 a group composed of Dandash al-Saqr, his five brothers, numerous cousins and nephews representing the Darwish, Shadid, Abu Tarraf, Mulham, Abu 'Ali Hasan, and Abu 'Ajib branches, other unnamed siblings, servants, and hangers-on, "and the entirety of the Banu Shamsin" (approximately 115 individuals in all) appeared before a deputy judge (*na'ib*) in the predominantly Sunni town of Draykish just to the north of Safita. Collectively and of their own free will, according to the *hujja* (court certificate), "they pronounced the dual profession of faith; confirmed their belief in God, His angels, His scriptures, His prophets, the final judgment and destiny, both good and bad, as coming from God; agreed to all articles of belief and accepted the obligatory precepts of the pillars of Islam; and promised to observe the rites of the true faith and adhere to the terms of Muhammadan law."

Most important in this regard, the 'Alawis committed themselves to performing the five individual daily prayers, seen by many pious Sunnis (then as now) as being the touchstone of whether they could be considered part of the community of Islam. Significantly, however, the proceedings also delve into the doctrinal and have the Shamsins abjure the central tenets of 'Alawi-Shi'i belief:

> They affirmed their doubt [*shubhatahum*] . . . that the noble imam 'Ali ibn Abu Talib had precedence, in terms of deputyship [*khilafa*] and

31 Al-'Awra, *Tarikh Wilayat Sulayman Basha*, 268–69.

merit, over the three caliphs by virtue of his kinship and leadership in war, and the truth was exposed to them and they returned to the standpoint of the Sunnis in according precedence to Abu Bakr..., then 'Umar, then 'Uthman, then 'Ali, then ... the rest of the Companions (may God be pleased with all of them). And they affirmed their doubt in transmigration and reincarnation [*tanassukh wa-taqmis*], whereby the soul, when it leaves the body, enters another. The matter was exposed to them and they reverted from their pretense and repudiated it, the belief in it, and the affirmation of it.... They likewise confessed to the prayers they held ... praying to the imams of the Ahl al-Bayt [the Prophet's family], acknowledged its error, repudiated it, and undertook to pray the five prayers [instead]; and they repudiated the celebration of Christmas [*'id al-milad*] and acknowledged its error; and together repented [*tabu*] of all the ways of the people of ignorance [*ahl al-jahala*].[32]

After receiving their certification as good Muslims, the Tripoli registers furthermore indicate, the Shamsins sent Süleyman Paşa two petitions (*arzuhal*) lauding him in the most radiant terms for having sent *'ulama* to guide them on the straight path and informing him of their intention to destroy their former places of worship and build a mosque. The petitions, which essentially confirm 'Awra's claim that the "conversion" occurred under duress from the governor, again emphasize the negation of their confessional identity and can only have been experienced as a humiliation by the 'Alawis:

> Through his praiseworthy munificence, our joy has become perfect as he deigned to favor us with imams who are the suns of Islam and the lights of mankind, and who have inculcated us with the *shahada*, sworn us to Islam, ... spurred us on to what is right and prohibited us from what is wrong; and spoken to us of belief and explained to us the law; and we have undertaken the rites of Islam, born witness to the *adhan* [call to prayer], and held the five prayers at their appointed times and collectively on Friday. We have torn down the places of error [*al-amakin al-mudilla*] and surrendered the books which were the cause of fallacy, and they [the imams] have lifted our doubts and led us from ruin. We have agreed on a site where to build a mosque [*jami'*] in order to accomplish the rites of the exalted religion, and we have pledged to read the Qur'an, we the whole of the Banu Shamsin, young and old.[33]

These documents are rather exceptional within the court record genre in that they dwell at length on questions of theological truth and doubt,

---

32 TShCR 45:243.
33 TShCR 45:242–43.

personal repentance and salvation, as well as the interiorizing of moral discipline, reminiscent indeed of confessionalization in early modern Europe. One may of course ask how genuine it all was. There is no more reference in the documentation to the Shamsins' religious identity, and over the next years Shaykh Dandash and then his brother Safi Saqr al-Mahfuz continued to receive the Safita *iltizam* on much the same terms as before.[34] The Shamsins do, on the other hand, seem to have taken the construction of mosques seriously. In September 1827, for example, an imperial *berat* (patent) was issued to turn "the mosque built by the charitable Shamsin family" in Barmana village near Safita into a full congregational mosque (*cami*), since it was serving the needs of the local population for Friday and holiday prayers.[35] The building of mosques, however, in any case served *ayan* such as the Shamsins to bolster their social capital—and was not necessarily incompatible with 'Alawism. Contemporary observers including H. A. al-Shihabi, at any rate, continued to regard the Shamsin shaykhs and the people of Safita as "Nusayris."[36]

If the southern highlands around Safita remained noticeably quiet until the Egyptian occupation ("les Anssariés ne se font plus tirer la manche pour acquitter le miri," the French consul at Tripoli wrote in 1830),[37] the northern part of the province around Latakia came to witness nearly constant sectarian warfare during the 1820s. On the one hand, tensions were stoked by the usual political rivalries among top-level Ottoman provincial administrators and their local supporters. Thus in 1822 the governor of Sayda, Abdullah Paşa, was officially accused of joining with the "Nusayris, Druze, and Kızılbaş" (the standard term for Twelver Shi'is) in a bid to seize the governorship of Damascus, severely defeating the Damascene army just outside the city. While a Hama court even sentenced Abdullah Paşa to death for colluding with heretics, the Sublime Porte quietly also approved his rival's proposal to "conciliate little by little" the 'Alawis and Shi'is in order to win them over to the Ottoman-Damascene side.[38] On the other hand, sectarian ressentiment against the Greek Orthodox Christians in Syria, but also against the 'Alawis, was driven to new heights in these years by Russia's intervention in the Greek struggle for independence. Whereas French diplomats repeatedly stated that Muslim bigotry was making life nearly impossible for the Greek Orthodox community in Latakia, in 1822 an

---

34 TShCR 30:12, 117; TShCR 49:7, 143; TShCR 50:18, 71; al-Qaht, "Al-Tarikh al-Ijtima'i wa'l-Iqtisadi," 25.

35 TShCR 30:200.

36 Shihabi, *Lubnan*, 841; see also MAE: Correspondance politique des consuls [CPC] Turquie 245, fol. 406b.

37 CPC Turquie-divers 1, fol. 107a ("The Anssariés no longer have to be pulled by the sleeve to pay the miri").

38 HAT 20647; HAT 35473.

envoy of the Egyptian governor Mehmed Ali Paşa (whose help in defending the Syrian coastline the Ottomans were imploring) alleged in Istanbul that "the sinister Greek nation, in order to advocate their corrupt thought and be joined in imposing their evil and contemptuous designs on the people of Islam ... have not failed to correspond and communicate with the Nusayri and Druze sects—who have no part in the ornament of Islam and are perhaps worse than combatant infidels—so as to establish the necessary friendship and unity between them."[39]

Regardless of the fact that Mehmed Ali had every interest in exaggerating the local threat (ironically, his asking price for helping the Ottomans included a royal pardon for the same Abdullah Paşa who had been accused of allying with the 'Alawis only shortly before), this document is also interesting in that it appears to be the first in modern times to reprise the discourse of Ibn Taymiyya's fatwas in qualifying the 'Alawis as "worse than" the external enemies of Islam. In any event the propaganda appears to have proven effective: the charge of the 'Alawis' complicity with the Greeks, however unlikely, is repeated without further elaboration in Ahmed Cevdet Paşa's *Tarih*.[40]

Abdullah Paşa was indeed amnestied in 1823, and it is in this double context of provincial rivalries and mounting sectarian tension that Latakia witnessed one of the most serious urban revolts in its history: in the night of 5 May 1824 Mehmed (Muhammad) Paşa ibn al-Mann, a native of the Latakia region who had worked his way up through the Ottoman janissary corps before being named governor of Tripoli/Latakia province just that spring, was hunted down and assassinated, along with his cousin, a Greek Orthodox secretary (*katib*) and other members of his household, by a lynch mob breaking into his residence. According to the French vice-consul, the attack was led by the *ayan* in response to "a few tyrannical acts" on Mehmed's part or might even have been engineered by his "jealous and ambitious neighbor" Abdullah Paşa.[41] Somewhat more to the point, local chronicler Ilyas Salih notes that Mehmed had taken the side of a French consular protégé in a dispute with a number of Muslim dignitaries, going so far as to banish the *qadi* to the island fortress of Arwad and thus incurring the wrath of the city's Muslims—who were already angry that he seemed to hold the 'Alawis in high esteem, and now suspected him of being one himself. "It was said that they had become convinced of this because of the Nusayris' association with him, and from his accent in Arabic which was like theirs. Some claimed

---

39 HAT 20671a; see also Winter, "The Nusayris before the Tanzimat," 101–3.

40 Ahmed Cevdet Paşa (d. 1895), *Tarih-i Cevdet*, 2nd imprint (Istanbul: Matbaa-ı Osmaniye, 1891–92), 12:74. On the importance of the *Tarih* in the context of the Ottoman reforms, see Christoph Neumann, *Das Indirekte Argument: Ein Plädoyer für die Tanzīmāt vermittels der Historie* (Münster: Lit, 1994).

41 Süreyya, *Sicill-i Osmanî*, 1036; 'Uthman, *Tarikh al-Ladhiqiyya*, 68–69; CCC Lattaquié 3, fol. 314a–315a.

with certainty that he had secretly married a Nusayri girl. So they awaited their chance to destroy him."[42]

In a petition addressed to the Sublime Porte, the notables of Latakia had openly disparaged Mehmed Paşa as a *zindiq* (heretic), who on account of his foul beliefs recruited 'Alawi soldiers to domineer and oppress Sunni-inhabited districts.[43] If Mehmed Paşa's 'Alawi roots were mainly speculative,[44] his good rapport with the community was not. As a result of his killing, Latakia's countryside erupted in violence as "the Ansaries, whom the Pacha protected and loved, and who were furious over a murder that deprived them of a cherished master, began to devastate the surroundings." Two-and-a-half weeks later, the same vice-consul reports, the 'Alawis had "spread out in numerous bands throughout the Latakia area, stopping and robbing not only caravans but even messengers. They seize Turkish [i.e., Sunni] villages and unpityingly massacre the inhabitants. A few days ago, the city expected to be attacked by ten thousand Ansaries who were said to be assembled and ready to take over Latakia. The population had taken up arms and begun to prepare for a rigorous defence. Happily these rumors were without issue."[45]

Even more critically, the inhabitants of Latakia lived in fear of an attack by Ottoman forces to punish them for the killing of the governor (so that the French vice-consul himself fled the city for a month). Surprisingly, however, the Sublime Porte preferred to defuse the situation by appointing a member of the much respected 'Azm family, Azemzade Süleyman Paşa, as a replacement governor acceptable to all. By early July 1824 Guys could report with satisfaction that the urban revolt leaders (and most notably a local janissary *agha*) had received official letters of amnesty, while "the rebel chiefs in the mountains came one after another to lay down their arms at the feet of our new governor and be dressed in honorary furs, as a sign of reconciliation and friendship."[46] Indeed the last *iltizam* contract for the northern 'Alawi highlands preserved in the Tripoli records, a concession on the Samt al-Qibli awarded to the local *muqaddam* and payable to Süleyman Paşa at Latakia, dates from these, his first days in office.[47]

Unfortunately, peace did not prevail. Already in mid-July Süleyman Paşa reported to Istanbul that the "entire Nusayri-inhabited *mukataa* of Bayt al-Shillif has revolted," with its denizens profiting from the difficult terrain to refuse paying taxes and descending on the nearby roads to rob travelers. A force had been sent out to confront them, which in the course of an eight- or ten-hour battle succeeded in inflicting heavy casualties and putting the rest

42 Salih, "Athar al-Hiqab," 1:108.
43 HAT 25480.
44 Cf. Al Ma'ruf, *Tarikh al-'Alawiyyin fi Bilad al-Sham*, 3:204–5.
45 CCC Lattaquié 3, fol. 315a–b, 320a–321a, 330b.
46 Ibid., fol. 330a, 332b–333a.
47 TShCR 50:17.

of them to flight.⁴⁸ It appears, however, that the rebels were targeting specific enemies rather than engaging in wanton brigandage. In early August the French vice-consul reported that "the Anssariés have attacked a camel caravan that left Latakia for Aleppo, taking only the merchandise that concerns the local population." The constant risk prompted the vice-consul to write to *muqaddam* 'Ali of Bahluliyya (the district dominating the Latakia-Aleppo road through the Nahr al-Kabir valley, immediately adjoining the Bayt al-Shillif), reminding him of their good rapport in the past and asking him to continue to "respect" French caravans bound for Aleppo. 'Ali indeed became one of the nation's most stalwart friends in the area, providing its caravans with free escorts whenever the roads were too unsafe.⁴⁹ The 'Alawis' relations with the state authorities, meanwhile, were far less cordial, especially after the appointment of Ali Paşa al-As'ad to replace Süleyman Paşa, recently deceased, in January 1825. Throughout the spring and early summer, the new governor took the field to "pacify the Anssariés" and reopen the roads, though failing to collect much by way of tax arrears.⁵⁰ His forces were, on the other hand, able to reconquer the Samt al-Qibli district, which according to a contemporary Lebanese observer had also "risen up" again that year.⁵¹

The conflict did not end there, however, but escalated dramatically through the autumn, as first *muqaddam* 'Ali of Bahluliyya was arrested, thrown in jail and subjected to daily beatings (for the sole reason of having successfully restored his finances after the last campaign, according to the French), and six 'Alawis including another *muqaddam* were publically executed in Latakia to avenge the murder of a group of Muslim travelers near Jisr al-Shughur.⁵² The vice-consul placed the blame for all the violence and tyranny, "not seen in Latakia since the days of Dgezzar-Pacha," squarely on the shoulders of the "current government that is continually making war against [the 'Alawis]" and noted that the deputy governor's "barbarous conduct ... has pushed the entire mountain into revolt." The crisis reached a head in late November when Sa'id al-Atrash, the *muqaddam* of the Hammam district (part of Jabala), kidnapped fourteen "Turks" in order to press the release of his sons, who were evidently being held in Tripoli as security hostages; upon setting out for Latakia the following spring, Ali Paşa had one of the sons, "a child of 10 or 12 years," impaled after his father and the other *muqaddam*s failed to present themselves to take out their regular *iltizam* contracts.⁵³

48 HAT 24468d.
49 CCC Lattaquié 3, fol. 344b, 379a.
50 CCC Lattaquié 4, fol. 16a, 20b, 32b.
51 Tannus al-Shidyaq (d. 1859), *Akhbar al-A'yan fi Jabal Lubnan* (Beirut: Lebanese University, 1970), 520–21.
52 CCC Lattaquié 4, fol. 46b, 54b, 66a.
53 Ibid., fol. 69b; CPC Turquie 244, fol. 257a–b; CPC Turquie 257, fol. 13a.

Unable to break the 'Alawis' resistance directly, Ali Paşa (a native of the 'Akkar in northern Lebanon) seems to have tried to manipulate sectarian divisions in the region to his own advantage. In December 1825 the French vice-consul reported that the *mütesellim* of Latakia had recruited Muslim peasants from the Jabal al-Aqra' district (in Aleppo province on the coast north of Latakia), supplied them with a canon, and sent them to fight the 'Alawis on the Nahr al-Sinn River near Jabala, where the latter were attempting to demolish a bridge.[54] In an official account of the campaign, sent along with fresh heads to Istanbul almost two months later, Ali Paşa, again attributing the 'Alawis' contumacy to Greek incitement, claimed that his forces (in combination with *sekban* irregulars) had killed thirteen insurgents and destroyed several villages near the major roadways after his "investigations" (*istihbar*) had revealed that the 'Alawis were planning to knock down other "*vakıf* bridges" and attack innocent wayfarers and "people of honor" in the area, who were in need of official protection.[55]

The result, as far as can be inferred from the few references available, appears to have been a full-fledged war between 'Alawis from the Bayt al-Shillif and Sunnis from the Sahyun district.[56] Ali Paşa himself, according to the French, attempted to quell the conflict at one point, once it had begun to harm agriculture and after hearing of the pillage of al-Talla, which, even though 'Alawi-inhabited, was under the authority of the (Sunni) *agha* of the "Kerad" (Jabal al-Akrad; essentially the Sahyun district).[57] In another lengthy account sent to Istanbul in June 1826, possibly the longest single archival document dealing with the 'Alawis in the prereform period, Ali Paşa paints a dire picture of conditions in the Sahyun. According to a petition made by the local population, seven to eight thousand fighters from the Bayt al-Shillif under the leadership of "Sultan" Hasan and his brother Barakat had attacked the district, killing upward of three hundred Muslims, plundering villages and farms, torching mosques and other buildings, and scattering refugees as far as Damascus and Aleppo. Criticizing his predecessor Mehmed Paşa for always having ignored the 'Alawis' transgressions, and depicting the latest campaign as just revenge, Ali Paşa proudly announces the capture and "putting to death by the extreme punishment of impalement" the *muqaddam* of Bahluliyya and twelve of his relatives, before sending their heads on to Istanbul.[58] In a short comment written at the top of the dispatch, Sultan Mahmud takes note of its content and advises the grand vezir to interrogate an imperial foundry official passing through the region on his way from Damascus to Istanbul about the

---

54 CCC Lattaquié 4, fol. 70a–b.
55 HAT 40823.
56 See also Al Ma'ruf, *Tarikh*, 3:207.
57 CCC Lattaquié 4, fol. 71a, 79b; CPC Turquie 245, fol. 9a–b.
58 HAT 24973.

situation on the ground. A few days later, having read the official's testimony, the sultan could only conclude that "the aforesaid paşa was not exaggerating."[59]

The aforesaid pasha, according to an incredulous Vice-Consul Guys, "being in need of heads," subsequently had fifteen innocent 'Alawis decapitated simply in order to be able "to write the Porte that the castle of Sahyun had been retaken by force." Throughout the autumn of 1826 his troops continued to pillage 'Alawi villages, raising the specter that "cette population ne périsse de faim ou de misère"; as late as November, the vice-consul indicated that "Anssariés are being executed every day in Latakia."[60]

SHAYKH AL-MOGHRABI

Beyond the general need to ensure provincial order and security, the sectarian troubles in Latakia do not seem to have elicited much interest in Istanbul. In July 1828, according to the Antioch law court records, the Sublime Porte sent orders to the government divan of Aleppo, announcing the empire's entry into war with Russia and instructing the authorities to verify the state of preparedness of the harbors of Suwayda (Suwaydiyya) and Kassab as well as the temperament of the local population.[61] Three weeks later the governor wrote back saying that since "the people of most of the villages around these harbors are Nusayris," he would personally lead a company to investigate their level of support, but this never appears to have become a cause for concern.[62]

By coincidence, several of the empire's leading statesmen in precisely these years happened to be of 'Alawi origin. The most illustrious of them was Kara Mehmed Paşa (d. 1828–29), a native of Antioch who worked his way up through the palace guard and imperial artillery before being named government inspector in Rumelia. In 1821 he was appointed governor of the province of Biga (Çanakkale) in the rank of full vezir, followed by a promotion to commander of the Mediterranean forces and finally, in the summer of 1822, to grand admiral (*kapudan-ı derya*) of the Ottoman navy—tasked among other things with guarding the Morea during the Greek uprising. In the *Sicill-i Osmani*, Kara Mehmed is described indifferently as a Nusayri and as being "foresighted." He seems to have owed his career in some measure to an advantageous marriage to the daughter of the former grand vezir, Halil Hamid Paşa. This pedigree is likely also what enabled their son, Mahmud Bey (d. 1841), to secure a post as deputy secretary at the Sublime Porte.[63]

---

59 HAT 32670.
60 CPC Turquie 245, fol. 61a–b, 220a, 313b.
61 AŞSD 20:16; Stefan Winter, "La révolte alaouite de 1834 contre l'occupation égyptienne: perceptions alaouites et lecture ottomane," *Oriente Moderno* 79 (1999): 69.
62 HAT 17679.
63 Süreyya, *Sicill-i Osmani*, 909; Winter, "Nusayris before the Tanzimat," 110–11.

Mehmed Emin Vahid (d. 1828), an 'Alawi born in Kilis but raised in Istanbul, also attained high office in this period. Appointed ambassador to France by Sultan Selim III in 1806, he subsequently served in the imperial finance administration before being promoted to pasha and made governor of Hanya (Crete) and finally Aleppo, in 1826–27.[64] If the famous reformist statesman and historian Ahmed Cevdet Paşa was somewhat uncharacteristically given to making disparaging remarks about 'Alawis in this time, this may in large part have been due to the power wielded by certain 'Alawi individuals within the state—not least of which the in-laws of another grand vezir, his great rival and nemesis Fuad Paşa.[65] Other 'Alawis of the time are known to have worked in the Ottoman tobacco Régie and in the Foreign Ministry.[66]

If the impulse for sectarian discrimination against 'Alawis thus did not primarily originate in Istanbul, it was not purely local either. As in the Lebanon, the communities of the Syrian coastal highlands had shared a long history of coexistence in which confessional identity could be a key mobilizing factor in times of crisis but did not determine the basic social and political order.[67] It is rather the destabilization of this order on a regional scale—the increasingly obvious decline of the empire's military prospects; the economic and cultural penetration of the Levant by European and American interests; Ottoman efforts to reassert central control through new measures of fiscal and administrative coercion—that sparked nativist reactions, including religious fundamentalism on a regional scale, and in turn led to a backlash against newly constructed *taife*s or "sectarian groups" such as the 'Alawis. We have already referred to Wahhabism, an Islamic reform movement (largely inspired by the teachings of Ibn Taymiyya) that made important inroads especially among the newly immigrated Arab tribal populations of southern and central Syria in the early nineteenth century. In the province of Latakia, the main agent of Islamic revivalism was a certain Muhammad al-Maghribi (or "al-Moghrabi," as per the local pronunciation), a religious preacher from Sus (Tunisia) who was himself the product of a wide but as yet understudied movement of migration that saw the arrival in western Syria of numerous North African scholars, mercenaries, tradesmen, and later refugees from French occupation. Shaykh al-Moghrabi appears to have lived for a number of years in Damascus after coming from Tunisia on pilgrimage around 1802,

---

64 Süreyya, *Sicill-i Osmanî*, 1648–49; Necati Alkan, "Fighting for the Nusayrī Soul: State, Protestant Missionaries and the 'Alawīs in the Late Ottoman Empire," *Die Welt des Islams* 52 (2012): 29–30.

65 İlber Ortaylı, "Groupes hétérodoxes et l'administration ottomane," in *Syncretistic Religious Communities in the Near East: Collected Papers of the International Symposium "Alevism in Turkey and Comparable Syncretistic Religious Communities in the Near East in the Past and Present,"* ed. Krisztina Kehl-Bodrogi et al. (Leiden: Brill, 1997), 209–10.

66 Hasan, *A'lam*, 1:102–3; Winter, "Nusayris," 110.

67 Makdisi, *Culture of Sectarianism*, 6, 46–47.

then moved on to other parts of Syria, and eventually settled in Latakia. There he gained a certain notoriety for his conservative teachings and acquired a devoted following among the local underclass, before dying of the plague in April 1827.[68] (The mosque where he lies buried carries his name to this day.) Much of his appeal among the urban population may have been his uncompromising stance vis-à-vis the 'Alawis of the surrounding countryside: qualifying him as a "vile and ignorant fanatic" who may though be considered the "patron saint" of Latakia, Samuel Lyde suggests that the shaykh "gave a fetwa for which his memory is accursed among the Ansaireeh, that the lives and property of the Ansaireeh were at the disposal of the Mussulmans."[69] While there is nothing to indicate that the likes of Berber Mustafa or 'Ali As'ad referred to any religious rulings in their harsh treatment of the 'Alawis, the fact that the precise terms of Ibn Taymiyya's fatwas suddenly begin cropping up in administrative documents of the 1820s is indeed likely attributable to Muhammad al-Moghrabi's scholarly activity and influence in the area.

Al-Moghrabi may have begun playing a direct political role in 1824, when Ilyas Salih affirms that Sunni partisans in Latakia consulted him about killing governor Mehmed Paşa, and he indicated his assent with a discreet hand gesture.[70] This could, however, be a backward projection of his later importance, as the local French vice-consul does not account for him as one of the leaders of the revolt but rather refers to him for the first time in 1826, as the cause of "all these cruel scenes" the people of Latakia were taking pleasure in: "They are fanaticized by a Maghribi shaykh who is telling them every day that it is a meritorious act before God to drench their hands in the blood of a Christian or an Anssarié."[71] Over the next few months the vice-consul refers repeatedly to Moghrabi's lead role in the persecution of 'Alawis in Latakia (now usually executed by being crucified upside down) and finally characterizes him as one of the three members of the "triumvirate" effectively governing the city (besides the *mütesellim* and a chief merchant).[72] After Moghrabi's death the following spring, the *mütesellim* seems to have returned to the more pragmatic policy of extorting money from the surrounding 'Alawi villages;[73] the French report several more tax revolts in the 'Alawi-inhabited districts of Latakia the following years but no more of the "barbarity" that is associated with al-Moghrabi.[74] In an 'Alawi prayer reproduced in the Bakura

---

68 'Uthman, *Tarikh al-Ladhiqiyya*, 68–71; Salih, "Athar al-Hiqab," 1:110; CPC Turquie 257, fol. 169b.

69 Lyde, *Asian Mystery*, 196; see also Dick Douwes, "Knowledge and Oppression: The Nusayriyya in the Late Ottoman Period," in *La Shi'a nell'Impero Ottomano* (Rome: Accademia Nazionale dei Lincei, 1993), 165.

70 Salih, "Athar al-Hiqab," 1:108–9.

71 CPC Turquie 245, fol. 61b.

72 CCC Tripoli 18, fol. 62b; CPC Turquie 245, fol. 382b, 405b–406a.

73 CPC Turquie 257, fol. 150a–b, 169b; CCC Tripoli 18, fol. 155a.

74 CCC Tripoli 18, fol. 215a; CPC Turquie 258, fol. 67a, 181a. 193b, 216b, 223b–224a.

al-Sulaymaniyya, the first text (from the mid-nineteenth century) to publicly disclose the tenets of the religion (see below), there is an express call to curse al-Moghrabi's name.[75]

In the final analysis, it was a combination of factors that conspired to press the 'Alawis, much like other rural confessional communities of western Syria, into an ever more sectarian mold in the opening decades of the nineteenth century: On one level, the participation of certain 'Alawi forces in the constant clashes between regional Ottoman governors raised the political profile of the population as a whole; the ascent of locally rooted provincial satraps such as Berber Mustafa Agha or 'Ali As'ad Paşa who were left to dominate secondary towns like Tripoli and Latakia over many years in turn contributed to entrenching preexisting sectarian enmities as a matrix of Ottoman government in the area. On another level, in an imperial Mediterranean context increasingly favorable to the interference of French, Russian, and other European interests, often in the optic of "protecting" specific religious groups, the 'Alawis progressively came to be represented by both foreign observers and Ottoman administrators in terms of what Ussama Makdisi has characterized as the "single greatest fallacy" in the historical understanding of sectarianism, "the notion of the pure communal actor."[76] And finally, the unprecedented ideological attacks on 'Alawism itself these years are thinkable only within the nascent international context of Islamist reformism and anti-imperialism—and in a sense therefore already foreshadowed, one might venture in conclusion, the even greater pressures that would be brought to bear on the 'Alawi community under the sign of pan-Islamism, later during the Hamidian period.

THE EGYPTIAN OCCUPATION, 1831–1841

The ten-year occupation of "Suriya" (a Latin loanword tellingly used for the first time in the Egyptian administrative correspondence of the day) by the forces of Mehmed Ali Paşa under the command of his son Ibrahim Paşa marks a watershed in the modern history of the 'Alawis. In Egypt the government of Mehmed Ali had wrought a veritable revolution, drawing inspiration from European (mainly French Napoleonic) models to reform and centralize the administration, introduce "modern" schooling and hospital care, create a state-controlled industrial sector (essentially for the commercial production of cotton), and finally train and discipline a vast new army of popular conscripts as the basis of Egypt's growing "national" power.[77] From the very beginning,

---

75 Salisbury, "The Book of Sulaimân's First Ripe Fruit," 273.
76 Makdisi, *Culture of Sectarianism*, 68–69.
77 See esp. Khaled Fahmy, *All the Pasha's Men: Mehmed Ali, His Army, and the Making of Modern Egypt* (Cairo: American University in Cairo Press, 1997).

Mehmed Ali's quest for aggrandizement had carried an important Syrian dimension. As early as 1810 he began to side with certain *valis* of the area against others or intervene on their behalf at the Sublime Porte, and having been called on by the empire first to deal with the Wahhabis and then to quell the Greek revolt, he repeatedly asked for the rich province of Damascus to be added to his domains as well. By 1828 it was clear to local observers that Mehmed Ali, frustrated over the Porte's obdurate refusals as well as its incompetent handling of the Greek crisis, would sooner or later simply seize Syria by force.[78]

The most tangible consequence of Egyptian rule for the 'Alawis and other tribal hinterland populations was a massive increase in taxation, disarmament, and conscription into the state army. As a result the Egyptians encountered sometimes fierce resistance in places like Nablus, the Kurdish districts of Aleppo, and finally southern Lebanon, where British arms shipments to the Druze and Shi'is helped break the occupation's back in 1838–40. The first major revolt against Ibrahim Paşa, however, took place in the 'Alawi mountains in the autumn of 1834, leading to serious destruction in Latakia and appearing for a moment as an opportunity to launch a wider Ottoman government offensive to reconquer the whole region. Yet at the same time, many individual 'Alawis actually supported the new regime, which among other things expressly forbade their discrimination and instead afforded them unprecedented rights and opportunities for social advancement. The 'Alawis' ambivalence toward the experience of Egyptian rule is reflected in Syrian and Turkish historiography down to the present day and can be seen as typical of the community's overall ambivalence toward the larger project of Ottoman modernism in the nineteenth and early twentieth centuries.

The 'Alawis' positive rapport with the Egyptian regime already predated the 1831 occupation. As early as 1817 Jabarti notes the presence in Cairo of "all kinds of newcomers," including "Druzes, Matawila [Twelver Shi'is], Nusayris, and others whom the pasha [Mehmed Ali] has brought to work as craftsmen, farmers, silk producers, and as workers on his reclamation projects in the eastern valley."[79] Many 'Alawis, according to Muhammad Ghalib al-Tawil, therefore embraced Ibrahim Paşa's invasion with open arms, seizing the chance to enroll freely in the military and playing a major role in the construction of Egypt's forward defensive positions in the Gülek Pass and the Taurus mountains above Adana. In this way the entire Cilician plain became extensively settled by 'Alawi migrants during the Egyptian interregnum.[80] In his *History* of Latakia, Syrian 'Alawi historian Hashim 'Uthman furthermore

---

78 Muhammed Kutluoglu, *The Egyptian Question (1831–1841). The Expansionist Policy of Mehmed Ali Pasa in Syria and Asia Minor and the Reaction of the Sublime Porte* (Istanbul: Eren, 1998); Fahmy, *All the Pasha's Men*, 48–59; CPC Turquie 258, fol. 14a.

79 Jabarti, *Aja'ib al-Athar*, 4:281.

80 Al-Tawil, *Tarikh al-'Alawiyyin*, 451–53.

draws attention to the many technical innovations and improvements brought by Ibrahim Paşa, including the introduction of mechanical cotton presses, the professional supervision of the tobacco and lumber industry, the city's incorporation into the Egyptian postal network, and the founding of its first modern library. Most important, of course, the 'Alawis for the first time enjoyed full legal equality under the Egyptian regime, Mehmed Ali going so far as to order the execution of one of his own officers who had conspired to set up a trade in 'Alawi girls and arranging for the girls to be sent back to their villages.[81] According to the Egyptian state correspondence on Syria published by Asad Rustum, even at the height of the 'Alawi revolt in October 1834 Ibrahim's commander at Latakia, Selim Bey, publicly denounced al-Moghrabi's fatwa condoning the enslavement of 'Alawi women and children and threatened to punish anyone involved in the practice.[82]

The more traditional, gentry-led populations of the highlands, meanwhile, were considerably more averse to the new regime. Not least, it may be surmised, because Ibrahim Paşa had received the allegiance of Tripoli and Latakia (as well as Beirut and Aleppo) immediately after landing in Palestine in November 1831—and assigned the governorship of the province to none other than Berber Mustafa Agha, who after several years' service in lesser functions had perspicaciously turned his back on the Ottomans and joined the Egyptian side. In February 1832 Shaykh Zahir (Dahir) Saqr al-Mahfuz, the taxlord of Safita, therefore made contact with Osman Paşa, the legitimate Ottoman-appointed governor of Tripoli, encouraging him to retake the city and promising to provide three thousand 'Alawi fighters in support. In the ensuing battle, however, the superior forces of the Lebanese emir Bashir al-Shihabi, Ibrahim Paşa's key ally in the region, dealt the 'Alawi-Ottoman coalition a severe defeat. Shaykh Zahir, wounded by a cannonball to the thigh, died as he was being carried back to Safita; Osman Paşa, quickly abandoned by his 'Alawi and other local partisans "always ready to join the stronger side," was ignominiously put to flight; while Berber Mustafa proceeded to exact revenge on his remaining supporters in Tripoli.[83] A few weeks later, the nominal Ottoman *vali* of Aleppo is reported to have written Zahir's brother Dandash and son Khidr, informing them of his imminent arrival in Hama to lead another attempt to dislodge the Egyptians and exhorting them to steadfastness and loyalty to the empire.[84] According to H. A. al-Shihabi, however, Berber Mustafa Agha in the meantime managed to conciliate Zahir's cousin Darwish al-Saqr and invested him as shaykh

---

81 Asad Rustum (d. 1965), ed., *Al-Mahfuzat al-Malikiyya al-Misriyya: Bayan bi-Watha'iq al-Sham*, 4 vols., 2nd imprint (Beirut: al-Maktaba al-Bulusiyya, 1986–87), [*Mahfuzat*] #5100, 5149; 'Uthman, *Tarikh al-Ladhiqiyya*, 78–84.

82 *Mahfuzat* #3829; Winter, "La révolte alaouite," 63.

83 CPC Turquie-divers 1, fol. 333b, 374a–b; Shihabi, *Lubnan*, 841.

84 *Mahfuzat* #755.

of Safita in his place.⁸⁵ The Tripoli *shar'iyya* court registers, for their part, show that the *iltizam* for Safita was awarded in July 1832 to Khidr al-Saqr Mahfuz—at the almost incredible new price of 276,290 *guruş*, a more than sixfold increase over the previous recorded contract.⁸⁶ The French consul general (now based in Beirut) notes in January 1833 that "the Ansariés living in the high mountains of Latakia are refusing to pay their contributions, despite the threats that have been made against them in Ibrahim Pacha's name," but they relented two months later when it became clear, with the signature of the "Treaty of Kütahya" between the Ottoman Empire and Mehmed Ali, that Syria would indeed remain under Egyptian rule.⁸⁷ In the early summer the tax farm for Safita was once more given to Khidr ibn Saqr al-Mahfuz, for 350,000 *guruş*.⁸⁸

In addition to the unprecedented tax burden ("la montagne est vraiment à plaindre," the French consul wrote in regard to Mt. Lebanon in early 1834),⁸⁹ the 'Alawi highlands were beginning to suffer under the Egyptian regime in other respects as well. After initially focusing on the Arsuz region in the Alexandretta district (Hatay) as a possible new source of lumber for the Egyptian navy, the occupation authorities decided that the mountains above Latakia offered a better quality of wood and began with the improvement of roads into the area in November 1832.⁹⁰ But it is above all the stationing of troops and the collection of weapons in the northern highlands, undertaken once most of Palestine had been subdued in 1833, that generated unrest and ultimately led to the 'Alawi revolt. Ibrahim Paşa himself realized early on that the new measures of state control would elicit opposition in some quarters: in a letter addressed to his father in September 1833, he floats the idea of raising a regiment "composed of the sons of the great families of the Druze mountain, Nablus, 'Akkar, and the Nusayri mountains," under his personal command, so as to "rein in the Arab lands until they are firmly in his hand."⁹¹ This idea was apparently not pursued, however, and throughout the summer of 1834 the French consul reports a growing number of incidents involving the 'Alawis and the forces of Emir Khalil al-Shihabi, who had been dispatched by his father Bashir to "pacify" Latakia's hinterland on the Egyptians' behalf.⁹²

The actual revolt began in the early autumn when the Egyptian commander Selim Bey arrived from Tripoli on an express mission to "disarm the mountains." According to a detailed *bulletin hébdomadaire* (weekly report)

85 Shihabi, *Lubnan*, 843.
86 TShCR 52:43–44.
87 CPC Turquie-divers 2, fol. 159b, 205b.
88 TShCR 52:107.
89 CPC Turquie-divers 4, fol. 19a.
90 *Mahfuzat* #1604, #1613, #1975, #1988, #2050, #2094, #2162, #2416.
91 Ibid. #3201.
92 CPC Turquie-divers 4, fol. 103a, 106b, 112b, 133b.

submitted by the French consular agency in Latakia shortly after the events, Selim headed out from Marqab castle on 21 September, quickly overpowering the relatively low-lying Banu 'Ali district (the Samt al-Qibli, centered around 'Ayn al-Shaqaq), whose shaykh then joined Egyptians for the campaign against the Kelbiye district (the Banu 'Ali's traditional enemies). All the other cantons refused to disarm, so that by 25 September the entire highlands were in a state of rebellion.[93] The first major confrontation took place the following day at Bahluliyya, where 'Alawi fighters had massed to intercept an Egyptian column heading from Latakia to Aleppo, and which the Egyptian state papers confirm ended in a serious defeat for the government troops.[94] Worse was yet to come: as reported by a number of contemporary observers, on 27 September the 'Alawis descended on Latakia itself, which had been left empty of troops and where the rebels, gleefully supported this time by the Sunni population who resented the occupation regime just as much as they, attacked and plundered government warehouses, sprang open the prisons, and killed several military officers.[95] The unique, unpublished eyewitness account of Fathallah Ibn al-Sa'igh, an Aleppine traveler sojourning in Latakia at the time, indicates that the Egyptians had tried to create divisions among the local 'Alawi leaders but failed, so that the attack was in fact coordinated among several leading *muqaddam*s. Only once these realized that Selim Bey's forces would head straight into the mountains did they vacate the city to go back and defend their villages.[96]

Selim's first response was to execute Ahmad Qarqur of the Samt al-Qibli, the one district that had actually submitted to him, to retaliate against the other 'Alawi *mukataa*s involved in the rebellion and to punish the residents of Latakia who had supported them. This seems only to have strengthened the 'Alawis' resolve, so that throughout the month of October 1834 the Egyptians became mired in an increasingly hopeless guerrilla war, especially in the northern part of the mountain around Bahluliyya, waiting for the arrival of Khalil Shihabi's better-adapted Druze and Maronite highlanders to come relieve them.[97] By this time the revolt had spread and no longer involved only the 'Alawi population but also other parochial groups loath to surrender

93 Ibid., fol. 140a–141a.
94 *Mahfuzat* #3712, #3718, #3732.
95 Ibid. #3733, #3738; CPC Turquie-divers 4, fol. 151a–152a; anonymous, *Hurub Ibrahim Basha al-Misri fi Suriya wa-'l-Anadul*, ed. Asad Rustum (Heliopolis: Syrian Press, [1927]), 1:46–50; A. A. Paton (d. 1874), *A History of the Egyptian Revolution, From the Period of the Mamlukes to the Death of Mohammed Ali*, 2nd ed. (London: Trübner, 1870), 2:117–9; anonymous, *Tarikh al-Umara' al-Shihabiyyin bi-Qalam Ahad Umara'ihim min Wadi Taym*, ed. Salim Hasan Hashshi (Beirut: al-Mudiriyya al-'Amma li'l-Athar, 1971), 205–6; Salih, "Athar al-Hiqab," 2:1–2; see also Sulayman Abu 'Izz al-Din (d. 1932–33), *Ibrahim Basha fi Suriya,* new ed. (Cairo: Dar al-Shuruq, 2006), 190–95.
96 Fathallah Ibn al-Sa'igh, "Al-Muqtarab fi Hawadith al-Hadar wa'l-'Arab," Bibliothèque Nationale (Paris), Ms. Arabe 1685, fol. 61a–62b.
97 *Mahfuzat* #3736, #3746, #3757, #3758, #3762; CPC Turquie-divers 4, fol. 161a–64b.

their arms, in particular in the Sahyun, Jabal al-Akrad, and Qusayr districts northeast of Latakia; the band of Kurdish rebels led by Yunus ("Yunso") Agha, who for a moment seemed to be on the verge of capturing Antioch and Jisr al-Shughur, were said by Russian diplomats of the time to be making common cause with the 'Alawis.[98]

The seriousness of the insurrection in northwestern Syria throughout the autumn of 1834 led several observers to believe it was being coordinated as part of a wider Ottoman campaign to retake control of the region. On 22 October the French consul in Beirut related from "reliable sources" that the 'Alawis had revolted only "on the insistence" of Mehmed Reşid Paşa,[99] a former grand vezir who had been dispatched from Istanbul to set up base in Sivas and marshal a new army to reconquer Syria. A report from the Egyptian governor of Aleppo, coincidentally dated the same day, indicates that a spy from the border region of Rumkale (near 'Urfa) had been able to visit Mehmed Reşid's camp and learned that he was in contact with the 'Alawis; according to this particular account, the correspondence had been initiated by the 'Alawis and relayed by the Egyptian-appointed *mütesellim* of 'Ayntab (Antep).[100] Whatever the case may be, the fact of the 'Alawis' secret contacts with the Ottoman government appears to be substantiated by a remarkable archival letter from 5 December 1834 in which the anonymous writer describes the 'Alawi revolt in some detail and asserts that all the people of the region are waiting for Mehmed Reşid to come deliver them from Ibrahim Paşa's tyranny. "The Egyptian side is losing because the Nusayris are very numerous and powerful. They are looking toward your honor and declare openly that they will rise up collectively when you set out."[101] While the letter might have been overly optimistic in its assessment of the 'Alawis' military prospects (the claim that they destroyed Jisr al-Shughur bridge is, for example, not corroborated by other sources), the uprising may indeed have constituted the Ottomans' best hope for retaking the country on their own and without European intervention. "The emperor of Stamboul could easily have driven his rebellious vassal out of Syria," the French traveler Baptistin Poujoulat commented a short time later, "if he would have sent an army in 1834 to save the peoples of Palestine and Syria who were reaching their arms out to him."[102]

By this time, however, the 'Alawis were no longer in a position to offer any help. After the arrival on 5 November of Emir Khalil al-Shihabi and his forces, estimated at between five and ten thousand men, the combined Lebanese-Egyptian army proceeded to ravage the Bahluliyya district, taking

98 *Mahfuzat* #3767, #3774, #3781; René Cattaui (d. 1994), ed., *Le règne de Mohamed Aly d'après les Archives russes en Egypte* (Cairo: Institut français d'archéologie orientale, 1933), 2-i:182.
99 CPC Turquie-divers 4, fol. 159b.
100 *Mahfuzat* #3769; see also Cattaui, *Le règne de Mohamad Aly*, 2-ii:16.
101 HAT 22354c; transcription in Winter, "La révolte alaouite," 64–66, 71.
102 Baptistin Poujoulat (d. 1864), *Voyage dans l'Asie Mineure* (Paris: Ducollet, 1841), 2:349.

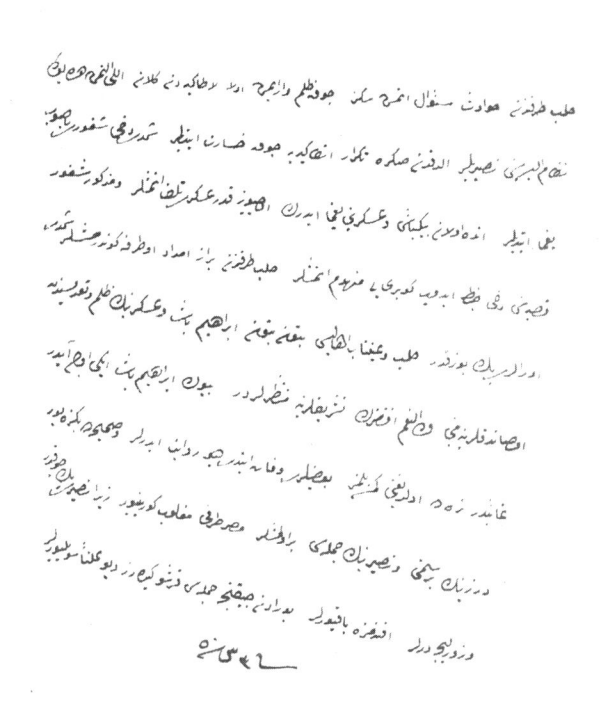

FIGURE 5.2. Ottoman spy report on the 1834 uprising HAT 22354 C
(Başbakanlık Archives, Istanbul)

a huge amount of grain and other plunder and beheading five elderly men, the only villagers to have remained behind, before heading higher up into the Sahyun. The ancient castle of Sahyun, where the rebels had chosen to make their final stand, was invested on 10–11 November, sending the last 'Alawi defenders fleeing with their families to the Bayt al-Shillif. The entire Sahyun district was put to sack, though Khalil is tellingly reported to have given three 'Alawi women at Sahyun their liberty after Bedouin irregulars had tried to keep them as booty.[103] Even while every village was systematically being burned down, the *muqaddam*s of the Kelbiye, Muhalaba, and Banu 'Ali districts came to bring their weapons and offer their submission but disappeared into the forests again once it became clear that Selim Bey was not honoring his promises of safe conduct and was willfully ruining their livelihoods. According to the new French consular agent at Latakia, Lucien Geofroy, the Egyptian administration was, in the end, very displeased with Selim's handling of the revolt, with Ibrahim Paşa issuing him specific orders to stop devastating the area so that the insurgents would more readily lay

103 *Mahfuzat* #3790, #3806; CPC Turquie-divers 4, fol. 164b–67a, Salih, "Athar al-Hiqab," 2:2.

down their arms, pay their tax arrears, and return all that they had stolen in the assault on Latakia two months earlier.[104]

Selim Bey's actions, however, followed a clear economic rationale. In the first place, the large quantities of wheat, barley, and honey taken from the 'Alawi villages allowed him to provision his own forces, which either were billeted in Latakia and causing the local population considerable hardship or remained camped in the mountains, where the advancing season and plentiful rainfall that year made it difficult to bring supplies up by caravan. Some eight hundred head of cattle were also stolen, most of which were apparently shipped abroad.[105] For weeks afterward, moreover, the 'Alawi *muqaddam*s coming to offer their submission in Latakia were obliged to bring several loads of produce from their villages, which Selim Bey immediately reserved for his army. For Ramadan, which began on 1 January 1835, the villagers were furthermore forced to supply the soldiers every day with butter, eggs and chickens. "In all the buyruldus [official patents of safety] which Selim Bey issued the rebels there is never any question of the losses suffered by individuals," Geofroy remarks acidly in one of his weekly reports, "there is only talk of what belongs to the government."[106] Even the disarmament of the highlanders seems to have been largely motivated by profit: carefully noting the population of each village, Selim Bey required the *muqaddam*s to surrender one gun for each individual in the district—even if they had never owned any and now had to purchase one to give the authorities.[107] Perhaps most critical, certainly in the eyes of the French, was the Egyptian regime's apparent attempt to capitalize on the devastation of Latakia's countryside in order to impose its own commercial monopoly on the province. In addition to methodically ruining the Kelbiye district, which had not actually been a center of the revolt but which, as Geofroy notes, was the primary source of Abu Riha tobacco, Latakia's key export commodity traditionally traded by foreign merchants, in late December the government also slapped new customs duties on oil, cotton, and cereals and proceeded to buy up the region's entire yield of gall nuts and pistachios to send on to Egypt. "There is no doubt that Mehmed Ali will soon control all business here, just like in Egypt. He will become the absolute ruler and sole merchant in all the lands under his dominion."[108]

In addition to the economic burden, the Egyptian government also sought to impose its control on the 'Alawi mountains through military conscription. The local population saw this as even worse than disarmament, so that many parents reportedly maimed their children to prevent them from being drafted when the

---

104 CPC Turquie-divers 4, fol. 166b–170a, 191a–196b.
105 Ibid., fol. 165b, 166b, 168b, 192b–193a, 195a, 202a.
106 Ibid., fol. 168a–169a, 169b, 195b, 196a.
107 Ibid., fol. 194b, 195b; *Mahfuzat* #3833.
108 CPC Turquie-divers 4, fol. 191b, 192a, 196a.

Egyptians headed up into the *mukataa*s to round them up in the aftermath of the revolt.[109] Initially Ibrahim Paşa had envisioned taking up to five thousand boys from the northern highlands but in the end contented himself with about twenty-eight hundred—some of whom were sent to the front at Kilis, some of whom deserted soon after, and many of whom were simply garrisoned in the region because they were not considered apt to serve elsewhere.[110] Partially as a result of this first "conscription crisis," 'Alawi resistance continued in some pockets throughout the winter. In late November 1834 rebels from the Jabala district attacked a column of Lebanese reinforcements (including, oddly enough, some seventy Shi'i volunteers from around Bint Jubayl in southern Lebanon) at the Nahr al-Sinn bridge between Marqab and Jabala; at virtually the same time, other 'Alawis were said to be "committing excesses" around Antioch.[111] After the departure of the Lebanese troops in December, 'Uthman Jabbur, the *muqaddam* of the Kelbiye (Qardaha) district, which had been totally destroyed despite his submission, reentered into revolt, while in early February 1835 "brigands" from the Wadi al-'Uyun attacked and plundered a convoy carrying military uniforms near Safita, possibly in protest against conscription efforts in the area.[112] By late June, however, the last of the 'Alawi insurgency seems to have been wiped out, with all the rebels captured in the mountains "enrolled in the military the minute they are deemed fit to serve as soldiers."[113]

For the rest of the occupation, the Egyptians met with little trouble from the chastened 'Alawis. In early 1837 news of Ibrahim Paşa's temporary return to Egypt sparked a small-scale tax revolt in Qardaha, where there were still some rebels who had escaped disarmament two years before by hiding out in the back country. Several of their leaders were finally captured after "la horde de ces mécontens" succeeded in destroying a government-built mill on the road to Tripoli, but these slipped back into the woods after promising to collect their followers' weapons and never returning.[114] By the summer, the French consular agents in Latakia and Alexandretta reported that the local population had still not been entirely disarmed; taxes were so high, meanwhile, that the people of one area near Latakia had indeed been forced to sell their daughters to Egyptian officers to raise the money (apparently

---

109 Ibn al-Sa'igh, "Al-Muqtarab," fol. 78a–80a; Paton, *Egyptian Revolution*, 2:121–22.

110 *Mahfuzat* #3762; CPC Turquie-divers 5, fol. 8b, 10b; Yvette Talhamy, "Conscription among the Nusayris ('Alawis) in the Nineteenth Century," *British Journal of Middle Eastern Studies* 38 (2011): 30–32.

111 CPC Turquie-divers 4, fol. 169b–170b, 184b; *Mahfuzat* #3833; Shidyaq, *Akhbar al-A'yan*, 451–53; Salih, "Athar al-Hiqab," 2:2–3.

112 CPC Turquie-divers 4, fol. 191b, 194b, 211a, 221b, 240a; *Mahfuzat* #3829; Winter, "La révolte alaouite," 62, 67.

113 *Mahfuzat* #3962, #3931, #3988; CPC Turquie-divers 4, fol. 290a, 329a, 354b; CCC Tripoli 18, fol. 319a.

114 CPC Turquie-divers 7, fol. 55a, 120a; *Mahfuzat* #5021.

the incident that was brought to Mehmed Ali's attention, who ordered those responsible to be executed), while others would poke out an eye or cut off a finger or even a whole hand to escape the "barbaric" levying of recruits.[115] An American missionary recounts one of the tricks apparently used by "the wily Ibrahim" to conscript 'Alawis: having initially seized only a disappointing few, he released them again, pretending that "he did not want such—he wanted none for his armies but good Mohammedans." The "liberated Ansairi were greatly pleased at their escape, reported it to their brethren, who came down from their mountains, and were taken in great numbers. The person who related the fact saw nearly a thousand of them marched into Aleppo in chains, to be drilled and trained for soldiers."[116]

The following year, however, once the Druze revolt had begun that would hasten the end of Egyptian rule in Syria, the authorities began to loosen their grip on the 'Alawi mountains. In September 1838 the governor of Tripoli undertook an inspection tour through the 'Akkar and Safita region but does not appear to have attempted to raise troops; by June 1839 several small-scale rebellions were breaking out in the Latakia hinterland, and beginning in July the Egyptians lost control of the Latakia-Aleppo highway for more than a month, despite their stated intentions to keep it open at all costs on account of its strategic significance.[117] In September 1840, when the British navy arrived to bombard Egyptian positions along the coast to help dislodge Ibrahim from Syria and restore Ottoman rule, French diplomats speculated that they were also distributing guns to the 'Alawis as they had to the Druze. This has not been corroborated, however, and the 'Alawis' only contribution to the final revolt against the Egyptians appears to have been pillaging the army's warehouses in Ma'arrat al-Nu'man during its retreat from northern Syria in November.[118] Even if the 'Alawis therefore did not have a direct part in ending the occupation like the Druze (and Shi'is) of Lebanon, they nevertheless seem to have remained conscious of their own role in the steady undermining of Egypt's experiment in modern state control in the region—as suggested among other things by a slightly ambivalent anecdote still recounted years later in Qardaha: upon turning power back over to an Ottoman general at the conclusion of the war, Ibrahim Paşa is claimed to have told him, "You, with the assistance of the English, have expelled me; you have again put arms into the hands of the mountaineers. It cost me nine years and ninety thousand men to disarm them. You will yet invite me back to govern them."[119]

115 CPC Turquie-divers 7, fol. 181a–b, 301a; *Mahfuzat* #5100, #5149.
116 John D. Paxton (d. 1868), *Letters from Palestine: Written during a Residence There in the Years 1836, 7 and 8* (London: Charles Tilt, 1839), 90–91.
117 CPC Turquie-divers 9, fol. 22a; 10, fol. 28b, 100b, 131b.
118 Ibid. 12, fol. 108 b, 258a.
119 Frederick Walpole (d. 1876), *The Ansayrii, or Assassins, with Travels in the Further East, in 1850–51* (London: Richard Bentley, 1851), 3:127.

The place of Ibrahim Paşa in the collective memory of the 'Alawi community ultimately remains uncertain, an uncertainty increasingly colored today by the different historical perspectives of Syrian and Turkish 'Alawi writers. For Arabists such as Muhammad Ghalib al-Tawil and Hashim 'Uthman, as we have seen, Ibrahim Paşa's reign, despite its averred despotism, constitutes a turning point in the community's development, marking the first time 'Alawis became accepted and integrated on an equal footing into wider society and liberating them from the incessant cycle of state discrimination, homegrown feudal oppression, and social banditry. In Syrian 'Alawi historiography, incidentally much like in Lebanese Twelver Shi'i historiography, Ibrahim Paşa therefore represents, in somewhat idealized fashion, the starting point of the community's renaissance in modern times.[120] In contemporary Turkish writing, on the other hand—born, as it is, of the necessity to demonstrate the community's integration into modern republican society, more influenced by Ottoman sources and less preoccupied by sectarianism than its Arabic counterpart—Ibrahim Paşa was and remains a traitor. Mahmut Reyhani (1920–2015), for example, whose three-volume *Gölgesiz Işıklar* ("Shadowless Lights") provides one of the first inside accounts of the 'Alawi community of Hatay, relates to what degree Ibrahim's memory was deprecated in the local tradition. Around Alexandretta, according to the most vivid story of Reyhani's childhood, Ismail "paşa," a petty commoner who had rushed to organize the cutting of timber and forced his fellow 'Alawis into corvée labor on Ibrahim's behalf, was left destitute and ostracized upon the Egyptians' withdrawal. Despite centuries of poverty and mistreatment by Ottoman state officials, the 'Alawis were never anything but the most loyal of the Turkish sultan's subjects.[121]

In the final analysis, the progressive economic and social measures which the Egyptians had hoped to bring to Syria may simply have been implemented too quickly to be accepted by the 'Alawis and other rural highland populations—not least, as Ibrahim Paşa had indeed suspected, by completely overriding and marginalizing their long-standing gentry class. "The Egyptian state worked hard to effect change in Syria, banish old tribal customs, and raise taxes like in any developing country, until most of the people became unhappy and wished for the return of the Turkish state, on account of their ignorance," the Christian Lebanese chronicler Mikha'il Mishaqa (d. 1888) later wrote in reference to the 'Alawi uprising.

> What caused this spirit to spread is what the shaykhs hammered into them at every turn, so that the poor, who are used to submitting to their

---

120 Sabrina Mervin, *Un réformisme chiite: Ulémas et lettrés du Ǧabal 'Āmil (actuel Liban-Sud) de la fin de l'Empire ottoman à l'indépendance du Liban* (Paris: Éditions Karthala, Cermoc et Iféad, 2000), 386.
121 Reyhani, *Gölgesiz Işıklar*, 2:99–101.

leaders [sing. *za'im*], were swayed and convinced to reject the Egyptian state that was spending all that effort to improve and elevate them by weakening the shaykhs' power over them. If the state had followed a policy of flattery and kept the shaykhs or other leaders in their position until it gained the people's hearts, made them feel safe and given them confidence, like in England and every other advanced nation, it could have trusted in and had the support of the people, who would have turned against and rejected their oppressive leaders. Had it followed this policy the result would have been better. Instead, every time it conquered an area it undertook to cut the head but let the body heal itself. The people are naturally predisposed to blind submission to their leader, so that being independent is the worst thing that can happen to them. The Turkish state understood the situation of the people better than the Egyptian state.[122]

The success of the Ottomans' own reform efforts would depend in large part on their ability to avoid the mistakes of the Egyptians and work within the parameters of 'Alawi society and its traditional leaderships.

A WORLD RESTORED

With the departure of the last Egyptian troops in 1841, northwestern Syria became a theater of conflict and instability as Ottoman officials and local feudal factions scrambled to reassert their former power. The disarray is partially reflected in the paucity of sources for the first decade after the Ottomans' return. In principle the imperial government had announced the end of *iltizam* tax farming with the Gülhane reform decree of 1839; in practice it soon had to revert to its former intermediaries in many hinterland areas such as the 'Alawi mountains. In Safita, as already indicated, the *shar'iyya* court records suggest that the Bayt Raslan were again dominant and behaving oppressively toward the local population in 1847; a battle between them and the Shamsin family necessitated the intervention of the governor of Homs in the fall of that same year.[123] In the neighborhood of Homs itself, 'Alawi factions were colluding with Bedouin from the desert interior to attack and plunder farmers, or fighting turf battles against the Dandashli clan of Tall Kalakh, henceforth their most serious adversaries in the area. At the same time, according to British consular officials (who had become very active in the region after the Egyptian withdrawal and increasingly competed with

---

122 Mikha'il Mishaqa, *Mashhad al-'Iyan bi-Hawadith Suriya wa-Lubnan* (Cairo: n.p., 1908), 115.
123 TShCR 33:263; Joseph Catafago, "Die Drei Messen der Nossairier," *Zeitschrift der Deutschen Morgenländischen Gesellschaft* 2 (1848): 388–89.

the French for the "protection" of minorities), other 'Alawi villagers were being victimized by sectarian violence in the foothills west of Hama or being oppressed along with the rest of the rural population in Antioch.[124] The governing council of Aleppo for its part complained that 'Alawi brigands from across the border in Damascus or Sayda were once again attacking Qal'at al-Madiq in Aleppo province.[125]

Be that as it may, the restoration of Ottoman rule was not merely a return to the status quo ante. The Ottomans were aware of the weakness of their government in the region and began to intervene more directly and often with greater nuance in local affairs, as documented in a wealth of new records compiled and kept by the Sublime Porte (more precisely the grand vezirate, usually referred to now as the Sadaret) and its increasingly specialized bureaus in the Tanzimat reform era. Still in 1848, to cite one salient example, an exchange of missives between the Chancery Office (Mektubi Kalemi), the Provincial Correspondence Office (Amedi Kalemi), and the newly instituted Supreme Judicial Council (Meclis-i Vala) refers to a minor factional dispute among 'Alawis in Safita, where one of the leaders responsible was initially sentenced to the galleys (*kürek*) but then received a "writ of reconciliation" (*istilamname*) to present to the governor of Sayda and was released, after his adversary had been captured and sent into punitive exile at Sinop on the Black Sea. (His family was finally given formal permission to return home to Safita six years later, in 1854).[126] The reformist government's primary means of infiltrating, rearranging, and colonizing local society, to reprise Timothy Mitchell's terms, was of course still military conscription. The Ottoman Nizamiye or regular army, inspired in large part by the Egyptian experience and predominantly manned by conscripts, was created in 1843; precise rules governing the levying of troops in each province by drawing lots (*kura*) were established in 1848.[127] The state's first task was to carry out a complete new census of the population that could be drawn on, the first such undertaking since the Tahrir tax surveys of the sixteenth and seventeenth centuries. In the coastal mountains the new Nüfus Defterleri (population registers) begin to record the 'Alawi military service–age population of the Cebel-i Kelbiye and other districts attached to the province of Hama in December 1846.[128]

---

124 National Archives, London (Kew): Foreign Office [FO] 78/1118, unnumbered folios, Dec. 23, 1854, Jan. 20, 1855, March 15, 1855.

125 İ.DH 265/16558.

126 BOA: A.MKT 103/44; A.MKT 139/12; A.AMD 5/16; İ.MSM 76/2173, 2174, 2175; A.MKT. UM 169/55; see also Hasan, *A'lam*, 1:104–5.

127 Erik J. Zürcher, "The Ottoman Conscription System in Theory and Practice, 1844–1918," in *The Young Turk Legacy and Nation Building: From the Ottoman Empire to Atatürk's Turkey*, ed. Zürcher (London: I. B. Tauris, 2010), 156–60.

128 BOA: NFS.d 3746.

Needless to say, the actual conscription did not proceed as smoothly as hoped for in 'Alawi areas. Both British and French diplomats report considerable opposition as the Ottomans attempted to levy troops in Tripoli province in the autumn and spring of 1851–52, especially in the inaccessible northern districts of Bayt al-Shillif, Qardaha, Muhalaba, and Samt al-Qibli, as well as in the Wadi al-'Uyun near Safita, whose inhabitants were all "under arms" and refusing to provide any men.[129] Chancery and provincial correspondence records show that the sultan, Abdülmecid I, was personally informed of the troubles encountered with the Nusayris but had no advice other than to ask the (Beirut-based) *vali* of Sayda, under whose overall authority Latakia now fell, to redouble his efforts.[130] The French consul-general in Beirut, for his part, citing the failed campaign as yet more evidence of the weakness of Ottoman imperial government in Syria, claimed to know for sure that the resistance of the 'Alawis and other tribes of the interior was the work of 'Abbas Paşa, grandson of Mehmed Ali and viceroy (*khedive*) of Egypt.[131] The following year, when the reverend Lyde arrived in Latakia to commence his mission among the 'Alawis of the Qardaha area, the city and countryside were again in upheaval over the levies being made in view of the impending Crimean War.[132]

Even in the midst of the Crimean War, the state authorities continued to take an interest in local affairs in the mountains and manage societal conflicts rather than just impose order. In the late fall of 1854 the Sublime Porte took notice of a violent quarrel which had been brewing for some time (originally over a stolen cucumber, according to Lyde) between the Muhalaba and Qardaha districts, ordering the deputy governor (*kaimakam*) of Latakia to raise popular troops (*nefir-i amm*) in the adjoining districts and go and mediate; he was promptly killed in an engagement with the belligerents.[133] Both Lyde, who wound up arranging for his burial and that of numerous other fighters killed the same day, and the French consul in Beirut recount the almost farcical chain of events that had led to this disaster: the *kaimakam* had originally summoned the shaykhs of Qardaha to Latakia on the pretext of wanting to talk with them, thinking he would quiet things by throwing them in jail, then headed into the mountains to collect their outstanding tax dues. During his absence, however, a party of seventy or more 'Alawi raiders had descended on the city to break open the *saray* prison and reclaim their hostages, whereupon the *kaimakam* flouted his orders to exercise restraint and undertook the ill-fated attack on Qardaha. His precipitate actions were

---

129 FO 78/910, fol. 58b, 244a, 272a–273b; CPC Turquie-Beyrouth 10, fol. 28b; Salih, "Athar al-Hiqab," 2:6–7.
130 A.MKT.MHM 46/19; A.AMD 37/70.
131 CPC Turquie-Beyrouth 10, fol. 43b, 63b.
132 Lyde, *Asian Mystery*, 193–94; see also Al Ma'ruf, *Tarikh*, 3:233–39.
133 A.MKT.UM 178/24; MVL 284/69.

subsequently condemned by the reformist governor of Sayda, Vamık Paşa, who appointed a new *kaimakam* to Latakia in the hopes of restarting the mediation process among the 'Alawi population, though apparently to little avail.[134]

Over the next two years the Ottoman authorities struggled to maintain control over the northern highlands, appointing a *müdir* (director) or state tax collector to each district, in replacement of the old tax-farming system, and repeatedly sending troops, particularly against the ever-refractory Qardaha and Bayt al-Shillif districts, when their payments fell in arrears.[135] Just as often, however, the Meclis-i Vala judicial council in Istanbul (the principle organism tasked with elaborating and instituting the Tanzimat) or the foreign consular corps in Syria bemoaned the fact that various 'Alawi factions were always fighting each other and thereby causing harm to commerce and the general welfare of the region.[136] Nor did things improve after the conclusion of the Crimean War. In late 1857 the Shillif clan continued to attract attention with their robberies in the Latakia area; throughout the spring and summer of 1858, imperial records deplore numerous acts of 'Alawi brigandage against (predominantly Sunni) villages around Antioch, Badama (Qusayr), and Jisr al-Shughur, detail the deployment of Nizamiye troops, and direct the restitution of the stolen goods to the villagers.[137] Around the same time, the British vice-consuls at Damascus and Latakia report on 'Alawi attacks on Christian villages near Hama and begin to speculate openly about the division of the entire coastal mountain region into sectarian statelets, should the Ottoman government finally lose control and be forced to concede it independence.[138] In November 1858 the Sublime Porte ordered four companies of reinforcements to be sent to Qardaha after an assault on government troops, and a year later the French could report that the 'Alawis had been severely reduced,[139] but after another winter of internecine warfare, brigandage, and punitive campaigning, even the imperial chancery had to admit, in February 1860, that the "Nusayri faction's abominable actions have only gotten worse," and that yet more troops would be necessary.[140] "Such a thing as a just uniform system of government is a thing unknown in the outlying provinces of Turkey," Reverend Lyde remarked in typically pessimistic manner at the time. "The Ottomans only retain Syria by setting tribe against tribe, making use of

---

134 Lyde, *Asian Mystery*, 194, 198–205; CPC Turquie-Beyrouth 10, 333b–336a; MVL 287/67; see also Salih, "Athar al-Hiqab," 2:9–11.
135 A.MKT.MVL 74/84; A.MKT.MHM 757/110.
136 MVL 310/98; FO 78/1297, fol. 118a–119a.
137 İ.DH 389/25724; İ.DH 393/26006; İ.DH 409/27058; MVL 750/107.
138 FO 78/1388, fol. 233b–234a, 237b–238a, 320a–321a; FO 195/601, unnumbered fol., 6 April 1858.
139 İ.DH 415/27493; İ.DH 416/27528; CPC Turquie-Beyrouth 11, fol. 304a; Al Ma'ruf, *Tarikh*, 3:243–45.
140 MVL 754/87; A.MKT.UM 395/98.

one to weaken and subdue the other, thus fostering desolating feuds among neighbors, which the forces at the command of government are utterly unable to check, even when desirous of doing so."[141]

If the northern 'Alawi mountains descended into seemingly total anarchy in this period, the South around Safita witnessed what might be considered the last incarnation of classical *ayan*-based Ottoman provincial rule. Isma'il Khayr-Bey was the most celebrated 'Alawi leader of his time, not least on account of the somewhat histrionic, forty-page article on his career published by the French vice-consul in Tripoli, Isidore Blanche, in the *Revue européenne* immediately after his death in 1858.[142] Isma'il was the son of 'Uthman Khayr-Bey, head of the Matawira "tribe" and sometime *mültezim* of Qardaha (see chapter 4). Along with his older brother Khayri (or Khayr-Bey, leading to the frequent confusion of the two brothers in the sources), he had supposedly been one of the most famous robbers of the entire mountain, corresponding squarely in Blanche's description to the archetypical Mediterranean social bandit of the time, "un brigand émérite et redouté qui passa toute sa vie à désobéir aux ordres de la Sublime Porte ... il est connu au loin dans le pays par toutes les qualités qui constituent le vrai brigand du désert: pilleur infatigable, vindicatif, brave, généreux, fidèle à ses compagnons."[143] British reports agree that Isma'il "has for some time past sent his people to plunder" the villages of the Hama region, his example leading other "Anserians" of the Kelbiye mountains to follow suit.[144] Local legend moreover claims the Ottomans intermittently recognized him as an irregular troop commander (*delibaşı*); that he was endowed with magical abilities; or that he and his brother were for a while imprisoned in Istanbul, before their sister managed to infiltrate the harem of some high officeholder and set them free.[145]

In fact Isma'il owed his rise to an attempt at administrative reform in Safita: in the spring of 1855, Vamık Paşa, the *müşir* (the new Tanzimat-era term for provincial field marshal, equivalent to governor) of Sayda, realizing that his government appointees were unable to keep the peace in the district, ordered it to be subdivided into four individual *müdirlik*s or tax collectorships, and assigned to the leading branches of the Shamsin family—in essence a return to the *hilla* system of the eighteenth century. This, according to Blanche, wakened the jealousies of some lesser family members, who promptly sought the Khayr-Beys' help. Accompanied by three hundred or more men, Isma'il set out

---

141 Lyde, *Asian Mystery*, 208–9.
142 Charles-Isidore Blanche (d. 1887), "Études sur la Syrie: L'ansarié Kaïr-Beik," *Revue européenne: Lettres, sciences, arts, voyages, politique* 2/12 (1860): 384–402, 582–601.
143 CPC Turquie-Beyrouth 10, 346b–347a ("An accomplished, redoubtable brigand who spent his whole life disobeying the Sublime Porte ... he is known far and wide for all the qualities that make a real desert brigand: indefatigable pillager, vindictive, brave, generous, loyal to his companions").
144 FO 195/601, unnumbered fol., 6 April 1858; 14 June 1858.
145 Blanche, "L'ansarié Kaïr-Beik," 390–91; Dussaud, *Histoire et religion*, 34–37; Hasan, *A'lam*, 2:33–34.

from his robber den in the Kelbiye district to take control of Safita, reparcel it into six or even eight *müdirlik*s to bestow on his clients (who trembled in fear of him themselves), and generally subjugate the entire area. Eager to avoid further disorder, the Ottomans accepted Isma'il's profession of loyalty and formally named him *müdir* of Safita in April 1855.[146] Blanche, who had intervened with the authorities in Tripoli and Beirut to guarantee Isma'il's safety and later had every interest in sensationalizing his deeds, describes with evident delight how Isma'il reigned *"en maître absolu"* over 120,000 highlanders, building himself an absurdly sumptuous palace at Draykish, collecting huge amounts of taxes, and styling himself "pacha" or "muschir" (*müşir*) of the entire mountain.[147]

Of course he was never recognized as such by the Ottomans. In July 1857 the Sublime Porte ordered an investigation into reports that Isma'il, in addition to his usual tyranny and oppression of the local population, had recently begun to build or restore a number of fortresses in the southern highlands between Safita and Qal'at al-Husn (Hisn al-Akrad); around the same time, the French also had a change of heart, owing to his alleged mistreatment of Christians, and began to take up contact with Shaykh 'Abbas, an 'Alawi religious shaykh critical of Isma'il, about secretly stirring up strife against him.[148] What is true is that the Ottomans, in hopes of placating or appeasing (*celb*) not only Isma'il but the entire 'Alawi community as well, in July 1858 decided to confer on him the Order of Merit (*nişan*), fifth degree, for his services as *müdir* of Safita.[149] Isma'il's greatest conflict was in the end not with the government of Sayda but with the Dandashli clan, with whom he had a long-standing feud and who especially resented his efforts to extend his influence in Qal'at al-Husn, part of the *sancak* of Homs and therewith under the overall authority of the governor of Damascus.[150] In late October the British consul in Damascus could report that a "collision" had occurred between Isma'il Khayr-Bey and the Dandashlis, "the latter assisted by the regular troops and Bashee Bozooks [mounted irregulars] in the pay of the government, in which a good many lives were lost"; ten days later the Ottoman commander Tahir Paşa and eight thousand men joined in the pursuit of Isma'il and his adherents, "who are retreating from Safita into the

---

146 CPC Turquie-Beyrouth 10, fol. 346a–47b, 357a–b, 359a–60b, 368b.

147 Blanche, "L'ansarié Kaïr-Beik," 392–97; cf. Yvette Talhamy, "The Nusayri Leader Isma'il Khayr Bey and the Ottomans (1854–58)," *Middle Eastern Studies* 44 (2008): 897–98.

148 BOA: HR.MKT 197/48; CPC Turquie-Beyrouth 11, fol. 159a–60b, 227a–b. The message was intercepted by the governor of Sayda, Hurşid Mehmed Paşa, who shared it with the British; see FO 195/587, unnumb. fol., May 13, 1858.

149 A.AMD 83/17; İ.HR 157/8341.

150 A.MKT.UM 337/3; FO 195/601, unnumbered fol., 20 Oct. 1858; Dussaud, *Histoire et religion*, 37–38; see also Caesar Farah, *The Politics of Interventionism in Ottoman Lebanon, 1830–1861* (London: I. B. Tauris, 2000), 540; Talhamy, "Nusayri Leader," 900.

fastnesses of the Ansayrié Mountains facing the plain of Hama."[151] Hated by much of the local population (of whom a number apparently responded to calls to wage "jihad" against him) and abandoned by most of his erstwhile supporters, Isma'il was finally surrounded by Damascene troops in the 'Alawi village of 'Ayn al-Kurum and killed through the treachery of his own uncle. On 15 November Isma'il's severed head as well as those of a brother and several of his children were brought to Damascus to be displayed before the government *saray*.[152] A year later, seven of his last remaining followers were captured and also sent to Damascus to be executed, with an imperial firman ordering "that one day's interval should be allowed ... to give the prisoners an opportunity to embrace Mohamedanism. They were decapitated in different parts of the town.... The people looked on the executions with indifference, regarding the men as infidels."[153]

Despite the great notoriety of Isma'il Khayr-Bey's challenge to the establishment, it essentially changed very little for the 'Alawis. The main beneficiaries of his demise, as noted by the British consul in Damascus, were the Shamsins, who had sided with the "Sultan's Commanders" and now stood to be reappointed to their traditional post in Safita.[154] The French, for their part, were principally concerned that Isma'il still owed one of their protégés—the Algerian emir 'Abd al-Qadir—considerable sums of money, which they now asked the Ottoman government to collect from his heirs. "The principal debtor, Mohamed Havach [Hawwash] son of Ismail Khaÿri-Bey, is rich and perfectly capable of paying this sum," internal correspondence between French diplomats in November 1859 reveals. "This Havach is an employee of the caïmacam [district governor] of Homs and Hama, and consequently within reach of the Damascus authorities."[155] The Khayr-Bey family was certainly not wiped out: one of Isma'il's grandsons would apply to enter Sultan Abdülhamid's "tribal school" toward the end of the century (see next chapter). If anything, the episode once again demonstrated the community's greatest weaknesses, namely, the complete lack of unity among its various district or clan leaderships that precluded any sort of joint response to the challenges posed by creeping government imposition, increasing foreign interference, and better organized local rivals; as well as the ultimate refusal of the British and French, despite their constant lamentation over the 'Alawis' situation

---

151 FO 78/1388, fol. 50a–b, 52a–53a; FO 78/1386 and FO 195/587, unnumbered fol., 26 Oct., 27 Oct., 1 Nov. 1858.

152 FO 78/1386 and 195/587, unnumbered fol., 22 Nov., 23 Nov. 1858; CPC Turquie-Beyrouth 11, fol. 244a–245b; Blanche, "L'ansarié Kaïr-Beik," 593–600; Talhamy, "Nusayri Leader," 902–5; Al Ma'ruf, *Tarikh*, 3:327–38.

153 FO 195/601, unnumbered fol., 27 April, 20 Dec. 1859.

154 FO 78/1388, fol. 58b; FO 195/601, unnumbered fol., 16 Nov. 1858.

155 Centre des archives diplomatiques, Nantes [CADN]: Représentations diplomatiques et consulaires, Damas-Consulat 72, 17 Oct., 4 Nov. 1859.

under Ottoman rule, to defend them in the same way as the Druze and Catholics of the region. What little improvement in the 'Alawis' condition could be expected would finally have to come from within the parameters of the Tanzimat themselves.

THE STRUGGLE OVER SCHOOLING

The years before and after the Hatt-ı Hümayun of 1856, the imperial rescript that extended full legal equality to the empire's non-Muslim populations, were marked by political instability and considerable sectarian tensions throughout western Syria. Adopted in large part at the urging of Britain and France, who had come to the Ottomans' aid in the war against Russia, this key measure of the Tanzimat reforms not only consecrated the Great Powers' decisive influence over the hereafter "sick man of Europe" but also went significantly further in the way of upending the traditional hierarchies of power and standing among the confessional groups of the region. In Lebanon a Maronite peasant revolt in the Kisrawan in 1858 turned into an open sectarian war among Druze and Maronites and ultimately led to a massacre of Christians in Damascus in 1860; in Latakia the Greek Orthodox population, fearing similar attacks by their Muslim neighbors, fled their homes to take shelter at the French and Austrian consulates or even with 'Alawi families in the hills.[156] In this generalized atmosphere of sectarian hostility, local officials felt free to commit numerous exactions against the 'Alawi population as well over the next years.[157] In 1866, after the entire region—minus the governorate of Mount Lebanon—had been reorganized in the Ottoman provincial reform of 1864 as the "*vilayet* of Syria," the mountains above Latakia witnessed another conscription crisis that could only be put down by force in the Kelbiye district.[158] A source of tension remembered as particularly significant by the 'Alawis and other rural communities in Syria today was the Land Law of 1858, which led to many agricultural areas being registered in the names of urban-based absentee landowners and the peasants reduced to the status of tenants, if not serfs.[159] In the spring of 1870, furthermore, the governor of Syria, Râşid Mehmed Paşa, dealt the "malfaiteurs Ansariés" of both Safita and the Kelbiye a devastating blow, taking two infantry battalions and two mortars to subjugate a number of inaccessible villages that had apparently never been under true state control before. In addition to a

156 FO 226/133, "Xtian massacres: Repercussions at Latakia, + elsewhere," passim.
157 BOA: HR.TO 287/4; A.MKT.MHM 349/68; A.MKT.MHM 357/39; İ.DH 559/38933; Salih, "Athar al-Hiqab," 2:13–24.
158 A.MKT MHM 405/92; A.MKT.MHM 419/14; DH.MKT 1311/27.
159 Al-Tawil, *Tarikh al-'Alawiyyin*, 459–61; Fabrice Balanche, *La région alaouite et le pouvoir syrien* (Paris: Karthala, 2006), 30–32; Al Ma'ruf, *Tarikh al-'Alawiyyin fi Bilad al-Sham*, 3:242–43.

heavy war indemnity and outright plunder, the Ottoman forces also took dozens of 'Alawi shaykhs as prisoners, leaving the area, at least according to French and Russian diplomats, in more abject misery than ever before.[160]

At the same time, however, there are signs of a new angle in the government's approach toward the 'Alawi population. Rebels seized during these campaigns were no longer condemned on the basis of their religious identity but were subjected to some sort of due process, as supervised and recorded by the Interior Ministry (Dahiliye Nezareti).[161] In May 1862, moreover, the *müdir* of Jisr al-Shughur himself, a Sunni Muslim, was ordered arrested, and his fortress-residence destroyed, after he had too mercilessly pursued the local 'Alawis over taxes the previous month. (He was nevertheless able to escape and took refuge with the British vice-consul in Latakia).[162] In the spring of 1867 a specially constituted Meclis-i Deavi (Judicial Assembly), one of several new administrative councils created on the municipal level with the provincial reform of 1864, held a formal inquest in Homs into the activities of the 'Alawi brigand Sulayman al-Salit and his band around the towns of Shin and Hisn al-Akrad. A thick dossier, containing an extensive transcript of Salit's interrogation by the Meclis, an Ottoman-Turkish translation of the same, and a detailed *jurnal* (official report) of the investigation, was forwarded to Istanbul for approval.[163] In early 1868 the *mutasarrıf* (deputy governor) of Tripoli put down another revolt in the Banu 'Ali and Bayt al-Shillif districts but left the equally bothersome Qarahala, Saramita, and Bayt Yashut areas untouched after he had restored order. Shortly after, 'Alawi notables from the Bahluliyya, Jabal al-Akrad, Sahyun, and other districts petitioned the *mutasarrıf* in order to reduce the number of conscripts demanded from them.[164] His successor's policy was even described by the French consul as one of "douceur et persuasion," unfortunately taken as a sign of weakness by the 'Alawis and therefore to blame for their renewed sedition in 1870.[165]

Even more important was education. In principle the Tanzimat purposed the introduction of universal elementary schooling and the development of modern institutions of higher learning in the empire, particularly in fields deemed vital for military and technological advancement. In practice, however, the state did not have the wherewithal to compete against the extensive network

---

160 DH.MKT 1311/32; DH.MKT 1311/40; İ.DH 612/42642, 42686; CPC Turquie-Beyrouth 19, fol. 147a–157a, 160a–164a; Salih, "Athar al-Hiqab," 2:30–35; Dussaud, *Histoire et religion*, 38; Al Ma'ruf, *Tarikh*, 3:246–97.
161 DH.MKT 1311/40.
162 A.MKT.UM 566/12; Salih, "Athar al-Hiqab," 2:22.
163 İ.DA 1/9.
164 A.MKT.MHM 419/14; Talhamy, "Conscription," 37.
165 CPC Turquie-Beyrouth 19, fol. 157a–b; see also Salih, "Athar al-Hiqab," 2:31–33; Max Gross, "Ottoman Rule in the Province of Damascus, 1860–1909" (PhD diss., Georgetown University, 1979), 132–33.

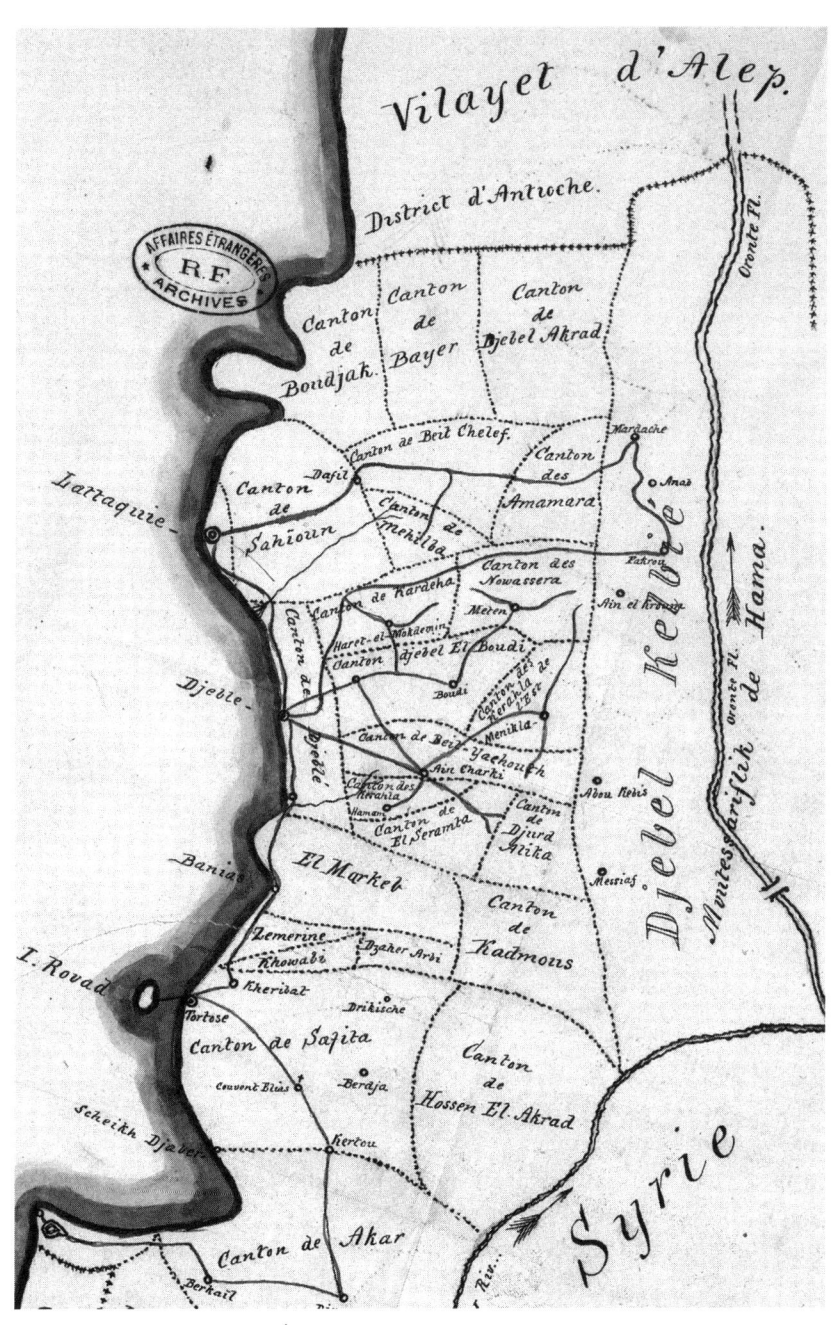

FIGURE 5.3. French sketch map of Latakia province, 1870 (Ministère des Affaires étrangères, La Courneuve: CPC Turquie-Beyrouth 19, fol. 164a)

of private confessional schools being implanted by foreign missionaries since the start of the century. It is only with the promulgation of the "Statute of General Education" (Maarif-i Umumiye Nizamnamesi) in 1869 that the government began in earnest to put in place a "national" system of secular education throughout its territory.[166] In certain sensitive areas the first state schools had been founded earlier. Already in December 1867, most notably for our purposes, the Supreme Administrative Council recommended the building of a secondary school (*mekteb-i rüşdiye*) in Latakia specifically "for the children of the Islamic, Nusayri, and Christian sects" and asked the Ministry of Education (Nezaret-i Maarif) to set aside moneys for teachers in the district.[167] After his campaign into the 'Alawi mountains in the spring of 1870, Raşid Paşa stayed on for two months to oversee the construction of not only military fortifications and new government buildings but schools as well.[168] In Antioch, an imperial order (*irade*) was given to build schools and mosques for the local 'Alawi community in May 1870. This appears to have resulted from the intervention of the mufti of Aleppo, after a number of 'Alawis around Antioch had lawfully embraced Islam but continued to have their use of mosques in the district "looked upon coldly" by the Sunnis. In July 1871 the governor of Aleppo was alerted a second time that the 'Alawi converts were still being excluded.[169]

If the mufti's rationale for providing modern schools was, in his own terms, "to lift the Nusayri sect out of the vale of ignorance and segregation" and thereby favor their integration into the Islamic communion, the Ministry of Education was above all concerned with countering the growing presence of foreign-sponsored confessional institutions. The pioneers of Christian caritative and evangelical work among the 'Alawis were American Protestants under the supervision of the American Board of Commissioners for Foreign Missions (ABCFM). ABCFM ministers first began to distribute bibles in the hinterland of Latakia in 1830–31 and over the next years repeatedly called for the establishment of a permanent mission to "that very peculiar ... and most needy people, the Nusairiyeh.... An outcast, degraded, oppressed people, without books, schools or guides of any kind, they offer a large field, and present strong claims upon Christian benevolence. Some of us have travelled among them extensively, and ... they professed a willingness to receive missionaries and to send their children to school."[170] The ABCFM's plans were

---

166 Niyazi Berkes, *The Development of Secularism in Turkey*, facsimile ed. (London: Hurst, 1998), 100, 106, 173–74, 179–80; Selçuk Akşin Somel, *The Modernization of Public Education in the Ottoman Empire, 1839–1908: Islamization, Autocracy and Discipline* (Leiden: Brill, 2001), esp. 83–99.
167 MVL 567/25.
168 Gross, "Ottoman Rule," 163; see also 'Uthman, *Tarikh al-Ladhiqiyya*, 91–93.
169 İ.DH 611/42613 (catalog description); BEO AYN.d 867.
170 Kamal Salibi and Yusuf Khoury, eds., *The Missionary Herald: Reports from Ottoman Syria, 1819–1870* (Amman: Royal Institute for Inter-Faith Studies, 1995), 4:17–19; Winter, "Nusayris before the Tanzimat," 99.

interrupted by the Egyptian occupation, the turmoil of 1860, and finally the American Civil War. When they began founding their first schools in northern Syria in the mid-1850s, in a period that has been described as "the decade of many missions," it was in competition with English Presbyterians and Anglicans such as Samuel Lyde, who already in the summer of 1852 had undertaken an extended trip throughout the coastal mountains to report on the possibilities of setting up a Church of England school among the 'Alawis.[171] Catholic missionary efforts in this time were overwhelmingly focused on Lebanon, where both Britain and France were already committed to the "protection" of the Druze and Maronites, respectively. The American Protestant missions therefore perhaps indeed constituted "the closest the Alawites came to enjoying a foreign benefactor" in the region.[172]

This was, however, a challenge to imperial authority that the Ottomans intended to meet. In late December 1872 the new governor of Syria, Abdüllatif Subhi Paşa (himself a historian, translator of Ibn Khaldun, and former minister of education), sounded the alarm over the failure of state education in Syria and over how many children (especially in Beirut) were enrolled in foreign institutions:

> Because there are no schools for the subjects of His Majesty the Padişah other than small and disorganized boys' schools [*sıbyan mekatibi*], everyone is forced to send their children to the aforesaid foreign schools, and these children do not learn the foundations of religion and the stipulations of faith, nor how to distinguish between right and wrong. Syria's non-Muslims are in any case inclined toward the foreigners because many of them are in the care of Catholic, Protestant or Orthodox teachers. As for the Nusayri, Druze and Mütevali sects, who outwardly show themselves to be Muslim and do not display their particular beliefs, they are prepared to accept any religion or sect and then forget it again. With all sorts of incitement and false representations the teachers of these schools therefore proselytize the Christians, Nusayris and Druze (or in the case of the Iranians, the Mütevalis, whose beliefs are close to the Imami religion) and convert them to their confessions, with which they themselves are in agreement.

---

171 A. L. Tibawi, *American Interests in Syria, 1800–1901: A Study of Educational, Literary and Religious Work* (Oxford: Clarendon Press, 1966), 150–59; Samuel Lyde, *The Ansyreeh and Ismaeleeh: A Visit to the Secret Sects of Northern Syria; with a View to the Establishment of Schools* (London: Hurst and Blackett, 1853).

172 Leon Goldsmith, "'God Wanted Diversity': Alawite Pluralist Ideals and Their Integration into Syrian Society 1832–1973," *British Journal of Middle East Studies* 40 (2013): 398; see also Yvette Talhamy, "American Protestant Missionary Activity among the Nusayris (Alawis) of Syria in the Nineteenth Century," *Middle Eastern Studies* 47 (2011): 215–36; Alkan, "Fighting for the Nusayrī Soul," 33–41.

The governor goes on to cite the example of an 'Alawi village near Qardaha, where several locals had ostensibly converted after the opening of a Protestant school (the reference is likely to Samuel Lyde's mission), as well as to a number of schools opened illegally in Druze villages in the Hawran (southern Syria), which should immediately be shut down and replaced with teachers paid for by the provincial government.[173] A year later the Sublime Porte indeed ordered all the Protestant schools in Syria closed, including twenty-five run by the American Reformed Presbyterian Mission in the mountains east and southeast of Latakia. "The persecution near Latakia was brutal and violent," a leading member of the American mission asserted at the time. "[T]he Turks have closed the door to all Christian light for the pagan Nusairiyeh, resolved on making them Moslems."[174]

The schools were eventually reopened after British diplomats began to intervene more aggressively on the 'Alawis behalf, defending their need for Western education and securing military exemptions for 'Alawis deemed to have truly converted to Christianity.[175] For the 'Alawi community there were of course certain risks in being too closely associated with foreign interests. Conversions to Islam, as we have seen, were met with skepticism; conversions to Christianity, with outright hostility. In September 1873, for example, the Foreign Ministry (Nezaret-i Hariciye) followed up complaints by the foreign consular corps that an 'Alawi convert who had found work in a local missionary school was summarily arrested and sent to jail in Damascus, where he was subjected to insults and beatings; a presumably 'Alawi resident of Maraş who had likewise "turned Christian" (*tenassur etmesi üzerine*) was seized and taken to prison in Aleppo and his family deported to Izmir.[176] Certainly the most famous 'Alawi proselyte of this period was Sulayman al-Adani. Following his conversion, al-Adani in 1863 published *Al-Bakura al-Sulaymaniyya*, a detailed exposition of 'Alawi beliefs, initiation, and ritual that long formed the only basis of Western knowledge about the religion as such. The correspondents of the American *Missionary Herald* reported breathlessly how Adani had converted first to Islam, then to Greek Orthodoxy, and then to Judaism, before embracing the truth of Protestantism—only to realize resentfully, in early 1864, that "Soleyman, the *professedly* converted Nusairy, after printing his book in Beirut, . . . has gone over to the Greek church and the bottle, hoping to secure the daughter of a Greek priest in marriage. His *book* will doubtless do good, but *he* bids fair to go to ruin."[177] "There have been several defections

---

173 A.MKT.MHM 450/53.

174 Henry Harris Jessup (d. 1910), *Fifty-Three Years in Syria* (New York: Fleming H. Revell, 1910), 2:436.

175 FO 78/2282, 26 May, 19 Sept., 12 Oct., 27 Oct. 1873; İ.HR 266/15960–61.ii–iii; Talhamy, "Missionary Activity," 227–28.

176 İ.HR 266/15960–61.i.

177 *Missionary Herald*, 5:59–61, 87, 97.

from the Protestant ranks in the past year ... in different parts of the land, one being that of Soleyman Effendi, who ... has now given himself up to the habits of drunkenness, embraced the Greek church again, and written a book against Protestantism."[178] By 1866 the Americans were admitting that a good 50 percent of their converts, "among whom are all the Nusaireeyeh," had turned away and relapsed into their old faith.[179]

It was not his rejection of Protestantism, however, that proved Sulayman al-Adani's undoing. In 1875 a fifty-page précis of the *Bakura* in Ottoman Turkish was prepared by Mustafa bin Ebi Bekir el-Kayseri, a minor religious scholar from Adana, at the behest of the local Sunni clergy. The manuscript, entitled "Damigü'n-Nusayriye" ("Refutation of Nusayrism") and augmented by a description of 'Alawi feasts in various different neighborhoods of Adana, was apparently never published.[180] Sometime later Sulayman is reported to have been murdered by his former 'Alawi coreligionists in Tarsus for having divulged the secrets of the faith, though there has never been any concrete evidence of this.[181] Many of the claims made in his book are anyhow contested by Syrian 'Alawis or dismissed as ridiculous down to the present day.[182]

THE PLIGHT OF THE MINORITIES

The Protestant crusade to educate (and proselytize) the 'Alawis was only one aspect of the Western powers' own progressive infiltration and rearrangement of local society in Syria in the closing decades of the nineteenth century. British and French consular reports from the 1870s demonstrate not only an unprecedented firsthand, insider knowledge of Syrian provincial politics, and readiness to interfere in the appointment of Ottoman government officials, but also a new level of cooperation with each other in what sometimes literally amounted to gunboat diplomacy. In the opinion of the (honorary) British vice-consul at Latakia, to illustrate the first point, not only had the building of roads and schools in the district been badly neglected, but a tax abatement scheme originally promised the 'Alawis by Raşid Paşa had been revoked by his inept successor Subhi Paşa—creating disorder in the entire area, which the deputy governor's periodic raids did little to eradicate, while pushing a steady stream of 'Alawi families to emigrate to Adana.[183] The situ-

178 Ibid., 117.
179 Ibid., 144.
180 Atatürk Kitaplığı, Istanbul: ms. Osman Ergin 97.
181 Dussaud, *Histoire et religion*, xiii.
182 Al-Tawil, *Tarikh al-'Alawiyyin*, 447–48; al-Ibrahim, *Al-'Alawiyyun bayna'l-Ghuluw wa'l-Falsafa*, 126–27; see also Kais Firro, *Metamorphosis of the Nation (al-Umma): The Rise of Arabism and Minorities in Syria and Lebanon, 1850–1940* (Eastbourne, UK: Sussex Academic Press, 2009), 102–3.
183 FO 78/2282, 12 July, 31 Oct. 1873; FO 78/2493 and FO 195/1113, 18 Jan. 1876.

ation possibly reached its nadir with the start of the Russo-Ottoman War in the spring of 1877, when roving bands of *redif* (reserve) soldiers and robbers from the hills made life in the villages of the coastal plain around Jabala and Latakia unbearable. The war, which had started over an alleged massacre of Christians in Bulgaria, more than ever polarized confessional relations within the empire and vis-à-vis the non-Muslim communities' foreign backers. In Syria too, European diplomats were predominantly concerned with depicting the plight of the local Christian community but were nonetheless judicious enough to note that many 'Alawis were affected by the violence as well, that the 'Alawis by and large remained on good terms with the Christians, and that many Christians were sending their valuables to relatives in 'Alawi villages for safekeeping.[184] Who was actually exercising authority in the area, on the other hand, is made clear in a dispatch of the French consul in Beirut, who writes in June 1877 that in the face of the governor's enmity and inaction, he was "obliged" to send a corvette which had just returned from another such mission to Mersin back to Latakia, where it would furthermore be accompanied by a British corvette, "because a Christian village near the city has just been attacked by a band of Ansariés and Muslims."[185]

The degree of French-British coordination in these years is also suggested by the fact that the British too now received regular consular dispatches, in French, from Isidore Blanche, who had since been promoted to vice-consul of France in Tripoli and whose experience was unequaled in the field—particularly inasmuch as the most dangerous 'Alawi robber band threatening the Christian population was commanded by none other than Hawwash Bey of the Matawira tribe, son of the famous Isma'il Khayr-Bey whom Blanche had known so well (see above).[186] Hawwash Bey, according to Blanche, had evidently embarked on the same "career" as his father, leading companies of twenty to thirty men to pillage and ransom villages around Safita, Qal'at al-Husn, and Marqab, stealing livestock and burning crops. More acts of violence involving Christians, various opposing 'Alawi factions, or local Ottoman troops in Safita, Tartus, Latakia, Sahyun, and the Bayt al-Shillif are reported throughout the summer and fall of 1877 and winter of 1878;[187] the Ottoman authorities, for their part, understandably also concerned with the Muslim victims of the war-related anarchy in the area, signaled an attack by 'Alawi brigands on Qal'at al-Madiq (northwest of Hama) in July 1878.[188]

---

184 FO 195/1113, 11 Dec. 1876; FO 195/1153, 22 May, 24 May 1877; FO 226/189 7 May 1877.

185 CPC Turquie-Beyrouth 21, fol. 73a–b, 75b–76a, 78a–b. Another French corvette had been diverted from Salonika to intimidate the Muslims of Beirut the year before; see CPC Turquie-Beyrouth 20, fol. 325b–328a.

186 FO 195/1153, 29 May, 5 June, 14–20 June 1877.

187 FO 195/1154, 8 July, 16 July, 14 Aug. 1877; FO 226/189, 3 Sept. 1877; CPC Turquie-Beyrouth 21, fol. 187b–188a, 231a–b.

188 BOA: Şura-yı Devlet 2215/26.

The end of Russo-Ottoman hostilities in 1878 brought little relief in Syria. The war had proved an unmitigated disaster for the Ottomans, who suffered important territorial losses in both the Balkans and eastern Anatolia, with Russian troops advancing to within a few kilometers of Istanbul, and who struggled to restore peace and stability in the remaining imperial provinces. At the international peace conference which opened under German auspices in Berlin in June 1878, moreover, the Great Powers agreed that Britain would effectively annex (by placing under "protectorate") Egypt and Cyprus while France would get Tunisia, and it is from this point onward that France and Britain began to seriously envision the partition of Syria as well. In the summer of 1881, following what the French consul-general in Beirut characterized as the "happy conquest of Tunis," the entire Syrian coastal region was again in turmoil. In particular, Hawwash Bey was once more attacking villages and defying Ottoman forces in the southern 'Alawi highlands around Abu Qubays (near Hama); reversing his earlier appraisal, Blanche now saw in him an "intelligent, able, ambitious and matured" young leader who had not only broad support among the 'Alawi tribes but also connections inside the government at Damascus, where he had spent most of his youth. Rumors were going about that Hawwash and his clan had "become French" and intended to "surrender the Mountain to France in order to do what was done in Tunis." The Ottomans, the French consul concluded with satisfaction, "have perhaps too much contempt for the Syrians with no distinction for race or religion. If ever an understanding were to be reached between them, the Porte would have trouble to regain possession of the most important province still under its direct control."[189]

The point here is not whether the 'Alawis and other Syrians really would have supported foreign occupation and rule—Hawwash himself denied this was the case in a letter to the consul in Beirut—but that the French increasingly came to believe it themselves. In addition to the optimism of the diplomatic dispatches, leading contemporary orientalists such as Henri Lammens, who in any event regarded the 'Alawis as a distant offshoot of Christianity, later presented the events of 1870 and 1877 as specific proof of their rejection of both Ottoman religious and state authority.[190] To the Ottomans as well, the dangers conveyed by Western propaganda were anything but implausible: during the Anglo-French invasion of Egypt in August 1882, additional reserve

---

189 FO 195/1369, 6 June, 5 Oct., 13 Dec. 1881; CPC Turquie-Beyrouth 24, fol. 347a–348a; see also Al Ma'ruf, *Tarikh*, 3:338–42. The correspondence of French diplomats in the region suggests they in fact contemplated using Hawwash and others "to provoke a diversion in Syria capable of creating grave problems for the Ottoman government." See CADN Damas-Consulat 33, 5 July 1881.

190 Chantal Verdeil, "Une 'révolution sociale dans la montagne': la conversion des Alaouites par les jésuites dans les années 1930" in Heyberger and Madinier, *L'islam des marges*, 89–90. On claims that local notables were spearheading a "Syrian" independence movement in this period, see 'Abd al-Ra'uf Sinnu, *Al-Niza'at al-Kiyaniyya al-Islamiyya, 1877–1881: Bilad al-Sham, al-Hijaz, Kurdistan, Albaniya* (Beirut: Bisan, 1998), 40–44.

troops were ordered deployed to Syria to guard against "people like the Druze and Nusayris who are always ready to exploit any situation," after British agents had apparently tried to incite local tribes against the government, at least in the south of the country.[191] In the end the 'Alawis never did revolt against the empire but on the contrary engaged in a massive resistance together with both Emir Faysal's Arab army and Turkish Kemalist forces against the French at the end of World War I (to be seen in the following chapter). By this time, however, the Western powers had been successfully convincing themselves for at least forty years that their educational institutions, faith, infrastructure, and system of government best corresponded to the 'Alawis' and other Syrians' true needs and aspirations.

ADMINISTRATIVE MODERNITY

What is common to the Western European and Ottoman perceptions is that the 'Alawis tend to appear in both as politically passive, as the eternal victims of sectarian oppression on the one account and as the guileless targets of imperialist manipulation on the other. French and British consular sources in particular continue to describe the 'Alawis even in the Tanzimat period as fundamentally recalcitrant ("insoumis") rather than as participant subjects of Ottoman government: when a solemn ceremony to announce the promulgation of the Ottoman constitution was held in Latakia in January 1877, to take the most notable example, the British vice-consul (of the Levantine Vitalé family, writing in French) reported that while the Muslim population was generally hostile to the idea of a new law not sanctioned by religion, "The Ansaryéhs, not being able to appreciate or comprehend this event, are not paying it any heed. I can say, however, that they are delighted (especially those of the mountain) over the difficulties the Sultan's government has been facing."[192]

This condescending appraisal is challenged, however, by the numerous ways in which 'Alawis appropriated and engaged the opportunities offered by the Tanzimat. As already indicated, the imperial authorities recommended the construction of state schools specifically for the 'Alawis of Latakia as early as 1867. In December 1873 the Ministry of Education transmitted a memorandum to the imperial State Council (Şura-ı Devlet) regarding the need for schools in other 'Alawi-inhabited areas, proposing the construction of a secondary (rüşdiye) school in each of the three district centers of Bahluliyya, Sahyun, and Bayt al-Shillif and a boys' school in each village with more than twenty houses, later to be increased to each village with more than ten. The government of Damascus was thereupon instructed, in the spring of 1874,

---

191 BOA: Y.EE 40/6–7; see also Gross, "Ottoman Rule," 347, 350–51.
192 FO 195/1153 and FO 226/189, 30 Jan. 1877.

to set up a locally constituted education commission (*mahallince bir maarif komisyonı teşkili*) to organize the construction of schools with resources from the villages themselves and provide for the training and payment of local teachers.[193] While it is not clear to what extent 'Alawis were already implicated in this process, only two years later the 'Alawi community as such was also explicitly demanding representation on Latakia's new administrative and judicial councils (İdare Meclisi and Deavi Meclisi). The establishment of these representative (partially appointive and partially elective) bodies of local government was doubtless one of the centerpieces of the Tanzimat. First introduced on the *eyalet* level in 1840, standing administrative councils (as well as the more ad-hoc judicial assemblies) were further instituted on the *sancak* and *kaza* (district) levels in subsequent years and then regularized with the Ottoman Provincial Reforms of 1864 and 1871.[194] The *meclis*es marked the beginnings of both formal political representation and a standardized (*nizami*) court system in the empire, but in joining together appointed state officials with indirectly elected representatives of both the Muslim and non-Muslim communities, they also continued to reflect and accommodate local societal realities. In this fashion the councils were "dynamic sites of social and political interactions ... involving the imperial government, members of the local elite, and the wider population. Local notables served in both judicial and administrative councils at the same time, while identifying the new opportunities for exercise of power that were embodied in the new councils."[195]

Needless to say, the 'Alawi notables of the Latakia region did not wish to get left behind. In 1852 the Ottoman authorities had caused great consternation by insisting on the appointment of an 'Alawi to the local municipal council for the first time;[196] in late 1871 members of the "Kalaziyya" clan complained that 'Alawi appointees to the *meclis* were always chosen from the rival "Shamaliyya" (or "Haydariyya") clan and requested that there be some alternance. The following year Shaykh Musallam Hatim of the Shamalis could nevertheless impose himself once again as the 'Alawi candidate.[197] A more important dispute erupted in 1876, when representatives of the 'Alawi community were actually to be elected to the administrative and judicial *meclis*es for the first time. A petition in which 'Alawi leaders of both factions united to protest their exclusion from the elections in strikingly modern

---

193 A.MKT.MHM 475/44.

194 Roderic Davison, *Reform in the Ottoman Empire, 1856–1876* (Princeton, NJ: Princeton University Press, 1963), 48–49, 140–42, 147–48, 315, 374–75; Stanford and Ezel Kural Shaw, *History of the Ottoman Empire and Modern Turkey*, vol. 2: *Reform, Revolution, and Republic: The Rise of Modern Turkey, 1808–1975* (Cambridge: Cambridge University Press, 1977), 84–85, 88–90.

195 Avi Rubin, *Ottoman Nizamiye Courts: Law and Modernity* (New York: Palgrave Macmillan, 2011), 29.

196 Douwes, "Knowledge and Oppression," 163.

197 Salih, "Athar al-Hiqab," 2:55–56.

terms, appealing to principles of both proportional representation and fiscal accountability, was received at the Sublime Porte in early April:

> During the selection of candidates for the election [*intihab*] that was lately ordered by imperial ferman and noble instruction to be held for the Administrative and Judicial Councils in the *kaza* of Latakia, a number of Nusayri candidates from among the Kelaziye and Hayderiye factions were chosen. While eight Muslim and Christian candidates were elected to the stated *meclis*es, only one candidate from the Nusayri community, to which we belong, was appointed to serve on the Judicial Council. In the *kaza* of Latakia, the Muslims and Christians together make up 3,000 households [*hane*] and the Nusayris more than 6,000. Furthermore, two-thirds of all regular fiscal and military contributions in the *kaza* are assigned to and imposed on the Nusayris, so that the situation whereby others than we can form the majority [*ekseriyeti*] is inequitable and unfair. Inasmuch as that is contrary to the wishes of the illustrious Ministry, and in order to attain the satisfaction of all the subject classes [*sunuf-ı tebaa*], we humbly beseech and implore that noble orders be given for there to be two Nusayri members on both the aforesaid Administrative and Judicial Councils.[198]

The problem, as reported by the British vice-consul a short while later, was that the Muslims of Latakia absolutely refused the idea of seeing any 'Alawis elected. The 'Alawis, "claiming this right in their quality as Shi'i Muslims," sought half of the seats reserved for the Muslim community and in principle had the support of the Ottoman *mutasarrıf* of Latakia, who continued to try to convince the Sunnis so that the election could proceed as planned. His inability or unwillingness to overcome the Sunnis' opposition, however, was then taken by the 'Alawis as just one more sign of the government's latent discrimination.[199]

Latakia's relations with the surrounding 'Alawi highlands appear to have become one of the major preoccupations of the local government in the following years. In his history of Latakia, Ilyas Salih takes the position that the provincial capital, Tripoli, was too distant to exert its authority in the region, that the city was therefore suffering from the constant chaos and anarchy in its hinterland, and that it should be made the capital of an independent *sancak* in order to better keep the 'Alawis in check.[200] Seemingly against all odds, considering the empire's dire condition in the late 1870s, the imperial authorities appear to have taken the Latakians' concerns seriously and undertook concrete steps to improve the situation locally. Much of the initiative

---

198 HR.TO 516/24.
199 FO 78/2493, 1 April, 11 April 1876.
200 Salih, "Athar al-Hiqab," 2:132–36.

in this regard was attributable to one individual, Ahmed Şefik Midhat Paşa, one of leading men of the Tanzimat and key architect of both the provincial reform of 1864 and the constitution, who was appointed *vali* of Syria in October 1878. Midhat Paşa immediately set about restructuring the state administration in Latakia, including the installation of a modern police force (*zabtiye*) and a complete overhaul of the province's finances together with the final abolition of *iltizam* tax farming, which still weighed on a good part of the rural population.[201] In August 1879, Salih recounts, Midhat Paşa came to visit Latakia to gauge the progress of the reforms, meeting with the captain of the local *zabtiye* precinct and other officials. On his second day there he summoned the 'Alawi *muqaddam*s and harangued them at length over how they would have to submit to his authority: "I consider you a sick man, and I have now prepared an effective, beneficial medicine for you. Use it well and it will make you healthy and improve your condition. If you don't, if you misuse it and continue in your ways, I will resort to a treatment of a different sort." Two days later, however, he gathered the 'Alawi leaders again, following a meeting of the town's Administrative Council, to discuss the reestablishment of Latakia as a separate province and its division into new *kaza* districts. The new *sancak* (or *mutasarrıflık*) was proclaimed to great fanfare a few days after.[202]

Midhat Paşa's reign as governor of Syria, albeit brief, appears to have been experienced by many 'Alawis as a turning point. Muhammad Amin Ghalib al-Tawil quotes at length a speech that Midhat allegedly made to an assembly of five hundred 'Alawi leaders in the Hama area, similar in substance to that quoted by Salih, in which he nonetheless recognized that the community's disenfranchisement was the result of centuries of government neglect and pledged to furnish the area with roads and schools; according to al-Tawil, Midhat in fact intended to turn the entire 'Alawi mountain into an autonomous *sancak* along the lines of Mt. Lebanon, possibly under the leadership of Hawwash Khayr-Bey.[203] Like much of al-Tawil's writing, this is uncorroborated and seems excessively fanciful, but other sources also support the notion that Midhat's tenure in office marked a new departure in the Ottoman state's position vis-à-vis the 'Alawis. According to Salih, for example, the lower court (*mahkama ibtida'iyya*) of Latakia was split into two sections, with Sulayman Hatim copresiding the penal section (*da'irat al-jaza'*). Hatim and another 'Alawi shaykh were furthermore named to a special committee that the *mutassarıf*, following Midhat Paşa's advice, had set up to supervise the improvement of the road to Aleppo and the dredging of Latakia's harbor. The three new *kaza*s into which the hinterland was divided were all somewhat conspicuously centered on Sunni towns (Jabala, Babanna for the *kaza* of Sahyun, and Marqab).

201 Gross, "Ottoman Rule," 253–56, 261–65.
202 Salih, "Athar al-Hiqab," 2:138–39; see also CPC Turquie-Beyrouth 22, fol. 126a.
203 Al-Tawil, *Tarikh al-'Alawiyyin*, 454–60.

Already in November 1879, however, the *kaimakam* of Jabala was dismissed specifically for his "tyranny and bad conduct toward the population" and replaced by a Druze official from Lebanon.[204] Finally, one of Midhat's key innovations in the province of Syria, being confronted with a permanent budget deficit, had been to prod wealthy notables to contribute money for the building and upkeep of schools in order to compete with those of the foreign missions. There are conflicting reports whether such schools were built in the Latakia region, but in 1884 Rida al-Sulh, who had just founded the first privately financed school for a Shi'i clientele in Nabatiyya (southern Lebanon), was made *kaimakam* of Latakia.[205]

Even in times of tension the authorities tended to act with greater circumspection. During a tribal conflagration in the mountains in the autumn of 1880, the local garrison commander refused to send troops so as not to provoke more violence; the French for their part also credited Hamdi Paşa, who had succeeded Midhat Paşa as governor of Syria, for continually proceeding "with wise deliberation" and not lending the 'Alawi mountaineers' inherent rebelliousness more importance than it actually deserved.[206] In October 1881, likewise, the provincial government requested permission from the Sublime Porte to "exceptionally and temporarily" be allowed to take cash payments (*bedel*) in lieu of military service, though in contravention of the *kura* conscription law, from the families of recruits in the Nusayri and Kelbi mountains who had absconded from duty.[207] Documents from the State Council and Interior Ministry over the following years indicate that 'Alawis accused of various crimes in Adana, Mersin, Antioch, or Homs were usually sent into internal exile, preferably somewhere where there was no 'Alawi population.[208] Hawwash Bey himself was arrested and sentenced to fifteen years in the galleys in September 1886 but subsequently banished to Rhodes instead.[209] Instructions were regularly transmitted to the government of Syria over the next years to provide for his and his family's sustenance there.[210]

The reformist administration's desire to deal with the 'Alawis on their own terms and work toward their integration into Ottoman society is best exemplified by the inclusion of the province of Latakia in the new *vilayet* of Beirut in 1888. The *vilayet* of Beirut was a "geographic oddity," uniting the coastal *sancak*s of Latakia and Tripoli in the North, and Acre and Balqa

204 Salih, "Athar al-Hiqab," 2:141–42.
205 Gross, "Ottoman Rule," 269–81; Mervin, *Un réformisme chiite*, 142.
206 CPC Turquie-Beyrouth 23, fol. 313b–14a, 340a.
207 Y.MTV 7/54.
208 Şura-yı Devlet 2483/9; DH.MKT 1355/3; DH.MKT 1358/7; DH.MKT 1368/44.
209 DH.MKT 1364/106; DH.MKT 1485/32; see also Gross, "Ottoman Rule," 362.
210 DH.MKT 1767/68; DH.MKT 1778/130; DH.MKT 1796/106; DH.MKT 1823/102; DH.MKT 1831/58.

(Nablus) in the South, all of which the capital Beirut was physically separated from by Mt. Lebanon, which continued to have the status of an autonomous *mutasarrıflık* (that is, under the direct control of Istanbul). The creation of the new *vilayet*, apparently the last such jurisdiction to be formed in the Ottoman Empire, responded to both administrative and strategic concerns. Jens Hanssen has shown that the initiative was above all that of the Beiruti merchant classes themselves, who had for years lobbied for the "capitalization" of their city as a platform to extend their commercial domination into the coastal interior.[211] At the same time, the central government also sought to counter increasing foreign influence in areas where missionary schools and European business interests were proliferating, promote its own "civilizing mission" to the rural hinterland population, and remake Beirut into a showcase of modern Ottoman governance.[212]

Latakia shared closely in Beirut's political and economic development in the final years of Ottoman rule; the two cities were connected by numerous family ties, particularly among Orthodox Christians, with Beirut's new weekly *al-Manar* being copublished by the patriarch of Latakia toward the end of the century. Latakia's emergence as an intermediate Ottoman Arab provincial center in its own right still awaits a thorough study.[213] That the decision to include Latakia in the new *vilayet* was indeed motivated in large part by the desire to better supervise the 'Alawis, however, is evoked by Ottoman sources from the period. In May 1887, almost a year before the creation of the *vilayet* was definitively decided, the Interior Ministry sent a preliminary order to the Syrian authorities in Damascus, steeped in the language of the Tanzimat, asking them to

> undertake, in the first instance, a complete investigation of the number of people in the *kaza*s and *nahiye*s which are to be formed anew in the Nusayri mountains, following the decision ... of the Interior Bureau of the State Council and a special session of the Council of Ministers, with a view to elucidating the ways and means of reform [*esbab-ı ıslahiye*] required in the said mountains and reconstituting the *kaza*s and *nahiye*s and proceeding with new subdivisions.[214]

Surprisingly, the same order had to be repeated in January 1888 after the government of Damascus, no doubt unhappy with the prospect of losing

---

211 Jens Hanssen, *Fin de Siècle Beirut: The Making of an Ottoman Provincial Capital* (Oxford: Oxford University Press, 2005), 40–53.
212 Ibid., 14, 63; Gross, "Ottoman Rule," 391–94.
213 See 'Uthman, *Tarikh al-Ladhiqiyya*, 112–20; Kinda Wazzan, "La production de la périphérie nord de Lattaquié (Syrie): Stratégie d'acteurs et formes produites" (Doctoral thesis, Université François-Rabelais, 2012), 40–52.
214 DH.MKT 1416/29.

these territories to the new province of Beirut, had failed to execute the initial request.[215]

There is no question that the Ottomans' wish to embrace the 'Alawis in the reforms had a strong disciplinary component. Soon after the founding of the *vilayet*, the authorities in Beirut determined that the 'Alawis continued to live in "a state of savagery," stealing and endangering the welfare of their neighbors, so that "the government does not really profit from their existence"; orders were once again given to gather taxes and seize military conscripts by force—that the region may at long last "benefit materially from the reform initiatives."[216] As late as September 1892 a special commission was charged with counting and eventually punishing 'Alawis in the hinterland of Latakia who had escaped the earlier census.[217] More liberal Ottoman statesmen continued to see parochial rivalries, economic inequities, and supposedly ancient religious hatreds as the real obstacles to the region's development. Shortly after being appointed governor of Beirut in January 1891, for example, Ismail Kemal Bey, a leading reformer and former protégé of Midhat Paşa, embarked on an inspection tour of the province's northern territories. There he was struck by the "unjust treatment meted out to the Noussairi," later characterizing this "tribe" in terms that have nothing to envy those of European orientalism: "These mountaineers were as a race remarkable for their physical beauty, but, having been the objects of persistent persecution for centuries, they naturally felt but little sympathy for their neighbours." According to Kemal Bey's enlightened understanding, the 'Alawis had often been subject to repressive measures and had, at some indeterminate point in time, lost the rights to their land on which they were now exploited as tenants; "I took steps to remedy this deplorable state of affairs by restoring their lands to them, and ordering the local authorities to treat them more justly in the future, which I was sure would not only render them more contented, but would go far towards attaching them to the Government."[218]

Kemal Bey's personal application on the 'Alawis' behalf appears to be corroborated to some extent by Interior Ministry documents, which, for example, show that the *muqaddam*s of the Cebel-i Kelbiye and Qardaha were exempted from military service, in return for the payment of a *bedel* fee, following a petition by leading members of the 'Alawi community to the government in Beirut in the summer of 1891.[219] His deputy governor in Latakia, Ziya Bey, was credited with constructing numerous schools and mosques for 'Alawis in the region—though at the price, as will be seen in the

215 DH.MKT 1475/100.
216 DH.MKT 1670/20; DH.MKT 1691/55.
217 DH.MKT 1999/43.
218 Ismail Kemal Bey (d. 1915), *The Memoirs of Ismail Kemal Bey*, ed. Sommerville Story (London: Constable, 1920), 199–200.
219 DH.MKT 1851/93.

following chapter, of increasing pressure from the Abdülhamid regime in Istanbul to convert to Sunni Islam. The Ottomans' "civilizing mission," like those of other empires active in western Syria, was of course never selfless and disinterested. Whether schools, roads, censuses, or district rezoning, Ottoman measures of social engineering were always aimed at raising productivity, levying more taxes and recruits, and perhaps more than anything increasing the state's grip on a region where its sovereignty was being sorely put in question by Western imperialism. These very challenges, however, the very fact that isolated, heretical, historically marginalized populations could now count as a sphere of contention with other would-be protectors, as an economic resource and as a test case for modern Ottoman government, also proved to be an opportunity for the 'Alawis. Inasmuch as the Tanzimat were perhaps above all a great project of standardization—the introduction of uniform law codes, educational norms, military service obligations, and representative administrative bodies for all the "citizens" of the empire—there was ultimately no other alternative but to admit 'Alawis to the schools, mosques, *meclis*es, and educational commissions that embodied the reform process. This did not spare the 'Alawis of the hostility of local competitors, who attempted to invoke traditional, pre-Tanzimat social hierarchies as a reason to discriminate against them in thoroughly modern institutions, nor of increasing social disparities, which, if anything, became even more accentuated with the land reforms and continuing commercial development in the second half of the nineteenth century. It did, however, provide them with a window on the wider Ottoman universe, with a political education that would lay the basis for future claims, whether individual, communal, or national, in the twentieth.

CONCLUSION: 'ALAWI OTTOMANISM AND COMPATRIOTISM

For the 'Alawis, the incorporation of Latakia and its hinterland into the *vilayet* of Beirut in 1888 marked the culmination of a long process of integration into the Ottoman state. Whereas the reign of the provincial *ayan* had been characterized by the near total absence of central government authority in the highlands of western Syria, the need to institute far-reaching structural changes in order to better comprehend, oversee, and utilize local society to the empire's advantage was recognized by successive imperial and provincial administrations from Mahmud II to the Egyptian occupation regime, through the actual Tanzimat period and into the reign of Abdülhamid II. The various new measures adopted in this time—the elimination of tax farming, the levying of popular conscripts, the standardization of legal practices, the establishment of a public school system, the introduction of representative political bodies—aimed at replacing the de facto sovereignty of a rural-based feudal notability with a modern bureaucratic state, knowledgeable of and responsible to its individual constituents. This rearrangement and colonization of local society in western Syria may not have specifically targeted the 'Alawis, but in extending the rights and privileges of citizenship to all of the empire's subjects regardless of religion, the secularizing reforms of the nineteenth century put the 'Alawis on a fundamentally new footing vis-à-vis the rest of society.

This process, however, was neither uniform nor linear nor irreversible. If leading provincial governors such as Genç Yusuf Paşa, Abdullah Paşa, or Mehmed Paşa al-Mann (who was suspected of being 'Alawi himself) early on realized the advantages of conciliating and accommodating rebellious highlanders rather than prosecuting them indiscriminately, it was precisely the weakness of central Ottoman authority in Syria and incessant rivalry between various governorships of the region that produced intercommunal violence on a previously unseen scale. The same period that saw the 'Alawi gentry, for example, in Safita enjoy an unprecedented degree of power over indigenous society, and that saw individual 'Alawis rise to the highest levels of state service in Istanbul, ironically also witnessed the unparalleled repression of the 'Alawi mountain populace at the hands of local despots like Berber Mustafa Agha, as well as a new intensity of polemics against 'Alawism per se and pressure to convert to Sunni Islam. Similarly, while numerous individual 'Alawi families appear to have welcomed the Ibrahim Paşa occupation in 1831, profiting from the new opportunities offered by the progressive Egyptian regime to find employment in state industries, serve in the military, and further the 'Alawi colonization of the Adana region and Cilicia, the more traditional *muqaddam*-based leaderships in the mountains of Latakia spearheaded the resistance against Egyptian state encroachment and thereby emerged as the Ottoman Empire's most reliable pillar in the region.

Ultimately, the various state interventions of the nineteenth century may have precipitated greater changes within 'Alawi society than in the 'Alawis' rapport with Ottoman society at large. The discourse of reform was unquestionably egalitarian, affording both Muslims and non-Muslims, and by extension non-orthodox Muslims, constitutional recognition as "Ottoman" nationals (*osmanlı*) in their own right, rather than as members of a particular religious community (*taife* or *millet*); calling for their universal education in state institutions, in order to undercut the influence of the foreign missionary schools; and finally, in an expression made popular throughout the empire by the Young Turk poet, playwright, and political activist Namık Kemal (d. 1888), elevating them to the status of "*vatandaş*," or Ottoman compatriots.[220] Some 'Alawis, however, inevitably became more equal than others.

---

220 Şerif Mardin, *The Genesis of Young Ottoman Thought: A Study in the Modernization of Turkish Political Ideas* (Princeton, NJ: Princeton University Press, 1982), 326–32; Davison, *Ottoman*

While the masses were indeed pressed to contribute not only to the state treasury and army but also to the new schools and infrastructure being built in the region, many peasants effectively lost their lands when these became registered as the private property of urban landowners, who were in some cases 'Alawis themselves, after the land reform of 1858. The late nineteenth century thus witnessed the emergence of a veritable 'Alawi landowning bourgeoisie (including the likes of the Hatims and 'Abbas in Latakia or the Arsuzis and Jabbaras in Antioch), whose social standing was furthermore consecrated by the very political institutions of the Tanzimat, in which they were called on to "represent" their communities, and who would sometimes come to play a critical role, to be seen in the final chapter, in the region's tumultuous transition from Ottoman imperial to French mandatory and Turkish republican rule.

For all the revolutionary change doubtless attending the Ottomans', and the 'Alawis', "longest century," it is therefore also important to keep in mind the historical continuities. Even radical reform, as already suspected by Ibrahim Paşa in 1833, had a better chance of succeeding when the state took into account and employed the traditional notable classes as mediators; the Ottomans, perhaps more pragmatically, applied this lesson when they named the "brigand" Isma'il Khayr-Bey *müdir* of Safita or received petitions from the Kalaziyya of Latakia to be admitted to the local Administrative Council. At the other end, if the Tanzimat reforms provided the political will and legal framework for 'Alawi integration and compatriotism, their actual enactment continued to depend on local, imperial, or even international circumstances. Ottoman statesmen repeatedly had to take the side of the 'Alawis against their feudal rivals, urban detractors, and religious bigots, insisting on their admission to the newly built mosques and schools (occasionally contingent on their conversion) or on their nomination to the local *meclis*es and other committees. In the face of ancient parochial conflicts, modern religious revivalism, and finally nationalist ideology, the 'Alawis' acceptance as true *vatandaşlar* always remained precarious—and would continue to be so in the twentieth century.

Reform, 56, 194–96, 298; Shaw and Shaw, *History of the Ottoman Empire*, 157, 177, 182.

* 6 *
NOT YET NATIONALS
ARABISM, KEMALISM, AND THE ALAOUITES
(1888–1936)

The manifold administrative and legal reforms of the Tanzimat, and in particular the principle of "Ottomanism" (*osmanlılık*) by which all subjects of the empire could be deemed equal citizens irrespective of their religion, raised broad expectations among the 'Alawis for their continuing integration and acceptance into wider Syrian and Ottoman society. Despite important material progress in the 'Alawis' situation, however, these expectations were to be repeatedly frustrated in both the final years of Ottoman rule and the mandate period. As successive regimes tried their hand at elevating and civilizing the 'Alawis, from the caliph-sultan Abdülhamid II, through the CUP (Young Turk) Revolution, the French colonial administration in Syria, and the Kemalist government in republican Turkey, the 'Alawis were made to realize time and again that they still had conditions to meet before they could be considered fully equal members of their respective new political entities, that their own wishes mattered little in the decisions ostensibly being made in their name, and that their very identity was subject to definition and redefinition by others.

Historians of Western imperialism have characterized as the "waiting room of history" the argument by which modernist colonial powers have habitually sought to convince subject peoples that they are "not yet civilized" or "not quite modern" enough themselves to participate in the political process and determine their own futures; writing on the Armenian refugees who were brought to settle in Aleppo after World War I, Keith Watenpaugh has shown how the French did everything in their power to ensure that they remained a distinct entity that could be considered "not quite Syrian."[1] France pursued a similar strategy vis-à-vis the 'Alawis after taking over the region in 1920,

---

1 Dipesh Chakrabarty, *Provincializing Europe: Postcolonial Thought and Historical Difference* (Princeton, NJ: Princeton University Press, 2000), 8–9, 13, 31; Keith Watenpaugh, *Being Modern in the Middle East: Revolution, Nationalism, Colonialism and the Arab Middle Class* (Princeton, NJ: Princeton University Press, 2006), 281–82, 288–91.

setting up the independent "Territoire des Alaouites" (later "État des Alaouites" and "Gouvernement de Lattaquié") as a means to obstruct Syrian unity and independence and ensure that the local 'Alawis would not identify with Syrian nationalist forces in Damascus, or encouraging those of Alexandretta to seek union with Kemalist Turkey. Essentially the same positions had been taken by Hamidian officials, however, for whom the 'Alawis were never quite Ottoman enough until they converted to Sunni Islam; by the Committee for Union and Progress (CUP), for whom 'Alawis, as Arabs, remained potentially subversive; and finally by the Turkish Kemalist government, which hoped to reconstruct the 'Alawis as "Hittite Turks" in order to hasten their assimilation and disappearance into the greater Turkish nation.

The purpose of this chapter is to document the 'Alawis' ambivalent relationship with the Syrian Arab, Ottoman/Turkish, and French colonial projects at the threshold of the contemporary era. The study ends with their uncertain futures in both the Syrian and Turkish polities in the mid-1930s; the conclusions and interpretative framework proposed here therefore remain provisional and open-ended and may ultimately raise more questions than they answer. The decision to leave the community's contemporary history, in particular its rise to prominence within independent Syria, down to the civil war today, to other specialists is dictated both by the rupture occasioned by the disappearance of the Ottoman Empire and by the nature of the sources at our disposal. The subject of the first part of the chapter, the educational policies of the Abdülhamid regime toward the 'Alawis, generated what was probably the most extensive documentation ever in their regard. This material has been examined in several recent studies, both of late Ottoman administrative practice and of the 'Alawi community per se, and an exhaustive reappraisal is neither necessary nor possible in the scope of the present contribution. The object here will instead be to draw attention to the social, rather than to the religious, vector of Hamidian policies. The second and third sections analyze ongoing control and development measures in the region under both Abdülhamid and the CUP government (1908–14) but also seek to show how the 'Alawis capitalized on the opportunities provided by modern schooling and increasing contact with the outside world to promote a distinctly local, 'Alawi "reformism." The theme of their political maturation is then carried over into the discussion of their stance during and after the "Great War," from the Arab Revolt in 1916 through the Turkish War of Liberation in 1922, where documents from the ATASE military archives show to what extent the famous 'Alawi resistance leader Salih al-'Ali was in fact coordinating with the Kemalist government in Ankara. The final section, in turn, concludes with a discussion of the contrast between France's separatist, confessionalist policies and Turkey's resolve to incorporate and assimilate the 'Alawis of Cilicia and the Alexandretta (Hatay) district, reaching ahead to take a brief look at republican and CHP party sources regarding education and eugenics as a way to render the 'Alawi population fully Turkish.

Much more, of course, remains to be said of the 'Alawis after the effective end of French rule over Syria, as well as of the community's later progression in Turkey (and to a lesser extent in modern Lebanon and even Israel). Important fieldwork-based studies on the rise of the 'Alawi peasant notability within the Syrian state and Ba'th Party apparatus and the rising fortunes of the 'Alawi-inhabited coastlands have been undertaken by the likes of Hanna Batatu, Nikolaos Van Dam, and Fabrice Balanche;[2] the density of primary archival documentation already drawn on for the foregoing chapters, however, is either not available for the more recent periods of Syrian history or inaccessible. Even more important, perhaps, the 'Alawis' integration into the formally secular Syrian and Turkish republics makes their treatment as a separate confessional "community" increasingly questionable or irrelevant, their further social evolution better being looked at in the more universal frameworks of rural modernization, mass-movement political mobilization, economic and military clientelism, and so on. These new and radically different chapters in the history of the 'Alawis remain to be written; it is hoped that the present contribution on their unique, often ignored secular development up to the contemporary period, rather than the mere fact of their religious distinctiveness, will have provided some useful background to that endeavor.

HAMIDIAN REEDUCATION

The building of schools in the 'Alawi coastal regions of Syria and southern Anatolia received a new impetus under the reign of Sultan Abdülhamid II. Several overlapping reasons account for this. For one, the Hamidian administration made public education a central priority—universal primary instruction, an overhaul of the secondary school curriculum, and the reinforcement of religious values being seen as vital to both social cohesion and the legitimacy of the imperial state. Areas where foreign missionaries were active of course received special attention: not just in Syria, but also in eastern Anatolia where Protestant missions had been targeting the Armenian as well as the Turkish and Kurdish Alevi populations, Abdülhamid regarded their influence as a key threat to his vision of an Ottoman-Muslim national community under his leadership as caliph.[3] With the loss of most of the Balkans after

---

2 Batatu, *Syria's Peasantry*; Nikolaos Van Dam, *The Struggle for Power in Syria: Sectarianism, Regionalism and Tribalism, 1961–1978* (London: I. B. Tauris, 1979); Balanche, *La région alaouite*, 39–78.

3 Selim Deringil, *The Well-Protected Domains: Ideology and the Legitimation of Power in the Ottoman Empire 1876–1909* (London: I. B. Tauris, 1998), 93–95; Somel, *Modernization of Public Education*; Hans-Lukas Kieser, *Der Verpasste Friede: Mission, Ethnie und Staat in den Ostprovinzen der Türkei, 1839–1938* (Zürich: Chronos, 2000), 163–68, 170–78.

the 1876–78 war, Ottoman statecraft became more focused than before on Islamic symbolism, the codification of shariʻa law, and pan-Islamist solidarity with other Muslim countries and gave new precedence to the Arab-speaking provinces and their better insertion, notably in the field of education, into the empire. Local officials had repeatedly deplored that investment in the state school system was not keeping pace with Western institutions; in 1887 an inspectorate of non-Muslim and foreign schools was established for the first time, and measures were taken to prevent Muslim children (including ʻAlawis) from attending non-Ottoman facilities.[4]

Beyond the need to meet the social and political challenges posed by the missionary presence, however, educational policies toward the ʻAlawis also acquired a decidedly more sectarian bent under Abdülhamid. Under the sign of both pan-Islamism and Salafi reformism, Abdülhamid began to assert his role as caliph in the 1880s and accord greater importance to the buttressing of Islamic orthodoxy and concord in his realm. The biggest threat in this regard emanated from Iraq, where Iranian propaganda, the conversion and sedentarization of Bedouin tribes around Najaf and Kerbala, and the large amounts of income generated by the pilgrimage and funerary industry as well as from religious bequests from as far away as India had led to a significant expansion of the Imami (Twelver) Shiʻi community since the early decades of the century. While ostensibly seeking a rapprochement with the Shiʻi *mujtahids* (clerics) and their Iranian sponsors, Abdülhamid in reality hoped to reduce their social power by providing for the instruction of the local Shiʻis in Ottoman state schools, which would ultimately help erode the differences between the Shiʻi and Sunni communities, redefine *osmanlılık* or membership in the Ottoman national community in terms of Muslim ecumenism, and strengthen his own claim to universal Islamic leadership. "His Imperial Majesty will accomplish more by education," a report circa 1891 on the proposed schooling and conversion of the Shiʻi population in Iraq foresaw, "than his illustrious ancestor Selim I did by the sword."[5]

This government initiative for the "rectification of belief" (*tashih-i akaid*), as it was later termed, was of course extended to other nonorthodox communities as well. In 1891–92 the Ottomans carried out a major campaign to convert

---

4 Deringil, *Well-Protected Domains*, 104–6, 114–18; François Georgeon, *Abdulhamid II: Le sultan calife* (Paris: Fayard, 2003), 183–86, 207–12; Benjamin Fortna, *Imperial Classroom: Islam, the State, and Education in the Late Ottoman Empire* (Oxford: Oxford University Press, 2002), 48–60; Talhamy, "Missionary Activity," 229–31; Y.EE.KP 1/80.

5 Selim Deringil, "The Struggle against Shiism in Hamidian Iraq: A Study in Ottoman Counter-Propaganda," *Die Welt des Islams* 30 (1990): 45–62; see also Gökhan Çetinsaya, *Ottoman Administration of Iraq, 1890–1908* (London: Routledge, 2006), 99–126; İsmail Safa Üstün, "The Ottoman Dilemma in Handling the Shiʻi Challenge in Nineteenth-Century Iraq," in *The Sunna and Shiʻa in History: Division and Ecumenism in the Muslim Middle East*, ed. Ofra Bengio and Meir Litvak (New York: Palgrave Macmillan, 2011), 87–103.

the Yezidi Kurds of eastern Anatolia to Hanafi Islam (the official law school of the empire), building schools and mosques in the area but also resorting to the army's "Reform Division" (Fırka-ı İslahiye) to impose Sunnism by force if necessary. In subsequent years, similar conversion efforts were made with the Zaydi population in Yemen; among the Alevis and other groups in central Anatolia and the Black Sea region; as well as in what remained of the Balkan provinces.[6] Among the first targets of the *tashih-i akaid* campaign, however, were the 'Alawis. From October 1889 onward a vast collection of chancery documents attests to the resources spent to educate and, where possible, re-educate the 'Alawi population to Hanafism.[7] Initially the Ministers' Council (Meclis-i Vükela), which included the empire's chief cleric, the *şeyhü'l-islam*, requested that the government of Latakia build enough elementary schools in the *sancak* and hire an approved Sunni cleric as a roving school inspector in order to compete with the Christian missionaries and "pull the Nusayris over toward the Islamic faith." The funds had to be raised locally, with 50 percent of the so-called educational contribution tax (*maarif hisse-i ianesi*), however, being reserved for the Ministry of Education.[8] Already a few months later, in the spring of 1890, the Interior Ministry could report with great satisfaction (and some likely exaggeration) to Yıldız Palace that fifteen thousand 'Alawis in Latakia and forty thousand in Marqab had converted to Islam and should therefore have mosques and schools built for them; this time the Minister's Council agreed to forgo their share of the *hisse* and contribute instead to their construction and appointment.[9] Additional mosques and schools were ordered to be built in the Sahyun district in anticipation of further conversions there.[10] In July 1893 the Interior Ministry, considering that "the totality of the *sancak* of Latakia's residents have adopted the Hanefi *mezheb*," ordered sixty thousand new identity cards (*tezkere*) "with the rubric of their confessional affiliation being corrected" to be made available to them free of charge.[11]

If the "rectification of belief" was a matter of imperial policy, much of the movement in this regard, however, depended on local officials. Mehmed Ziya Bey, who served as *mutasarrıf* of Latakia from 1885 to 1892 (and lies buried in the al-Moghrabi cemetery), is remembered as having been particularly keen on raising the condition of the 'Alawi population.[12] As Necati Alkan has shown, Ziya used his authority to close down Protestant missionary schools in the area

---

6 Deringil, *Well-Protected Domains*, 69–82; Kieser, *Verpasste Friede*, 168–70.

7 See Ortaylı, "Groupes hétérodoxes," 209–10; Deringil, *Well-Protected Domains*, 83–84; Somel, *Modernization*, 222–23; Uğur Akbulut, "Osmanlı Arşiv Belgelerinde Lazkiye Nusayrîleri (19. Yüzyıl)," *Türk Kültürü ve Hacı Bektaş Veli Araştırma Dergisi* 54 (2010): 119–22.

8 MV 48/32. On the *hisse* contribution, see Somel, *Modernization*, 120–22, 145–53.

9 İ.DH 1182/92449, 92451; MV 54/37; DH.MKT 1741/10.

10 İ.MMS 114/4867; DH.MKT 1744/33.

11 İ.DH 1306/9.

12 Al-Tawil, *Tarikh al-'Alawiyyin*, 459; 'Uthman, *Tarikh al-Ladhiqiyya*, 113–14; Sari, *Safahat*, 102–3.

and in some cases even restitute the property to the original 'Alawi inhabitants. He was then approached by a number of 'Alawi shaykhs who sought to "return" their community to Islam and lift it out its "slumber of ignorance" with modern schools and mosques, and he interceded for them repeatedly in Istanbul.[13] For all his efforts, Ziya, as well as the elementary school inspector in Latakia, Shaykh 'Ali Rashid al-Miqati, were later nominated for an official commendation.[14] Around the same time Hakki Paşa, *mutasarrıf* of Tripoli, sent a lengthy report to Istanbul on how best to win over the 'Alawis of the southern highlands. He not only proposed the building of mosques and schools, and eventually even a military college, but also insisted on the importance of instruction in both Arabic and Turkish, as well as suggesting that certain 'Alawi shaykhs receive stipends and other awards in order to gain their loyalty.[15]

By Ziya Bey's reckoning, there were "over 120,000 people in the Nusayri sect spread between Anatolia and Arabistan, from the Kozan Mountains to Mount Lebanon, in the districts of Antioch and Latakia" who were in need of reeducation into Islam.[16] The entire *tashih* project cannot be covered in full detail here, but two points merit consideration. The first is the extent to which efforts appear to have become focused on the 'Alawis of the Adana (Cilicia) and Antioch region. If local officials in Latakia continued to lobby for schools (another seven were opened in Marqab, Sahyun, and Jabala in 1892, all of them with the word "Hamid" as an element in their name) and signal conversions among the 'Alawi population,[17] the great mass of Başbakanlık documents in the 1890s concern areas beyond the province of Beirut. There are several possible reasons for this. For one, Protestant missionary activities seem to have been significantly curtailed in the coastal mountains by this time, Ottoman records indicating only one problem with the proselytization of 'Alawis by a Catholic monk in Safita in November 1894.[18] (A few weeks later, interestingly, the imperial Ministers' Council issued orders to investigate and if necessary interdict the reportedly continuing practice of 'Alawis renting out their daughters as maidservants in Latakia, suggesting the government remained highly sensitive to criticism in this regard.)[19] In Adana, Mersin, and Suwaydiyya, on the other hand, the Americans continued to open schools unabatedly, often without permission and by all evidence targeting the 'Alawi

---

13 İ.MMS 113/4821; Y.PRK.UM 19/58; Alkan, "Fighting for the Nusayrī Soul," 41–42, 45–46.
14 DH.MKT 1823/38; DH.MKT 1767/69; DH.MKT 1958/80.
15 Y.PRK.AZN 4/57.
16 Y.PRK.UM 19/70. A contemporary French diplomat, promoting the "nation Ansarié" as a potential market for French textiles, puts their number in the region at an implausibly high 500,000; see CCC Lattaquié 5, fol. 31b (7 Feb. 1887).
17 Y.A.HUS 266/97; MF.MKT 162/54; MF.MKT 174/24.
18 Y.PRK.MŞ 5/83. Some thirty 'Alawi girls continued to be schooled for free at the Anglo-American mission school in Latakia; see CPC Turquie-Beyrouth 40, fol. 88b–89a.
19 MV 83/72.

as well as the Armenian community.[20] The growing American presence seems to have impelled the authorities to pay greater attention to the region: the single most convoluted issue confronting the government of Adana in these years, to judge by the available documentation, and one of several that it would no doubt be worthwhile to follow up in the American archives, involved the school of Dr. Metheny in Mersin, where three 'Alawi girls from the same family were reported "abducted" in 1893 and shipped to the United States to be educated, against the wishes of both their parents and local officials.[21]

The second point, related to the first, is that many of the measures regarding the 'Alawis in the North, while dealing on the surface with their religious affiliation, in fact seem to have been concerned more than anything with their social integration. Unlike the more traditional *ayan*-led feudal clanships in the highlands of Tripoli, Hama, and Latakia, most of the 'Alawis in Adana and Antioch were relatively recent immigrants who had come as individual families in the service of the Egyptian regime, or who worked as tenant farmers on large commercial estates and were thus more amenable to state control. The Çukurova plain of Adana, where 'Alawis had begun to move in the time of Ibrahim Paşa, became somewhat of a model reform province with the commercial cotton boom of the 1860s, when the Fırka-ı Islahiye was employed to settle numerous additional tribes from Anatolia in order to better develop and exploit the area's agricultural potential.[22] In key parts of the Antioch region as well, 'Alawi immigration was a late result of Ottoman modernization efforts. The town of Alexandretta (Iskenderun) in particular, though serving as one of Aleppo's maritime outlets since the sixteenth century, developed into a major commercial port and began to attract a growing number of Arab ('Alawi) settlers only in the final decades of the nineteenth century, after the improvement of the highway leading over the Beilan Pass. Oddly enough, the 'Alawi-settled *nahiye* of Arsuz (immediately south of Alexandretta) was also the first place in the Ottoman Empire where oil was discovered, in 1880–81. After further exploration, a drilling concession was granted to Ottoman investors in 1889, but the occurrence was finally too small to warrant commercial production.[23]

Numerous documents from this period deal with 'Alawis from Latakia who had settled in Antioch and Alexandretta and converted to Islam. The problem was that they were encountering considerable resistance on the part

20 Y.MTV 87/44; DH.TMIK.M 168/7.
21 BEO 314/23496, 23495; A.MKT.MHM 700/5; Y.PRK.MF 3/11; MF.MKT 237/20.
22 Georgeon, *Abdulhamid*, 268; Uğur Pişmanlık, *Tarsus İşçi Sınıfı Tarihi: 19. Yüzyıldan Günümüze* (Istanbul: Yazılama, 2013), 25–59; see also Ali Sinan Bilgili, "Osmanlı Arşiv Belgelerinde Adana, Tarsus ve Mersin Bölgesi Nusayrîleri (19–20. Yüzyıl)," *Türk Kültürü ve Hacı Bektaş Veli Araştırma Dergisi* 54 (2010): 52–54.
23 Mehmet Tekin, *Hatay Tarihi: Osmanlı Dönemi* (Ankara: Atatürk Yüksek Kurumu Atatürk Kültür Merkezi Başkanlığı, 2000), 114–19.

of the local Sunni population, much as had already occurred in Antioch in 1870, when trying to worship in mosques. In late 1891 local *'ulama* wrote the government in Aleppo claiming that the 'Alawis had only converted outwardly but continued to cling to their traditional, heretical, beliefs; specifically, landowners in the Antioch area on whose farm plots and gardens the 'Alawis were living as tenants feared that they were only posing as Muslims so that they could eventually seize ownership of the property. The matter was referred to Istanbul, but the response of the imperial Fetvahane (bureau of the *şeyhü'l-islam*) and the State Council was swift: inasmuch as the 'Alawis had submitted to Islam, even if it was out of *taqiyya* (dissimulation), they could not be denied the right to perform their prayers and should instead be provided with further mosques and schools in their villages to ensure they be properly instructed in the true faith and did not relapse into error. Remarking that "there is no such thing as a Nusayri mosque or a Nusayri school," the State Council ordered the long-delayed construction of state institutions to be pursued, the mufti of Antioch to be dismissed, and traditional 'Alawi shaykhs who persisted in misguiding their people to be banished.[24]

Throughout the autumn of 1892 and first half of 1893, the authorities in Istanbul continued to supervise the setting up of new schools in the area, relieving their constant budgetary shortfalls by "temporarily" assigning the building costs to the local municipalities and ordering additional funds and materials to be collected among the population. At the same time, they also repeatedly stressed that 'Alawi children could go to other schools as well and should indeed be made to learn together with Muslim children so as to better assimilate the fundamentals of the religion.[25] In Antioch there nevertheless appear to have been persistent tensions with the Sunnis. In April 1893 an Interior Ministry report on the situation claimed that "some self-seeking individuals are keeping Nusayris to work for them as slaves in a state of quasi-captivity" in the area; they should instead be considered—like the Zaydis of Yemen—full members of the Islamic communion.[26] Ottoman policy toward the 'Alawis was essentially one of desegregation, and it ultimately had to be backed up by force: the following October, when Sultan Abdülhamid gave his blessing for the grand opening, at the start of the school year, of twenty-five new primary schools for 'Alawis in Antioch and another five in Alexandretta, the Interior Ministry ordered an infantry unit to be sent to the region to guard against potential trouble.[27]

---

24 İ.MMS 130/5563; DH.MKT 1958/80; DH.MKT 1993/3; Alkan, "Fighting for the Nusayrī Soul," 47–48.
25 MF.MKT 150/12; MV 73/38; BEO 142/10630; DH.MKT 2049/13; MF.MKT 181/109; MF.MKT 187/1; Y.PRK.MF 2/57.
26 BEO 294/21989; DH.MKT 31/9 i–ii.
27 MV 76/93; DH.MKT 31/9 iii–iv; İ.MF 2/10.

The 'Alawi migrants' relationship with other groups continued to be a cause for concern. In Adana, a major incident occurred on the occasion of Laylat al-Qadr, the holiest night of the Muslim year, celebrated near the end of Ramadan (mid-April 1893), when some 'Alawis coming to the Great Mosque to visit a relic of the Prophet's beard were driven away by an angry mob ("a gang of stupid, malicious Turks"). Fortunately some far-sighted Sunni *'ulama* on the scene were able to step in and prevent further violence and, together with a local 'Alawi notable and court official, Garib-zade Cemal Efendi, managed to stem an outburst of anger in the 'Alawi villages of Tarsus and Mersin afterward by proposing the construction of additional schools and mosques. The Sublime Porte quickly acceded and awarded each of them decorations for their civic action, though not without criticizing them for not having brought the matter to the state's attention even quicker.[28] In September 1896, similarly, some fifty to sixty Sunni military conscripts from Antioch who had gathered in Alexandretta to be sent to Yemen attacked a group of 'Alawis in a mosque after Friday prayers, beating and insulting them and then battling with local gendarmes and police who had rushed to the scene. Reinforcements were sent to restore order until the troop transport ships could arrive in port.[29] A few months later, in March 1897, the local authorities again had to step in, this time after a fight between an 'Alawi and an Armenian had led to a generalized brawl and forced the closure of Alexandretta's market.[30]

The Hamidian regime's educational policies toward the 'Alawis remained very much a work in progress. If the "correction of belief" had been a top priority in 1889, mainly on account of the alarmist reports about the progress of Shi'ism in Iraq, a chronic lack of funds and ongoing discrimination on the local level continued to militate against true 'Alawi integration. According to historian and former statesman Yusuf al-Hakim (1879–1969), himself a native of Latakia, the mosques and schools built under Ziya Bey quickly fell into disrepair after his death or were turned into dwellings, as the 'Alawi highlanders were subjected to the same oppression by local officials as before.[31] The Ministry of Education confirmed in January 1895 that many of these *mekteb*s did indeed remain empty and suggested turning some of them into *rüşdiye* secondary schools.[32] The ministry's *salname* (yearbook) for 1898 still only notes the existence of three *rüşdiye*s in the province's rural districts, however—those of Marqab and Jabala having thirty-one and sixteen pupils,

---

28 BEO 201/15050; Y.MTV 77/10; Bilgili, "Adana, Tarsus ve Mersin Bölgesi," 57–58.
29 Y.A.HUS 358/80.
30 Y.PRK.UM 37/24; DH.TMIK.M 29/47.
31 Yusuf al-Hakim, *Suriyya wa'l-'Ahd al-'Uthmani* (Beirut: Al-Matba'a al-Kathulikiyya, 1966), 70–71.
32 MF.MKT 246/56; İ.MF 4/7.

respectively, while that of Sahyun was no longer in operation.[33] In January 1905 local education officials were still complaining that the two elementary schools ordered built for the 'Alawis of Safita twelve years earlier had not yet materialized.[34]

The provincial authorities in Aleppo, meanwhile, began to carry out a financial review and inspection (*teftiş*) of all the schools built for the 'Alawis of Antioch and Alexandretta and recommended that the teachers receive a salary cut in order to reduce costs. This was summarily rejected by the Ministry of Education, however, which for its part suggested that the inspectors sent by Aleppo were a waste of money.[35] On the other hand, the inspections did turn up evidence of continuing gross misconduct toward the 'Alawi population: in October 1897 the provincial director of education (*maarif müdiri*) reported that many of the *rüşdiye* schools in Antioch and Alexandretta were not yet finished, and that local officials were forcing 'Alawi children to work on their construction, even under torture, and then preventing them from enrolling in the schools or participating in mosque prayers. Similarly, in the districts of Arsuz and Suwaydiyya, where the 'Alawis constituted 90 percent of the population and supposedly showed great enthusiasm for the new schools, notables from Antioch were employing thugs to attack and intimidate the 'Alawis since they wished them to remain uneducated to continue using them as servants. Several months later the governor of Aleppo once again indicated that even the mufti was impeding 'Alawis from converting to Islam because this did not suit the needs of the local landowners who preferred to keep them indentured.[36]

Despite growing financial problems in the 1890s, as Akşin Somel has indicated, the Hamidian government continued to pay special attention to public state schooling in peripheral, politically sensitive areas.[37] In early 1899 Yıldız Palace noted with anguish that some 'Alawis in the Antioch region were threatening to convert to Christianity and ordered both the provincial government and the Education Ministry to mobilize additional resources in order to retain them in Ottoman schools;[38] the following year the leading imams of Alexandretta petitioned the court, saying that the town had grown so large in recent years, and so many 'Alawis had turned Muslim, that the great mosque could no longer accommodate everyone ("part of the congregation has to pray out on the street in the rain and the mud"), and

---

33 *Salname-i Nezaret-i Maarif-i Umumiye: İkinci Sene* (Istanbul: Darü'l-Hilafeti'l-Aliye, 1899/1900), 1082.
34 MF.MKT 825/73.
35 MF.MKT 273/59; MF.MKT 333/21.
36 MF.MKT 374/12; Y.EE 132/38.
37 Somel, *Modernization*, 159–60, 165.
38 Y.PRK.BŞK 58/35, 44; MF.MKT 437/33.

more had to be built.[39] Around the same time, in February 1900, the ministry noted that the schools in Latakia's hinterland remained empty for want of qualified teachers and called for the construction of a boarding school in the city where 'Alawi children would be housed for free. As late as July 1904, when the *tashih-i akaid* program had already lapsed in most other areas of the empire, the Interior Ministry was still rewarding local school officials in Antioch and Alexandretta for their efforts to "righten the beliefs" of the 'Alawi population.[40]

LOYALTY AND CONTROL

For all the energy spent on the 'Alawis' education and religious enlightenment, the Ottoman authorities remained decidedly ambivalent about their political reliability. Mosques and schools were of course only one aspect of the wider strategy to discipline and domesticate heterodox and other rural hinterland populations and turn them into malleable, productive members of society, and many documents concerning the 'Alawis in the late Hamidian period continue to focus as before on more mundane problems of brigandage, taxes, and tribalism. In the summer of 1890, for example, just as the first schools were being founded in the Sahyun, the governor of Beirut and Justice Ministry (Adliye Nezareti) officials stepped in to mediate in a clan war between 'Alawis and Bedouin Arabs of the district, arranging for the 'Alawis to pay 40,000 *guruş* blood money for the Bedouins killed and thus averting a criminal trial.[41] In March 1892 the governor of Syria sent soldiers to subdue 'Ayn al-Kurum in the *kaza* of Hamidiye west of Hama, where a notorious gang of robbers from the Latakia region had found refuge; a few months later his colleague in Beirut followed suit against alleged bandits in Qardaha.[42] In Homs, a group of eleven 'Alawis were arrested for the murder of two Muslims in March 1893 but managed to bribe local court officials to release them, sparking a Justice Ministry investigation into the latter's conduct.[43] In January 1896 the French consul in Beirut reported that the 'Alawis of Qardaha had revolted on account of their continual harassment by state tax collectors, causing the governor of Latakia to dispatch two hundred reservists to raid the district. The governor had previously assured Istanbul that the 'Alawis were all converted to Islam and therefore docile, but "there is reason to think that these mountaineers, even if they have become Muslim

---

39 Y.PRK.AZJ 39/117.
40 MF.MKT 496/33; DH.MKT 866/56.
41 İ.DH 1207/94486.
42 Y.A.HUS 257/26; DH.MKT 1981/40.
43 DH.MKT 2060/105.

in appearance, remain very indisposed to suffer the blatant injustices of the Turkish officials."[44]

Ottoman policy toward the 'Alawis under Abdülhamid was neither solely religion-based nor solely repressive but also aimed, much like in previous periods, at increasing the efficacy of local administration and co-opting the population through its own indigenous leaderships. As a solution to the problem of constant lawlessness in 'Ayn al-Kurum, the Interior Ministry proposed in December 1892 to turn it into the center of a new district, complete with budgetary autonomy and authority over thirteen adjoining villages;[45] some years later, in 1901, the 'Alawi shaykh Isma'il Junayd was rewarded with the rank of *kapucı başı* for his steadfast service as member of the Administrative Council of the *kaza* of Hamidiye.[46] To cite yet other examples: In September 1895 the government of Beirut was asked to look into a somewhat bizarre case where an 'Alawi shaykh from the hills above Hisn al-Akrad, together with a notable from Tripoli (who allegedly had contacts with the vastly influential religious ideologue Abu'l-Huda Efendi in Istanbul), was diverting water away from the villages below and asserting ownership over it, leading the Dandashlis and other local Arab tribes to launch a desperate petition for help.[47] A few years later, in April 1899, it was the turn of the 'Alawis of Latakia, now styling themselves the "rightly-guided sect" (*taife-i hüdaiye*), to petition "their beloved padişah" and denounce the constant oppression they continued to suffer at the hands of his officials. Interestingly they now also claimed to number 120,000 followers, a figure taken of course from earlier official sources.[48] The discourses and institutions of provincial government may have changed over the course of the nineteenth century, from townships and tax farming to municipal councils, population statistics, and education, but the rationale behind acknowledging and integrating the 'Alawis regardless of their actual beliefs or sectarian identity remained largely the same.

Perhaps the best illustration of the state's continuing ambivalence vis-à-vis the 'Alawis in the late Ottoman period was the question of enrollment in that most Hamidian of institutions, the Aşiret Mektebi or imperial "Tribal School." Established in 1892, the school aimed to bring together the sons of the most prominent Arab tribal shaykhs under Abdülhamid's patronage in Istanbul, where they would be taught Turkish and love of the faith and the fatherland—to partake in "the light of knowledge and the fruit of civilization" and be "saved from the darkness of ignorance and the abyss of barbarism." At first only a limited number of boys aged twelve to sixteen were to be selected

---

44 CPC Turquie-Beyrouth 40, fol. 8a–9a.
45 DH.MKT 2031/114; DH.MKT 2045/97.
46 DH.MKT 2522/65.
47 DH.MKT 430/70.
48 DH.TMIK.S 26/31.

from the principal Arab provinces, but demand soon proved so high that the sons of many more rural notables from Kurdistan, Albania, and Mt. Lebanon were admitted as well.[49] The most famous 'Alawi family of the century was not to be left aside: in December 1892, only shortly after the school's opening, the government of the Aegean province (Cezair-i Bahriye) forwarded a request from Muhammad Hawwash Bey, "one of the chiefs of the Nusayri mountains" (and former rebel leader) now living in exile in Rhodes, to enroll both his son 'Abid and his grandson 'Abd al-'Aziz.[50] The Interior Ministry transmitted the application to the Ministry of Education, but there does not appear to be any evidence that it was granted. The Hawwash family, in any event, continued to arouse much suspicion in Istanbul. Hawwash and two of his brothers had originally been arrested in 1883, according to British diplomats, for their continuing complicity with France.[51] They were sentenced to fifteen years in the galleys or to exile three years later, in 1886, and it was indeed not before May 1901 that Hawwash's brothers were finally pardoned and allowed to return home to Syria.[52] Almost immediately, however, they began to attract notice for their renewed "untoward behavior" and for trying to bring their sons over from Rhodes as well. "It having been officially stated time and again that the return of the Hevvaş Bey family to their homeland would be a cause of utmost worry," the Interior Ministry expressed its regret that they had not been separated upon their release from Rhodes and ordered the governors of both Syria and the Aegean to keep it abreast of the situation.[53] There is no more indication of how the family fared with the Ottoman state; 'Aziz ('Abd al-'Aziz) Hawwash certainly did return to Syria, however, and together with Salih al-'Ali would go on to lead the 'Alawi revolt against the French occupation twenty years later.

The authorities' uncertainty about the 'Alawis was no doubt also colored by the rampant instability in Anatolia in the mid-1890s, in particular by the ever greater thrust of Armenian revolutionary activities and the repeated massacre of Armenian civilians by Kurdish irregulars in the eastern provinces between 1894 and 1896.[54] Although not reflected in official reports of the time, rumors were rife within the Christian/Levantine community of Aleppo in August 1895 that the 'Alawis of the Qusayr, Jabal al-Aqra', Jabal Musa, and Amanus mountains around Antioch would soon rise up in support of the Armenians there as well.[55] That the authorities did take such rumors seriously is suggested

49 Somel, *Modernization*, 238–40; see also Deringil, *Well-Protected Domains*, 101–4.
50 MF.MKT 164/159.
51 FO 195/1448, 17 Aug., 13 Oct., 5 Nov. 1883.
52 DH.MKT 1865/20; DH.MKT 1919/122.
53 DH.MKT 2490/75.
54 See Stephen Duguid, "The Politics of Unity: Hamidian Policy in Eastern Anatolia," *Middle Eastern Studies* 9 (1973): 147–50; Georgeon, *Abdulhamid*, 286–95.
55 Poche-Marcopoli Archives, Aleppo: FP 2005, 17 Aug. 1895.

by the fact that orders sent to governments of Aleppo, Baghdad, and Basra to guard against the illegal importation of modern cartridge-loading rifles, a key factor in the Armenian revolts of the time, were later also extended to Beirut, Tripoli, and other ports along the Syrian coast, lest they fall into the hands of 'Alawi, Druze, or Bedouin troublemakers.[56] Most striking, perhaps, considering how the state had labored since the Tanzimat to integrate the 'Alawis into both the educational system and the army, was the suspicion expressed even late in the century toward 'Alawi military officers. In the fall of 1899 Abdülhamid, who had only narrowly escaped an assassination attempt by Armenian extremists in Istanbul a few years earlier, appears to have demanded assurances that there would be no 'Alawis assigned to his retinue during an upcoming visit to Beirut. Military officials in Damascus sent their assurances to Yıldız Palace forthwith.[57]

In the final years of Abdülhamid's reign, the imperial government's policy toward the 'Alawis appears once again to have been less concerned with education or the rectification of religious belief than with maintaining law and order. As such there is actually very little that distinguishes the late Hamidian period from the ostensibly more progressive regime of the CUP, which took power and reestablished the Ottoman constitution in 1908. Throughout the early years of the twentieth century the authorities struggled with the problem of brigandage in the coastal mountains, a problem that, however, invariably also had political overtones. Thus in the summer of 1901 a major clan war erupted between the 'Alawis of the southern Safita area and the *bey*s of the 'Akkar, who had taken to raiding 'Alawi villages and carrying off their livestock. According to the French consul in Beirut, the Ottomans were increasingly allowing the 'Akkar *bey*s as well as the Dandashlis to dominate the region as a check against the local Christian and 'Alawi populations they deemed potentially disloyal—leading the French to intervene heavily in favor of the Christian notables of Safita, who stood accused of having fomented the dispute.[58] In September 1904 the Foreign Ministry in Istanbul had to deal with a petition by the widows of two victims of the Safita-based 'Alawi bandits Iskandar Agha al-Maw'i and his brother Salim Agha, who were infesting the roads and raiding villages in the area.[59] Further north, the governments of Beirut and Aleppo had to put together a joint task force in the summer of 1902 to fight 'Alawi brigands from Latakia and Sahyun who had been attacking villages around Jisr al-Shughur, on the border between the two provinces.[60] The area was strategically important, at

---

56 DH.MKT 1823/38; DH.MKT 2204/18; DH.MKT 2251/77.
57 Y.PRK.MYD 22/105; Y.PRK.ASK 157/45; Y.PRK.BŞK 61/45.
58 MAE: Correspondance politique et commerciale, Nouvelle Série [NS] Turquie 108, fol. 62a–69a.
59 DH.TMIK.M 182/69, 75.
60 DH.MKT 529/38.

the junction of the Orontes and Nahr al-Kabir river valleys, but notoriously difficult to monitor. In April 1909 the sultan personally asked the Interior Ministry to investigate reports of 'Alawi depredations in the Jisr area "on the old hajj route from Payas and Antioch"; as late as July 1915 the ministry was handing out cash awards to officers who had helped capture the 'Alawi brigand Ahtif ibn Kiloş and an associate at Jisr.[61]

A good illustration of the state's ongoing challenges in asserting control in this period is provided by the extended dossier dealing with the establishment of a military post in the Kelbiye district. In April 1900, following a central government directive to station soldiers in refractory areas, the *kaimakam* and members of the Administrative Council of Jabala wrote the governor of Latakia recommending the construction of a *kışla* (army barracks) or *karakolhane* (police station) in Qardaha, "on account of its inaccessible location and the uncouthness of its people," to put an end to the "violence and aggression they forever and habitually commit against each other, the disputes and killings between them and the inhabitants of neighboring villages, and the stealing and plundering of livestock and the ruining of crops, whether those of their enemies or of other individuals."[62] The proposal, which interestingly never makes mention of the population's confessional identity, was mulled over for many months on the provincial level. In August 1901 Latakia's infrastructure engineer (*nafıaları mühendisi*) produced a detailed cost estimate as well as an architectural blueprint for barracks that could accommodate one hundred men. The governor of Beirut eventually forwarded them to the High Command (Seraskerlik) in Istanbul, along with a suggestion to the Interior Ministry to make Qardaha the center of a *nahiye*, which would make it easier to secure the necessary financing. There the planning came to an abrupt end: in April 1902 the bureau of the General Staff (Umum Erkan-ı Harbiye) let it be known that its forces in Latakia were already engaged in protecting the coast, pursuing brigands, and supporting the local authorities and could not spare any men whatsoever for a new station post in Qardaha. Indeed, nothing resembling the blueprint drawings was to our knowledge ever built there.

The Abdülhamid government's wariness of groups such as the 'Alawis was also reflected in its extensive censorship and domestic spying program.[63] In September 1898, for example, the Interior Ministry prohibited a number of religious and ethnographic studies published in England and France, including both Samuel Lyde's *Asian Mystery* and his *The Ansyreeh and Ismaeleeh: A Visit to the Secret Sects of Northern Syria*.[64] In May 1902 a police commissioner extraordinaire was sent to Cairo to investigate an

61 Y.EE 36/55; DH.EUM.4.Şb 2/57.
62 DH.TMIK.S 36/50; see also İ.DH 944/74757.
63 See Georgeon, *Abdulhamid*, 159–64.
64 DH.MKT 2110/24.

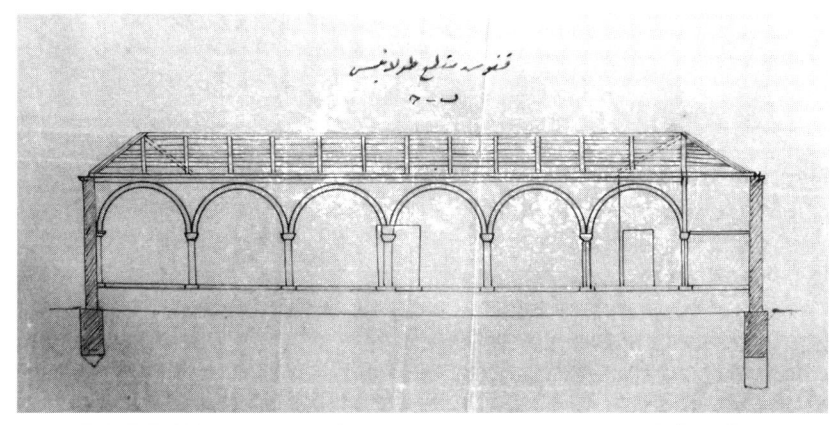

FIGURE 6.1. Blueprints of planned police station in Qardaha
(DH.TMIK.S 36/50, Başbakanlık Archives, Istanbul)

'Alawi from Adana who had recently moved there and begun publishing *Anadolı*, a paper critical of the sultanate, in which he decried all sorts of misdoings by the authorities in Adana, including land expropriations and the unending harassment of 'Alawis, which is what had pushed him into exile. The police commissioner estimated that 70–80 percent of the allegations were probably true and should be further investigated in Adana.[65] In Syria the provincial government continued to apprise Yıldız Palace of foreigners traveling in the coastal mountains and stirring up the 'Alawi population, or of the influence still being exerted by foreign missionaries.[66] In June 1914 an informant (*muhbir*) identified only as "Ahmed" notified the Sublime Porte that two court officials were trying to provoke clashes between 'Alawis and Muslims in Antioch; the following month, only weeks before the outbreak of World War I, the Bureau of Public Security (Emniyet-i Umumiye Müdiriyeti) received word from the Justice Ministry that

65 Y.EE 129/79.
66 Y.PRK.UM 49/76; Y.EE 43/103.

some 'Alawi shaykhs of the 'Umraniye district of Hama were undermining the state's authority through their excessive influence over their flock and needed to be curtailed.[67]

At the same time, these sources imply, the Ottomans did try to address 'Alawi concerns in an effort to reinforce their governance over the community. In October 1902 the Tripoli garrison commander reported that a group of 150 'Alawis had been occupying the local government house (*konak*) for the past seven days to protest against their ill-treatment at the hands of the *kaimakam* of Safita; in the end their headmen were invited to come to the garrison "because so long as their complaints and grievances are not heard, the incidence of conditions that are detrimental to public peace and contrary to the royal wish cannot be excluded."[68] For all their acrimony toward local state officials, 'Alawis increasingly resorted to sending the central government petitions by telegram. Thus in May 1907 the Interior Ministry received a cable from Latakia from 'Ali ibn Darwish Saqr, in which he describes, in heavily colloquial Arabic, how domestic strife had led to the ruin of their crops in the Bayt al-Shillif and Muhalaba districts that year: if the peasants were not granted a tax reprieve, something which the local government refused to do, they would have to abandon their fields and move away.[69] Another time 'Alawis from the Hama area requested help after Bedouin of the Khalifa tribe had raided their villages.[70] In March 1909 the 'Alawis of Latakia complained that they were once again suffering discrimination and being excluded from serving on the administrative and judicial councils on both the *sancak* and *kaza* levels, claiming this as their "constitutional right."[71] As always, Ottoman efforts to better integrate the 'Alawis were hampered more than anything else by a lack of resources. The conundrums the authorities sometimes faced in trying to govern the 'Alawis according to the modern standards they had set are exemplified in a last case from September 1913, where Beirut officials informed the imperial Ministers' Council (Meclis-i Vükela) that they lacked the means to summon and prosecute up to 280 members of the Qarahala and Khayyatin tribes who had been involved in a vicious war "with many dead and injured" in the district of Jabala two years prior. Instead they proposed to "resolve and decide the suit according to tribal conditions," that is, essentially to let the defendants go and settle things among themselves. The council, however, while recognizing that too much time had elapsed (and that the local gendarmerie was lax in the performance of its duties), nonetheless "considered it not appropriate to release the detained persons, which

67 DH.EUM.EMN 80/21; DH.EUM.7.Şb 1/1.
68 Y.MTV 235/127.
69 DH.TMIK.M 244/40.
70 DH.MKT 2647/38.
71 DH.MKT 2792/76.

would be seen as a failure of justice," and enjoined the provincial authorities to pursue with the case.[72]

The CUP government's somewhat haphazard efforts to engage the 'Alawis extended right into World War I.[73] There is of course no question that the war brought enormous suffering to the entire population of western Syria, where conscription, military requisitions, and the forced sale of staple foods to the government at artificially low prices led to acute famine and the spread of deadly diseases such as typhus fever. As always the draining of scarce resources toward the political and economic nerve centers of the coast left the hinterland particularly vulnerable. Entire swaths of the Lebanon and 'Alawi mountains became depopulated during the war, with the latter mired in even deeper poverty on account of their pronounced underdevelopment. Al-Tawil, who was a witness to events, furthermore reports that in Adana, the government foodstuff commission, which controlled the sale of bread, prevented its distribution in 'Alawi neighborhoods, while many of the 'Alawi men were drafted into the infamous sixteenth army division that was sent to the killing fields of Çanakkale.[74]

It is in this context of generalized misery and resentment against the Ottomans that Cemal Paşa, commander of the Fourth Army and governor of all Syria during the war, took special care to propitiate certain 'Alawi leaders. In Latakia, for example, the properties of Christian notables who had fled the city under French auspices were seized and redistributed, often by legally dubious means, to local village and neighborhood bosses. One of the main beneficiaries of this expropriation was Saqr Khayr-Bey.[75] Even more, Cemal Paşa was concerned lest the 'Alawi notability throw in their lot with the Arab nationalist movement taking shape in Beirut and Damascus, or with the "Arab revolt" commencing under the leadership of Sharif Husayn of Mecca. In August 1916 the district governor of Beirut reported the capture of 'Umar Rafi'i, a minor nationalist figure from Tripoli thought to be organizing secret meetings with supporters of the Arab cause in Beirut. His account, striking in its direct, distinctly modern language, provides one of the last assessments of the 'Alawis' standing as Ottoman subjects:

---

72 MV 180/30.
73 A lengthy situation report on the province of Latakia made to the Fourth Army in Syria at the beginning of the war notes that the Nusayris continued to live in a state of ignorance and poverty under the thumb of their own *mukaddem*s, whereas "sacred things such as fatherland, government, and army have not yet begun to inspire them anything." See ATASE Archives, Ankara: Birinci Dünya Harbi koleksiyonu [BDH] 170–736.
74 Al-Tawil, *Tarikh al-'Alawiyyin*, 462–68.
75 'Uthman, *Tarikh al-Ladhiqiyya*, 122–23.

The said individual was caught and arrested. I am sending the results of his interrogation by mail. There is no change in the mood and situation in Tripoli. The surroundings are calm and secure. However, the Sharif [Husayn] is in contact with the Nusayri tribes of Latakia through an intermediary, and I think he is trying to attain [their support]. I have sent my directives to the area and am returning to the city tomorrow. The gratification of the Nusayri shaykhs has been undertaken together with his excellency, the Commander [Cemal] Paşa. Only it will be necessary to give each one a valuable gift on behalf of the government. I submit that if you also give a bit of money, the gifts will have a very good effect.[76]

A few weeks later the Interior Ministry recommended bestowing the Mecidiye Order on several provincial notables in Latakia, including the chief of the Banu 'Ali and two other 'Alawi shaykhs, for their "service and loyalty above all suspicion."[77] Around the same time funds were covertly transferred to Beirut to be distributed to various 'Alawi shaykhs in the province.[78] This policy of co-optation appears to have been maintained to the very end of the war. In November 1918, a full month after the armistice of Mudros, Sultan Mehmed Vahieddin followed the War Ministry's recommendation and awarded the Mecidiye Order, fifth degree, to Shaykh Ma'ruf Efendi, a leading 'Alawi landowner and notable of Suwaydiyya near Antioch.[79] Even though the empire was effectively at its end, the measure helped secure important long-term benefits: in the 1930s, as will be seen below, the Ma'ruf family would emerge as ardent proponents of the Alexandretta district's annexation to republican Turkey.

In conclusion, the state's policies toward the 'Alawis in the late Hamidian and Young Turk period demonstrated time and again that they were still looked at askance and "not yet" considered full and equal citizens. Religion, however, had little to do with it. If anything, the "rectification of belief" offered an occasion for disseminating Ottomanist state ideology through the medium of modern education, an opportunity eagerly seized upon by a significant proportion of the 'Alawi population itself. In some cases 'Alawis willingly converted to Islam or otherwise demonstrated their fidelity to the imperial state; in many other cases, our sources suggest that their sectarian identity was simply not relevant to the more immediate concerns of maintaining order and defending the empire's integrity. Rather, what conspired against greater 'Alawi enfranchisement in the twilight years of Ottoman rule were a number

76 DH.EUM.4.Şb 7/39.
77 İ.DUİT 66/52.
78 DH.EUM.4.Şb 7/60; DH.ŞFR 531/87; DH.ŞFR 68/8.
79 İ.DUİT 68/20.

of interrelated political and economic factors: the state's increasingly d international situation, coupled with the growing fear and hostility within provincial society toward groups which, like the Armenians, appeared to have the favor of foreign interests; the continuing power of local gentry leaderships, whether 'Alawi or non-'Alawi, who remained intent on preserving their socio-economic dominance in the area; the heavy-handedness of CUP policies in the provinces and the concomitant rise of an Arab nationalist ideology, with which the 'Alawis were partially becoming identified; and, perhaps more than anything, a perpetual lack of state resources to counter these challenges and bring to fulfillment the promises and expectations raised by the secularizing reforms of the late nineteenth and early twentieth centuries.

There is a temptation to see the vehement opposition that the 'Alawis continued to meet on the local level against their conversion, their use of mosques and schools, or their election to the provincial *meclis*es as an expression of ancient sectarian or tribal animosities, which could be overcome only by the enlightened rule of a strong central authority. This is indeed how the Ottomans themselves tended to see their "civilizing mission" in the region, as Ussama Makdisi has argued with respect to Mt. Lebanon, by bringing modern government to a society deemed backward and forever wracked by parochial conflict.[80] The same basic reading was made of the coastal hinterland further north: in a far-ranging report on the *vilâyet* of Beirut commissioned by the Sublime Porte and published simultaneously in Turkish and Arabic in September 1917, two Ministry of Education inspectors expound at length on the 'Alawis' religious idiosyncrasies, tribalism, and economic deprivation, blaming the provincial notability for continually exploiting the peasantry and pressing the government to take more action to lift the 'Alawis and others out of this state of barbarity and oppression.[81]

Yet the struggle 'Alawi society faced in the late Ottoman period was in reality less about overcoming timeless religious and tribal prejudices than about competition for distinctly modern resources. Conflict with Sunni neighbors, landowners, or municipal rivals, though often expressed in a sectarian idiom, resulted above all from large-scale 'Alawi labor migration to the new industrial centers of Tarsus, Mersin, and Alexandretta; from 'Alawi wage slavery on the new commercial cotton-farming estates of the Çukurova or the Amık Plain near Antioch; and from legal disputes over rural property (itself only a commodity since 1858) or irrigation rights in new highland farming ventures. Even in the antiquities trade—by definition one of the most "modern" commercial activities imaginable—there was competition involving 'Alawis: in November 1902 a landowner from Arsuz near Alexandretta complained

---

80 Makdisi, *Culture of Sectarianism*, 28, 147–49, 151–52.
81 Mehmed Behcet and Refik Temimi, *Beyrut Vilayeti*, vol. 2, Şemal Kısmı (Beirut: Vilayet Matbaası, 1917), 120–61, 221–24; see also Hanssen, *Fin de Siècle*, 80–81.

to the Education Ministry that a local 'Alawi shaykh and his helpers had dug up an ancient column along with some coins and other antiques from his fields at night, and he demanded his fair share of their value. (The ministry, for its part, immediately sent orders to Aleppo to have the artifacts seized for the state.)[82] The means by which these conflicts were brought before the authorities, and the political claims being made on them, were equally modern: the sending of telegram petitions, the contestation of election results, the invocation of constitutional rights, and the protestation of "loyalty" (*sadakat*) were all part of the new register of Ottoman political discourse in the last years of empire. As such there was never a simple, binary opposition between "the 'Alawis" and "the state" or between "the 'Alawis" and "the Sunnis" on the communal level but rather a question of which 'Alawi actors stood to gain from what kind of patronage relations with which state officials or business associates. The form these relations took changed significantly over time, from tax farming to commercial sharecropping, military recruitment, school enrollment, and local political office. It is nevertheless these relations that would continue to define, more than any religious or tribal aspect, the 'Alawis' standing vis-à-vis the rest of society, both in the late Ottoman period and into the mandate and early republican era.

THE 'ALAWI AWAKENING

The new social and economic vistas opening before the 'Alawis in the late nineteenth and early twentieth centuries of course brought about important changes within the 'Alawi community itself. Up to this point we have mainly dealt with 'Alawi society as reflected in the sources of others, in the normative archives of the imperial authority, in the often deprecatory chronicles of an urban elite, and in the self-interested reports of foreign observers. The final decades of Ottoman rule, however, witnessed an upsurge in literary production by 'Alawis themselves, which, like the wider Arabic literary revival (or *nahda*) of which it was part, served to define and delineate the community's identity like never before. If 'Alawi literature in the past had been mainly religious and poetical, beginning in the late nineteenth century a new class of secular intellectuals such as Husayn Mayhub Harfush and Muhammad Amin Ghalib al-Tawil undertook to inventory and narrate 'Alawi history as such, to reach out to and educate the 'Alawi hinterland population, and thus to lay the groundwork for the formulation of properly political claims as a sectarian community in the post-Ottoman period. Borrowing from an article published by the reformist cleric 'Abd al-Rahman al-Khayyir in the journal *Al-Nahda* in 1937, contemporary writers have therefore consecrated

[82] MF.MKT 672/36–48.

this cultural revival in retrospect as the "awakening" (*yaqza*) of the 'Alawi community per se.[83]

The roots of the 'Alawi awakening were multiple. On the one hand, 'Alawi religious scholars themselves recognized the need, beginning as early as the first half of the nineteenth century, to revitalize the faith and reassert their own role as the spiritual leaders, teachers, and judges of their community—not least in the face of Ottoman, Egyptian, and European efforts to impose their own respective versions of "modernity" on provincial society. As Sabrina Mervin has demonstrated with regard to the Shi'is of southern Lebanon, the heterodox Muslim *'ulama* grappled with basically the same questions as their Sunni colleagues—how to reconcile traditional learning with science and technology; how to cleanse the religion of illegitimate innovation and use it instead to reinvigorate and guide the community—and thereby participated actively in the wider Ottoman project of "renewal" (*tecdid*) and "reform" (*ıslah*) of the period.[84] Indeed, while the 'Alawi oral tradition recalls only a handful of religious shaykhs from the first few centuries of Ottoman rule, it preserves the memory of numerous clerics who came to play an important social and educational role within the community in the nineteenth century: 'Abd al-'Al al-Hajj Mu'alla is credited with having built one of the first mosques in the Tartus area after his return from pilgrimage to Mecca in 1838; Yusuf Miyy and others are remembered for their medical skills, their teaching efforts and interest in astronomy, or their helping the poor and building windmills to benefit the local population.[85]

A key factor in the 'Alawi awakening was also the willingness of some shaykhs to seize on the new educational and administrative opportunities offered by the state's Tanzimat reforms. Thus 'Ali Badra, a shaykh from the Safita area, apparently served as a *qadi* (judge) and teacher on the village level; other members of his family are noted to have studied Hanefi jurisprudence and Turkish, to have served as secretary in the court of Safita, or to have been appointed to an official government school in Latakia under Ziya Bey.[86] Perhaps the best illustration of how 'Alawi *'ulama* embraced Ottoman modernism is provided by Husayn Mayhub Harfush, author of the *Khayr al-Sani'a*, and the extended Harfush family of Maqaramda village in the district of Qadmus. According to 'Ali 'Abbas Harfush (d. 1981), nephew of Husayn and editor of the first modern publication to be based on his uncle's biographical dictionary, the family forebear Salman ibn Muhammad Harfush moved to Maqaramda from Banyas after legally purchasing it from

---

83 'Abd al-Rahman al-Khayyir (d. 1986), *Yaqzat al-Muslimin al-'Alawiyyin fi Matla' al-Qarn al-'Ashrin*, ed. Hani al-Khayyir (Damascus: Matba'at al-Kitab al-'Arabi, 1996); see also al-Musa, *Al-Imam 'Ali wa'l-'Alawiyyin*, 203–33.

84 Mervin, *Un réformisme chiite*, esp. 13–14, 49, 109–20, 159.

85 Al-Khayyir, *Yaqza*, 21–22; Hasan, *A'lam*, 1:75–78.

86 Al-Khayyir, *Yaqza*, 22–24; Hasan, *A'lam*, 1:125.

the people of Qadmus around 1865. There he built a mosque and study room that soon attracted visitors from the entire area, turning Maqaramda into an important center of 'Alawi learnedness. Growing up in this milieu, Salman's son Mayhub (ca. 1866–1917) become a noted scholar and poet in his own right and used his extensive social skills not only to maintain contact with brethren as far away as Tarsus (southern Turkey) but also to improve relations with the Ismailis of the district with whom there were lingering communal tensions.[87] Mayhub's son Husayn, who was born in Maqaramda around 1892, followed in his father's and grandfather's footsteps and devoted his early life to teaching, before spending the final decades of his life compiling the *Khayr al-Saniʿa*, the most monumental work of all 'Alawi historiography. Around 1917 he and Shaykh 'Ali 'Abbas Salman founded a new school for 'Alawi children in al-'Anaza (near Banyas), then collected money from private donors to build another school at Barmana in the district of Safita. His efforts to bring modern education to the highland population were supported by Salih al-'Ali, himself the son of a local shaykh considered a reformist scholar, and who sent his family to live under the Harfushes' care in Maqaramda during his revolt against the French in 1918–21. After the revolt Husayn financed and built another school in Maqaramda itself, this time with the help of Shaykh 'Ali Hasan of the famous al-Khayyir family of Qardaha, and was eventually given an official teaching appointment by the French mandate government.[88]

Other members of the family participated in these endeavors as well. According to a manuscript "Supplement" (*Mustadrak*) to the *Khayr al-Saniʿa* compiled by Husayn's great-nephew Ibrahim Ahmad Harfush, Husayn's elder cousin Muhsin 'Ali Harfush (d. 1936), who had been educated at a state school in Hattaniyya village in Qadmus, was among the first to recognize the need for modern reforms in the region and played a key part in collecting money from the local villages to pay for teachers' salaries and student bursaries in al-'Anaza.[89] The *Mustadrak* also provides evidence of other 'Alawi reformists serving as Ottoman functionaries. 'Ali 'Abbas Salman (d. 1971), one of the leading intellectuals of his generation and on whose recollections the account of the 'Anaza school is largely based, was formally appointed director of the school by the Ottoman government and given responsibility for the staff of six teachers it employed.[90] And 'Ali Hamdan al-Zawi (d. 1945), originally a religious scholar from the Safita district and graduate of the Ottoman state school in Draykish, went on to a long and distinguished career in both the Ottoman and French mandate civil service. In 1909–10 he was named director

87 Harfush, *Al-Maghmurun al-Qudama*, 13–19.
88 Ibid., 21–23, 64–65; see also Hasan, *Aʿlam*, 1:77–78, 143–49; Khonda, *Tarikh al-ʿAlawiyyin*, 247–49.
89 Ibrahim Harfush, *Al-Mustadrak fi Khayr al-Saniʿa* (Library of the Institut français du Proche-Orient, Damascus: photocopy of manuscript dated 1991), 421–24.
90 Ibid., 424–25, 376–84; al-Khayyir, *Yaqza*, 24–25; Harfush, *Al-Maghmurun*, 23.

of the Safita branch of the Ottoman Agricultural Bank (Ziraat Bankası), which had been founded in 1888 to provide low-cost loans to farmers throughout the empire. A few years later he was elected head of the local municipality (*ra'is al-baladiyya*) in Safita and subsequently served as state inspector or prosecutor (*mustantiq*) at the *kaza* level. Under the French he was appointed justice of the peace (*hakim al-sulh*) in the troublesome Tall Kalakh district in the southern coastal mountains, where the 'Alawi peasantry was frequently at odds with the Sunni *agha*-class landowners, and in 1932 he was named to the Appeals Court in Latakia.[91]

Perhaps most significantly, Muhammad Amin Ghalib al-Tawil (d. 1932), author of the landmark *History of the 'Alawis*, likewise began his career as an Ottoman functionary. Born in Adana to a family of 'Alawi émigrés from Antioch, al-Tawil recounts that he studied law and administration and subsequently served as a director of police in the *vilayet*. In the course of his work he was called on to travel to numerous other provinces of the empire as well, and at one point even participated in an official Ottoman mission to gather charitable donations in India. After the French withdrawal from Cilicia in 1919 (see below), he emigrated first to Antioch, then accepted an appointment to the district court in Latakia and later also served as justice of the peace in Tall Kalakh.[92] According to his own account, al-Tawil first wrote his opus in Turkish while still in Adana, before translating it into Arabic and publishing it Beirut in 1924; the original version is, however, not known to be extant. Because of his secular background, al-Tawil was never regarded as a "shaykh" and is therefore often not included in the historiography of the *yaqza* today. The *Tarikh al-'Alawiyyin*, despite its many flaws, nonetheless constitutes a pioneering attempt to construct an 'Alawi identity as such and should probably be seen as the historically most important work of all 'Alawi literature.

A third aspect of the 'Alawi awakening was more properly religious or ecumenical. In seeking to reform and modernize their community, the leading 'Alawi *'ulama* of the day were also working toward a rapprochement (*taqrib*) with other Muslim denominations, starting with Twelver Shi'ism. The Shi'i scholarly community of Lebanon and Damascus, unlike the 'Alawis, had an established jurisprudential tradition, an institutional base in the Shi'i shrine cities of Iraq, and an extensive network of contacts with other families throughout the region that allowed it to assume its full share in the Shi'i reform movement of the second half of the nineteenth century. It also had the resources to finance its own confessional schools and, perhaps most important, to support a modern literary and societal

---

91 Harfush, *Mustadrak*," 354–61.
92 'Abd al-Rahman al-Khayyir, introduction to al-Tawil, *Tarikh al-'Alawiyyin*, 6–11; Hasan, *A'lam*, 2:87–97.

journal such as *al-'Irfan*, which began publication in 1909 (following the restoration of press freedom by the CUP government) and played a key part in the precipitation of a distinctly Shi'i sectarian identity.[93] *Al-'Irfan* also functioned, as Sabrina Mervin writes, as a vital link between the Lebanese Shi'i and the 'Alawi scholarly communities. In 1911 the 'Alawi reformists Sulayman al-Ahmad and Ibrahim 'Abd al-Latif Mirhij traveled to Sayda to meet with the editors and other secular Shi'i writers, as well as with the Najaf-based religious scholar Muhammad Husayn Al Kashif al-Ghita', who subsequently sent them books of Imami jurisprudence that later served as an important reference for 'Alawi law. Al-Ahmad and Mirhij began a contributing correspondence with *al-'Irfan* and saw to its distribution back in the 'Alawi highlands. A year later, when the journal was on the point of folding for lack of funds, al-Ahmad pledged to find two hundred new subscribers in the North, thanks to whom it was indeed finally able to survive and even turn a profit for the first time.[94]

Sulayman al-Ahmad (d. 1942) was doubtless the driving force behind the 'Alawi-Shi'i rapprochement, and the 'Alawi awakening as a whole. Raised in a traditional religious family in the Qardaha area and highly literate at an early age, al-Ahmad at forty was seen as the most learned and accomplished scholar of his generation. He traveled widely throughout the highlands to mobilize other clerics to the modernist cause, while his reputation as a linguist earned him an honorary appointment to the Arab Academy (Al-Majma' al-'Arabi) in Damascus in 1919.[95] In addition to helping introduce the Ja'fari (Imami Shi'i) *madhhab* of Islamic jurisprudence to the 'Alawi community, he also fought to reduce the influence of popular superstitions and magical practices within 'Alawi society and advocated for the education of girls; his own daughter Jumana studied medicine and became the first woman doctor of Latakia. Under the French he later agreed to serve as chief *qadi* of the 'Alawi confessional court system and remained at the forefront of efforts to create a unified 'Alawi religious leadership.[96] Thanks in large part to al-Ahmad's organizational efforts, the leading 'Alawi clergy of Syria issued a declaration in early 1936 stating unequivocally that true 'Alawism subscribes to all the precepts of Islam and that 'Alawis have always been loyal defenders of the Muslim, and Arab, community; in a spirit of pan-Islamic and anticolonial solidarity, Amin al-Husayni, the mufti of Jerusalem and leading Sunni

---

93 Silvia Naef, "Aufklärung in einem schiitischen Umfeld: Die libanesische Zeitschrift al-'Irfan," *Die Welt des Islams* 36 (1996): 365–78; Mervin, *Un réformisme chiite*, 154–58; Max Weiss, *In the Shadow of Sectarianism: Law, Shi'ism and the Making of Modern Lebanon* (Cambridge, MA: Harvard University Press, 2010).

94 Mervin, *Un réformisme chiite*, 155, 322–24.

95 Harfush, *Mustadrak*, 370; Al-Khayyir, *Yaqza*, 33–34; Hasan, *A'lam*, 1:126–43.

96 Mervin, *Un réformisme chiite*, 324–26.

political figure of the time, responded that same year with a fatwa formally recognizing them as such.[97]

A fourth and final aspect of the *yaqza* was thus simply also political. From the very start, reformist 'Alawi shaykhs had seen education, religious modernism, and ecumenism as a way of overcoming sectarian and tribal divisions,[98] and no doubt of consolidating their own leadership position within society at the expense of the traditional feudal classes. Particularly in the North, they also sought to overcome tensions with other communities that were laid bare even more by the suffering and deprivation brought by World War I and then the French occupation. Shortly after the end of the war, the Latakia highlands witnessed violent clashes between the 'Alawis and the Kurds and Turkmen of the area, for example, which Sulayman al-Ahmad tried to calm, among other things, with a public appeal to Muslim brotherliness.[99] Many Sunnis (and Christians) had in fact taken refuge in the 'Alawi mountains during the war to escape the oppression of the Cemal Paşa government,[100] while Sharif Husayn, as already indicated, had also begun to solicit contacts in support of Arab nationalism. It is therefore not surprising that 'Alawi reformists came to play a central role in the Salih al-'Ali revolt against the French in 1918–21, nor that modern writers regard this revolt as an integral part of the 'Alawi awakening per se. Salih al-'Ali (d. 1950), the 'Alawi biographical sources agree, was himself a recognized scholar, devout, and sought after as a teacher.[101] During the revolt he relied on numerous friends and colleagues to rally support in the region, gather money, and help in planning; the aforesaid 'Ali 'Abbas Salman, according to his own account, served as the *amin al-sirr* or general secretary of the operation.[102]

The intellectual ferment of the 'Alawi awakening did not end with the defeat of the revolt or the start of French mandatory rule. Several key 'Alawi figures embraced the establishment of the separate "Alaouites" regime in Latakia, while others continued to cooperate with other Syrian nationalists against the French. Nor were all 'Alawi shaykhs single-mindedly obsessed with religious reformism or a rapprochement with other sects: the biographical sources also preserve the memory of poets and clerics who cleaved to a more traditional, nonpolitical "Khasibi" path of 'Alawi mysticism and asceticism.[103] Modernist 'Alawi clerics nevertheless continued to forge ties with their Lebanese Shi'i counterparts and even began to participate in joint study

---

97 Ibid., 326–27; see also Firro, *Metamorphosis of the Nation*, 112–13.
98 Al-Khayyir, *Yaqza*, 24, 26–27; Harfush, *Maghmurun*, 70–72.
99 Hasan, *A'lam*, 1:131; see also al-Tawil, *Tarikh al-'Alawiyyin*, 506–11.
100 Al-Hakim, *Suriyya wa'l-'Ahd al-'Uthmani*, 71.
101 Harfush, *Mustadrak*, 208–9; Hasan, *A'lam*, 1:35, 77–78, 128; Qays Ibrahim 'Abbas, *Al-Shaykh Salih al-'Ali: Awraq wa-Shahadat* (Damascus: Dar al-Takwin, 2005), 32–38.
102 Harfush, *Mustadrak*, 174, 390–91.
103 Ibid., 137–43, 157–69, 400–403, 495–532.

trips to the Shi'i shrine cities in Iraq; of particular note are the visitations undertaken by Habib Al Ibrahim (d. 1965) of Baalbek, who came to meet with countless 'Alawi shaykhs in Homs, Hama, and Latakia in the later 1940s and played a key role in the propagation of Ja'fari legal thought in the region.[104] This process can be said to have reached its logical conclusion in 1951, when the 'Alawi clerical leadership finally gave itself a full-fledged institutional framework with the founding of the Ja'fari Islamic Aid Society (al-Jam'iyya al-Khayriyya al-Islamiyya al-Ja'fariyya). The following year the community was officially recognized as one of the constituent *madhhabs* of the Syrian republic.[105]

The notion of 'Alawi reformism therefore also casts a different light on the question of 'Alawi "conversion" to orthodox Islam. From the late Ottoman period onward, as we have seen, the 'Alawis' local antagonists (especially in Antioch) as well as Western observers were often quick to assume that their profession of orthodox faith, their use of mosques, or their intended rapprochement with Shi'ism were merely tactical or a display of *taqiyya* (dissimulation). This charge has stuck with them in a lot of the literature, both polemical and academic, down to the present day. Ever since 'Alawis have given written expression to their own claims, however, from the petitions of the Abdülhamid era to the explicit literature of the *yaqza*, they have consistently maintained that whatever doctrinal divergences exist concern only minor points of allegorical interpretation (*ta'wil*) or are the result of centuries of isolation and neglect and can therefore be overcome by better access to education and integration into Muslim society. There is little gain in debating the theological validity of the 'Alawis' desire to be recognized as part of the wider community; socially and historically, it is in need of no further demonstration.

SALIH AL-'ALI AND THE GÜNEY CEPHESI (SOUTHERN FRONT)

The Salih al-'Ali revolt against the French stands out as the most celebrated event in modern 'Alawi history. For almost three years Salih al-'Ali and his followers were able to prevent France's colonial troops from "pacifying" the Latakia hinterland, dealing them a number of outright military defeats and building ties to other anti-French insurgencies in northern Syria, in particular to that of Ibrahim Hanano. However, the revolt or even "revolution" (*thawra*), as it is often termed, remains subject to greatly differing interpretations. While

---

104 Ja'far al-Muhajir, "Al-Rajul alladhi Hazama al-Isti'mar Marratayn" in *Al-Mu'tamar al-Takrimi li'l-'Allama al-Muqaddas wa'l-Da'iya al-Mujahid al-Muhajir al-'Amili al-Shaykh Habib Al Ibrahim* (Beirut: Al-Mustashara al-Thaqafiyya li'l-Jumhuriyya al-Islamiyya al-Iraniyya, 1997), 39–48.

105 Mervin, *Un réformisme chiite*, 327–28.

many 'Alawi writers have proudly drawn attention to its grounding in a local, sectarian milieu, in part to demonstrate their community's contribution to the wider Syrian cause, nationalist historiography particularly in the 1960s began to appropriate Salih al-'Ali as a leading exponent of the "popular struggle" against imperialism in Syria and make little or no reference to his 'Alawi identity.[106] Some contemporary historians of the mandate period, currently one of the most active fields of Syrian historiography, have suggested that the likes of Salih al-'Ali and assorted Druze and Bedouin resistance leaders were not motivated by an ideology of Arab nationalism but rather by a *"patriotisme des terroirs"* (regionalist patriotism) to defend traditionally peripheral areas against the encroachment of a non-Muslim occupying state;[107] others, by contrast, have argued that the actions of seemingly preideological rebel or robber "bands" (Turk.: *çetes*; Arab. *'isabat*) did in fact demonstrate the beginnings of a national consciousness.[108] The present section, however, will draw on French and Turkish military sources in order to shed light on an aspect of the revolt that has often been neglected, namely, its connection with the no-longer-Ottoman but not yet exclusively Turkish "War of Liberation" (Kurtuluş Savaşı) being fought under the auspices of Mustafa Kemal (the later Atatürk) in southern Anatolia at the same time.

Salih al-'Ali's relationship with the Turks is the subject of some controversy. According to 'Abd al-Latif al-Yunus (1914–2013), whose nearly contemporary biography constitutes our principal narrative source for the period, Salih al-'Ali hailed from an important landowning family in the Murayqib/Shaykh Badr region of Tartus. In December 1918 he convened a meeting of twelve other leading notables in order to mount a resistance movement against the French forces, which had by then begun to occupy the coastal band of Lebanon and Syria. Even before that, however, he had supposedly been engaging for several years in guerrilla attacks against the Turkish army in the area.[109] In a recent survey of local lore regarding the revolt, Qays Ibrahim

---

106 See Adham Al Jundi, *Tarikh al-Thawrat al-Suriyya fi 'Ahd al-Intidab al-Faransi* (Damascus: Matba'at al-Ittihad, 1960), 30–60; Faris Zarzur, *Ma'arik al-Hurriyya fi Suriyya* (Damascus: Dar al-Sharq, 1964), 56–81.

107 Philip Khoury, *Syria and the French Mandate* (London: I. B. Tauris, 1987), 100–102; Jean-David Mizrahi, *Genèse de l'État mandataire: Service des Renseignements et bandes armées en Syrie et au Liban dans les années 1920* (Paris: Publications de la Sorbonne, 2003), 123–24; see also Fred Lawson, "The Northern Syrian Revolts of 1919–1921 and the Sharifian Regime: Congruence or Conflict of Interests and Ideologies?" in Philipp and Schumann, *From the Syrian Land*, 257–74.

108 Michael Provence, *The Great Syrian Revolt and the Rise of Arab Nationalism* (Austin: University of Texas Press, 2005), 14–22; Nadine Méouchy, "Rural Resistance Movements and the Introduction of New Forms of Consciousness in the Syrian Countryside, 1918–1926," in Philipp and Schumann, *From the Syrian Land*, 275–89.

109 'Abd al-Latif al-Yunus, *Thawrat al-Shaykh Salih al-'Ali* (Damascus: Wizarat al-Thaqafa, 1961), 28–29, 67–85, 105–6; Al Jundi, *Tarikh al-Thawrat*, 58; Hasan, *A'lam*, 2:60–65; Mundhir al-Mawsili, *Al-Bahth 'an al-Dhat: Al-Judhur* (Damascus: Dar al-Muruwwa, 2008), 162–200.

FIGURE 6.2. Shaykh Salih al-'Ali and cover illustration depicting mountain and desert rebel types, from Faris Zarzur, *Ma'arik al-Hurriyya fi Suriyya* (Battlefields of Freedom in Syria) (Damascus, 1964)

'Abbas denies that Salih al-'Ali was in essence a "feudalist" and claims instead that he was a social revolutionary, who in coordination with the Sharif Husayn had begun to lead an outright insurrection against Ottoman Turkish oppression as early as the spring of 1918. After months of harassing the Turkish forces in the highlands region, he was able to deal them a devastating blow in the so-called battle of Wadi al-'Uyun, during which they lost up to eighty or ninety men. Only the following year did Mustafa Kemal initiate contact with Salih al-'Ali, not out of love for the Arabs and 'Alawis, nor to support their national aspirations, but rather to get their help in putting additional pressure on the French in southern Anatolia, so that "yesterday's enemies became today's friends."[110]

There are a number of problems with this narrative, which seems above all designed to provide Salih al-'Ali with the same sort of anti-Ottoman pedigree that the Druze initiators of the "Great Syrian Revolt" of 1925–27 already enjoy in Syrian historiography. Not only are claims that Mustafa Kemal was already coordinating with Arab nationalists in 1919 spurious, as Sina Akşin has argued, since he was not yet in sole control of the Turkish independence movement, and the Society for the Defense of Rights (Müdafaa-ı Hukuk

110 'Abbas, *Awraq wa-Shahadat*, 39–50.

Cemiyeti) that would coordinate the struggle in Anatolia was not formed before September of that year,[111] but it is also unlikely that Salih al-'Ali could have been such a prodigious social bandit (and slaughterer of Turkish soldiers) without this being addressed in one way or another in their correspondence only a short while later. In the already-cited Ottoman Fourth Army report on the province of Latakia, the 'Alawis, though generally labeled as rebellious and unreliable, are expressly noted not to have been the authors of recent violence afflicting the highland region.[112] In any event, al-Yunus's account indicates that Salih al-'Ali's rebel career began in earnest in January–February 1919, when the French attempted to arrest him near Qadmus, where they were benefiting from the collaboration of the Ismaili population, but were defeated twice in short order. Thereafter the movement began to gather more and more followers throughout the area, with constant attacks on military convoys and Ismaili villages forcing the French to temporarily retreat and sue for peace in July 1919.[113]

It is unclear to what extent the Salih al-'Ali revolt was aligned at this early stage with other nationalist movements in the coastal region. Starting in early 1919 a number of insurgents from the Jabal al-Akrad, Qusayr, Antioch, and Harem areas had united under Ibrahim Hanano's leadership to coordinate efforts against the French, particularly in the newly organized "sandjak" (*sancak*; Arab., *liwa'*) of Alexandretta.[114] The French, while recognizing that the insurgency had the backing of Sharifian forces in the vicinity of Antioch, claimed that most of the 'Alawi chiefs of the northern mountains had in fact offered their submission by February 1919.[115] 'Alawi sources, on the other hand, state that Sharif Husayn's son and representative in Syria, Faysal, entered into contact with Salih al-'Ali in October 1919 with a view to supplying the latter with weapons against the French,[116] and it is indeed after the reprisal of hostilities with the 'Alawis toward the end of the year that the French begin in earnest to address his potential contacts with outside sponsors. According to the "Rapports hébdomadaires de l'Armée du Levant,"

---

111 Sina Akşin, "Turkish-Syrian Relations in the Time of Faisal (1918–1920)" in *Essays in Ottoman-Turkish Political History*, ed. Akşin, (Istanbul: Isis Press, 2000), 34.

112 ATASE: BDH 170–736.

113 Al-Yunus, *Thawra*, 107–12; see also al-Tawil, *Tarikh al-'Alawiyyin*, 512–16; Moosa, *Extremist Shiites*, 282–83.

114 Nadine Méouchy, "Le mouvement des *'isabat* en Syrie du Nord à travers le témoignage du chaykh Youssef Saadoun (1919–1921)," in *The French and British Mandates in Comparative Perspective / Les mandats français et anglais dans une perspective comparative*, ed. Nadine Méouchy and Peter Sluglett (Leiden: Brill, 2004), 659–60; see also Dalal Arsuzi-Elamir, *Arabischer Nationalismus in Syrien: Zakī al-Arsūzī und die arabisch-nationale Bewegung an der Peripherie Alexandretta/Antakya 1930–1938* (Münster: Lit, 2003), 31–35, 81.

115 MAE: Correspondance politique et commerciale, E-Levant Syrie-Liban [ELSL] 112, no. 2; ELSL 115, no. 4.

116 Al-Yunus, *Thawra*, 123–24; Hasan, *A'lam*, 66–68.

the French occupation zone had been "like an island of calm between the area of Kemalist influence in the North and that of Sharifian agitation in the South," but already in February 1920 French officials had to take note of an attack by five hundred 'Alawis on an army warehouse in Tartus and on Christian villages of the surroundings, while Latakia was once more emerging as a theater of "extremist" (that is, pro-Sharifian and Arab nationalist) propaganda and disturbances.[117] To the French, these acts were not to be construed as an "actual uprising" but were merely "instigated" by Salih al-'Ali in collaboration with a Sunni Muslim notable from Tartus. The French did have to admit, however, that the 'Alawi rebels were being armed by Syrian "extremists" from Homs who were in turn members of the Damascus-based "Committee of National Defense," and also that they had been supported by "Sharifian regular troops" armed with machine guns in another recent attack on Qadmus.[118]

In March 1920 the Syrian National Congress, with elected representatives from all over Syria, met in Damascus to declare the country's independence within its "natural" and historical borders, to proclaim Faysal king, and to refuse any power-sharing agreement with the French. There were no 'Alawi delegates at this congress, a fact often remarked upon by outside observers and taken as a possible sign of 'Alawi acquiescence in the French mandate.[119] Indeed, shortly after the congress, France's high commissioner in Syria and Lebanon, General Henri Gouraud, congratulated himself that the notables of Safita and other parts of the northern coastal range supposedly wanted nothing to do with the congress's "arbitrary declarations," which had been rejected "not only by our Christian clientele, but by Muslim, Alaouite, and Ismaili groupings too, even in places that are occupied by the Sharifians and despite the terror they are causing to reign there."[120] Such statements are belied, however, by the control Faysal evidently did exercise over the 'Alawi rebel movement. The French themselves relate that Salih al-'Ali received orders from Faysal to return properties which had been stolen in recent raids on Christian villages; throughout the spring and early summer of 1920, further intelligence reports indicate that Salih al-'Ali's "bande," already over a thousand men strong, would soon get additional Sharifian reinforcements; that they had received support from fifty regular soldiers "wearing khaki uniforms," several machine guns, and a mortar canon in their attacks in the Banyas and Shaykh Badr area; and finally that the "Sharifian authorities are putting pressure on Cheikh Saleh and encouraging him to continue the resistance."[121] By June

117 ELSL 121, no. 14, 17, 51–52, 60–61.
118 ELSL 115, no. 60; ELSL 121, no. 61, 63, 74, 88; ELSL 125, no. 154.
119 Yusuf al-Hakim, *Suriyya wa'l-'Ahd al-Faysali* (Beirut: Al-Matba'a al-Kathulikiyya, 1966), 94–95; Moosa, *Extremist Shiites*, 284; cf. Al Ma'ruf, *Tarikh*, 3:503, 510–12.
120 ELSL 121, no. 126; ELSL 125, no. 157.
121 ELSL 115, no. 126; ELSL 117, no. 6; ELSL 121, no. 127, 156–57, 177–78, 181, 205, 239.

the French noted that "the situation is worsening in the Ansarieh region" as two thousand 'Alawi insurgents equipped with machine guns were preparing a major offensive against French police columns operating in the Qadmus and Masyaf area. At the same time, Faysal is reported to have dispatched his cousin, the Sharif Nasir, to convince the remaining 'Alawi shaykhs who had been neutral up to this point to join Salih al-'Ali's cause.[122]

The tragic defeat of Sharif Faysal's nationalist forces at Maysalun on 24 July 1920 of course marked the end of his support for the rural insurrections in northern Syria as well. Already before the battle, however, the French had remarked that the Kemalist government in Turkey was mounting an ever greater propaganda effort in the region, not only around Kilis and in the Alexandretta district but among various tribes in the coastal mountains as well, funneling money through agents in Egypt to encourage local "*tchétés*" (*çete*s) and "*moudjehids*" to continue the struggle against foreign occupation.[123] Most of the rebel operations in the North were now being coordinated by the Aleppine notable and landowner Ibrahim Hanano (d. 1935), who is said to have begun receiving arms and Turkish stipends in June before signing a full-fledged cooperation agreement with the Kemalists in September 1920. 'Alawi sources indicate that Salih al-'Ali was also in contact (through his in-laws) with Ibrahim Hanano by this time and was consequently solicited by Mustafa Kemal directly to pursue with his campaign against the French.[124] In any event, the 'Alawi revolt appears to have entered a new phase in September, as rebel units now under the command of both Salih al-'Ali and 'Aziz Bey Hawwash, scion of the famous Khayr-Bey family, inflicted serious losses on the French at Masyaf.[125] All available French units were needed at this time to stem Kemalist advances along the Adana-Toprakkale line further north. The French claimed to be making headway in disarming the 'Alawi mountains through the late autumn, but with the spectacular seizure of Jisr al-Shughur by Ibrahim Hanano together with rebel bands from the Sahyun and regular Kemalist soldiers in early December, the 'Alawi insurgents returned to the offensive as well.[126] French field dispatches from the time note that Salih al-'Ali was beginning to concentrate his troops in the Jabala area, where he had been sent Turkish personnel and had issued a call for "holy war" against the enemy;[127] an extended situation report from the following spring, for its

---

122 ELSL 115, no. 190; ELSL 121 no. 249–50, 263–64, 276, 289, 304.
123 ELSL 121, no. 209, 219, 220; see also al-Yunus, *Thawra*, 180–89.
124 Ömer Osman Umar, *Osmanlı Yönetimi ve Fransız Manda İdaresi Altında Suriye (1908–1938)* (Ankara: Atatürk Araştırma Merkezi, 2004), 472–76; 'Abbas, *Al-Shaykh Salih al-'Ali*, 27, 51–54; Al Ma'ruf, *Tarikh*, 3:524–25.
125 ELSL 113, no. 146; ELSL 116, no. 48; ELSL 117, no. 111–12; Khonda, *Tarikh*, 250–60.
126 ELSL 113, no. 228; ELSL 116, no. 73, 78, 111, 118–19.
127 ELSL 113, no. 235–40; ELSL 116, no. 122, 126, 137.

part, admits that with the help of the Kemalists, Salih had indeed "created an exceptional government" and raised the entire coast in revolt.[128]

The notion of direct ties between Salih al-'Ali and the Kemalists is corroborated by the archives of the Turkish General Staff's Directorate for Military History and Strategic Studies (ATASE) in Ankara. Turkish-French confrontation had begun as early as November 1918, when the first units of the French "Légion d'Orient" landed at Mersin and Alexandretta and proceeded inland to occupy all of Cilicia including Adana. Whereas the Mudros armistice had only foreseen allied control of the railway lines and tunnel system underneath the Taurus mountains, France's heavy reliance on Armenian legionnaires, its inclusion of the region in its occupation plans for "Syria in its entirety" (*la Syrie intégrale*), and the swift inauguration of direct colonial rule immediately raised the ire of the local Muslim population, which together with the retreating Ottoman army began to stockpile weapons and organize local Kuva-ı Milliye (National Forces) militias in order to fight the French and their Armenian partisans.[129] Around the same time that Britain ceded full control over the area to France in the autumn of 1919, essentially under the reiterated terms of the Sykes-Picot agreement, the diverse local militias and Müdafaa-ı Hukuk (Defense of Rights) committees were incorporated into a single resistance movement under the direction of the Young Turk general and hero of Gallipoli, Mustafa Kemal Paşa, who on 6 November 1919 issued a *tamim* (encyclical) in which he warned of France's annexationist designs for the whole region and called for a united defense of the "Muslim" homeland. Thus did Cilicia and the northern Alexandretta district crystallize as the opening battleground of what would ultimately be recalled as the Güney Cephesi or "Southern Front" in an increasingly Kemalist-led "national" War of Independence.[130]

The Salih al-'Ali revolt was first brought to the Ankara government's attention in April 1920, when Kemalist agents in Antalya transmitted a report from a former officer in the Ottoman army regarding the situation in the Arab provinces, according to which "the Nusayri shaykh Salih has repeatedly attacked the French in the Tripoli area, and given them much trouble."[131] It is

---

128 Service historique de la Défense [SHD], Vincennes (Paris): 4H 249, dossier 2d.

129 Vahé Tachjian, *La France en Cilicie et en Haute-Mésopotamie: Aux confins de la Turquie, de la Syrie et de l'Irak (1919–1933)* (Paris: Karthala, 2004), 27–36; Robert Zeidner, *The Tricolor over the Taurus: The French in Cilicia and Vicinity, 1918–1922* (Ankara: Turkish Historical Society, 2005), 61–174. On the *Kuva-ı Milliye*, see also Ryan Gingeras, *Sorrowful Shores: Violence, Ethnicity and the End of the Ottoman Empire, 1912–1923* (Oxford: Oxford University Press, 2009), 74–78.

130 Yaşar Akbıyık, *Milli Mücadelede Güney Cephesi: Maraş* (Ankara: Kültür Bakanlığı, 1990), 68–122; T. C. Genelkurmay Başkanlığı, *Türk İstiklal Harbi IV'üncü Cilt Güney Cephesi* (Ankara: Genelkurmay Basımevi, 2009), 60–89.

131 ATASE: İstiklal Harbi koleksiyonu [İSH] 868-4.

unlikely the Kemalists envisaged relying more systematically on the 'Alawis at this point. In Cilicia the leading 'Alawi notables had welcomed the allied occupation and expressed a clear preference to the American King-Crane Commission for a French protectorate over the region; in a report to the Interior Ministry in Istanbul from August 1920 (the last Ottoman imperial document to deal with the 'Alawis), the governor of Adana indicated that the 'Alawis there had "embraced the French army with white flags" and were asking to be placed under a separate administrative regime along with their brethren in Antioch and Latakia.[132] The commander of the Kuva-ı Milliye division in Tarsus during the War of Independence likewise states in his memoirs that the local *"Fellahs"* ('Alawis) were principally regarded as supporters of the French.[133] According to al-Tawil, however, 'Alawi enthusiasm for the occupation soon turned to fear as they were literally caught in the middle of a violent struggle between Armenian returnees attempting to claim Cilicia for an independent homeland and the Turkish Muslim population of Adana. In the final pages of the *Tarikh al-'Alawiyyin*, a unique third-party perspective on the events in Cilicia that has hitherto gone largely unnoticed, al-Tawil describes eloquently from his own experience how the 'Alawi community was subject to indiscriminate attacks by Armenian irregulars, many of them genocide survivors from other parts of Anatolia. Largely unarmed and initially rebuffed by the Turkish nationalists, the 'Alawis of Adana finally came to play a key role in protecting the property and lives of their fellow Muslims during an all-out Armenian attack on their neighborhood on 10–11 July 1920. The French, desperate to restore peace and order, in the end sent armored units to quell the strife, rejected the Christian militias' declaration of independence, and instead appointed three non-Kemalist Muslims (including al-Tawil himself, in his capacity as spokesman of the local 'Alawi organization İntibah-ı Milli or "National Awakening") to head a provisional city council.[134]

The 'Alawi notables of Cilicia, French army bureau reports suggest, were deeply divided among themselves. Several had held low-level administrative posts under the Ottomans and now supported the Kemalist cause. Others cooperated wholeheartedly with the French authorities (who for their part intimated that the violence suffered by the 'Alawis of Adana in July 1920 was primarily due to the Kemalists' forced evacuation of the city's Muslim population). Selami Bey, for example, the leading pro-French 'Alawi notable of Tarsus (a scion of the nineteenth-century Egyptian immigration) was even

---

132 Tachjian, *La France en Cilicie*, 94–95; DH.İ.UM 20–25/14.
133 İsmail Ferahim Şalvuz (d. 1977), *Kurtuluş Savaşı'nda Kahraman Çukurovalılar (Adana, Tarsus, Mersinliler): Hatıra*, ed. Halil Atılgan (Ankara: T.C. Kültür Bakanlığı, 2002), 29, 51, 57, 109.
134 Al-Tawil, *Tarikh al-'Alawiyyin*, 469–97; see also Reyhani, *Gölgesiz Işıklar*, 2:123–25.

recruited to travel to Latakia in February 1920 in order to mediate with Salih al-'Ali.[135] Around Antioch, 'Alawi bands (including one led by the father of the later Arab nationalist leader Zaki al-Arsuzi) by turns battled the retreating Ottoman army, the French occupiers, and finally Kemalist insurgents, who on several occasions attacked the Harbiye and 'Affan neighborhoods and villages in the Suwaydiyya area. More traditional pro-Ottoman 'Alawi landowners such as Khalil Ma'ruf, meanwhile, worked to reconcile the local 'Alawi and Sunni communities. Even in the hinterland of Jabala, a number of 'Alawi villages initially sided with the French and supported them against the Sunni Muslim *çete*s of the Sahyun, their long-standing enemies, before joining the rebel side.[136]

The 'Alawi reaction vis-à-vis the Turkish resistance movement was therefore far from uniform. The Salih al-'Ali revolt, in any event, owing to its sponsorship by Ibrahim Hanano starting in the fall of 1920 and its continuing success in northwestern Syria, was drawn ever closer to the Kemalist camp. Early the following year, Salih al-'Ali appears to have initiated direct contact through a middleman in Aleppo, proposing that they coordinate their efforts and asking for supplies to use against the French. This follows from a remarkable return letter in the Turkish military archives dated 29 January 1921, in which the contact, Salah al-Din 'Adil, addresses Salih al-'Ali as a "*mujahid*" and assures him both of Turkey's national and religious solidarity: "There is no doubt that the Turkish and Arab nations (*milletleri*) will continue to walk hand in hand in fighting the foreigners' aggression, until the liberation of our homeland (*vatanımız*), and that we will not fail to provide the necessary help in this matter. . . . We honor and salute our brothers fighting jihad for the people of Islam."[137] The letter was accompanied by a list of weapons and ammunition to be sent to Salih, material aid that Kemalist officials in Maraş, the de facto headquarters of the Southern Front, confirmed the following month.[138]

The Kemalists were also well aware of the political significance of Salih al-'Ali's revolt, acknowledging his declaration of an independent administration in northwestern Syria in March 1921.[139] Shortly after, the officials in Maraş also took note of a petition that had been signed by "several hundred people" in the area under Salih's control (designated as zone 5 of Kemalist operations in Syria) and adjoining areas to protest against French injustices. This petition was to be transmitted to the Italian and American consuls in Aleppo to be "sent to the League of Nations secretariat in London and all

---

135 Tachjian, *La France en Cilicie*, 95–97, 148–51.
136 Al-Tawil, *Tarikh al-'Alawiyyin*, 502–11; Arsuzi-Elamir, *Arabischer Nationalismus*, 31–37.
137 İSH 809-68.
138 İSH 809-63; İSH 805-58; Umar, *Suriye*, 484–85.
139 İSH 664-141.

neutral countries, which will have a very good political effect."[140] The French *renseignements* (intelligence) bureau itself realized that "an insurrection movement where Turks and Arabs are joined in the name of Islam has been organized particularly in the mountainous region between the plain of Aleppo and Latakia"; by early May 1921 it was feared the "Ankara government" was preparing a major offensive in the region as Ibrahim Hanano joined forces with Salih al-'Ali to field an army of almost four thousand men at Sqaylbiyya in the Ghab valley.[141]

Already in March, however, the French had resolved to abandon Cilicia and Maraş (where they had suffered a major defeat at the hands of the Kemalists the year before) so as to better concentrate their forces in the occupation of northern Syria. Throughout the spring, three army columns were thus engaged in the coastal mountains, disarming the villagers and "cleaning out" the last points of resistance against French rule.[142] In June the Kemalist command in Maraş appears to have received a request for additional men and arms to help the beleaguered 'Alawi rebels.[143] By this time, however, most of the local leadership (including Salih al-'Ali's uncles, one of whom was supposedly his liaison with the Kemalists) had had to submit, while Salih himself, whom the French claimed "reports directly to Kemalist general headquarters," was cornered near Shaykh Badr.[144] A month later, on 17 July 1921, Salih personally addressed a final entreaty to Mustafa Kemal and the Büyük Millet Meclisi (Grand National Assembly) in Ankara, in language no longer reflecting his status as an autonomous political actor but rather the desperation of his situation:

> We repeat the supplication we made earlier to send us soldiers together with sufficient amounts of war supplies. Under the auspices of your favor our success will be certain, for with the arrival of your soldiers and the necessary amount of supplies for our people, the country will be set to rise up. In the opposite case, we will blame you before God and his Prophet.... The whole country—men and women, big and small, everybody—is hoping for help from their government, victorious Turkey, and we pray to God that He make you triumph. We are here, without news and under the enemy's bombs and bullets, awaiting the return of our emissary. If we receive what we have asked for, we will all

---

140 İSH 809-91. The other operational zones were (1) the Qusayr and Amık Plain; (2) the Sahyun and Jabal al-Akrad; (3) Harem; and (4) Jabal al-Zawiya.
141 ELSL 114, no. 87–90; ELSL 117, no. 74; ELSL 126, no. 134.
142 ELSL 114, no. 153; ELSL 117, no. 84–85, 91, 94, 96, 101, 106.
143 İSH 1321-124.
144 SHD 4H 249, dossier 2a–c.

FIGURE 6.3. Salih al-'Ali's letter to Mustafa Kemal, 17 July 1921 (ATASE archives, Ankara)

together be ready to pursue with the holy jihad. If not, we will have nothing left but to walk straight into the desert.[145]

Salih al-'Ali's dire predictions essentially proved true. With neither Sharifian nor Turkish aid, his undertaking soon faltered. By early August most of the 'Alawi notables in the area had lain down their arms or even rallied to the French side, while the signature of the Ankara accord between Turkey and France on 20 October 1921 effectively ended all hope of outside support to the rebels. Salih al-'Ali's last remaining lieutenants surrendered in mid-October; he himself was able to hold out in the mountains for several more months before finally coming to Latakia to offer his submission on 2 June 1922.[146] Most of the classical 'Alawi gentry were by then already won over to the idea of French colonial rule. As early as February 1922 former revolt leader 'Aziz

145 İSH 1169-66; İSH 629-125.
146 ELSL 114, no. 153, 180–81, 183; ELSL 117, no. 114, 116, 132–35; see also documents reproduced in 'Isa Abu-'Allush, *Safahat Majhula min Thawrat al-Shaykh Salih al-'Ali* (Latakia: Dar Dhu'l-Fiqar, 2007), 236–37.

Bey Hawwash had sent the newly appointed French prime minister Poincarré a telegram of effusive congratulations in which he signed himself the "chef tribus des Métaouras [Matawira] à Safita Territoire des Alaouites Syrie" and declaimed that "all the tribes express their sincere attachment to noble and generous France." In July the "État des Alaouites" was constituted as a separate mandate province with first Jabir ʿAbbas and then Ibrahim al-Kanj (Genç), another former rebel turned French auxiliary during the revolt, heading its Representative Council.[147] Salih al-ʿAli, confined to house arrest in Shaykh Badr, ceased to play any role in the politics of Syria or the larger region.

A final aspect of his letter to Mustafa Kemal, however, merits consideration: the fact that it is not signed Salih "al-ʿAli," but rather Salih "al-ʿAlawi." Much has of course been written on the question of when the term "ʿAlawi," or its French equivalent "Alaouite," was first used to designate the community. Most authors have posited that it was essentially a French invention, eagerly adopted by the ʿAlawis themselves in an effort to shake off the historical opprobrium of the word "Nusayri." Indeed, as already indicated in the introduction, "Nusayri" was traditionally used as a pejorative term by the sect's detractors and never figures in their own literature. In isolated cases, writers such as Husayn Mayhub Harfush employed the term "Khasibi" to identify specifically the Syrian branch of the wider Shiʿi gnostic calling, whereas "ʿAlawi," though sometimes used in medieval times to distinguish Imami from Ismaili-leaning Shiʿis, gained wider currency as a group name only after the appearance of al-Tawil's *Tarikh al-ʿAlawiyyin*. The French themselves continued to use "Ansarieh" (from "al-Nusayriyya") and "Monts Ansariehs" in their administrative decrees as late as August 1920, substituting the term "Alaouite" in systematic fashion only after the separation of "Greater Lebanon" from Syria later that same month.[148] "Les Alaouites" in the plural simply also served as the administrative shorthand for the coastal mandate province (the "Territoire" and later the "État" des Alaouites) stretching between the Alexandretta district in the North and the border with Lebanon in the South. On the other hand, Necati Alkan has recently called attention to the fact that some ʿAlawi shaykhs had already started using the term themselves in late Ottoman times, addressing various petitions to the Sublime Porte in Istanbul not only in the name of the "rightly guided sect" (*taife-i hüdaiye*) as cited above but occasionally also in the name of the Arab "Alevi [ʿAlawi] taife."[149]

What needs to be noted in this context is that the word "Alevi" (the same as "ʿAlawi" in Ottoman script) was also in use by the late nineteenth century to designate the heterodox Shiʿi populations of Anatolia formerly referred to

---

147 ELSL 127, no. 1–5, 126, 128.
148 *Recueil des actes administratifs du Haut-Commissariat de la République française en Syrie et au Liban*, vol. 1: *Années 1919–1920* (Beirut: Imprimerie Jeanne d'Arc, n.d.), 23, 130, 131.
149 MD 2739/90; Alkan, "Fighting for the Nusayri Soul," 49–50.

as Kızılbaş or Bektaşis.[150] If Salih al-'Ali similarly chose to present himself not as a local or tribal notable but as an "'Alawi" leader to the Kemalists in 1921, this was moreover a conscious attempt to cast himself as the agent of a larger Islamic denomination participating in the joint post-Ottoman anticolonial project. Thus while some 'Alawis may already have appropriated the term before, its generalized use—or the use of any one precise appellation, for that matter—to name and define the entire community ultimately has to be seen as originating in the context of a three-way contest for the 'Alawis' political allegiance during and immediately after World War I. The Sharifians, as we have seen, were the first to approach the 'Alawis collectively in their capacity as "Arabs" and potential vectors of Arab nationalism. In March 1920 the French reported that Faysal, in seeking to overcome the 'Alawis' "particularism," had promised to make Salih al-'Ali the head of an "'Alawi Confederation,"[151] likely the first time the term was deployed in a political sense. After the eclipse of the Sharifians, Salih al-'Ali's ties with the Güney Cephesi were predicated on the notion of a shared "jihad" in the defense of faith and fatherland, in which he represented the most important Muslim collective operating against the French in the northern coastal region. Of primordial significance for the development of an 'Alawi communal identity in Syria, however, this concept proved of only limited and temporary interest to the Kemalist regime in Turkey. In the end, of course, it was the French construction of the "Alaouites" as a historically separate (and therefore oppressed) religious "minority" in need of enlightened foreign rule and protection that was enshrined in the Syrian mandate system.

MANDATE VS. REPUBLIC

The defeat of the Salih al-'Ali revolt marked an important rupture in the history of the 'Alawis. With the cessation of hostilities between France and Turkey in October 1921 and the creation of the État des Alaouites on 31 August 1922, the 'Alawi population of the region was to become permanently divided between the modern Turkish and Syrian states. The profound social and economic transformation of the 'Alawi community under French rule in Syria has been discussed in various studies of the mandate period; more recently historians have also begun to address its fate in the Alexandretta district, which formed a separate mandatory state under French control until it was essentially ceded to Turkey in 1938, as well as in Cilicia, where the 'Alawis became subject to extensive and often repressive integrationist

---

150 Markus Dressler, *Writing Religion: The Making of Turkish Alevi Islam* (Oxford: Oxford University Press, 2013), 1–5.
151 ELSL 121, no. 100, 116.

measures. The goal of this final section is not to provide an exhaustive portrait of the 'Alawis' evolution throughout the region, something that would require an analysis of an even greater variety of documentary and other sources within the increasingly divergent political contexts of modern Turkey and Syria (and Lebanon and Israel) and should best be left to subsequent studies. Rather, the purpose here is to highlight the contrast between France's policies of ethno-religious differentiation and Turkey's radical ethno-national assimilationism and suggest, by way of a tentative conclusion, that neither strategy ultimately succeeded in the long run in securing for 'Alawis the recognition as full and equal citizens that they had coveted since the late Ottoman period.

The État des Alaouites formed in August 1922 was initially included in the "Fédération syrienne" together with Aleppo and Damascus (later also Alexandretta). Already the following year, however, 'Alawi notables co-opted by the French authorities, starting with Jabir 'Abbas, began to lobby for more power, lauding the "*effet merveilleux*" that French direct rule was having on the area and demanding autonomy vis-à-vis the Syrian federation.[152] In January 1924, incidentally just after the foundation of the new Turkish Republic, 'Abbas and the local Administrative Council in Latakia succeeded in having the Alaouites removed from the federation, and over the next years they continued to insist that benevolent France help it attain independence separately from the rest of Syria.[153] In 1930, however, the "state" was renamed to the more secular-sounding "Gouvernement de Lattaquié" and finally reincorporated into Syria in 1936, as France began negotiations with the home-rule "National Bloc" (Kutla Wataniyya) government with a view to granting the country full national sovereignty. This set off a new round of petitions (after similar negotiations in 1933 had failed) from Jabir 'Abbas, Ibrahim al-Kanj, 'Aziz Hawwash, Sulayman Murshid, and other 'Alawi notables to denounce the Syrians' "unionist propaganda," "Sunni fanaticism," and the "crime" that fusion with Syria would represent, and to propose instead that the Alaouites be joined to Lebanon.[154] The most famous of these petitions, in which the 'Alawis compare the oppression they have suffered throughout history with that of the Jews peaceably settling in Palestine and refuse once again to be incorporated into Syria, was purportedly also signed by Hafiz al-Asad's grandfather Sulayman al-Asad. Said to be registered as "file no. 3547" in the

---

152 ELSL 267, no. 1–6, 14–15, 18, 27–28.
153 ELSL 267, no. 31, 33, 35–44; SHD 4H 84 dossier 1a.
154 ELSL 492, no. 193–204; ELSL 493, no. 7–9, 53–57, 98, 106–7, 113–16, 165; Benjamin White, *The Emergence of Minorities in the Middle East: The Politics of Community in French Mandate Syria* (Edinburgh: Edinburgh University Press, 2011), 54–55, 87–88.

French Foreign Ministry archives, this petition appears to be known, however, only through an Arabic copy preserved at the Asad Library in Damascus.[155]

The, in many aspects, advantageous treatment of the Alaouites under French mandatory rule has been highlighted in countless publications, often in the polemical intent of demonstrating the community's irreconcilability with the rest of Syrian society; this literature need not be reviewed here. Among the greatest and most lasting benefits to the 'Alawis was certainly their recruitment in large numbers into the state's armed forces. Though the French aimed to maintain a proportional representation of all communities, according to N. E. Bou-Nacklie, the poverty of the coastal mountains, the new prospect of social advancement, and various local communal conflicts meant that 'Alawis enrolled in such numbers as to become the relatively best-represented community in the Syrian colonial army (the "Syrian Legion" or the "Troupes spéciales du Levant") in the 1920s and 1930s.[156] Just as important was the formal recognition of a separate 'Alawi common law in 1922, by which personal status cases as well as those regarding 'Alawi religious endowments (*waqf*) were no longer heard by ordinary Sunni judges but at state-accredited 'Alawi tribunals. Thus did the previously cited reformist scholar Sulayman al-Ahmad, who had already done much to bring 'Alawi practice in line with Muslim and specifically Ja'fari law, briefly come to serve as the first-ever *grand juge des musulmans alaouites* in Latakia.[157] Seizing on the unique opportunities afforded by French rule, the 'Alawis also began to participate wholeheartedly in what has been termed the "politics of demand," pressing for the construction of schools, courts, and other institutions in the name of their confessional community, as well as for a proportional share of government jobs. Much as in contemporary Lebanon, it was fundamentally the new legal status granted the "minorities" as a social category, together with the unprecedented bureaucratization of their customary legal practices, that defined them for the first time as actual political entities.[158]

While French government sources of course tend to emphasize 'Alawi support for the mandate regime, the community was nonetheless far from unanimous in its embrace of French rule and rejection of Syrian unity and

---

155 Abu Musa al-Hariri, *Al-'Alawiyyun al-Nusayriyyun: Bahth fi'l-'Aqida wa'l-Tarikh* (Beirut: n.p., 1980), 230–33; Moosa, *Extremist Shiites*, 286–89, 508; Daniel Le Gac, *La Syrie du général Assad* (Brussels: Éditions Complexe, 1991), 69–71, 269.

156 N. E. Bou-Nacklie, "Les Troupes spéciales: Religious and Ethnic Recruitment, 1916–46," *International Journal of Middle East Studies* 25 (1993): 645–60; also Batatu, *Syria's Peasantry*, 157–59.

157 Raymond O'Zoux, *Les États du Levant sous mandat français* (Paris: Larose, 1931), 130–35; Sabrina Mervin, "'L'entité alaouite', une création française" in *Le choc colonial et l'islam: les politiques religieuses des puissances coloniales en terres d'islam*, ed. Pierre-Jean Luizard (Paris: La Découverte, 2006), 352–53; 'Uthman, *Tarikh al-'Alawiyyin*, 59–62.

158 Weiss, *Shadow of Sectarianism*, 59, 112, 155, 162; White, *Emergence of Minorities*, 153–54, 168–69.

FIGURE 6.4. Ruins of French barracks near Shillif (Latakia)

independence. In May 1927, for example, French military intelligence worried that the leaders of the "great revolt" which had broken out in southern Syria two years before were targeting the 'Alawi population with propaganda mailed from Buenos Aires; around the same time they also took strident measures to prevent nationalist rebel bands, in particular that of Fawzi al-Qawuqji, from making inroads into 'Alawi territory.[159] A year later, in June 1928, *renseignements* officers reported that numerous 'Alawi notables in Safita and Latakia were either openly unionist and had signed a petition demanding the Alaouites' reincorporation into Syria or were loath to alienate the unionists and had adopted a wait-and-see approach.[160] Indeed, a number of 'Alawi public figures who had initially been sympathetic to French rule gradually favored the struggle for national self-determination. Thus Sulayman al-Murshid (d. 1946), the founder and self-appointed prophet of the 'Alawi "Murshidiyya" sect, both clashed with the mandate authorities over his tax collection activities and supported calls for the Alaouites' continuing autonomy under French rule—but then in 1936 threw his considerable weight behind the nationalist camp during elections to the Syrian parliament in Damascus.[161] Similarly, Muhammad Sulayman al-Ahmad (d. 1981), a renowned poet (writing under the pen-name of Badawi al-Jabal, "Bedouin of the Mountain"), son of Sulayman al-Ahmad, and member of the Latakia Representative Council, in 1933 authored a lengthy historical exposé on

159 SHD 4H 84, dossier 1a (1–15 May 1927).
160 SHD 4H 84, dossier 1a (1–15 June 1928).
161 Gitta Yaffe, "Suleiman al-Murshid: Beginnings of an Alawi Leader," *Middle Eastern Studies* 29 (1993): 624–40; Patrick Franke, *Göttliche Karriere eines syrischen Hirten: Sulaimān Muršid (1907–1946) und die Anfänge der Muršidīyya* (Berlin: Klaus Schwarz, 1994), 89–104.

why the 'Alawis should not be confused with, nor made to relive the persecution by, other Muslim sects. Later on, however, he joined the National Bloc movement and was arrested several times for his anti-French activities; he became a leading proponent of Arab nationalism and was finally elected to the parliament of independent Syria.[162]

The debate between 'Alawi "unionists" and "separatists" naturally came to a head with the renewed treaty negotiations between France and the National Bloc in 1936.[163] In addition to the pleas for maintaining French rule and 'Alawi autonomy, the High Commission in Beirut also received numerous petitions from 'Alawis condemning the French government's attempts to sow division and discord, rejecting the notion that they were not in fact real Muslims, disapproving of the "minority pretext," and clamoring that "200,000 'Alawis await the day of redemption when it will finally be announced to them that unity, independence, and the Franco-Syrian treaty are a done deal."[164] The *'ulama* statement and the Hajj Amin al-Husayni fatwa declaring 'Alawis to be Muslims (see above) also came about in this context. The French themselves realized that the Bloc had significant support among the 'Alawis, noting the presence of an 'Alawi delegation at Maysalun Day celebrations in Damascus in July 1936, for example, and warned local officials against encouraging the demands for autonomy or union with Lebanon too much, as these were only bound to be frustrated when the treaty was eventually signed.[165]

And if the separatist petition allegedly signed by Sulayman al-Asad remains elusive, a blistering attack against the separatists, also written in July 1936 and unmistakably bearing the signature not of Sulayman but of 'Ali Sulayman al-Asad, the father of the later Syrian president, as well as eighty-six other 'Alawi notables from the Raslan, Hawwash, 'Abbas, al-Khayyir, and other leading families, is indeed conserved in the archives of the French Foreign Ministry at La Courneuve. Vocally denouncing the constant "manipulation" as well as the "capricious dictatorship" and "disloyal despotism" of the Alaouites governor Ernest Schoeffler and other French colonial officials, the petition goes on to ridicule the claims of certain coreligionists, "made in bad faith and out of personal cupidity," to the effect "that 'Alawis are not Muslims nor Arabs, but rather descendants of the crusaders, and that a war of religion and of interest separates them from the inhabitants of Syria." If this were true, the petition asks, "then how does one explain the presence among us—advocates of Syrian unity and independence—of all the leading 'Alawi notables, both

---

162 ELSL 485, no. 46–54; Al Ma'ruf, *Tarikh al-'Alawiyyin*, 3:546–54. In a poem published in *al-'Irfan* in 1921, Badawi went so far as to mock Salih al-'Ali and his fight against the French; see Salih al-'Adima, *Hadha Huwa Badawi al-Jabal* (Beirut: Dar al-Mahajja al-Bayda' and Maktabat al-Sa'ih, 2010), 5, 13–16, 302–5, 319–23.
163 See 'Uthman, *Tarikh al-'Alawiyyin*, 62–73; al-Musa, *Al-Imam 'Ali wa'l-'Alawiyyin*, 246–64.
164 ELSL 493, no. 34, 126–38, 157–58; ELSL 494, no. 61.
165 ELSL 493, no. 35 a–b, 68–72, 161–64; ELSL 494, no. 31–32, 47–48.

religious and civil, who famously represent the overwhelming majority of their coreligionists in the Government of Latakia region?"

> Everyone here ... is convinced of the unfeasibility of joining our territory to Lebanon, as it has always been an integral part of Syria.... These suggestions are clearly in contradiction with historical, geographic, ethnic, linguistic, and religious realities, which all prove that our territory has never been but one with Syria. It is put forward that the majority of the inhabitants here are of the 'Alawi faith. On one hand, however, religion cannot be the basis of the constitution of a people; and on another, 'Alawis are Muslims just as the Greek Orthodox and Protestants are Christians. Are there not, in every city in Syria, a large number of inhabitants of all the religions professed in this country? ... In a word, in what country in this world do all the inhabitants practice one and the same religion? ... Circumstances have proven that the Syrian delegation in Paris represents the opinion and the hope of the great majority of the population of Syria, a majority which will turn into a perfect unanimity once the French authorities ... will have stopped twisting the normal course of events.[166]

In the end, of course, it was not the Franco-Syrian agreement, signed with the National Bloc in 1936 but never ratified by the French government, but

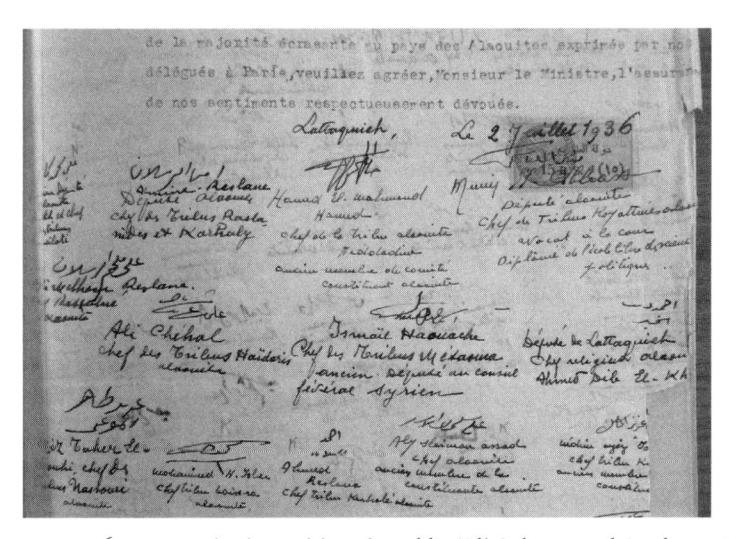

FIGURE 6.5. Pro-unionist petition signed by 'Ali Sulayman al-Asad, 1936 (Ministère des Affaires étrangères, La Courneuve)

166 ELSL 493, no. 36–40.

rather France's defeat at the beginning of World War II that heralded the end of the mandate and Syria's independence in 1946. How perfect a unanimity was finally established between the 'Alawis and the rest of Syria must be left for another discussion; how difficult a task this would prove to be, in any event, can yet be traced in the civilian and military archives of the French colonial administration, which pursued a policy of ethnic and confessional differentiation until the very end. At the other end of the spectrum, however, there is also a large and growing body of domestic sources which remain to be exploited in order to show the 'Alawi hinterland population's gradual integration into wider Syrian society, from the nationalist recollections of Salih al-'Ali's comrade and biographer 'Abd al-Latif al-Yunus, for example, to the recently edited memoirs of Ahmad Nihad al-Sayyaf, who as a Bloc activist and later as a government official in Latakia spent his career building bridges between the local 'Alawi elite and the national regime in Damascus.[167] In many ways, this process can be said to be ongoing still today.

In Turkey, in contrast, the Kemalist authorities saw to the 'Alawis' integration into the newly founded republic immediately and with great resolution. A number of 'Alawi notables who had been collaborators of the French in Cilicia left as soon as the treaty of Ankara was signed in October 1921 to move to the Territoire des Alaouites. Much of the 'Alawi population in the region, however, which French officials put at 100,000 members, had indeed supported the Kemalist side and today proudly recalls the role that individual 'Alawi shaykhs ostensibly played in the struggle against the French. Thus the August 1920 battle of Ziyarettepe ("Sanctuary Hill") near Tarsus is connected in local lore with the hilltop shrine of Shaykh Badr al-Ghafir, who is claimed (even though his real grave is actually in Syria) to have fired off artillery rounds at French ships 6 km offshore and otherwise made their ammunition explode spontaneously.[168] Another 'Alawi shaykh, Ibrahim al-Asir (Esiroğlu; "the prisoner"), whose shrine is in nearby Kazanlı village, is said to have been captured while fighting the French but was able to prevent the ship onto which he was taken from moving until he was finally released. His family later adopted the surname "Kurtuluş" in honor of his contribution to the War of Liberation.[169]

Be that as it may, starting in 1924 the Cilician 'Alawis became the target of extensive Turkification measures, as the Ankara government's focus turned from overthrowing the Ottoman sultanate and fighting off the allied occupation in the name of all Muslims to consolidating the Turkish nation-state.

---

167 'Abd al-Latif al-Yunus, *Mudhakkirat* (Damascus: Dar al-'Alam, 1992); Ahmad Nihad al-Sayyaf (d. 1992), *Shu'a' Qabl al-Fajr: Mudhakkirat*, ed. Muhammad Jamal Barut ([Aleppo]: n.p., 2005).
168 Procházka-Eisl and Procházka, *Plain of Saints and Prophets*, 227–29.
169 Abdulkerim Kurtuluş, *Şıh İbrahim Esir'in Esaretten Kurtuluşu: Şıh Yusuf Esir'in Mersiyesi ve Vasiyeti* (Mersin: n.p., 2000); Procházka-Eisl and Procházka, *Plain of Saints and Prophets*, 300.

According to French intelligence claims, the Kemalist authorities initially foresaw deporting large numbers of Cilician 'Alawis to provinces in eastern Anatolia where they would not constitute more than 10 percent of the population. Though no such plan was ever put into effect, the 'Alawis remained subject to other pressures and discrimination, including the systematic denial of government jobs as well as a sustained propaganda campaign, both in the press and by the Türk Ocakları, the nationalist "Turkish Hearth Society" that acted as a relay of Turkish state culture and ideology in the provinces, against the use of the Arabic language.[170]

The French reports, though by their nature negative and to some degree overwrought, are nevertheless corroborated by early republican archival sources. In an executive order (*karar*) signed "*reisicümhur* [president] Gazi M. Kemal" (later "Atatürk") in April 1930, for example, an 'Alawi notable from Mersin, described as "a subject of the abrogated Ottoman government, who did not participate in the War of Independence and who has remained abroad and to this day not returned to Turkey," was formally stripped of his Turkish citizenship; similar measures were taken against individual 'Alawi émigrés from Hatay (Alexandretta) after the district's separation from Syria in 1938.[171] The key impulse for the assimilation of the 'Alawis, however, appears to have come less from the government per se than from the Cumhuriyet Halk Partisi (Republican People's Party; CHP). Thus it was no longer so much the nationalist but nonpartisan Hearth Society that pursued the Turkification of Arabic-speaking (and Kurdish-speaking) groups in Anatolia as the Halk Evleri (People's Houses), a network of community and adult-education centers established by the CHP in 1932 to school the masses in Kemalism and foster ideological unity between the population and the party, and where linguistic homogeneity became a primary objective after İsmet İnönü declaimed at a party congress in 1935 that "We will no longer be silent; all citizens living together with us will henceforth speak Turkish."[172] In early 1937 the specially constituted Hars Komitesi (Culture Committee) in the province of Seyhan (Adana), an institution reporting directly to party headquarters in Ankara, went so far as to declare it "a national crime for our [Nusayri] blood-and-soil brothers to speak any other language than Turkish,"[173] and over the next months the party leadership of both Seyhan and İçel (Mersin) sought and received funding to construct schools for 'Alawis

---

170 Tachjian, *La France en Cilicie*, 157, 168–69, 243–47. On the Türk Ocakları, see also Shaw and Shaw, *History of the Ottoman Empire*, 309–10; Mizrahi, *Genèse*, 133.

171 Başbakanlık Cumhuriyet Archives, Ankara [BCA]: 030.18.1.2/9.19.7; BCA 030.18.1.2/127.100.4.

172 Shaw and Shaw, *History of the Ottoman Empire*, 383; Bünyamin Kocaoğlu, "Ulus-Devletin İnşası Sürecinde bir Türk(çe)leştirme Politikası: 'CHP Hars Komitaları' (1937–1938)," *Muhafazkar Düşünce* 3 (2007): 23–46.

173 BCA 490.01.0.0/583.11.1, no. 93.

"who speak a foreign language and do not know Turkish" or who had indeed "forgotten Turkish, their mother tongue."[174]

Thus while France was deploying all the machinery of the modern state available to it in Syria (foreign legions, Service des renseignements, press censorship, etc.) to prevent "minorities" such as the 'Alawis from identifying and associating with the national leadership, in Turkey, on the contrary, the government, the Hearths, the party, the People's Houses, the press, and academia all worked together in the interest of subsuming peripheral groups into the nation-state. The assimilation of the 'Alawis in this regard took on a special urgency in 1936, when the signature of the Franco-Syrian treaty raised the specter of the Alexandretta district's inclusion in an independent Syria. To press its own claims to the district, Ankara expanded the official "Turkish History Thesis," according to which the Turks were related to the ancient Hittites (and were thus the legitimate occupants of Anatolia), to state that the "Nusayris" too were not in fact Arabs but rather the direct descendants of the Hittites and therefore the most authentic of all Turks; the Hittites' homeland or "Hatay" (the newly coined name for the Alexandretta district) was in consequence the most ancient of Turkish soil. Largely ignored by Turkish scholars and intellectuals up to that point, the overriding political imperative of "reclaiming" the Hatay led to the appearance of numerous books and scientific studies over the following months regarding the 'Alawis and their purported historical, geographic, anthropological, and cultural contiguity with the rest of Turkey.[175]

The CHP leadership and the Hars Komitesi in Mersin and Adana naturally appropriated this discourse, no longer labeling the local 'Alawi population as "Nusayris" but as "Hittite Turks" (Eti Türkleri). Much like the term "mountain Turks" that was used to deny the Kurds a distinct ethnic identity, the racialized concept of Eti Turks technically does not appear in official government documents but rather in those of the party—which of course exercised nearly complete hegemony over the state in this time. Thus the CHP party chief of Mersin/İçel (who was concomitantly the provincial governor) reported in May 1937 that good progress was being made in the "cultural situation and literacy

---

174 BCA 490.01.0.0/583.10.1, no. 41–42; BCA 030.18.1.2/73.29.1; BCA 030.18.1.2/76.60.20; BCA 490.01.0.0/583.11.1, no. 126, 130–31.

175 Ahmet Faik Türkmen, *Mufassal Hatay: Tarih, Coğrafya, Ekalliyetler, Mezhepler, Edebiyat, İçtimai Durum, Lengüistik Durum, Folklor, Etnografya ve Hatay Davcasını ihtiva eden 4 cild* (Istanbul: Cumhuriyet Matbaası, 1937–39); Hasan Reşit Tankut, *Nusayriler ve Nusayrilik Hakkında* (Ankara: Ulus Basımevi, 1938); Cemal Alagöz, "Coğrafya gözüyle Hatay," *Ankara Üniversitesi Dil ve Tarih-Coğrafya Fakültesi Dergisi* 2 (1943–44): 203–16; see also Winter, "Nusayris before the Tanzimat," 98–99; Soner Cagaptay, *Islam, Secularism and Nationalism in Modern Turkey: Who Is a Turk?* (London: Routledge, 2006), 118; Erdal Aksoy, "Nusayrîlerin Sosyal Yapıları ve Cumhuriyetinin İlk Yıllarında Türkiye'de Yaşayan bu Topluluğa Devletin Yaklaşımları," *Türk Kültürü ve Hacı Bektaş Veli Araştırma Dergisi* 54 (2010): 205–11.

rate" of the Eti Turks, particularly in the central district of Mersin where they were relatively better "intermixed" (*ıhtilatlı*) with the rest of society than in the villages of the Tarsus district; in September he again invoked positive results in the education and "amalgamation" (*kaynaşma*) of the Hittites and requested additional funding both for schools and to support local "intermarriage" (*karşılıklı kız alub vermege*).[176] What exactly was meant by this "amalgamation" and "intermarriage," and what illustrates the full thrust of Kemalist racial ideology and social engineering in the 1930s, is a similar report from the CHP leadership in Adana, which contains a requisition of 2,000 lira "to arrange marriages between the Eti and the Oğuz" ("*Etilerle Oğuzları evlendirmek*"), that is, between 'Alawis and real, Anatolian Turks.[177] Executive orders from as late as July 1938 and August 1939 (bearing the signatures of presidents Atatürk and İnönü, respectively) formally allocate moneys to "teach Eti Turk Nusayris who do not know Turkish their mother tongue and contribute financially to the trousseaus of mixed marriages, and thereby support the amalgamation process."[178]

To what extent can the Turkish Republic be said to have been successful in its efforts? Like their Ottoman forebears, CHP officials claimed, no doubt with some justification, that the 'Alawis themselves were eager to embrace the educational efforts deployed on their behalf.[179] An early test of the 'Alawis' attitude toward Turkish political rule presented itself with the Alexandretta crisis of 1936–39, an event which does not figure in the scope of the present study but has been extensively treated in several important recent publications. The lead role in raising national sentiment among the Arabic-speaking majority of the district (newly created as the "sandjak d'Alexandrette" or "*liwa' Iskandarun*") and pushing for its reunification with Syria, as is well known, was played by a French-educated 'Alawi philosopher and schoolteacher from Antioch, Zaki al-Arsuzi (d. 1968). Cofounder of the League of National Action ('Usbat al-'Amal al-Qawmi) in the district, and later of the Ba'th Party, Arsuzi rejected France's policy of confessional differentiation, including the separate administration of Sunni and 'Alawi *waqf*s, and campaigned tirelessly to convert the Sunni Arab, 'Alawi, and Greek Orthodox population to a notion of shared "'Arabism" (*'uruba*) in the face of Kemalist efforts to claim a Turkish majority for the district.[180] Turkish intelligence reports apparently take note of Arsuzi for the first time in November 1936, when he was arrested after a group of young 'Alawi activists attacked the government serail in Antioch,

---

176 BCA 490.01.0.0/583.10.1, no. 32–35; BCA 490.01.0.0/583.10.1, no. 21.
177 BCA 490.01.0.0/583.11.1, no. 72.
178 BCA 030.18.1.2/84.68.11; BCA 030.18.1.2/88.77.16.
179 BCA 490.01.0.0/583.11.1, no. 70.
180 Keith Watenpaugh, "'Creating Phantoms': Zaki al-Arsuzi, the Alexandretta Crisis, and the Formation of Modern Arab Nationalism in Syria," *International Journal of Middle East Studies* 28 (1996): 363–89; Arsuzi-Elamir, *Arabischer Nationalismus*, 41–77, 102–38.

breaking windows and fighting with the Turkish gendarmes; he subsequently managed to escape from jail with the activists' help.[181]

Arsuzi, however, did not represent all of 'Alawi opinion in the district, which was split between Arabist, autonomist, and outright pro-Turkish positions. Leading 'Alawi notables such as Hasan Jabbara, for example, one of the region's wealthiest landowners, had a vested interest in preserving the district's autonomous administration under French rule (in which he furthermore served as local finance director) and therefore bitterly opposed Arsuzi's unionist and socialist agenda. Jabbara was apparently able to get Arsuzi dismissed from his teaching post, owing to the latter's supposed "corruption" of the youth under his care, joining with other 'Alawi notables in the misnamed "National Union" (Ittihad Watani) Party in 1938 to campaign against the district's unification with either Syria or Turkey.[182] Sadiq Ma'ruf (Sadek Maruf), another landowner, for his part became closely identified with the Turkish camp. In 1918, as we have seen, he or his father was awarded the Mecidiye Order by the Ottoman War Ministry. During the Alexandretta crisis the sandjak's main Kemalist leader, Abdülgani Türkmen, solicited Sadek to help convince the 'Alawis that they were in fact Turks and should register as such for elections to the local parliament; Sadek subsequently beat Arsuzi in a runoff election for one of the 'Alawi seats in 1936. Later on both he and his son were suspected of importing weapons from Turkey as the clash between pro-Syrian and pro-Turkish factions turned violent; after the Turkish-dominated *meclis* voted to make the "Hatay" an independent state in 1938 (so that it could be annexed to Turkey the following year), Sadek Maruf became its first (and last) ceremonial vice-president.[183]

While no 'Alawis of the time actually appear to have cast themselves as "Hittite Turks," enough seem to have accepted the idea (eagerly promoted by Turkey, at least as far as non-Turks were concerned) that national identity was in fact malleable, and that they could chose to register for the elections as (Sunni) Arabs, 'Alawis, or Turks based on their political interests rather than on timeless, mutually exclusive religious or linguistic identities. In consequence the 'Alawi community of the sandjak was deeply divided as to its ultimate national allegiance and became the site of considerable internecine bloodletting, recently chronicled by Sarah Shields, as 'Alawi adepts of Arabism, autonomism, and Kemalism jockeyed to register members in the fateful election spring of 1938.[184] How far the Turkish authorities themselves would then genuinely regard the 'Alawis as fellow citizens, on the other hand, was questionable: in July 1938, as Turkish troops prepared to enter the sandjak, the Turkish consul

181 ATASE: İkinci Dünya Harbi koleksiyonu [İDH] 7–80, no. 2.
182 Arsuzi-Elamir, *Arabischer Nationalismus*, 68–69, 103, 138–42; cf. Reyhani, *Gölgesiz Işıklar*, 2:164–69.
183 Sarah Shields, *Fezzes in the River: Identity Politics and European Diplomacy in the Middle East on the Eve of World War II* (Oxford: Oxford University Press, 2011), 40, 50, 125–26, 135–36, 234, 263.
184 Ibid., 72, 124–26, 129, 151, 165–67, 178–79, 182, 189, 195, 198, 203, 207–9, 213–15, 228, 247.

warned, in a letter harking back to Ottoman times, that serious altercations were likely to occur between the military troops and the 'Alawis in the local gendarmerie—who therefore needed to be removed.[185] Indeed, together with most of the Christian population, scores of (mainly better-off) 'Alawi families left the district the following months to become *liwa'i* refugees (from the *liwa'* Iskandarun) in Syria; Zaki al-Arsuzi and Hasan Jabbara themselves ended their careers in virtual exile and obscurity in Damascus and Aleppo, respectively.

For many 'Alawi transplants, however, identity continued to depend more than anything on context—a context that would witness a renewed shift only a few years later, from French colonial to Syrian national rule, on one side of the border, and from Kemalist one-party dictatorship to the prospect of free multiparty elections in Turkey, on the other. Thus in early 1947, by way of provisionally concluding this account, an estimated one thousand *liwa'i* 'Alawis who had earlier fled to Syria revised their political outlook once more and put into practice the only ideology of belonging that perhaps really matters in the end. They requested permission (and received the full support of the local CHP chapter) to reclaim their rights of citizenship and move back to the Hatay; back to their home.[186]

CONCLUSION: THE DOUBLE DISSERVICE

The 'Alawis, and the Middle East overall, continue to cope today with the twin legacy of France's policies of sectarian essentialism in Syria and the Kemalists' radical assimilationism in Turkey in the first decades of post-Ottoman statehood. In Syria the promotion of an "Alaouites" identity may have paved the way for their increasing participation in local government, modern education, the military, mass party mobilization, economic development, and finally politics at the highest level of state. To what degree these successes have equated with veritable acceptance and integration in Syria, however, or to what degree they have merely hidden and even accentuated the 'Alawis' historical standing on the sidelines of mainstream "orthodox" society, is too early to tell. That legacy was being fought out in the villages above Jisr al-Shughur and in the suburbs of Aleppo at the time of writing and will likely not be settled for a long time yet.

In Turkey too, the 'Alawi community still struggles to find its voice. In many ways the Kemalist state continued in line with the policies of the Hamidian and Young Turk era, offering the 'Alawis unprecedented opportunities for social advancement (and ultimately more security than in Syria), at the price of forsaking the very religious or linguistic specificities that defined

---

185 BCA 030.10.0.0/224.511.2.
186 BCA 490.01.0.0/584.17.1.

them as 'Alawis. Many 'Alawis were nevertheless ready to enter the bargain, not just in Cilicia and later the Hatay but even in the 'Alawi heartland of northern Syria, where the great 'Alawi resistance leader Salih al-'Ali had in the end proved willing, under the difficult circumstances of the day, to trade his autonomous enclave for an ill-defined, secular Muslim political union under post-Ottoman Turkish leadership. Today the 'Alawis of Cilicia and the Hatay are in an identity limbo, having long ago rejected the appeals of Arab nationalism and largely embraced the Kemalist state,[187] having for the most part lost the use of the Arabic language but still refusing to be assimilated as "Turks." They are doubly marginalized as "Arap Aleviler" (Arab Alevis), and are in fact neither. If the democratization of Turkish politics since the 1980s brought increasing recognition and respect for non-Sunni minorities, to the point that the Diyanet (Turkish religious affairs directorate) reportedly proceeded with the construction of *cem evleri* (Alevi meeting halls) in the Hatay on the pretext that 'Alawis must be Alevis (and therefore Turkish), a decade of neoconservative Ak Parti rule, plans to introduce obligatory religion courses at the high school level, ethnicity-based settlement projects in the Hatay, and the extraordinary sectarian tensions wrought by the Syrian Civil War just across the border have all conspired to call into question the 'Alawi community's integration once more.[188] As always, there is no one single consensus among the 'Alawis here either; the history of their past as well as of their present in Turkey is still being written.

---

187 Reyhani, *Gölgesiz Işıklar*, 2:107–13, 117–22.
188 See the comprehensive new study by Hakan Mertcan, *Türk Modernleşmesinde Arap Aleviler (Tarih, Kimlik, Siyaset)* (Adana: Karahan Kitabevi, 2014).

CONCLUSION

Producing a history of the 'Alawis, or of any group essentially identified by its religion, entails confronting the confessionalist bias of the sources themselves. Any written text, be it a theological treatise, heresiography, narrative chronicle, imperial decree, or travel report, which names the 'Alawis (or Nusayris) as such automatically directs attention to their singularity and potential opposition with the rest of society. As a result, any history based on such texts will necessarily concentrate on the undeniable but ultimately isolated instances where their religious beliefs were a factor in their interactions with others, magnifying episodes of sectarian strife, interpreting fiscal repression as persecution, and taking the pejorative opinions of orthodox religious scholars for actual lived experience. This is how it has become normal, in most of the academic literature as well as in much of the journalism on Syria today, to present a millennium of 'Alawi history as if it were epitomized and summed up by a single fatwa of Ibn Taymiyya or by a massacre in Aleppo that never actually occurred. Just as sectarianism has become a self-fulfilling prophecy in the current civil war, constructing the history of the 'Alawis as one of marginalization and persecution is in reality a circular argument.

To break out of the sectarian loop, this study has attempted to demonstrate, two things are necessary. First, the documentary basis must be significantly widened to include not only religious texts and event-based narrative chronicles but 'Alawi prosopographical literature and day-to-day administrative documentation as well. In particular, four hundred years' worth of Ottoman tax records, executive orders, and *iltizam* contracts that deal directly with the 'Alawi population of northwestern Syria, its geographic distribution, economic activity, legal status, and political integration cannot simply be passed over in silence. A significant proportion of this material does not actually identify 'Alawi village headmen, tax farmers, or entrepreneurs by their confessional affiliation, precisely because it was not at issue in their dealings with the state authorities and other societal groups. By interpolating what is known from other sources, however, it becomes possible to see just how much of the documentation from Tripoli and Istanbul did in fact concern 'Alawi individuals and communities, even when this was not stated explicitly. Second, therefore, the sources that do make mention of their religion, whether on account of particular tax obligations, clashes with other communities, dealings with

European missionaries, or specific educational needs, must be placed in their respective historical context rather than assumed to be an expression of a timeless and unchanging policy of discrimination. When Mamluk sources account for exactly one punitive campaign in 250 years of history, not coincidentally just after the first tax census was carried out in the area; when the same 'Alawi notable who is decried by the Ottomans as a Nusayri heretic one year is reappointed to his *iltizam* concession by the provincial court the next; or when 'Alawi reformists demand equal representation on local municipal councils in the name of their community's democratic rights, it becomes clear that religious nonconformity was not the only, or even a primary, factor in their relationship with the state.

Rather, this study has attempted to highlight the more long-term social and economic factors that have conditioned the 'Alawis' situation within Syria and the wider Middle East. In the first chapter it was argued that 'Alawism was not actually a radical departure from Imami Twelver Shi'ism but only came to be seen as such with the institutionalization of Imamism in Iraq in the eleventh century. Rather, the 'Alawi "mission" (*da'wa*), specifically its Khasibi branch in Syria, was an integral part of the general movement of Shi'i outreach and conversion of the time, benefiting from the protection especially of the Hamdanid dynasty of Aleppo (947–1003) to establish itself as one of the dominant branches of Islam in numerous towns of the interior, and spreading northward into the coastal mountains throughout the later middle ages. The rise of various Bedouin principalities and especially the Crusades of the twelfth century brought this age of expansion to an end, however, forcing the 'Alawis to yield to their Ismaili rivals and take refuge within their own increasingly bounded, compact sectarian community. Reinvigorated and reorganized along more pronouncedly tribal lines by the 'Alawi scholar-warlord Makzun al-Sinjari (d. 1240), this community, as chapter 2 attempted to show, became the site in the thirteenth century of a protracted theological dispute between the new 'Alawi orthodoxy and the popular following of older "incarnationist" ideas, a dispute that ultimately served to crystallize the social leadership of an emerging 'Alawi *'ulama* class. Far from having been driven into the mountains by physical persecution, it was this local consolidation of 'Alawi identity, on the one hand, and the rise of the self-consciously Sunni medieval state in Aleppo, Damascus, and Cairo, on the other, that left the 'Alawis in the position of a "heterodox" minority within wider Syrian and Middle Eastern society.

If the emergence and growing bureaucratization of the late medieval Ayyubid and Mamluk regimes placed new political and fiscal constraints on the 'Alawis, Ismailis, and other non-Sunni population groups, the sources at our disposal do not support the claim of increasing radicalization or generalized religious persecution. In particular, the legal opinions of Ibn Taymiyya and other piety-minded orthodox scholars were demonstrably neither followed by the Mamluk regime nor taken into consideration by Ottoman scholars before the eighteenth century; a single instance of state-organized violence against the 'Alawis in 1318, one that furthermore shows a wide range of interpretations by religious and nonreligious historians of the time, followed from a single fiscal-millenarian revolt and cannot be taken as evidence of constant sectarian oppression. Rather, it was suggested that late Mamluk and early Ottoman "policy" toward the 'Alawis should be deduced not from individual chronicles but from the Ottoman-era Tahrir censuses, which indicate that both regimes levied a customary, 'Alawi-specific *dirhemü'r-rical* tax on most of the 'Alawi villages in the region as part of their overall tax obligation. The progression (and occasional suspension) of *dirhem* dues as well as the application of other taxes specifically on 'Alawi wine production, and finally the co-optation of individual 'Alawi notables as Ottoman *mültezims* or tax farmers, were taken to indicate the extent to which the community was in reality integrated in the Ottoman provincial administration during the early modern period.

The eighteenth century can be seen as the heyday of 'Alawi autonomy in northwestern Syria, as leading local families not only benefited from the decentralization or privatization of Ottoman provincial administration as tax concessionaries but also profited from the rapid growth of commercial tobacco farming particularly in the northern coastal mountains around Latakia. If the region's unprecedented economic development and the 'Alawi community's overall expansion northward toward the Hatay and Cilicia are attested in the central state archives as well as by a wealth of *shar'iyya* court records from Tripoli and Antioch, the rise of a new landed gentry such as the Shamsins of Safita or the Shillifs of Bahluliyya, and their effective recognition as "tribal" leaders, it was suggested, also points to the increasing stratification of 'Alawi society itself. Thus in the early nineteenth century the Shamsin family patriarch Saqr ibn Mahfuz al-Shibli could emerge as one of the most powerful factional leaders of the entire Syro-Lebanese coastal region, an importance and visibility which, however, exposed the entire community to increasing conflict with quasi-independent local Ottoman authorities as well as the proponents of modern Sunni Islamic revivalism in Latakia and other cities of the region. The brief interregnum of modern Egyptian state rule over Syria (1832–1840) was welcomed by many 'Alawis as an opportunity for increased legal rights and social advancement; more traditional, old-guard feudalists such as the Shamsins or later the Khayr-Beys of Qardaha, on the other hand, actively defended the more diffuse, indirect suzerainty of the Ottoman Empire.

The Tanzimat reforms brought the promise of greater enfranchisement through education and political representation, while at the same time subjecting the 'Alawi community to unprecedented new levels of government intervention and control through conscription, co-optation into the local administration, and finally religious proselytization. Under Sultan Abdülhamid in particular, the 'Alawis were subject to an official "rectification of belief" program. Especially in the newly settled agricultural regions of Cilicia and Antioch, however, this appears to have aimed at their social integration as much as at their actual conversion to orthodoxy. Despite the growing appeal of Arab nationalism and a cultural *prise de conscience* or awakening within the community itself, a good number of 'Alawis therefore continued to support the Ottoman state, finally casting their lot with the Kemalist-led "jihad" or "War of Liberation" against the French occupation of southern Anatolia and northern Syria at the conclusion of World War I. After the failure of the 'Alawi rebel leader Salih al-'Ali's revolt in 1921–22, the 'Alawi community of both Turkey and Syria remained divided as to its political loyalties, jealously defending their autonomy in the "Alaouites" mandate and in the Alexandretta district (Hatay) in some cases but campaigning for their respective attachment to the independent Syrian and Turkish republics in others. Both France's promotion of a separate 'Alawi legal and political identity in Syria and the CHP's radical assimilationist policies in Turkey ultimately seem to have failed in making the 'Alawis fully equal nationals in either country. That discussion must be left to future, and likely separate, analyses of 'Alawi society in contemporary Syria and Turkey (as well as Lebanon and Israel). Advantaged neither by the once trendy discourse of "minorities" nor by nationalist policies designed to negate their religious and historical specificity, the 'Alawis have in each case sought, and will likely continue to seek, to constitute and define their community as best befits their material and moral interests.

FROM THE SECTARIAN TO THE LOCAL

If this ultimately rapid overview of a thousand years of 'Alawi history has been able to show anything, it is that the multiplicity of lived 'Alawi experiences cannot be reduced to the sole question of religion or framed within a monolithic narrative of persecution; that the very attempt to outline a single coherent history of "the 'Alawis" may indeed be misguided. The sources on which this study has drawn are considerably more accessible, and the social and administrative realities they reflect consistently more mundane and disjointed, than the discourse of the 'Alawis' supposed exceptionalism would lead one to believe. The challenge for historians of 'Alawi society in Syria and elsewhere must therefore be not to use the specific events and structures these sources detail to merely add to the already existing metanarratives of religious oppression, Ottoman misrule, and national resistance but rather to come to a newer and more intricate understanding of that community, and its place in wider Middle Eastern society, by investigating the lives of individual 'Alawi (and other) actors within the rich diversity of local contexts these sources reveal. It is precisely in the field of local history, as a modern historian of Safita has for example noted, that so much remains to be done, with many Syrian (and Turkish) writers consciously avoiding seemingly too parochial themes for fear of accentuating sectarian, tribal, or communal divisions and thus undermining national unity.[1] Until historians of 'Alawism reconcile themselves to the practice of local history, however, to the use of Ottoman administrative sources, and to the very mundanity of this historical record, it is not only the socioeconomic dimension of the 'Alawi community but the national histories of Syria and Turkey as such that will remain incomplete, incomprehensible, and implausible to the very audience for which they are intended, and thus prey to the outrageous, divisive interpretations of radicals of all persuasions.

There is less sense today than ever before, as the devastation of Syria reaches ever newer and more intolerable levels, in seeking to conclude on the nature of 'Alawi history. While it remains sadly impossible to envision the end, let alone the long-term consequences, of the current conflict in Syria, one thing, based on the recent experiences of other countries in similar situations, seems certain: the war will end, and when it does, the people of Syria, whether they continue to live within the same geopolitical parameters or not, will have to collectively rebuild, resume some measure of commercial and economic cooperation, and ultimately, perhaps far in the future, seek some measure of truth and reconciliation. When that day comes, the 'Alawis, and the Syrians together, will have a choice to make regarding the historical models on which to draw—whether the 'Alawis' place within wider society is historically to be defined by the likes of Ibn Taymiyya and Muhammad al-Moghrabi or better by Midhat Paşa and Ziya Bey; whether one will choose to "remember" the Jabala uprising of 1318 and the Aleppo massacre of 1516, or whether one will find cause for optimism in the careers of 'Ali al-Shillif and Kara Mehmed Paşa, in the joint education commissions and municipal councils of the Ottoman reform era, and in the political vision of a Salih al-'Ali or a Sulayman al-Ahmad. The past is neither dead nor even past, as we know, and it is vital that the 'Alawis, their neighbors, and countrymen reclaim theirs.

---

1 Georges Jabbour, "Safita et son environnement," in *Histoire économique et sociale de l'Empire Ottoman et de la Turquie (1326–1960)*, ed. Daniel Panzac (Paris: Peeters, 1995), 606.

BIBLIOGRAPHY

ARCHIVAL MATERIALS

Unpublished

Aleppo—Poche-Marcopoli Archives
Fonds Poche [FP] 2005.

Ankara—Başbakanlık Cumhuriyet Arşivi [BCA]
Bakanlar Kurulu Kararları 030.10.1.2/9.19.7; 030.18.1.2/73.29.1; 030.18.1.2/76.60.20; 030.18.1.2/84.68.11; 030.18.1.2/88.77.16; 030.10.1.2/127.100.4.

Başbakanlık Muamelât Genel Müdürlüğü 030.10.0.0/224.511.2.

Cumhuriyet Halk Partisi Evrakı 490.01.0.0/583.10.1; 490.01.0.0/583.11.1; 490.01.0.0/584.17.1.

Ankara—Genelkurmay Askeri Tarih ve Stratejik Etüt Başkanlığı Arşivi [ATASE]
Birinci Dünya Harbi koleksiyonu [BDH] 170-736; 2681-216.

İstiklal Harbi koleksiyonu [İSH]] 629-125; 664-141; 805-58; 809-63, 68, 91; 868-4; 1169-66; 1321-124.

İkinci Dünya Harbi koleksiyonu [İDH] 7-80.

Ankara—Vakıflar Genel Müdürlüğü [VGM]
Register nos. 284, 339, 354.

Istanbul—Başbakanlık Osmanlı Arşivi [BOA]

    Pre-Tanzimat Series

    Başmuhasebe Kalemi/Trablus-Şam Mukataası [D.BŞM.TŞH] 11, 13.

    Halep Ahkam Defteri [HAD] 1, 4.

    Hatt-ı Hümayun [HAT] 3784i, 17679, 20647, 20671a, 22354c, 24372, 24282, 24295, 24468d, 24973, 25480, 32670, 35473, 40823.

    Maliyeden Müdevver [MAD] 602, 842, 4455, 9833.

    Mühimme Defteri [MD] 3-4, 6, 19, 23, 26, 36, 39, 42, 46-48, 52-54, 102, 112, 127, 130-31, 136, 139, 147, 151, 157, 160.

    Mühimme Zeyli Defteri [MZ] 9, 12.

    Şam-ı Şerif Ahkam Defteri [ŞŞAD] 1-4.

Şikayet Defteri [ŞD] 4, 99.

Tahrir Defteri [TD] 68, 281, 421, 502, 513, 1017, 1107.

Tanzimat-Era Series

Bab-ı Ali Evrak Odası [BEO] 142/10630; 201/15050; 294/21989; 314/23496, 23495.

Bab-ı Ali Evrak Odası Ayniyat Defterleri [BEO.AYN.d] 867.

Cevdet Maliye [C.ML] 11/461.

Dahiliye Nezareti Emniyet-i Umumiye Müdüriyeti Emniyet Kalemi [DH.EUM.EMN] 80/21.

Dahiliye Nezareti Emniyet-i Umumiye Müdüriyeti 4. Şube [DH.EUM.4.Şb] 2/57; 7/39, 60.

Dahiliye Nezareti Emniyet-i Umumiye Müdüriyeti 7. Şube [DH.EUM.7.Şb] 1/1.

Dahiliye Nezareti İdare-i Umumiye [DH.İUM] 20–25/14.

Dahiliye Nezareti Mektubi Kalemi [DH.MKT] 31/9; 430/70; 529/38; 866/56; 1311/27; 1311/32; 1311/40; 1355/3; 1358/7; 1364/106; 1368/44; 1416/29; 1475/100; 1485/32; 1670/20; 1691/55; 1741/10; 1744/33; 1767/68, 69; 1778/130; 1796/106; 1823/38, 102; 1831/58; 1851/93; 1865/20; 1919/122; 1958/80; 1981/40; 1993/3; 1999/43; 2031/114; 2045/97; 2049/13; 2060/105; 2110/24; 2204/18; 2251/77; 2490/75; 2522/65; 2647/38; 2739/90; 2792/76.

Dahiliye Nezareti Şifre Kalemi [DH.ŞFR] 68/8; 531/87.

Dahiliye Nezareti Tesri-i Muamelat ve Islahat Komisyonu [DH.TMIK.M] 29/47; 168/7; 182/69, 75; 244/40; [DH.TMIK.S] 26/31; 36/50.

Hariciye Nezareti Mektubi Kalemi [HR.MKT] 197/48.

Hariciye Nezareti Tercüme Odası [HR.TO] 287/4; 516/24.

İrade Dahiliye [İ.DH] 265/16558; 389/25724; 393/26006; 409/27058; 415/27493; 416/27528; 559/38933; 611/42613; 612/42642, 42686; 944/74757; 1182/92449, 92451; 1207/94486; 1306/9.

İrade Divan-ı Ahkam-ı Adliye [İ.DA] 1/9.

İrade Dosya Usulü İrade Tasnifi [İ.DUİT] 66/52; 68/20.

İrade Hariciye [İ.HR] 157/8341; 266/15960–61.

İrade Maarif [İ.MF] 2/10; 4/7.

İrade Meclis-i Mahsus [İ.MMS] 113/4821; 114/4867; 130/5563.

İrade Mesail-i Mühimme [İ.MSM] 76/2173–75.

Maarif-i Umumiye Nezareti Mektubi Kalemi [MF.MKT] 150/12; 162/54; 164/159; 174/24; 181/109; 187/1; 237/20; 246/56; 273/59; 333/21; 374/12; 437/33; 496/33; 672/36–48; 825/73.

Meclis-i Vala [MVL] 284/69; 310/98; 567/25; 750/107; 754/87.

Meclis-i Vükela [MV] 48/32; 54/37; 73/38; 76/93; 83/72; 180/30.

Nüfus Defterleri [NFS.d] 3746.

Sadaret Amedi Kalemi [A.AMD] 5/16, 37/70; 83/17.

Sadaret Mektubi Kalemi [A.MKT] 103/44, 139/12.

Sadaret Mektubi Kalemi Meclis-i Vala [A.MKT.MVL] 74/84.

Sadaret Mektubi Kalemi Mühimme [A.MKT.MHM] 46/19; 349/68; 357/39; 405/92; 419/14; 450/53; 475/44; 700/5; 757/110.

Sadaret Mektubi Kalemi Umum Vilayet [A.MKT.UM] 169/55; 178/24; 337/3; 395/98; 566/12.

Şura-yı Devlet [ŞUD] 2215/26; 2483/9.

Yıldız Esas Evrakı [Y.EE] 36/55; 40/6–7; 43/103; 129/79; 132/38.

Yıldız Esas Evrakı/Kamil Paşa [Y.EE.KP] 1/80.

Yıldız Mütenevvi Maruzat [Y.MTV] 7/54; 77/10; 87/44; 235/127.

Yıldız Perakende Adliye ve Mezahib Nezareti Maruzatı [Y.PRK.AZN] 4/57.

Yıldız Perakende Arzuhal ve Jurnaller [Y.PRK.AZJ] 39/117.

Yıldız Perakende Askeri Maruzat [Y.PRK.ASK] 157/45.

Yıldız Perakende Başkitabeti [Y.PRK.BŞK] 58/35, 44; 61/45.

Yıldız Perakende Maarif Nezareti Maruzatı [Y.PRK.MF] 2/57; 3/11.

Yıldız Perakende Maiyet-i Seniye Erkan-ı Harbiye Dairesi [Y.PRK.MYD] 22/105.

Yıldız Perakende Meşihat Dairesi Maruzatı [Y.PRK.MŞ] 5/83.

Yıldız Perakende Umum Vilayetler Tahriratı [Y.PRK.UM] 19/58, 70; 37/24; 49/76.

Yıldız Sadaret Hususi Maruzat [Y.A.HUS] 257/26; 266/97; 358/80.

Istanbul—Topkapı Palace Archives

E. 2465

Istanbul (Üsküdar)—İslam Araştırmaları Merkezi (İSAM).

Antakya Şeriye Sicilleri Defteri [AŞSD] 5, 14, 20.

London (Kew)—National Archives

Foreign Office [FO] 78/910, 1118, 1297, 1386, 1388, 2282, 2493; FO 195/587, 601, 1113, 1153, 1154, 1369, 1448; FO 226/133, 189.

Nantes—Centre des archives diplomatiques de Nantes [CADN]

Représentations diplomatiques et consulaires, Damas-Consulat 33, 72.

Paris—Archives Nationales
Affaires étrangères B/I (Tripoli) [AE/BI] 1115–24.

Paris (La Courneuve)—Ministère des Affaires étrangères [MAE]
Correspondance consulaire et commerciale [CCC]

    Lattaquié 1–4.

    Tripoli 13–16, 18.

    Correspondance politique des consuls [CPC]

        Turquie 244–5, 257–8.

        Turquie-Beyrouth 10–11, 19–24.

        Turquie-divers 1–2, 4–5, 7, 9–10, 12.

    Correspondance politique et commerciale

        Nouvelle Série [NS] Turquie 108.

        E-Levant Syrie-Liban [ELSL] 112, 115, 121, 125.

Paris (Vincennes)—Service historique de la Défense [SHD]
4H 84, 4H 249.

Tripoli—Qasr Nawfal
Shar'iyya Court Records [TShCR], registers 1–12, 14–24, 26–30, 33, 45–46, 49–50, 52.

PUBLISHED

Akgündüz, Ahmed, ed. *Osmanlı Kanunnâmeleri ve Hukukî Tahlilleri*. 9 vols. Istanbul: FEY Vakfı/Osmanlı Araştırmaları Vakfı, 1990–96.

Ayhan, Rıza, et al., eds. *Osmanlı Arşiv Belgelerinde Nusayrîler ve Nusayrîlik (1745–1920)*. Ankara: Gazi Üniversitesi Türk Kültürü ve Hacı Bektaş Velî Araştırma Merkezi, 2010.

Cattaui, René (d. 1994), ed. *Le règne de Mohamed Aly d'après les Archives russes en Egypte*. Cairo: Institut français d'archéologie orientale, 1933.

Recueil des actes administratifs du Haut-Commissariat de la République française en Syrie et au Liban. Vol. 1: *Années 1919–1920*. Beirut: Imprimerie Jeanne d'Arc, n.d.

Rustum, Asad (d. 1965), ed. *Al-Mahfuzat al-Malikiyya al-Misriyya: Bayan bi-Watha'iq al-Sham*. 4 vols. 2nd imprint. Beirut: al-Maktaba al-Bulusiyya, 1986–1987. [*Mahfuzat*].

Salname-i Nezaret-i Maarif-i Umumiye: İkinci Sene. Istanbul: Darü'l-Hilafeti'l-Aliye, 1899/1900.

Tadmuri, 'Umar, et al., eds. *Watha'iq al-Mahkama al-Shar'iyya bi-Tarabulus: al-Sijill al-Awwal 1077–1078 h / 1666–1667 m*. Tripoli: Lebanese University, 1982.

UNPUBLISHED LITERARY SOURCES

Anonymous. "Risale der Redd-i Revafız." Süleymaniye Kütüphanesi, Istanbul: ms. Serez 1451.

Harfush, Husayn Mayhub (d. 1959). *Khayr al-Saniʻa fi Mukhtasar Tarikh Ghulat al-Shiʻa*. Library of the Institut français du Proche-Orient, Damascus: photocopy of ms. dated 1991.

Harfush, Ibrahim. *Al-Mustadrak fi Khayr al-Saniʻa*. Library of the Institut français du Proche-Orient, Damascus: photocopy of ms. dated 1991.

Ibn al-Saʼigh, Fathallah. "Al-Muqtarab fi Hawadith al-Hadar waʼl-ʻArab." Bibliothèque Nationale, Paris (Richelieu): ms. Arabe 1685.

el-Kayseri, Mustafa bin Ebi Bekir. "Damigüʼn-Nusayriye." Atatürk Kitapliği, Istanbul: ms. Osman Ergin 97.

al-Nashshabi al-Halabi, Yusuf ibn al-ʻAjuz. *Munazara*. Bibliothèque Nationale, Paris: ms. Arabe 1450.

PUBLISHED LITERARY SOURCES

Abuʼl-Fidaʼ, ʻImad al-Din Ismaʻil (d. 1331). *Al-Mukhtasar fi Akhbar al-Bashar*. Cairo: al-Matbaʻa al-Husayniyya al-Misriyya, 1968.

Abu Musa and Shaykh Musa, eds. *Majmuʻa al-Ahadith al-ʻAlawiyya, Silsilat al-Turath al-ʻAlawi*. Vol. 8. Diyar ʻAql, Lb.: Dar li-Ajl al-Maʻrifa, 2008.

Anonymous. *Hurub Ibrahim Basha al-Misri fi Suriya wa-ʼl-Anadul*. Edited by Asad Rustum. Heliopolis: Syrian Press, [1927].

Anonymous. *Tarikh al-Umaraʼ al-Shihabiyyin bi-Qalam Ahad Umaraʼihim min Wadi Taym*. Edited by Salim Hasan Hashshi. Beirut: al-Mudiriyya al-ʻAmma liʼl-Athar, 1971.

Asʻad, Munir al-Khuri ʻIsa. *Tarikh Hims: Min Zuhur al-Islam hatta Yawmina Hadha Sana 622–1977*. Homs: Matraniyya Hims al-Urthudhuksiyya, 1984.

al-ʻAsqalani, Ibn Hajar (d. 1449). *Inbaʼ al-Ghumr bi-Anbaʼ al-ʻUmr*. Damascus: Maktabat al-Dirasat al-Islamiyya, 1979.

al-ʻAwra, Ibrahim (d. 1863). *Tarikh Wilayat Sulayman Basha al-ʻAdil 1804–1819*. Edited by Antun Bishara Qiqanu. Beirut: Lahad Khatir, 1989.

Behcet, Mehmed, and Refik Temimi. *Beyrut Vilayeti*. Vol. 2: Şimal Kısmı. Beirut: Vilayet Matbaası, 1917.

al-Birzali, Qasim ibn Muhammad (d. 1338). *Al-Muqtafa ʻala Kitab al-Rawdatayn*. Edited by ʻUmar ʻAbd al-Salam al-Tadmuri. Saydaʼ: al-Maktaba al-ʻAsriyya, 2006.

Burckhardt, John Lewis (d. 1817). *Travels in Syria and the Holy Land*. London: John Murray, 1822.

Della Valle, Pietro (d. 1652). *Voyages de Pietro della Vallé, Gentilhomme romain, dans la Turquie, lʼEgypte, la Palestine, la Perse, les Indes Orientales & autres lieux*. Rouen: Robert Machuel, 1745.

al-Dimashqi, Muhammad Abu Talib (d. 1327). *Nukhbat al-Dahr fi ʻAjaʼib al-Barr waʼl-Bahr*. Edited by August Mehren. Leipzig: Harrassowitz, 1923.

Duwayhi, Istfan (d. 1704). *Tarikh al-Azmina 1095–1699*. Edited by Fardinan Tawtal. Beirut: Catholic Press, 1951.

al-Harawi, ʻAli ibn Abi Bakr (d. 1215). *Guide des lieux de pèlerinage*. Translated by Janine Sourdel-Thomine. Damascus: Institut français de Damas, 1957.

Hasan Agha al-ʻAbd (d. after 1826). *Tarikh Hasan Agha al-ʻAbd: Hawadith Bilad al-Sham waʼl-Imbaraturiyya al-ʻUthmaniyya, 1771–1826 m*. Edited by Yusuf Jumayyil Naʻisa. Damascus: Dar Dimashq, 1986.

Ibn Abi'l-Fada'il (d. after 1358). *Ägypten und Syrien zwischen 1317 und 1341 in der Chronik des Mufaddal b. Abi l-Fada'il.* Edited by Samira Kortantamer. Freiburg: Klaus Schwarz, 1973.

Ibn al-Athir, 'Izz al-Din 'Ali ibn Muhammad, al-Jazari (d. 1233). *Al-Kamil fi'l-Tarikh.* Edited by Muhammad Yusuf al-Daqqaq. Beirut: Dar al-Kutub al-'Ilmiyya.

Ibn Battuta, Muhammad ibn 'Abdallah (d. after 1368). *Rihlat Ibn Battuta: al-Tuhfat al-Nizar fi Ghara'ib al-Amsar wa-'Aja'ib al-Asfar.* Edited by 'Abd al-Hadi al-Tazi. Ribat: Akadimiyyat al-Mamlaka al-Maghribiyya, 1997.

Ibn al-Fuwati, 'Abd al-Razzak ibn Ahmad (d. 1323). *Majma' al-Adab fi Mu'jam al-Alqab.* Edited by Muhammad al-Kazim. Tehran: Danishmendan-e Islami, 1995.

Ibn Kathir, 'Imad al-Din (d. 1373). *Al-Bidaya wa'l-Nihaya fi'l-Tarikh.* Edited by Ahmad Abu Mulhim et al. Beirut: Dar al-Kutub al-'Ilmiyya, 1985.

Ibn Qadi Shuhba, Ahmad ibn Muhammad (d. 1448). *Tarikh.* Damascus: IFÉAD, 1997.

Ibn al-Qalanisi, Hamza ibn Asad (d. 1160). *Tarikh Dimashq 460–555.* Edited by Suhayl Zakkar. Damascus: Dar Hassan, 1983.

Ibn Taymiyya, Ahmad (d. 1328). *Majmu' Fatawa Shaykh al-Islam Ahmad ibn Taymiyya.* Edited by 'Abd al-Rahman ibn Muhammad ibn Qasim al-'Asimi. Riyad: n.p., 1961–66.

Ibn al-Wardi, 'Umar (d. 1348). *Tarikh.* Najaf: al-Matba'a al-Haydariyya, 1969.

Ibn Yahya, Salih (d. 1436). *Tarikh Bayrut.* Edited by Francis Hours and Kamal Salibi. Beirut: Dar al-Mashriq, 1969.

Ismail Kemal Bey (d. 1915). *The Memoirs of Ismail Kemal Bey.* Edited by Sommerville Story. London: Constable, 1920.

al-Jabarti, 'Abd al-Rahman (d. 1825). *Aja'ib al-Athar fi'l-Tarajim wa'l-Akhbar.* Translated by Thomas Philipp and Moshe Perlmann. Stuttgart: Franz Steiner, 1994.

al-Jazari, Muhammad ibn Ibrahim (d. 1338). *Hawadith al-Zaman wa-Anba'ihi wa-Wafayat al-Akabir wa'l-A'yan min Abna'ihi.* Edited by 'Umar 'Abd al-Salam al-Tadmuri. Beirut: al-Maktaba al-'Asriyya, 1998.

Jessup, Henry Harris (d. 1910). *Fifty-Three Years in Syria.* New York: Fleming H. Revell, 1910.

Karama, Rawfa'il ibn Yusuf (d. 1800). *Hawadith Lubnan wa-Suriya: min sanat 1745 ila sanat 1800.* Edited by Basilus Qattan. N.p:, Jarrus Pars, n.d.

Katib Çelebi (d. 1657). *Kitab-ı Cihannüma* (facsimile of 1732 Ibrahim Müteferrika edition, Istanbul: Büyükşehir Belediyesi, 2008). English translation edited by Gottfried Hagen. New Haven, CT: Yale University Press, forthcoming.

Lyde, Samuel (d. 1860). *The Ansyreeh and Ismaeleeh: A Visit to the Secret Sects of Northern Syria; with a View to the Establishment of Schools.* London: Hurst and Blackett, 1853.

———. *The Asian Mystery: Illustrated in the History, Religion, and Present State of the Ansaireeh or Nusairis of Syria.* London: Longman, Green, Longman and Roberts, 1860.

al-Makki, Muhammad (d. after 1722). *Tarikh Hims.* Edited by 'Umar Najib al-'Umar. Damascus: IFÉAD, 1987.

al-Maqdisi, Muhammad ibn Ahmad ibn Qudama (d. 1343). *Al-'Uqud al-Durriyya min Manaqib Shaykh al-Islam Ahmad ibn Taymiyya.* Edited by Muhammad Hamid al-Fiqi. Beirut: Dar al-Kutub al-'Ilmiyya, 1975.

al-Maqrizi, Taqi al-Din Ahmad (d. 1442). *Kitab al-Suluk li-Ma'rifat Duwal al-Muluk.* Cairo: Lajnat al-Ta'lif wa'l-Tarjama wa'l-Nashr, 1971.

Maundrell, Henry (d. 1701). *A Journey from Aleppo to Jerusalem, at Easter A.D. 1697.* Boston: Samuel Simpkins, 1836.

Mishaqa, Mikha'il (d. 1888). *Mashhad al-'Iyan bi-Hawadith Suriya wa-Lubnan*. Cairo: n.p., 1908.

al-Nabulusi, 'Abd al-Ghani (d. 1731). *Al-Haqiqa wa'l-Majaz fi Rihla Bilad al-Sham wa-Misr wa'l-Hijaz*. Edited by Riyad 'Abd al-Hamid Murad. Damascus: Dar al-Ma'rifa, 1989.

al-Nuwayri, Ahmad ibn 'Abd al-Wahhab (d. 1333). *Nihayat al-'Arab fi Funun al-Adab*. Edited by Muhammad 'Alawi Shaltut. Cairo: Dar al-Kutub al-Misriyya, 1998.

Paton, A. A. (d. 1874). *A History of the Egyptian Revolution, from the Period of the Mamlukes to the Death of Mohammed Ali*. 2nd ed. London: Trübner, 1870.

Paxton, John D. (d. 1868). *Letters from Palestine: Written during a Residence There in the Years 1836, 7 and 8*. London: Charles Tilt, 1839.

Poujoulat, Baptistin (d. 1864). *Voyage dans l'Asie Mineure*. Paris: Ducollet, 1841.

al-Qalqashandi, Shihab al-Din Ahmad (d. 1418). *Subh al-A'sha fi Sina'at al-Insha'*. Cairo: Al-Mu'assasa al-Misriyya al-'Amma, 1964.

Salih, Ilyas (d. 1885). "Athar al-Hiqab fi Ladhiqiyyat al-'Arab." Private manuscript, Syria, 1952. Recently published by Ilyas Jurjus Jurayj, ed. Beirut: Dar al-Farabi, 2013.

Şalvuz, İsmail Ferahim (d. 1977). *Kurtuluş Savaşı'nda Kahraman Çukurovalılar (Adana, Tarsus, Mersinliler): Hatira*. Edited by Halil Atılgan. Ankara: T.C. Kültür Bakanlığı, 2002.

al-Sayyaf, Ahmad Nihad (d. 1992). *Shu'a' Qabl al-Fajr: Mudhakkirat*. Edited by Muhammad Jamal Barut. [Aleppo]: n.p., 2005.

Seetzen, Ulrich Jasper (d. 1811). *Reisen durch Syrien, Palästina, die Tranjordan-Länder, Arabia Petraea und Unter-Aegypten*. Edited by Friedrich Kruse. Berlin: G. Reimer, 1854–59.

al-Shidyaq, Tannus (d. 1859). *Akhbar al-A'yan fi Jabal Lubnan*. Edited by Fu'ad Afram al-Bustani. Beirut: Lebanese University, 1970.

Shihabi, Haydar Ahmad (d. 1835). *Lubnan fi 'Ahd al-Umara' al-Shihabiyin*. Edited by Asad Rustum and Fu'ad Afram al-Bustani. Beirut: Lebanese University, 1969.

al-'Umari, Ibn Fadlallah (d. 1349). *Al-Ta'rif bi'l-Mustalah al-Sharif*. Edited by Samir al-Durubi. Karak: Mu'ta University, 1992.

Volney, Constantin-François (d. 1820). *Travels through Egypt and Syria in the Years 1783, 1784, and 1785*. New York: Evert Duyckinck, 1798.

Walpole, Frederick (d. 1876). *The Ansayrii, or Assassins, with Travels in the Further East, in 1850–51*. London: Richard Bentley, 1851.

al-Yunini, Qutb al-Din Musa (d. 1326). *Early Mamluk Syrian Historiography: Al-Yunini's Dhayl Mir'at al-Zaman*. Edited by Li Guo. Leiden: Brill, 1998.

REFERENCE WORKS

Encyclopaedia of Islam. 2nd ed. [*EI2*]. Leiden: Brill, 1960–2005.

Répertoire alphabétique des villages et hameaux. Latakia, [1924].

Talas, Mustafa, ed. *Al-Mu'jam al-Jughrafi li'l-Qutr al-'Arabi al-Suri*. Damascus: Al-Mu'assasa al-'Amma li'l-Masahat, 1992.

MODERN LITERATURE

'Abbas, Qays Ibrahim. *Al-Shaykh Salih al-'Ali: Awraq wa-Shahadat*. Damascus: Dar al-Takwin, 2005.

Abdel-Nour, Antoine (d. 1982). *Introduction à l'histoire urbaine de la Syrie ottomane (XVIe-XVIIIe siècle)*. Beirut: Librairie Orientale, 1982.

Abu-'Allush, 'Isa. *Safahat Majhula min Thawrat al-Shaykh Salih al-'Ali*. Latakia: Dar Dhu'l-Fiqar, 2007.

Abu-Husayn, Abdul-Rahim. *Provincial Leaderships in Syria, 1575–1650*. Beirut: American University of Beirut, 1985.

Abu-'Izz al-Din, Sulayman (d. 1932/33). *Ibrahim Basha fi Suriya*. New ed. Cairo: Dar al-Shuruq, 2006.

al-'Adima, Salih. *Hadha Huwa Badawi al-Jabal*. Beirut: Dar al-Mahajja al-Bayda' and Maktabat al-Sa'ih, 2010.

Akbıyık, Yaşar. *Milli Mücadelede Güney Cephesi: Maraş*. Ankara: Kültür Bakanlığı, 1990.

Akbulut, Uğur. "Lazkiye Nusayrîleri." *Türk Kültürü ve Hacı Bektaş Veli Araştırma Dergisi* 54 (2010): 111–26.

Akşin, Sina. "Turkish-Syrian Relations in the Time of Faisal (1918–1920)." In *Essays in Ottoman-Turkish Political History*. By Sina Akşin, 31–42. Istanbul: Isis Press, 2000.

Aksoy, Erdal. "Nusayrîlerin Sosyal Yapıları ve Cumhuriyetinin İlk Yıllarında Türkiye'de Yaşayan bu Topluluğa Devletin Yaklaşımları." *Türk Kültürü ve Hacı Bektaş Veli Araştırma Dergisi* 54 (2010): 199–212.

Al Jundi, Adham. *Tarikh al-Thawrat al-Suriyya fi 'Ahd al-Intidab al-Faransi*. Damascus: Matba'at al-Ittihad, 1960.

Al Ma'ruf, Amil 'Abbas. *Tarikh al-'Alawiyyin fi Bilad al-Sham: Mundhu Fajr al-Islam ila Tarikhina al-Mu'asir khilal Jami' al-'Usur wa'l-Duwaylat illati Marrat 'ala'l-Mintaqa al-'Arabiyya wa'l-Islamiyya*. 3 vols. Tripoli: Dar al-Amal wa'l-Salam, 2013.

Alagöz, Cemal. "Coğrafya gözüyle Hatay." *Ankara Üniversitesi Dil ve Tarih-Coğrafya Fakültesi Dergisi* 2 (1943–44): 203–16.

'Ali, As'ad Ahmad. *Ma'rifat Allah wa'l-Makzun al-Sinjari*. 1st ed., 1972; Damascus: Dar al-Su'al, 1990.

'Ali, Muhammad Ahmad. *Al-'Alawiyyin fi 'l-Tarikh. Haqa'iq wa-Abatil*. Beirut: Mu'assasat al-Nur, 1997.

Alkan, Necati. "Fighting for the Nusayrī Soul: State, Protestant Missionaries and the 'Alawīs in the Late Ottoman Empire." *Die Welt des Islams* 52 (2012): 23–50.

Allouche, Adel. *The Origins and Development of the Ottoman-Safavid Conflict (906–962/1500–1555)*. Berlin: Klaus Schwarz, 1983.

al-Amin, Muhsin (d. 1952). *A'yan al-Shi'a*. 2nd ed. Beirut: Dar al-Ta'arif, 1996.

Amir-Moezzi, Mohammed Ali. *Le guide divin dans le Shî'isme originel: aux sources de l'ésoterisme en Islam*. N.p: Verdier, 1992.

Arsuzi-Elamir, Dalal. *Arabischer Nationalismus in Syrien: Zaki al-Arsūzī und die arabisch-nationale Bewegung an der Peripherie Alexandretta/Antakya 1930–1938*. Münster: Lit, 2003.

Aslan, Cahit. *Fellahlar'ın Sosyolojisi: Arapuşakları, Nusayriler, Hasibiler, Kilaziler, Haydariler, Arap Alevileri*. Adana: Karahan Kitabevi, 2005.

Baer, Marc. Review of Tijana Krstíc, *Contested Conversions to Islam: Narratives of Religious Change in the Early Modern Ottoman Empire*. *Journal of Islamic Studies* 23 (2012): 391–94.

Balanche, Fabrice. *La région alaouite et le pouvoir syrien*. Paris: Karthala, 2006.

Bar-Asher, Meir, and Aryeh Kofsky. *The Nusayrī-'Alawī Religion: An Enquiry into Its Theology and Liturgy*. Leiden: Brill, 2002.
Batatu, Hanna (d. 2000). *Syria's Peasantry, the Descendants of Its Lesser Rural Notables, and Their Politics*. Princeton, NJ: Princeton University Press, 1999.
Bayat, Fadil. *Dirasat fi Tarikh al-'Arab fi'l-'Ahd al-'Uthmani: Ru'ya Jadida fi Daw' al-Watha'iq wa'l-Masadir al-'Uthmaniyya*. Tripoli, Libya: Dar al-Madar al-Islami, 2003.
Berkes, Niyazi. *The Development of Secularism in Turkey*. Facsimile ed. London: Hurst, 1998.
Beydoun, Ahmed. *Identité confessionnelle et temps social chez les historiens libanais*. Beirut: Lebanese University, 1984.
Bianquis, Thierry. *Damas et la Syrie sous la domination fatimide*. Damascus: IFÉAD, 1986–89.
Bilgili, Ali Sinan. "Osmanlı Arşiv Belgelerinde Adana, Tarsus ve Mersin Bölgesi Nusayrîleri (19–20. Yüzyıl)." *Türk Kültürü ve Hacı Bektaş Veli Araştırma Dergisi* 54 (2010): 49–78.
Bitar, Ghayad Ilyas. *Al-Ladhiqiyya 'ibra'l-Zaman: Min 'Usur ma qabla'l-Tarikh ila 'am 1963*. Damascus: Dar al-Majd, 2001.
Blachère, Regis, and Charles Pellat. "Al-Mutanabbī." *EI2*, 1993, 7:769–72.
Blanche, Charles-Isidore (d. 1887). "Études sur la Syrie: L'ansarié Kaïr-Beik." *Revue européenne: Lettres, sciences, arts, voyages, politique* 2/12 (1860): 384–402, 582–601.
Bonte, Pierre, and Édouard Conte. "La tribu arabe: approches anthropologiques et orientalistes." In *Al-Ansâb, La quête des origines: Anthropologie historique de la société arabe tribale*. Edited by P. Bonte (d. 2013) et al., 13–48. Paris: Maison des sciences de l'homme, 1991.
Bou-Nacklie, N. E. "Les Troupes spéciales: Religious and Ethnic Recruitment, 1916–46." *International Journal of Middle East Studies* 25 (1993): 645–60.
Broadbridge, Anne. "Apostasy Trials in Eighth/Fourteenth Century Egypt and Syria: A Case Study." In *History and Historiography of Post-Mongol Central Asia and the Middle East: Studies in Honor of John E. Woods*. Edited by Judith Pfeiffer and Sholeh Quinn, 363–82. Wiesbaden: Harrassowitz, 2006.
Burns, Ross. *Monuments of Syria: An Historical Guide*. London: I. B. Tauris, 1999.
Çagaptay, Soner. *Islam, Secularism and Nationalism in Modern Turkey: Who Is a Turk?* London: Routledge, 2006.
Canard, Marius. "Hamdānids." In *EI2*, 1971, 3:125–31.
Carré, Olivier, and Michel Seurat, eds. *Les Frères musulmans: Égypte et Syrie (1928–1982)*. Paris: Gallimard, 1983.
Catafago, Joseph. "Die Drei Messen der Nossairier." *Zeitschrift der Deutschen Morgenländischen Gesellschaft* 2 (1848): 388–94.
Çelik, Şenol. "XVI. Yüzyılda Hanedan Kurucu Bir Osmanlı Sancakbeyi: Canbulad Bey." *Türk Kültürü İncelemeleri Dergisi* 7 (2002): 1–34.
Çetinsaya, Gökhan. *Ottoman Administration of Iraq, 1890–1908*. London: Routledge, 2006.
Cevdet Paşa, Ahmed (d. 1895). *Tarih-i Cevdet*. Istanbul: Matbaa-ı Osmaniye, 1891/92.
Chakrabarty, Dipesh. *Provincializing Europe: Postcolonial Thought and Historical Difference*. Princeton, NJ: Princeton University Press, 2000.
Coşgel, Metin. "Ottoman Tax Registers (*Tahrir Defterleri*)." *Historical Methods* 37 (2004): 87–100.

Dadoyan, Seta. *The Fatimid Armenians: Cultural and Political Interaction in the Near East*. Leiden: Brill, 1997.
Daftary, Farhad. *The Ismāʿīlīs: Their History and Doctrines*. Cambridge: Cambridge University Press, 1990.
———. "Rāshid al-Dīn Sinān." *EI2*, 1995, 8:442–43.
Davison, Roderic. *Reform in the Ottoman Empire, 1856–1876*. Princeton, NJ: Princeton University Press, 1963.
Deringil, Selim. "The Struggle against Shiism in Hamidian Iraq: A Study in Ottoman Counter-Propaganda." *Die Welt des Islams* 30 (1990): 45–62.
———. *The Well-Protected Domains: Ideology and the Legitimation of Power in the Ottoman Empire 1876–1909*. London: I. B. Tauris, 1998.
Deschamps, Paul. *Les châteaux croisés en Terre Sainte*. Vol. 3: *La défense du Comté de Tripoli et de la Principauté d'Antioche*. Paris: Paul Geuthner, 1973.
D'Ohsson, Ignace Muradgea (d. 1807). *Tableau général de l'empire Ot[h]oman*. Istanbul: Isis, 2001.
Douwes, Dick. "Knowledge and Oppression: The Nusayriyya in the Late Ottoman Period." In *La Shiʿa nell'Impero Ottomano*. Rome: Accademia Nazionale dei Lincei, 1993.
———. *The Ottomans in Syria: A History of Justice and Oppression*. London: I. B. Tauris, 2000.
Dressler, Markus. *Writing Religion: The Making of Turkish Alevi Islam*. Oxford: Oxford University Press, 2013.
Duguid, Stephen. "The Politics of Unity: Hamidian Policy in Eastern Anatolia." *Middle Eastern Studies* 9 (1973): 139–55.
Dussaud, René (d. 1958). *Histoire et religion des Nosairîs*. Paris: Bouillon, 1900.
Ende, Werner. "Mutawālī" *EI2*, 1993, 7:780–81.
Fahmy, Khaled. *All the Pasha's Men: Mehmed Ali, His Army, and the Making of Modern Egypt*. Cairo: American University in Cairo Press, 1997.
Farah, Caesar. *The Politics of Interventionism in Ottoman Lebanon, 1830–1861*. London: I. B. Tauris, 2000.
Farhat, Yahya Qasim. *Al-Shiʿa fi Tarabulus: Min al-Fath al-ʿArabi ila'l-Fath al-ʿUthmani*. Beirut: Dar al-Malak, 1999.
Firro, Kais. *Metamorphosis of the Nation (al-Umma): The Rise of Arabism and Minorities in Syria and Lebanon, 1850–1940*. Eastbourne, UK: Sussex Academic Press, 2009.
Fortna, Benjamin. *Imperial Classroom: Islam, the State, and Education in the Late Ottoman Empire*. Oxford: Oxford University Press, 2002.
Franke, Patrick. *Begegnung mit Khidr: Quellenstudien zum Imaginären im traditionellen Islam*. Beirut: Franz Steiner, 2000.
———. *Göttliche Karriere eines syrischen Hirten: Sulaimān Muršid (1907–1946) und die Anfänge der Muršidiyya*. Berlin: Klaus Schwarz, 1994.
Fried, Morton (d. 1986). *The Notion of Tribe*. Menlo Park, CA: Cummings, 1975.
Friedman, Yaron. "Ibn Taymiyya's *Fatāwa* against the Nusayrī-ʿAlawī Sect." *Der Islam* 82 (2005): 349–63.
———. *The Nusayrī-ʿAlawīs: An Introduction to the Religion, History and Identity of the Leading Minority in Syria*. Leiden: Brill, 2010.
Fuess, Albrecht. *Verbranntes Ufer: Auswirkungn mamlukischer Seepolitik auf Beirut und die syro-palästinensische Küste (1250–1517)*. Leiden: Brill, 2001.

Gelvin, James. *Divided Loyalties: Nationalism and Mass Politics in Syria at the Close of Empire*. Berkeley: University of California Press, 1998.

Georgeon, François. *Abdulhamid II: Le sultan calife*. Paris: Fayard, 2003.

Gingeras, Ryan. *Sorrowful Shores: Violence, Ethnicity and the End of the Ottoman Empire, 1912–1923*. Oxford: Oxford University Press, 2009.

Goldsmith, Leon. "'God Wanted Diversity': Alawite Pluralist Ideals and Their Integration into Syrian Society 1832–1973." *British Journal of Middle East Studies* 40 (2013): 392–409.

Göyünç, Nejat, and Wolf-Dieter Hütteroth. *Land an der Grenze: Osmanische Verwaltung im heutigen türkisch-syrisch-irakischen Grenzgebiet im 16. Jahrhundert*. Istanbul: Eren, 1997.

Grehan, James *Everyday Life and Consumer Culture in 18th-Century Damascus*. Seattle: University of Washington Press, 2007.

Gril, Denis. "Ésotérisme contre hérésie: 'Abd al-Rahmân al-Bistâmî, un représentant de la science des lettres à Bursa dans la première moitié du XVe siècle." In *Syncrétismes et hérésies dans l'Orient seldjoukide et ottoman (XIVe-XVIIIe siècle): Actes du Colloque du Collège de France, octobre 2001*. Edited by Gilles Veinstein, 183–95. Paris: Peeters, 2005.

Gross, Max. "Ottoman Rule in the Province of Damascus, 1860–1909." PhD diss., Georgetown University, 1979.

Guyard, Stanislas (d. 1884). "Le fetwa d'Ibn Taimiyyah sur les Nosairis." *Journal Asiatique* 18 (1871): 158–98.

———. "Un grand maître des Assassins au temps de Saladin." *Journal Asiatique* series 7, 9 (1877): 324–489.

Haarmann, Ulrich (d. 1999). *Quellenstudien zur frühen Mamlukenzeit*. Freiburg: D. Robischon, 1969.

al-Hakim, Yusuf. *Suriyya wa'l-'Ahd al-Faysali*. Beirut: Al-Matba'a al-Kathulikiyya, 1966.

———. *Suriyya wa'l-'Ahd al-'Uthmani*. Beirut: Al-Matba'a al-Kathulikiyya, 1966.

Halm, Heinz. "Das Buch der Schatten: Die Mufaddal-Tradition der Gulat und die Ursprünge des Nusairiertums (I)." *Der Islam* 55 (1978): 219–66.

———. *Die Islamische Gnosis: Die Extreme Schia und die 'Alawiten*. Zurich: Artemis, 1982.

———. "Nusayriyya." *EI2*, 1995, 8:145–48.

Hamza, Nadim Nayif. *Al-Tanukhiyyun: Ajdad al-Muwahiddin (al-Duruz) wa-Dawruhum fi Jabal Lubnan*. Beirut: Dar al-Nahar, 1984.

Hanssen, Jens. *Fin de Siècle Beirut: The Making of an Ottoman Provincial Capital*. Oxford: Oxford University Press, 2005.

Harfush, 'Ali 'Abbas (d. 1981). *Al-Maghmurun al-Qudama' fi Jibal al-Ladhiqiyya*. Damascus: Dar al-Yanabi', 1996.

al-Hariri, Abu Musa. *Al-'Alawiyyun al-Nusayriyyun: Bahth fi'l-'Aqida wa'l-Tarikh*. Beirut: n.p. 1980.

Hartmann, Martin. "Das Liwa el-Ladkije und die Nahije Urdu." *Zeitschrift des Deutschen Palästinavereins* 14 (1891): 151–255.

Hasan, Dib 'Ali. *A'lam min al-Madhhab al-Ja'fari "al-'Alawi."* Beirut: Dar al-Sahil li'l-Turath, 1997–2000.

Hasan, Hamid. *Al-Makzun al-Sinjari bayna'l-Imara wa'l-Sha'r wa'l-Tasawwuf wa'l-Falsafa*. Damascus: Dar Majallat al-Thaqafa, 1972.

Hashi, Salim Hasan. *Al-Khazana al-Tarikhiyya fi'l-Isma'iliyyin wa'l-Duruz*. Beirut: Lahad Khatir, 1985.

Heidemann, Stefan. *Die Renaissance der Städte in Nordsyrien und Nordmesopotamien: Städtische Entwicklung und wirtschaftliche Bedingungen in ar-Raqqa und Harrān von der Zeit der beduinischen Vorherrschaft bis zu den Seldschuken.* Leiden: Brill, 2002.

Heyberger, Bernard. "Peuples 'sans loi, sans foi, ni prêtre': druzes et nusayrîs de Syrie découverts par les missionaires catholiques (XVIIe–XVIIIe siècles)," in *L'islam des marges: Mission chrétienne et espaces périphériques du monde musulman XVIe-XXe siècles*. Edited by B. Heyberger and Rémy Madinier, 45–80. Paris: Karthala, 2011.

Hodgson, Marshall (d. 1968). "How Did the Early Shî'a Become Sectarian?" *Journal of the American Oriental Society* 75 (1955): 1–13.

Honigman, E., and Nikita Elisséeff. "Masyad." *EI2*, 1991, 6:791.

Hourani, Albert (d. 1993). *A History of the Arab Peoples*. Cambridge, MA: Harvard University Press, 1991.

al-Ibrahim, 'Ali 'Aziz. *Al-'Alawiyyun bayna'l-Ghuluw wa'l-Falsafa wa'l-Tasawwuf wa'l-Tashayyu'*. Beirut: Mu'assasat al-A'lami, 1995.

Imber, Colin. "The Persecution of the Ottoman Shiites According to the Mühimme Defterleri, 1565–1585." *Der Islam* 56 (1979): 245–73.

Isma'il Basha al-Baghdadi (d. 1920). *Hadiyat al-'Arifin: Asma' al-Mu'allifin wa-Athar al-Musannifin min Kashf al-Zunun*. Istanbul: Wakalat al-Ma'arif, 1951.

Jabbour, Georges. "Safita et son environnement au XIXe siècle." In *Histoire économique et sociale de l'Empire Ottoman et de la Turquie (1326–1960)*. Edited by Daniel Panzac, 605–17. Paris: Peeters, 1995.

Jennings, Ronald. *Christians and Muslims in Ottoman Cyprus and the Mediterranean World, 1571–1640*. New York: New York University Press, 1993.

Kara, Adem. "Antakya ve Çevresi Hakkında Yapılan Çalışmalar." *Türkiye Araştırmaları Literatür Dergisi* 3 (2005): 733–52.

Kaufman, Asher. "'Let Sleeping Dogs Lie:' On Ghajar and Other Anomalies in the Syria-Lebanon-Israel Tri-Border Region." *Middle East Journal* 63 (2009): 539–60.

Kerr, Michael, and Craig Larkin, eds. *The Alawis of Syria: War, Faith and Politics in the Levant*. London: Hurst, 2015.

Khalaf, Taysir. *Al-Julan fi Masadir al-Tarikh al-'Arabi: Hawliyat wa-Tarajim*. Damascus: Dar Kan'an, 2005.

Khawanda, Muhammad. *Tarikh al-'Alawiyyin wa-Ansabuhum*. Beirut: Dar al-Mahajja al-Bayda', 2004.

al-Khuri, Ighnatiyus Tannus. *Mustafa Agha Barbar: Hakim Ayalat Tarabulus wa-Jabala wa-Ladhiqiyyat al-'Arab (1767–1834)*. Tripoli: Jarrus Bars and Dar al-Khalil, 1984.

al-Khayyir, 'Abd al-Rahman (d. 1986). *Yaqzat al-Muslimin al-'Alawiyyin fi Matla' al-Qarn al-'Ashrin*. Edited by Hani al-Khayyir. Damascus: Matba'at al-Kitab al-'Arabi, 1996.

Khoury, Philip. *Syria and the French Mandate*. London: I. B. Tauris, 1987.

Khowaiter, Abdul-Aziz. *Baibars the First: His Endeavours and Achievements*. London: Green Mountain Press, 1978.

Kieser, Hans-Lukas. *Der Verpasste Friede: Mission, Ethnie und Staat in den Ostprovinzen der Türkei, 1839–1938*. Zürich: Chronos, 2000.

Kimyongür, Bahar. *Syriana: La conquête continue*. Brussels: Investig'Action, 2011.

Koca, Ferhat. "İbn Teymiyye, Takıyyüddin." *Türkiye Diyanet Vakfı İslam Ansiklopedisi*. Istanbul: İSAM, 1999), 20:391–405.

Kocaoğlu, Bünyamin. "Ulus-Devletin İnşası Sürecinde bir Türk(çe)leştirme Politikası: 'CHP Hars Komitaları' (1937–1938)." *Muhafazkar Düşünce* 3 (2007): 23–46.

Krstíc, Tijana. *Contested Conversions to Islam: Narratives of Religious Change in the Early Modern Ottoman Empire*. Stanford, CA: Stanford University Press, 2011.

Kurayyim, 'Abd al-Latif. *Barbar Agha: Majd Tarabulus U'tiya Lahu*. Tripoli: Imbras, 2004.

Kurtuluş, Abdulkerim. *Şıh İbrahim Esir'in Esaretten Kurtuluşu: Şıh Yusuf Esir'in Mersiyesi ve Vasiyeti*. Mersin: n.p., 2000.

Kutluoglu, Muhammed. *The Egyptian Question (1831–1841). The Expansionist Policy of Mehmed Ali Pasa in Syria and Asia Minor and the Reaction of the Sublime Porte*. Istanbul: Eren, 1998.

Lambert, Malcolm. *The Cathars*. Oxford: Blackwell, 1998.

Landis, Joshua. "Alawi-Ismaili Confrontation in Qadmous: What Does It Mean?" 28 July 2005. http://syriacomment.com.

Laoust, Henri. *Essai sur les doctrines sociales et politiques de Takī-d-Dīn Ahmad b. Taimīya*. Cairo: Institut français d'archéologie orientale, 1939.

———. "Remarques sur les expéditions du Kasrawan sous les premiers Mamluks." *Bulletin du Musée de Beyrouth* 4 (1940): 93–115.

———. *Les schismes dans l'islam: Introduction à une étude de la religion musulmane*. Paris: Payot, 1965.

Lawson, Fred. "The Northern Syrian Revolts of 1919–1921 and the Sharifian Regime: Congruence or Conflict of Interests and Ideologies?" In *From the Syrian Land to the States of Syria and Lebanon*. Edited by Thomas Philipp and Christoph Schumann, 257–74. Würzburg: Ergon, 2004.

Le Gac, Daniel. *La Syrie du général Assad*. Brussels: Éditions Complexe, 1991.

Le Roy Ladurie, Emmanuel. *Montaillou, village occitan de 1294 à 1324*. 2nd ed. Paris: Gallimard, 1982.

Lewis, Bernard. "Ottoman Land Tenure and Taxation in Syria." *Studia Islamica* 50 (1979): 109–24.

Lewis, Norman. "Taïbe and El Kowm, 1600–1980." *Cahiers de l'Euphrate* 5–6 (1991): 67–78.

Little, Donald. "Did Ibn Taymiyya Have a Screw Loose?" *Studia Islamica* 41 (1975): 93–111.

———. "The Historical and Historiographical Significance of the Detention of Ibn Taymiyya." *International Journal of Middle East Studies* 4 (1973): 311–27.

———. *An Introduction to Mamluk Historiography*. Wiesbaden: Steiner, 1970.

Lowry, Heath. "The Ottoman Tahrîr Defterleri as a Source for Social and Economic History: Pitfalls and Limitations." In *Studies in Defterology: Ottoman Society in the Fifteenth and Sixteenth Centuries*, 3–18. Istanbul: Isis Press, 1992.

Makdisi, Ussama. *The Culture of Sectarianism: Community, History and Violence in Nineteenth-Century Ottoman Lebanon*. Berkeley: University of California Press, 2000.

al-Ma'luf, 'Isa Iskandar (d. 1956). *Diwani al-Qatuf fi Tarikh Bani al-Ma'luf*. 1908; new ed. Damascus: Dar Hawran, 2003.

Mantran, Robert, and Jean Sauvaget. *Règlements fiscaux ottomans: les provinces syriennes*. Beirut: Institut Français de Damas, 1951.

Mardin, Şerif. *The Genesis of Young Ottoman Thought: A Study in the Modernization of Turkish Political Ideas*. Princeton, NJ: Princeton University Press, 1982.

Masters, Bruce. *Christians and Jews in the Ottoman Arab World.* Cambridge: Cambridge University Press, 2001.

al-Mawsili, Mundhir. *Al-Bahth 'an al-Dhat: Al-Judhur.* Damascus: Dar al-Muruwwa, 2008.

Mazzaoui, Michel. *The Origins of the Safawids: Shi'ism, Sufism and the Ġulat.* Wiesbaden: Franz Steinter, 1972.

Meeker, Michael. *A Nation of Empire: The Ottoman Legacy of Turkish Modernity.* Berkeley: University of California Press, 1997.

Melville, Charles. "'Sometimes by the Sword, Sometimes by the Dagger': The Role of the Isma'ilis in Mamluk-Mongol Relations in the 8th/14th Century." In *Medieval Isma'ili History and Thought.* Edited by Farhad Daftary, 247–63. Cambridge: Cambridge University Press, 1996.

Méouchy, Nadine. "Le mouvement des *'isabat* en Syrie du Nord à travers le témoignage du chaykh Youssef Saadoun (1919–1921)." In *The French and British Mandates in Comparative Perspective / Les mandats français et anglais dans une perspective comparative.* Edited by Nadine Méouchy and Peter Sluglett, 649–71. Leiden: Brill, 2004.

———. "Rural Resistance Movements and the Introduction of New Forms of Consciousness in the Syrian Countryside, 1918–1926." In *From the Syrian Land to the States of Syria and Lebanon.* Edited by Thomas Philipp and Christoph Schumann, 275–89. Würzburg: Ergon, 2004.

Mertcan, Hakan. *Türk Modernleşmesinde Arap Aleviler (Tarih, Kimlik, Siyaset).* Adana: Karahan Kitabevi, 2014.

Mervin, Sabrina. "'L'entité alaouite,' une création française." In *Le choc colonial et l'islam: les politiques religieuses des puissances coloniales en terres d'islam.* Editd by Pierre-Jean Luizard, 343–58. Paris: La Découverte, 2006.

———. *Un réformisme chiite: Ulémas et lettrés du Ğabal 'Āmil (actuel Liban-Sud) de la fin de l'Empire ottoman à l'indépendance du Liban.* Paris: Éditions Karthala, Cermoc et Iféad, 2000.

Minorsky, Vladimir. "Ahl-i Hakk," *EI2*, 1960, 1:260–63.

Mirza, Nasseh Ahmad. *Syrian Ismailism: The Ever Living Line of the Imamate.* Surrey, UK: Curzon, 1997.

Mitchell, Timothy. *Colonising Egypt.* Berkeley: University of California Press, 1991.

Mizrahi, Jean-David. *Genèse de l'État mandataire: Service des Renseignements et bandes armées en Syrie et au Liban dans les années 1920.* Paris: Publications de la Sorbonne, 2003.

Momen, Moojan. *An Introduction to Shi'i Islam.* New Haven, CT: Yale University Press, 1985.

Moore, R. I. *The Origins of European Dissent.* 2nd ed. Oxford: Blackwell, 1985.

Moosa, Matti. *Extremist Shiites: The Ghulat Sects.* Syracuse, NY: Syracuse University Press, 1988.

Mortel, Richard. "The Husaynid Amirate of Medina during the Mamluk Period." *Studia Islamica* 80 (1994): 97–123.

———. "Zaydi Shi'ism and the Hasanid Sharifs of Mecca." *International Journal of Middle East Studies* 19 (1987): 455–72.

Mouton, Jean-Michel. *Damas et sa principauté sous les Saljoukides et les Bourides 1076–1154.* Cairo: Institut Français d'Archéologie Orientale, 1994.

al-Muhajir, Ja'far. "Al-Rajul alladhi Hazama al-Isti'mar Marratayn." In *Al-Mu'tamar al-Takrimi li'l-'Allama al-Muqaddas wa'l-Da'iya al-Mujahid al-Muhajir al-'Amili al-Shaykh*

Habib Al Ibrahim, 39–48. Beirut: Al-Mustashara al-Thaqafiyya li'l-Jumhuriyya al-Islamiyya al-Iraniyya, 1997.

———. *Al-Ta'sis li-Tarikh al-Shi'a fi Lubnan wa-Suriya*. Beirut: Dar al-Milak, 1992.

Mulder, Stephennie. "Sunnis, Shi'is and the Shrines of the 'Alids in the Medieval Levant." PhD diss., University of Pennsylvania, 2008.

Murphey, Rhoads. "Tobacco Cultivation in Northern Syria and Conditions of Its Marketing and Distribution in the Late Eighteenth Century." *Turcica* 17 (1985): 205–26.

al-Musa, 'Ali Muhammad. *Al-Imam 'Ali wa'l-'Alawiyyun: Dirasa wa-Tarikh wa-Tarajim*. Damascus: Dar al-Fatat, 2002.

Naef, Silvia. "Aufklärung in einem schiitischen Umfeld: Die libanesische Zeitschrift al-'Irfān." *Die Welt des Islams* 36 (1996): 365–78.

Na'isa, Haydar. *Suwar Rifiyya min al-Ladhiqiyya*. Damascus: Wizarat al-Thaqafa, 1994.

Nakash, Yitzhak. *The Shi'is of Iraq*. Princeton, NJ: Princeton University Press, 1994.

Nasrallah, Ibrahim. *Halab wa'l-Tashayyu'*. Beirut: Mu'assasat al-Wafa', 1983.

Neumann, Christoph. *Das Indirekte Argument: Ein Plädoyer für die Tanzīmāt vermittels der Historie*. Münster: Lit, 1994.

Nwyia, Paul. "Makzun al-Sinjarī, poète mystique alaouite." *Studia Islamica* 40 (1974): 87–113.

Ocak, Ahmet Yaşar. *Osmanlı Toplumunda Zındıklar ve Mülhidler (15.–17. Yüzyıllar)*. Istanbul: Tarih Vakfı, 1998.

Ortaylı, İlber. "Groupes hétérodoxes et l'administration ottomane." In *Syncretistic Religious Communities in the Near East: Collected Papers of the International Symposium "Alevism in Turkey and Comparable Syncretistic Religious Communities in the Near East in the Past and Present."* Edited by Krisztina Kehl-Bodrogi et al., 205–11. Leiden: Brill, 1997.

Osterhammel, Jürgen. *Die Entzauberung Asiens: Europa und die asiatischen Reiche im 18. Jahrhundert*. Munich: C. H. Beck, 1998.

———. *Die Verwandlung der Welt: Eine Geschichte des 19. Jahrhunderts*. Munich: C. H. Beck, 2009. Translated by Patrick Camiller as *The Transformation of the World: A Global History of the Nineteenth Century*. Princeton, NJ: Princeton University Press, 2014.

O'Zoux, Raymond. *Les États du Levant sous mandat français*. Paris: Larose, 1931.

Öztürk, Mustafa. "XVIII. Yüzyılda Antakya ve Çevresinde Eşkiyalık Olayları." *Belleten* 54 (1990): 963–93.

Paoli, Bruno. "La diffusion de la doctrine nusayrie au IVe/Xe siècle d'après le Kitāb Hayr al-sanī'a du šayh Husayn Mayhūb Harfūš." *Arabica* 58 (2011): 19–52.

Pişmanlık, Uğur. *Tarsus İşçi Sınıfı Tarihi: 19. Yüzyıldan Günümüze*. Istanbul: Yazılama, 2013.

Prager, Laila. "Alawi Ziyāra Tradition and Its Interreligious Dimensions: Sacred Places and Their Contested Meanings among Christians, Alawi and Sunni Muslims in Contemporary Hatay (Turkey)." *Muslim World* 103 (2013): 41–61.

Procházka-Eisl, Gisela, and Stephan Procházka, *The Plain of Saints and Prophets: The Nusayri-Alawi Community of Cilicia (Southern Turkey) and Its Sacred Places*. Wiesbaden: Harrossowitz, 2010.

Provence, Michael. *The Great Syrian Revolt and the Rise of Arab Nationalism*. Austin: University of Texas Press, 2005.

al-Qadi, Wadad. "The Development of the Term Ghulāt in Muslim Literature with Special Reference to the Kaysāniyya." In *Akten des VII. Kongresses für Arabistik und Islamwissenschaft, Göttingen*. Edited by Albert Dietrich, 295–319. Göttingen: Vandenhoeck & Ruprecht, 1976.

al-Qaht, Bassam 'Isa. "Al-Tarikh al-Ijtima'i wa'l-Iqtisadi li-Muqata'at Safita 1790–1832 m.: Qira'a fi Sijillat Mahkamat Tarabulus al-Shar'iyya." Graduate thesis, Lebanese University, 1997.
Qawsara, Fayiz. *Al-Rahhala fi Muhafazat Idlib: Itlaqa Tarikhiyya*. Aleppo: Matba'at al-Sharq, 1985–88.
Reyhani, Mahmut (d. 2015). *Gölgesiz Işıklar*. Vol. 2: *Tarihte Aleviler*. Istanbul: Can Yayınları, 1995.
Rosenthal, Franz (d. 2003). "Ibn al-Fuwatī." *EI2*, 1971, 3:769–70.
Rubin, Avi. *Ottoman Nizamiye Courts: Law and Modernity*. New York: Palgrave Macmillan, 2011.
Saadé, Gabriel. "Lattaquié au dix-huitième siècle." In *Orient et Lumières: Actes du Colloque de Lattaquié (Syrie)*, 3–9. Grenoble: Recherches et Travaux, 1987.
de Sacy, Antoine Silvestre (d. 1838). *Exposé de la religion des druzes, tiré des livres religieux de cette secte*. Paris: Imprimérie Royale, 1838.
Salati, Marco. "Toleration, Persecution and Local Realities: Observations on the Shiism in the Holy Places and the *Bilad al-Sham* (16th-17th Centuries)." In *La Shi'a nell'Impero Ottomano*. Rome: Accademia Nazionale dei Lincei, 1993, 123–32.
Salibi, Kamal. "The Buhturids of the Ġarb: Mediaeval Lords of Beirut and of Southern Lebanon." *Arabica* 8 (1961): 74–97.
———. *A House of Many Mansions: The History of Lebanon Reconsidered*. Berkeley: University of California Press, 1988.
———. "Mount Lebanon under the Mamluks." In *Quest for Understanding: Arabic and Islamic Studies in Memory of Malcolm Kerr*. Edited by Samir Seikaly et al., 15–32. Beirut: AUB, 1991.
Salibi, Kamal, and Yusuf Khoury, eds. *The Missionary Herald: Reports from Ottoman Syria, 1819–1870*. Amman: Royal Institute for Inter-Faith Studies, 1995.
al-Salih, Mahmud. *Al-Naba' al-Yaqin 'an al-'Alawiyyin*. Beirut: Mu'assasat al-Balagh, 1961.
Salisbury, Edward. "The Book of Sulaimân's First Ripe Fruit, Disclosing the Mysteries of the Nusairian Religion." *Journal of the American Oriental Society* 8 (1866): 227–308.
Salzmann, Ariel. *Toqueville in the Ottoman Empire: Rival Paths to the Modern State*. Leiden: Brill, 2004.
al-Samad, Qasim. "Nizam al-Iltizam fi Wilayat Tarabulus fi'l-Qarn 18 min khilal Watha'iq Sijillat Mahkamatiha al-Shar'iyya." In *al-Mu'tamar al-Awwal li-Tarikh Wilayat Tarabulus ibana'l-Hiqba al-'Uthmaniyya 1516–1918*, 59–95. N.p.: Lebanese University, 1995.
Sari, Yasir. *Safahat min Tarikh al-Ladhiqiyya*. Damascus: Wizarat al-Thaqafa, 1992.
Sauvaget, Jean. "Décrets Mamelouks de Syrie (III)." *Bulletin d'études orientales* 12 (1947–48): 5–60.
Seale, Patrick (d. 2015). *Asad of Syria: The Struggle for the Middle East*. Berkeley: University of California Press, 1988.
Shahid, Irfan. "Tanūkh." *EI2*, 2000, 10:190–92.
al-Sharif, Munir. *Al-'Alawiyyun: Man-hum wa-Ayna-hum?* [Damascus:] Al-Maktaba al-Kubra, 1946.
Shaw, Stanford, and Ezel Kural Shaw. *History of the Ottoman Empire and Modern Turkey*. Vol. 2: *Reform, Revolution, and Republic: The Rise of Modern Turkey, 1808–1975*. Cambridge: Cambridge University Press, 1977.

Shields, Sarah. *Fezzes in the River: Identity Politics and European Diplomacy in the Middle East on the Eve of World War II*. Oxford: Oxford University Press, 2011.

Sinnu, 'Abd al-Ra'uf. *Al-Niza'at al-Kiyaniyya al-Islamiyya, 1877–1881: Bilad al-Sham, al-Hijaz, Kurdistan, Albaniya*. Beirut: Bisan, 1998.

Sneath, David. *The Headless State: Aristocratic Orders, Kinship Society, and Misrepresentations of Nomadic Inner Asia*. New York: Columbia University Press, 2007.

Sohrweide, Hanna. "Der Sieg der Safaviden in Persien und seine Rückwirkung auf die Schiiten Anatoliens im 16. Jahrhundert." *Der Islam* 41 (1965): 95–223.

Somel, Selçuk Akşin. *The Modernization of Public Education in the Ottoman Empire, 1839–1908: Islamization, Autocracy and Discipline*. Leiden: Brill, 2001.

Sourdel, Dominique, and Janine Sourdel-Thomine. "Un Sanctuaire chiite de l'ancienne Balis." In *Mélanges d'Islamologie*. Edited by Pierre Salmon, 247–53. Leiden: Brill, 1974.

Stewart, Devin. "Popular Shi'ism in Medieval Egypt: Vestiges of Islamic Sectarian Polemics in Egyptian Arabic." *Studia Islamica* 84 (1996): 35–66.

Strothmann, Rudolf. "Festkalender der Nusairier: Grundlegendes Lehrbuch im syrischen Alawitenstaat." *Der Islam* 27 (1946).

Süreyya, Mehmed (d. 1909). *Sicill-i Osmanî*. Edited by Nuri Akbayar and Seyit Ali Kahraman. Istanbul: Türkiye Ekonomik ve Toplumsal Tarih Vakfı, 1996.

Tachjian, Vahé. *La France en Cilicie et en Haute-Mésopotamie: Aux confins de la Turquie, de la Syrie et de l'Irak (1919–1933)*. Paris: Karthala, 2004.

Talhamy, Yvette. "American Protestant Missionary Activity among the Nusayris (Alawis) of Syria in the Nineteenth Century." *Middle Eastern Studies* 47 (2011): 215–36.

———. "Conscription among the Nusayris ('Alawis) in the Nineteenth Century." *British Journal of Middle Eastern Studies* 38 (2011): 23–40.

———. "The *Fatwa*s and the Nusayri/Alawis of Syria." *Middle East Studies* 46 (2010): 175–91.

———. "The Nusayri Leader Isma'il Khayr Bey and the Ottomans (1854–58)." *Middle Eastern Studies* 44 (2008): 895–908.

Tankut, Hasan Reşit. *Nusayriler ve Nusayrilik Hakkında*. Ankara: Ulus Basımevi, 1938.

Tapper, Richard. "Anthropologists, Historians and Tribespeople on Tribe and State Formation in the Middle East." In *Tribes and State Formation in the Middle East*. Edited by Philip Khoury and Joseph Kostiner, 48–73. Berkeley: University of California Press, 1990).

al-Tawil, Muhammad Amin Ghalib (d. 1932). *Tarikh al-'Alawiyyin*. Beirut: Dar al-Andalus, 1979.

T. C. Genelkurmay Başkanlığı. *Türk İstiklal Harbi IV'üncü Cilt Güney Cephesi*. Ankara: Genelkurmay Basımevi, 2009.

Tekin, Mehmet. *Hatay Tarihi: Osmanlı Dönemi*. Ankara: Atatürk Yüksek Kurumu Atatürk Kültür Merkezi Başkanlığı, 2000.

Tezcan, Baki. *The Second Ottoman Empire: Political and Social Transformation in the Early Modern World*. Cambridge: Cambridge University Press, 2010.

Tibawi, A. L. *American Interests in Syria, 1800–1901: A Study of Educational, Literary and Religious Work*. Oxford: Clarendon Press, 1966.

Tsugitaka, Sato. *State and Rural Society in Medieval Islam*. Leiden: Brill, 1997.

Tümkaya, Yunus. *Farklılığa Rağmen Bir Olmak: Nusayri Alevi Dünyasında Bir Gezi*. Istanbul: Can Yayınları, 2004.

Türk, Hüseyin. *Nusayrilik (Arap Aleviliği) ve Nusayrilerde Hızır İnancı*. Ankara: Ütopya, 2002.

Türkmen, Ahmet Faik. *Mufassal Hatay: Tarih, Coğrafya, Ekalliyetler, Mezhepler, Edebiyat, İçtimai Durum, Lengüistik Durum, Folklor, Etnografya ve Hatay Davcasını ihtiva eden 4 cild*. Istanbul: Cumhuriyet Matbaası, 1937–39.

Umar, Ömer Osman. *Osmanlı Yönetimi ve Fransız Manda İdaresi Altında Suriye (1908–1938)*. Ankara: Atatürk Araştırma Merkezi, 2004.

'Umayri, Ibrahim. *Silsilat al-Jibal al-Sahiliyya: Qissat al-Tarikh al-Ghamid wa'l-Hadarat al-Mansiyya*. Damascus: al-Aqsa, 1995.

Üstün, İsmail Safa. "The Ottoman Dilemma in Handling the Shi'i Challenge in Nineteenth-Century Iraq." In *The Sunna and Shi'a in History: Division and Ecumenism in the Muslim Middle East*. Edited by Ofra Bengio and Meir Litvak, 87–103. New York: Palgrave Macmillan, 2011).

'Uthman, Hashim. *Tarikh al-'Alawiyyin: Waqa'i' wa-Ahdath*. Beirut: Mu'assasat al-A'lami li'l-Matbu'at, 1997.

———. *Tarikh al-Ladhiqiyya 637m-1946m*. Damascus: Wizarat al-Thaqafa, 1996.

———. *Tarikh al-Shi'a fi Sahil Bilad al-Sham al-Shamali*. Beirut: Mu'assasat al-A'lami, 1994.

Üzüm, İlyas. Comments in Irene Melikof et al., eds. *Tarihî ve Kültürel Boyutlarıyla Türkiye'de Alevîler, Bektaşîler, Nusayrîler*. Istanbul: Ensar Neşriyat, 1999, 199–208.

———. "Nusayrîlik." *Türkiye Diyanet Vakfı İslam Ansiklopedisi*. Istanbul: İSAM, 2007, 33:270–74.

Van Dam, Nikolaos. *The Struggle for Power in Syria: Sectarianism, Regionalism and Tribalism, 1961–1978*. London: I. B. Tauris, 1979.

Venzke, Margaret. "The Ottoman Tahrir Defterleri and Agricultural Productivity: The Case for Northern Syria." *Osmanlı Araştırmaları* 17 (1997): 1–13.

———. "Syria's Land-Taxation in the Ottoman 'Classical Age' Broadly Considered." In *V. Milletlerarası Türkiye Sosyal ve İktisat Tarihi Kongresi: Tebliğler*. Edited by Marmara Universitesi Türkiyat Araştırma ve Uygulama Merkezi, 419–34. Ankara: Türk Tarih Kurumu, 1990.

Verdeil, Chantal. "Une 'révolution sociale dans la montagne': la conversion des Alaouites par les jésuites dans les années 1930." In *L'islam des marges: Mission chrétienne et espaces périphériques du monde musulman XVIe–XXe siècles*. Edited by Bernard Heyberger and Rémy Madinier, 81–105. Paris: Karthala, 2011.

Vermeulen, Urbain. "The Rescript against the Shi'ites and Rafidites of Beirut, Saida and District (764 AH/1363 AD)." *Orientalia Lovaniensia Periodica* 4 (1973): 169–75.

———. "Some Remarks on a Rescript of an-Nasir Muhammand b. Qala'un on the Abolition of Taxes and the Nusayris (Mamlaka of Tripoli 717/1317)." *Orientalia Lovaniensia Periodica* 1 (1970): 195–201.

Voss, Gregor. *'Alawīya oder Nusairīya: Schiitische Machtelite und sunnitische Opposition in der Syrischen Arabischen Republik* (Hamburg: n.p., 1987).

Watenpaugh, Keith. *Being Modern in the Middle East: Revolution, Nationalism, Colonialism and the Arab Middle Class*. Princeton, NJ: Princeton University Press, 2006.

———. "'Creating Phantoms': Zaki al-Arsuzi, the Alexandretta Crisis, and the Formation of Modern Arab Nationalism in Syria." *International Journal of Middle East Studies* 28 (1996): 363–89.

Wazzan, Kinda. "La production de la périphérie nord de Lattaquié (Syrie): Stratégie d'acteurs et formes produites." PhD diss., Université François-Rabelais, 2012.

Weiss, Max. *In the Shadow of Sectarianism: Law, Shi'ism and the Making of Modern Lebanon*. Cambridge, MA: Harvard University Press, 2010.
Weulersse, Jacques (d. 1946). *Le Pays des Alaouites*. Tours: Arrault, 1940.
White, Benjamin. *The Emergence of Minorities in the Middle East: The Politics of Community in French Mandate Syria*. Edinburgh: Edinburgh University Press, 2011.
White, Sam. *The Climate of Rebellion in the Early Modern Ottoman Empire*. Cambridge: Cambridge University Press, 2011.
Whitehead, Neil. "Tribes Make States and States Make Tribes: Warfare and the Creation of Colonial Tribes and States in Northeastern South America." In *War in the Tribal Zone: Expanding States and Indigenous Warfare*. Edited by N. Whitehead and R. Brian Ferguson, 127–50. Santa Fe: School of American Research, 1992.
Winter, Stefan. "'Alawism and Islam: Whom Does the Debate about the Religious Legitimacy of the Syrian Regime Serve?" M.A. thesis, University of Erlangen, 1994.
———. "Aufstieg und Niedergang des osmanischen Wüstenemirats (1536–1741): Die Mawali-Beduinen zwischen Tribalisierung und Nomadenaristokratie." *Saeculum* 63 (2013): 249–63.
———. "Les Kurdes de Syrie dans les archives ottomanes (XVIIIe siècle)." *Études Kurdes* 10 (2009): 125–56.
———. "Les Kurdes du Nord-Ouest syrien et l'Etat ottoman, 1690–1750." In *Sociétés rurales ottomanes*. Edited by Mohammad Afifi et al., 243–58. Cairo: IFAO, 2005.
———. "The Nusayris before the Tanzimat in the Eyes of Ottoman Provincial Administrators, 1804–1834." In *From the Syrian Land to the States of Syria and Lebanon*. Edited by Thomas Philipp and Christoph Schumann, 97–112. Würzburg: Ergon, 2004. Published in French with editorial corrections as "Les nusayris au regard des administrateurs provinciaux ottomans d'avant les Tanzimat (1804–1834)." *Chronos* 9 (2004): 211–35.
———. "Osmanische Sozialdisziplinierung am Beispiel der Nomadenstämme Nordsyriens im 17.-18. Jahrhundert." *Periplus: Jahrbuch für außereuropäische Geschichte* 13 (2003): 51–70.
———. "La révolte alaouite de 1834 contre l'occupation égyptienne: perceptions alaouites et lecture ottomane." *Oriente Moderno* 79 (1999): 60–71.
———. "Shams al-Din Muhammad ibn Makki 'al-Shahid al-Awwal' (d. 1384) and the Shi'a of Syria." *Mamluk Studies Review* 3 (1999): 159–82.
———. *The Shiites of Lebanon under Ottoman Rule, 1516–1788*. Cambridge: Cambridge University Press, 2010.
Yaffe, Gitta. "Suleiman al-Murshid: Beginnings of an Alawi Leader." *Middle Eastern Studies* 29 (1993): 624–40.
Yüksel, Emrullah. "Birgivî." In *Türkiye Diyanet Vakfı İslam Ansiklopedisi*. Istanbul: İSAM, 1992, 6:191–94.
Yunus, 'Abd al-Latif (d. 2013). *Mudhakkirat*. Damascus: Dar al-'Alam, 1992.
———. *Thawrat al-Shaykh Salih al-'Ali*. Damascus: Wizarat al-Thaqafa, 1961.
Zarzur, Faris. *Ma'arik al-Hurriyya fi Suriyya*. Damascus: Dar al-Sharq, 1964.
Zeidner, Robert. *The Tricolor over the Taurus: The French in Cilicia and Vicinity, 1918–1922*. Ankara: Turkish Historical Society, 2005.
Zürcher, Erik J. "The Ottoman Conscription System in Theory and Practice, 1844–1918." Rev. ed. In *The Young Turk Legacy and Nation Building: From the Ottoman Empire to Atatürk's Turkey*. Edited by Erik J. Zürcher, 154–66. London: I. B. Tauris, 2010.

INDEX

Page numbers in *italics* refer to maps.

'Abbas family, 217; Jabir, 255, 257
'Abbas Paşa, Egyptian viceroy, 194
'Abbas, Qays Ibrahim, 245–46
'Abbasids, 14, 17–19, 21, 23, 25, 26, 32, 42, 69
'Abd al-Qadir, of Algeria, 198
Abdülhamid II, sultan, 9, 162, 198, 215, 218, 219, 220–21, 223, 225, 229, 231, 232, 244, 272. *See also* Hamidian regime
Abdullah Paşa al-'Azm. *See* 'Azm family
Abdullah Paşa, of Sayda, 173–74
Abdüllatif Subhi Paşa, 203
Abdülmecid I, sultan, 194
Abu Bakr, caliph, 13, 65, 131, 172
Abu Dhuhayba Isma'il ibn Khallad, 31, 45–46, 50
Abu Qubays castle/village, 35, 38, 39–40, 53, 82, 95, 207
Abu Riha tobacco, 139–40, 142, 188
Abu Rish emirs, 24–25
Abu'l-Fath al-Baghdadi, 27, 31, 47
Abu'l-Fida', historian, 58, 60, 64, 66–67
Abu'l-Huda Efendi, 229
Acre, 7, 163–64, 167, 212. *See also* Sayda province
Adana, 1, 26, 40, 77, 79, 146, 182, 205, 212, 216, 223–24, 226, 233, 235, 241, 249–51, 263–65
al-Adani, Sulayman. *See* Sulayman al-Adani
'Adil, Salah al-Din, 252
Adra'i emirs, 55
Aegean province, 230
'Affan neighborhood, 252
Ahl-i Haqq, 22
al-Ahmad family: Jumana, 242; Muhammad Sulayman ("Badawi al-Jabal"), 259, 260n162; Sulayman, 242–43, 258, 259, 273
Ahmad Pasha al-Jazzar. *See* Cezzar Ahmed Paşa
Ahmed Cevdet Paşa. *See* Cevdet Paşa

'A'isha, 23
Ak Parti (AKP), 268
'Akkar district, 1, 30, 32, 126, 128, 150, 155, 177, 184, 190, 231
Al Ibrahim, Habib, 244
Al Kashif al-Ghita', Muhammad Husayn, 242
Alamut, 34
Alaouites, French mandate state, 9, 219, 243, 255–60, 262, 267, 272
Albania, Albanians, 165, 230
Aleppo, 33, 36, 39, 41, 53, 65, 70, 77, 79, 82, 131, 137, 177, 190, 204, 211, 218, 224, 249, 252–53, 267, 270; and Hamdanid dynasty,7, 10, 21, 26–27, 41, 270; as center of Khasibi *da'wa*, 19–20, 23, 25, 27, 29, 31, 40, 45–46, 49–50; alleged massacre of 'Alawis at, 74, 76–78, 80, 269, 273; Ottoman province (*sancak* or *eyalet*) and government officials of, 112–14, 116, 131, 134, 144–46, 177, 178, 179, 183, 193, 202, 225, 227, 231, 238; Christians in, 138, 218, 230; trade with, 139, 163, 176, 224; Kurdish district of, 182; Egyptian government of, 183, 185–86, 190; mufti of, 202; as French mandate state, 257
Alevis, 1n1, 5n9, 220, 222, 255–56, 268
Alexandretta (Iskandarun), 79, 139, 189; 224–28, 237, 250; district of, 184, 191, 219, 249, 250, 255, 263; as French mandate state (*sandjak* or *liwa'*), 247, 256–57, 264–65, 267, 272; and annexation to Turkey, 219, 236, 264–66. *See also* Hatay
Alexandria, 112
'Ali (ibn Abi Talib), 3, 12–13, 15, 18, 22–23, 46, 48, 50, 64–65, 171–72
'Ali ibn Baqrat, 49–50
'Ali al-Hadi (10th Imam), 12
Ali Paşa, of Tripoli, 137
Ali Paşa al-As'ad, 176–78, 180, 181

295

'Alids, 14, 22–23, 27, 32; shrines of, 21, 23, 71
Ali-Ilahi sect, 22
al-'Aliyya, 55
Amanus mountains, 79, 230
American Board of Commissioners for Foreign Missions (ABCFM), 202–3
American Reformed Presbyterian Mission, 204
Americans, 139, 179, 190, 202–3, 204–5, 223n18, 224, 251, 252
Amık Plain, 237, 253n140
'Ammarids, 32
'Amuda, 81
Amyanus, 99
'Ana, 20, 23–25, 40, 48, 50; Ottoman province of, 85
Anatolia, Anatolians, 7, 75–77, 113, 115, 117, 120, 207, 220, 222, 223, 224, 230, 245–47, 251, 255, 263, 264, 265, 272
al-'Anaza, 240
Anglicans, 121, 203
Ankara: archive collections in, 6–7, 131, 143, 250, 254; as seat of Kemalist government, 219, 250, 253, 262, 263–64; treaty of, 254, 262, 264
'Annab, 135, 142–43
Antalya, 250
Antartus. *See* Tartus
Antioch, 1, 26–27, 79, 82, 113, 137, 141, 144–46, 178, 186, 189, 193, 195, 202, 212, 217, 223–28, 230, 232, 233, 236, 237, 241, 244, 265–66, 272; governor (*voivode*) of, 145; revolt against French in, 247, 252; *shar'iyya* court records of, 119, 131, 144, 178, 271
'Antit, 31
Aqqush al-Afram, Mamluk governor, 59–60
'Arab al-Mulk tribe, 168n23
Arab nationalism, 9, 76, 111, 219, 235, 237, 243, 245–46, 248, 252, 256, 260, 265–66, 268, 272
Arab tribes, tribal chiefs, 26–27, 28–29, 35, 86, 100, 115, 124, 129, 179, 229. *See also* Bedouin
Arap Aleviler, 268
Armenians, 21–22, 218, 220, 224, 230–31, 237, 250, 251; in northwestern Syria, 137, 226, 230
'Arqub, 83, 99
Arsuz, 184, 237–38; district (*nahiye*) of, 224, 227

al-Arsuzi family, 217; Zaki, 252, 265–67
Arwad island, 128, 130, 148, 174
al-Asad family, 26; 'Ali Sulayman, 260–61; Bashar, 1–2; Hafiz, 1, 122, 152, 257; Sulayman, 257–58, 260
Ascalon, 20, 30
Asfin, 46–47, 50
ashraf, 22–23, 69, 78; *naqib al-ashraf*, 22, 59
al-Asir, Ibrahim (Esiroğlu), 262
Aşiret Mektebi, 198, 229–30
'Assaf family, 113
ATASE archives, 219, 250, 252, 254
Atatürk. *See* Mustafa Kemal
Austrian consulate, Latakia, 199
al-'Awra, Ibrahim, historian, 171–72
'Ayn al-Kurum, 135, 142, 198, 228–29
'Ayn Ghajar. *See* Ghajar
'Ayn Shaqaq, 143, 185
'Ayntab (Antep), 20, 186
Ayyubids, 7–8, 36–37, 39, 41–42, 43–44, 46, 51, 52–54, 70, 270
Azerbaijan, 22, 39, 41
al-'Azm (Azemzade) family, 120, 138, 163; Abdullah Paşa, 156, 158, 165, 216; Sadeddin Paşa, 138; Süleyman Paşa, 175–76. *See also* Genç Yusuf Paşa

Ba'rin, 29, 39, 154–55
Ba'th Party, 1, 220, 265
Baalbek, 31, 32, 45, 58, 115, 154, 244
Babanna, 211
Badama, 195
Badawi al-Jabal. *See* al-Ahmad, Muhammad Sulayman
Badr al-Ghafir shrine, 262
Baghdad, 12–14, 17–21, 25, 39, 41–42, 44–45, 48–50; Ottoman province of, 231
Bahamra, 121
Bahluliyya, 82, 131, 140, 142, 185; district of, 133, 176–77, 186, 200, 271; schools in, 208
Bahram al-Asadabadi, 34
Bahram al-Dimashqi, Abu Bakr, 24
Bakarrama, 81, 99
Al-Bakura al-Sulaymaniyya, 180–81, 204–5
Bal'alin, 99
Balat, 100
Balis, 23–24
Balkans, 74, 111, 207, 220, 222
Balqa, *sancak* of, 212
Baluta River. *See* Khawabi River

296 * *Index*

Banu 'Ali: tribe, 40, 121–22, 143–44, 185, 236; district of, 133, 143, 185, 187, 200. *See also* Samt al-Qibli
Banu Hilal, 45
Banu Muhriz, 28–29, 42; 'Abdallah ibn Ja'far, 29, 35; Nasih al-Dawla Jaysh ibn Muhammad, 29
Banu Numayr, 14
Banu Qahtan castle, 81, 157
Banu Ruzzik, 21–22
Banu'l-'Arid, 28
Banu'l-Ahmar, 28
Banyas (Golan), 27, 31–32, 34–35
Banyas (northwest coast), 28, 31, 39, 48, *82*, 91, 95, 239–40, 248
al-Banyasi, 'Isa ibn Muhammad, 27, 31
Barakat (Malik) family, 86, 147–49, 151, 152; As'ad ibn Hasan, 151; Ahmad ibn Hasan, 147; Hasan ibn Muhammad, 147–48, 150–51; Ibrahim ibn Muhammad, 147; Muhammad, 147; Musa, 147
Barmana, 173, 240
Barsbay, Mamluk sultan, 53
Barza, tax district (*nahiye*), *82*, 88, 100, 106, 108, 111
Basawtar, 112
Bashamman, 95, 99
Bashraghi, 95, 99
Basnada, 28
Basra, 23, 35, 45, 49, 231
Bassin, 81, 99
Basuram, 150
Baybars, Mamluk sultan, 53–54
al-Bayda', 52, 95
Bayezid district, 130
Bayezid, Ottoman sultan, 77
Bayir district, 131, 145
Bayt al-Shillif district, 136, 175–77, 187, 194, 195, 200, 206, 208, 234; Bayt al-Shillif family (*see* Shillif family)
Bayt Maqsud, 150
Bayt Yashut, 81, 133, 200
Bedouin, 10, 14, 19, 24, 41, 99, 135, 154, 192, 221, 231, 234, 245, 270; of coastal mountains, 168n23, 187, 228, 259. *See also* Arab tribes
Beilan Pass, 224
Beirut, 26, 32, 58, 69, 183, 194, 203, 204, 206n185, 197, 231, 234, 235, 236, 241; province (*vilayet*) and government of, 212–14, 215, 223, 228–29, 231, 232, 235, 237; French consul general at, 184, 186, 194, 206–7, 228, 231; French High Commission in, 260
Bekaa Valley, 32–33, 69, 86
Bektaşis, 256
Berber Mustafa Agha, 156–58, 162, 164–69, 171, 180, 181, 183, 216
Berlin, 207
Bidlis, 22
Biga province, 178
Bint Jubayl, 189
Birgivi Mehmed, 61
al-Birzali, historian, 58, 64–68
al-Bistami, 'Abd al-Rahman, 61
Black Sea region, 193, 222
Blanche, Isidore, 196–97, 206, 207
Bogomil sect, 51
Boutin, Vincent, 168
Britain, 199, 203, 207, 250; armed intervention of, 162, 182, 190, 206; consular agents of, 192, 194–98, 204, 205, 208, 230; vice-consul in Latakia of, 195, 200, 205, 208, 210. *See also* England
Buenos Aires, 259
Buhturids, 59
Bulgaria, 206
Burckhardt, John Lewis, 31, 157
Burids, 34
Burqush, 31
Bursa, 61
Busayra, 23
Busaysil, 65
Buyids, 13–15, 17–21, 42
Byzantine Empire, Byzantines, 27–29, 41, 51

Cairo, 18, 20–21, 42, 53, 59–60, 63, 77, 112, 182, 232, 270
Çaldıran, 75
Çanakkale, 178, 235
Canpolad Bey, 112. *See also* Habib Bey Canpolad
Carmelites, 147
Cathars, 51
Catholics, 170, 199, 203, 223
Cebel-i Kelbiyun Dağı. *See* Kelbi mountains
Celali rebels, 114, 117, 118, 120
Cemal Paşa, 235–36, 243
*çete*s (rebel bands), 245, 249, 252
Cevdet Paşa, Ahmed, historian, 174, 179

Cezzar Ahmed Paşa, 155–56, 157, 163–65, 167, 176
CHP (Cumhuriyet Halk Partisi), 7, 10, 219–20, 263, 264–65, 267, 272
Christianity, 4, 11, 14, 51, 171, 204, 207; conversion to, 36, 227
Christians, 3, 4, 12, 20, 36, 42, 57, 59, 71, 73, 80, 111, 115, 125, 170, 180, 206, 261; in greater Syria, 27, 137, 138, 173, 191, 199, 230, 251, 267; in coastal highland region, 4, 86, 123, 127, 135, 140, 160, 195, 197, 203, 206, 231, 243, 248; in Latakia, 138, 163, 202, 210, 235. *See also* Anglicans; Catholics; Copts; Greek Catholics; Greek Orthodox; Maronites; missionaries; Protestants
Cilicia, 26, 40, 146, 182, 216, 219, 223, 241, 250–51, 253, 256, 262–63, 268, 271, 272
Circassian Mamluks, 53, 77, 80
conscription (recruitment), 9, 162, 181–82, 188–90, 193–94, 199, 200, 212, 214, 215, 235, 238, 258, 271
conversion, 26, 69, 77, 170, 221; to 'Alawism, 15, 17–18, 20, 21, 22, 25–27, 30, 32, 34, 35, 121, 270; of 'Alawis to Christianity, 36, 203–5, 227; of 'Alawis to Sunnism, 9, 158, 160, 169–73, 198, 202, 204, 215, 216, 217, 219, 222–29, 236–37, 244, 272
Copts, 67
Crac des Chevaliers. *See* Hisn al-Akrad
Crete, 179
Crimean War, 194–95
Crusades, 8, 10, 28, 32, 35–36, 40–42, 51, 52, 58–59, 62, 112, 260, 270; crusader castles, 86, 88, 91, 106, 168
Çukurova plain, 79, 224, 237. *See also* Cilicia
CUP (Committee for Union and Progress), 218–19, 231, 235, 237, 242. *See also* Young Turks
Cyprus, 53, 207; conquest of, 112–113

Dahbash, 150
Damascus, 21, 23–24, 27, 33, 34–35, 39, 59–60, 64, 66, 76, 128, 177, 179, 198, 199, 204, 258, 267, 270; religious scholars of, 28, 43, 56, 58, 64, 66, 68–69, 76, 80; province (*eyalet*) and Ottoman officials of, 113–14, 116, 120, 137, 156–57, 159, 163–65, 173, 182, 193, 197, 198, 207, 208, 213, 231; finance registers (*Ahkam Defterleri*) of, 136, 142, 153, 154; British vice-consul in, 195, 197–98; as French mandate state, 257; as center of Syrian nationalist movement, 219, 235, 242, 248, 259, 260, 262; Twelver Shi'i community of, 59, 71, 241
Damietta, 139–40
Dandashli clan, 128, 192, 197, 229, 231
Danniye. *See* Zanniyya district
Dara, 23n26
Darawish, 83
Dayr al-Zor/Rahba province, 135
Dayr Mama, 29, 142
Dayr Shama'il, 29
debt and usury, 130, 140–41, 147–50, 153, 159, 198
Della Vale, Pietro, 24–25
Dhahabi, historian, 67
dirhemü'r-rical tax, 8, 70-, 75, 78, 80, 82–111, 114, 117, 124–125, 136, 144, 146, 271
Diryus tribe, 121
Diyarbekir, 20, 22
Draykish, 153, 171, 197, 240
Druze, 12, 18, 20, 25, 26, 32, 33–34, 42, 43, 58, 59, 69, 84, 99, 116, 123, 124, 137, 160, 164–65, 169, 173–74, 182, 184, 185, 190, 199, 203–4, 208, 212, 231, 245, 246
Dulaybat, 100

Egypt, 20–21, 27, 35, 36, 68, 138, 158, 181, 189, 194, 207, 239, 249; and Fatimid dynasty, 18, 30, 33–34; scholars of, 70, 80, 158; Ottoman conquest of, 75–77, 112; Egyptian occupation of Syria, 9, 153, 156, 162, 163, 173–74, 182–93, 203, 215, 216, 224, 251, 271
England, English, 5, 131, 138, 168, 190, 192, 203, 223n18, 232. *See also* Britain
Erzincan, 22
Esiroğlu, 262
Eti Türkleri. *See* Hittite Turks
Euphrates region, 7, 22–23, 41, 45

Fakhr al-Din Ma'n, 137
Farshat river, 81
Fatima, 18
Fatimid dynasty, 8, 10, 17, 18, 20–21, 23, 25, 27, 30, 32, 33–34, 42
Faysal, emir, 208, 247, 248, 249, 256. *See also* Sharifian forces
fellahin, as term for 'Alawis, 5, 145, 146, 251
Fırka-ı İslahiye, 222, 224

France, 7, 10, 51, 138, 161, 162, 168, 176, 181, 186, 179, 193, 199, 203, 206–7, 230, 232, 235, 255, 264, 265, 272; French consuls and consular reports, 138, 158, 164–65, 167–70, 173–77, 180, 184–90, 194–201, 205–8, 212, 223n16, 228, 231, 263, 265; French mandate and mandate officials, 2, 9, 81n12, 217, 218–20, 240–43, 248, 255–62, 266, 267, 272; 'Alawi revolts against, 7, 230, 240, 243, 244–55, 262; relations with Kemalist Turkey, 208, 246–47, 250–51, 253, 254, 256, 262, 272; Foreign Ministry and military archives of, 7, 201, 245, 258, 260–61
Franks, 35–36, 41, 48, 52, 53, 58. *See also* Crusades
Fuad Paşa, 179
Funaytiq, 54
al-Furat family, 14

Gallipoli, 250
Garib-zade Cemal Efendi, 226
Gaza, 20
Genç (Kanj) Yusuf Paşa, 156–58, 165–66, 170, 216
Geofroy, Lucien, 187–88
Germans, 31, 207
Ghab valley and marshlands, 142, 253
Ghajar, 1, 31
Gharb mountains, 26
ghulat Shi'ism, 12–18, 22, 25, 27, 32, 39, 41, 44–45, 47, 49–50, 75, 80, 83
Giacinto di Santa Maria, Elia, 147, 151
Golan, 31–32, 34
Gouraud, Henri, 248
Greece, Greeks, 74, 111, 177; Greek revolt, 173–74, 178, 182
Greek Catholics, 154
Greek Orthodox, 137, 173, 174, 199, 203, 204–5, 213, 261, 265
Gülek Pass, 182
Gülhane decree, 192
Guys, Charles-Édouard, 165, 167, 175, 177

Habib Bey Canpolad, 112
al-Hadda, Abu'l-Khayr Ahmad ibn Salama, 27, 28–29, 30–31
Haddadin (Haddadiyya) confederation, 40, 143
al-Hakim bi-Amri'illah, 20, 33
al-Hakim, Yusuf, 226

Hakki Paşa, 223
Halbakko, 81, 99
Halil Hamid Paşa, 178
Halk Evleri, 263, 264
al-Hallaj, Mansur, 45, 49
Hama, 7, 18, 29, 33, 39, 49–50, 53, 58, 64, 71, 73, 78, 79, 82, 120, 128, 183; Hama region, 27, 29–30, 45–46, 48, 52, 55, 80, 95, 127, 135, 142, 154, 159, 193, 195–96, 198, 206, 207, 211, 224, 228, 234, 244; Ottoman province (*sancak*) and governor (*mütesellim* or *kaimakam*) of, 71, 85, 88, 95, 111, 128, 136, 157, 166, 193, 198, 234; province (*muhafaza*) of, 30; *shar'iyya* court of, 55, 119, 173
Hamad al-'Abbas, 135
Hamada family (Twelver Shi'i), 32, 86, 126
Hamdanids, 7–8, 10, 19–21, 25, 26–27, 41, 270
Hamdi Paşa, 212
Hamidian regime, 163, 181, 219, 223, 226–29, 236, 267. *See also* Abdülhamid II
Hamidiye district (*kaza*), 228–29
Hammam (al-Qarahala), 112; district of, 176
Hammin, 150–51
Hamza ibn 'Ali, 33
Hanafi school, 130, 222, 239
Hanano, Ibrahim, 244, 247, 249, 252–53
Hanbali school, 56, 59–61
Hanya, 179
Harbiye, 252
Harem, 247, 253n140
Harfush family ('Alawi), 239–40; 'Ali 'Abbas, 239; Husayn Mayhub, 7, 40, 47, 238, 239–40, 255; Ibrahim Ahmad, 49, 240; Mayhub, 240; Muhsin 'Ali, 240; Salman ibn Muhammad, 239–40
Harfush family (Twelver Shi'i), 32, 123; 'Ali ibn Harfush, 115–16
al-Harif, 55, 57
Harran, 19–22
Hars Komitesi, 263, 264
Hasan al-Ajrud, 23–24, 53
Hasan al-'Askari (11th Imam), 12–13, 15
Hasan Kafrun, 36–37
Hasan-i Sabah, 34
Hasbani River, 31, 34
Hasnayn, 100
Hatay, 1, 5n9, 9, 76, 120, 143, 146, 159, 184, 191, 219, 263, 264, 266, 267, 268, 271, 272
Hatim al-Judayli. *See* al-Judayli

Index ∗ 299

Hatim family, 217; Musallam, 209; Sulayman, 211
Hatimiyya sect, 48–50
al-Hatiriyya, 54, 56
Hattaniyya, 240
Hawran, 204
Hawwash family, 230, 249, 260; 'Abdi, 230; 'Aziz ('Abd al-'Aziz) Bey, 230, 249, 254–55, 257. *See also* Khayr-Bey family
Haydariyya sect, 209–10. *See also* Shamsi sect
Hearth Society (Türk Ocakları), 263–64
Hebron, 20
Hermel, 86
Hilla (Iraq), 19, 20
Hillat 'Ara, 81, 99
Hisn al-Akrad (Qal'at al-Husn), 82, 86, 91, 197, 200, 206, 229; tax district of, 82, 86–87, 116, 128
Hisn Yashut, 100
Hittite Turks, 219, 266, 264–65
Homs, 26, 28–30, 46, 48–50, 78, 79, 82, 86, 117–18, 128, 142, 154, 159, 200, 212, 228, 244, 248; Ottoman province (*sancak*) and governor of, 71, 75, 84–86, 111, 136, 192, 197, 198
hulul (incarnation), 13, 16, 46–49, 51; Hululi sect, 19, 23, 44, 50
Humayn, 95–96
Hurşid Mehmed Paşa, 197n148
Husayn River. *See* Khawabi River
Husayn, sharif, 235–36, 243, 246, 247. *See also* Sharifian forces
al-Husayni, Hajj Amin, 242–43, 260
al-Husayni, Muhammad ibn 'Adnan, 59
Husayniyya, 133

Ibn 'Amrun, Sayf al-Mulk, Arab chief, 35
Ibn al-'Arabi, 61, 76
Ibn al-Athir, historian, 34
Ibn al-Fuwati, historian, 38–39
Ibn al-Matraji. *See* Mataracı family
Ibn al-Sa'igh, Fathallah, 185
Ibn al-Wardi, historian, 67
Ibn Battuta, historian, 67
Ibn Hajar al-'Asqalani, historian, 70
Ibn Hanbal, Ahmad, 61. *See also* Hanbali school
Ibn Jandab, Muhammad, 17
Ibn Kathir, historian, 63, 68
Ibn Khaldun, 203
Ibn Khallad. *See* Abu Dhuhayba

Ibn Makki, Muhammad, al-Shahid al-Awwal, 33, 70
Ibn Muhannad, 100, 111, 117
Ibn Mushraf (Ibn Musharraf) al-Radufi, Nasr, 28
Ibn Nusayr, 3, 12–15, 17, 45
Ibn Qadi Shuhba', historian, 69
Ibn Ruzzik, Tala'i', Fatimid official, 21
Ibn Taymiyya, 2, 8, 44, 56–61, 68, 73, 80, 174, 179–80, 269, 270–71, 273
Ibrahim al-'Idda ibn Musa, 55, 57
Ibrahim Edhem, 64; *waqf* foundation of, 136, 140, 143–44
Ibrahim Paşa, of Egypt, 156, 181–84, 186–87, 189–91, 216, 217, 224
Ibrahim, shaykh, and brothers, 145–46
İçel province, 263–64
Ikhshidids, 27
Ilkhanids, 54, 60
Imami (Twelver) Shi'ism, Shi'is, 1, 3, 5, 7–8, 12–15, 17–21, 23, 25, 26, 32–33, 39, 41, 43, 54, 56, 59–61, 63–64, 73, 117, 171–72, 203, 270; in Aleppo, 19, 21, 41, 76n4, 77–78; in Damascus, 59, 71, 241; in Iran, 32, 60, 75, 78, 203; in Iraq, 18, 20, 41, 221, 226, 241–42, 244; in Lebanon, 26, 32–33, 42, 58–59, 69–70, 84, 99, 115, 123, 137, 164–65, 182, 189–91, 212, 239, 241–43; in Ottoman discourse, 123, 170, 173, 221; 'Alawi rapprochement with, 210, 241–42, 244, 255
India, Indian Ocean, 24, 75, 221, 241
İnönü, İsmet, 263, 265
Iran, Iranians, 18, 20, 22, 26, 32, 34, 54, 60, 61, 75, 77–78, 117, 203, 221. *See also* Persians
Iraq, 7, 17–23, 27, 33, 37, 38, 41, 48–49, 71, 221, 226, 241, 244, 270
Iraqanata, 100
Al-'Irfan, 241–42
Ishaq ibn Muhammad al-Nakha'i, 15, 45
Ishaqi sect, 7, 15, 19, 25, 31, 44–49, 50–51
Iskandarun. *See* Alexandretta
Isma'il, Shah, 75, 77
Ismail Kemal Bey, 214
Isma'il ibn al-Za'nabi, emir, 127, 133
Ismaili Shi'ism, Shi'is, 5, 7, 17–20, 23, 25, 27, 33–34, 58–59, 255; in Syria/Lebanon, 7, 8, 12, 28, 32, 34–37, 39, 41, 42, 43–44, 51, 53–56, 69, 71, 72, 88, 95, 127, 133, 135, 152, 156–58, 169, 240, 247, 248, 270
Israel, 1, 31, 220, 257, 272

Istafalin, 80–81
Istamo, 100, 133
Istanbul, 61, 112, 179, 196, 207, 216, 229, 231; archives in, 6, 127n24, 131, 158, 269; as seat of imperial government, 75, 132, 140, 142, 163, 166, 167, 174, 175, 177, 178, 186, 195, 200, 213, 215, 223, 225, 228–32, 251, 255; tobacco customs of, 139
Italy, Italians, 51, 147, 252
Izmir, 204

Ja'far al-Sadiq, 18
Ja'fari school, 242, 244, 258
Jabal al-Akrad district, 30, 177, 186, 200, 247, 253n140
Jabal 'Ali, 136
Jabal 'Amil, 19, 32–33
Jabal al-Aqra' district, 177, 230
Jabal al-Bahra', 28, 30
Jabal al-Lukkam, 30
Jabal al-Manasif, 48, 86. *See also* Manasif district
Jabal Musa, 230
Jabal al-Rawadif, 28, 30
Jabal Sahyun, 30. *See also* Sahyun
Jabal al-Sha'ra, 81. *See also* Sha'ra district
Jabal al-Shaykh. *See* Mt. Hermon
Jabal Sinjar. *See* Sinjar
Jabal Summaq, 30
"Jabal al-Turkman," 100
Jabal al-Zawiya, 253n140
Jabala, 44, 45, 63, 64–68, 79, *82*, *107*, 113, 131, 136, 143, 177, 189, 211, 273; Jabala region, 8, 29, 53, 64, 66, 73, 81, 112–13, 115, 117, 121, 139–40, 170, 206, 249, 252; province (*sancak*) and governor (*bey*) of, 75, 85, 88, 106, 111–115, 130, 136, 137; tax district (*nahiye*) of, 80, *82*, 88, 95, 99–105, 113, 121, 133–34, 136, 176, 189; municipal district (*kaza*) and deputy governor (*kaimakam*) of, 211–12, 232, 234; schools in, 223, 226
al-Jabarti, historian, 158, 182
Jabbara family, 217; Hasan, 266, 267
Janaro, 83
janissaries, 113, 118, 137, 174; of Antioch, 145; of Latakia, 175; of Tripoli, 164
Jaranana, 66, 112
Jaris, 50
al-Jazari, historian, 66
Jerusalem, 20, 36, 242

Jews, Judaism, 20, 57, 71, 73, 80, 170, 171, 204, 257
al-Jilli, Muhammad, 20–22, 27, 30–31, 35
Jisr al-Shughur, 79, *82*, 116, 131, 137, 176, 186, 195, 200, 231–32, 249, 267
al-Jisri, 'Ali, 19, 21
al-Judayli (al-Tubani), Hatim, 48–50, *52*. *See also* Hatimiyya
Junaynat Raslan, 153
al-Junbulani, 'Abdallah al-Jannan, 17

Kadizadelis, 61
Kafr Dibl, 140
Kafr Susa, 39
Kafrun, 36–37, 127
al-Kahf: castle, 28, 35, 62, 88, *91*, 169; tax district, 80, *82*, 88, 92–93, 133
Kalaziyya faction, 209–10, 217. *See also* Qamari sect
al-Kanj, Ibrahim, 255, 257
Kara Mehmed Paşa, 178, 273
Karak Nuh, 32
Karama, Rawfa'il, historian, 154
Karaman, 77
Karkid, 140
Kassab, 178
Katib Çelebi, 24, 61
Kazanlı, 262
kefalet (guarantee); *kefil*s, 116, 127, 134, 147, 151
Kelbi tribe, 75, 83, 99–100, 111, 113–16, 117, 121–22, 142–44, 149; mountains of (Cebel-i Kelbiye), 100, 133, 134, 196, 212; district of, 133, 143, 154, 165, 170, 185, 187–88, 189, 193, 197, 199, 214, 232
Kemal, Namık, 216
Kemalists, 7, 9, 208, 218–19, 248–53, 256, 262, 263, 265–68, 272. *See also* Mustafa Kemal
Kerbela, 221
Khalifa tribe, 234
Khalil al-Numayli, 154
Kharijis, 19, 68
al-Khasibi, Husayn ibn Hamdan, 15, 17–21, 23, 32, 47–48
Khasibi path (*da'wa*), 5, 10, 23, 32, 39, 41, 45, 50, 53, 243, 255, 270
Khawabi River, 88, 91
Khawabi: castle, 35, 88; tax district of, 80, *82*, 88, 92, 93–94, 132
Khayir Beğ, 77

Khayr al-Sani'a, 7, 16–17, 20, 22–23, 27–31, 35, 37, 44–45, 47–49, 51, 53–55, 70, 99, 112, 135, 154, 239–40
Khayr-Bey family, 143, 196, 198, 249, 271; Barakat 'Ali, 143; Hawwash Bey (Muhammad), 198, 206–7, 211, 212, 230, 249; Isma'il, 196–98, 206, 217; Khayri, 196; Saqr, 235; 'Uthman, 143, 196. *See also* Hawwash family
Khayyatin tribe, 31, 234
al-Khayyir family, 240, 260; 'Abd al-Rahman, 238; 'Ali Hasan, 240
Khidr, prophet, 16, 23–24, 146; feast of, 140
Khirbat Malik, 150
Khorasan, 35
Khuzistan, 18
Kilis, 40, 179, 189, 249; province of, 112
Kimin, 133–36
King-Crane Commission, 251
Kışlak, 145
Kisrawan, 58–60, 199
Kızılbaş, 75–78, 115, 117, 173, 256
Kozan Mountains, 223
Kurds, 22, 34, 37, 39, 111, 121; of Aleppo province, 112, 182; of Anatolia (Kurdistan), 220, 222, 230, 263, 264; of coastal highlands, 86, 106, 131–32, 134, 186, 243
Kurtuluş (war of liberation), 219, 245, 250, 251, 262–63, 272; as name of family, 262
Kütahya, treaty of, 184
Kutla Wataniyya. *See* National Bloc
Kuva-ı Milliye, 250–51

Lake Urmia, 21
Latakia, Latakia, 6, 7, 26–29, 31, 45, 53, 66, 79, 82, 100, 107, 114–16, 131–41, 142, 158, 159, 160, 162, 163, 166–67, 174–78, 179–81, 182–83, 185, 188, 194, 206, 208, 210–11, 213, 217, 223, 226, 234, 241, 242, 248, 254, 258, 262; coastal plain of, 45, 99, 142, 165, 175, 206; mountain hinterland of, 26, 28–30, 32, 39, 120, 132, 134–36, 139, 152, 158, 159, 175, 184, 186, 190, 195, 199, 202, 204, 209, 214, 216, 224, 228, 231, 243, 244, 253, 271; Christians of, 137, 163, 173, 199, 235; Sunnis of, 166, 180, 210, 271; tax district (*nahiye*) of, 80, 82, 88, 100, 108–9, 133–34, 145, 206; provincial division (*sancak, kaza*) and governor (*mütesellim, mutasarrıf, kaimakam*) of, 135–36, 138–40, 164, 168, 173–74, 177, 179–80, 194–95, 201, 209–10, 211–12, 213, 214, 215, 222–23, 228, 229, 232, 235n73, 236, 239, 244, 247, 251–52, 259; French consular agent or vice-consul at, 158, 165, 167, 168n23, 169, 185, 187, 189; British (honorary) vice-consul at, 195, 200, 205, 208, 210; French mandate state (Alaouites; Gouvernement de Lattaquié) and Representative Council of, 219, 243, 257, 259, 261
League of National Action ('Usbat al-'Amal al-Qawmi), 265
League of Nations, 252
Lebanon, Mount Lebanon, 1, 26, 30–32, 43, 79, 84, 99, 113, 124, 126, 128, 137, 138, 150, 154–56, 163, 170, 177, 179, 182, 184, 199, 203, 212, 220, 223, 230, 235, 237, 245, 271, 272; emirs of, 86, 131, 137, 138, 152, 154, 183, 235; and participation in Egyptian occupation, 186, 189; province (*mutasarrıflık*) of, 199, 211, 213; historians and historiography of, 5n9, 26, 32, 43, 58, 142, 164, 176, 176, 191; Druze of, 84, 164, 190; Twelver Shi'is of, 8, 26, 32, 33, 164, 189, 190, 191, 239, 241–42, 243; as French mandate state (Greater Lebanon), 248, 255, 257–58, 260–61
Légion d'Orient, 250
Levantine community, 208, 230
London, 252
Lyde, Samuel, 121, 168n23, 180, 194, 195, 203–4, 232

Ma'arrat al-Nu'man, 26, 36, 128, 190
Ma'nids, 116, 123, 124, 137
Ma'ruf (Maruf) family, 236; Khalil, 252; Ma'ruf Efendi, 236; Sadiq (Sadek), 266
Madiq castle. *See* Qal'at al-Madiq
Mağaracık, 145–46
Mahfuz lineage. *See* Shamsin family
Mahmud al-Qusayr, 54–56
Mahmud II, sultan, 162, 168, 177–78, 215
Majdalun, 150
Makdisi, Ussama, 170, 181, 237
Makhluf family, 122
Makzun al-Sinjari, 12, 22, 37–43, 45, 46, 47, 49, 51, 52, 95, 99, 119, 152, 270
Malikh family. *See* Barakat family
Mamluks, 2, 6–7, 8, 10, 16, 29, 42, 43–44, 52–54, 58–63, 66–73, 74–78, 80–81, 112, 117, 123, 170, 270–71
Al-Manar, 213

Manasif district, 82, 86–87. See also Jabal al-Manasif
al-Mandara, 150
Maqaramda, 239–40
al-Maqrizi, historian, 62–63, 68
Maraş, 204, 252–53
Mardin, 20
Marj Dabiq, 77
Maronites, 36, 58, 185, 199, 203
Marqab, 28, 35, 66, 91, 142, 168, 185, 189, 206, 211; district of, 80, 82, 88, 91, 96–97, 132; schools in, 222–223, 226
Mashtal Hilu, 36, 127
al-Maskana, 23
Masyaf, 35, 36, 53–55, 82, 88, 156–58, 249
Mataracı (Ibn al-Matraji) family, 137; Mataracı Ali, 137; Arslan Mehmed Paşa, 137; Kaplan Paşa, 137; Mehmed ibn Kaplan, 137
Matawira tribe, 40, 143, 196, 206, 255
Maundrell, Henry, 5, 131
mawali, 17–18, 41
Mawali (Mevali) confederation, 135, 154
Maysalun, battle of, 249, 260
Mecca (and Medina), 52, 69, 76–77, 235, 239
Mecidiye Order, 236, 266
meclis: municipal administrative (*Idare*) and judicial (*Deavi*) councils, 9, 200, 209–11, 215, 217, 229, 232, 234, 237, 273; supreme judicial (*Vala*) and Ministers' (*Vükela*) councils, 193, 195, 202, 213, 222–23, 234; provisional council of Adana, 251; parliament of Turkey, 253; constitutive assembly of Hatay, 266
Mediterranean, 51, 112, 123, 138, 178, 181, 196
Mehmed Ali Paşa, of Egypt, 174, 181–84, 188, 190, 194
Mehmed IV, sultan, 61
Mehmed Paşa ibn al-Mann, 174–75, 177, 180, 216
Mehmed Reşid Paşa, 186
Mehmed Vahieddin, sultan, 236
Mersin, 1, 40, 206, 212, 237, 250, 263–65; villages of, 226; schools in, 223–24
Metheny, Dr. David, 224
Métoualis (Mütevalis), 32, 203. See also Imami Shiʿis
Miʿar, tax district, 80, 82, 86–87, 89–90, 91, 124, 127
Midhat Paşa, Ahmed Şefik, 211–12, 214, 273
Mirdasiyya, 99

Mirhij, Ibrahim ʿAbd al-Latif, 242
Mishaqa, Mikhaʾil, 191
missions, foreign, and missionaries, 138, 147, 190, 202–3, 204, 212, 213, 220–21, 222, 233, 270
Mızraklı, 144
al-Moghrabi, Muhammad, shaykh, 162, 178–81, 183, 222, 273
Mongols, 24, 25, 53–54, 58, 59, 62
Mosul, 19, 23, 39
Mt. Hermon, 31–32, 34
Mt. Lebanon. See Lebanon
Müdafaa-ı Hukuk (Defense of Rights) Society and committees, 246–47, 250
müdir (district tax agent), 195, 196–97, 200, 217
Mudros armistice, 236, 250
Mufaddal ibn Abiʾl-Fadaʾil, historian, 67
Muhalaba: tribe, 40, 121–22, 143, 146, 158; castle (Qalʿat al-Muhalaba), 143 (*see also* Platanus); tax district of, 140, 143, 167, 170, 187, 194, 234
Muhammad al-Maghribi. See al-Moghrabi
Muhammad, Prophet, 3, 12–13, 26, 65, 167, 172, 226, 253
Muhriz family. See Banu Muhriz
al-Munayqa: castle, 35, 66, 107; tax district of, 80, 82, 88, 91, 95–98
*muqaddam*s, 115, 123, 126, 128–31, 133, 134, 140, 143, 149, 151, 154, 170, 171, 175–77, 185, 187–88, 189, 211, 214, 216, 235n73; in Mamluk *fidaʾi* forces, 54
Murayqib, 245
al-Murrayih, 50
Murshid, Sulayman, 257, 259
Murshidiyya sect, 16, 259
Musa al-Rabti, 39–40, 53
Musan tribe, 134
Mushayrifa, 140
Mushraqiyya, 144
Mustafa Agha Barbar. See Berber Mustafa Agha
Mustafa bin Ebi Bekr el-Kayseri, 205
Mustafa Kemal (Atatürk), 7, 245–46, 249, 250, 253–54, 255, 263, 265. See also Kemalists
al-Mutanabbi, Abuʾl-Tayyib, 19, 26–27
Mutawwar, 81, 99
Muzayraʿa, 114, 135–36

Nabatiyya, 212
Nablus, 20, 182, 184, 213

al-Nabulusi, 'Abd al-Ghani, 28
Al-Nahda, 238
Nahr al-Kabir river (north), 30, 79, 100, 131, 176, 232
Nahr al-Kabir river (south), 28, 79
Nahr al-Sinn river, 177, 189
Najaf, 20, 71, 221, 242
Namiris, 14, 17
Nani, 112
al-Nashshabi, Yusuf ibn al-'Ajuz, 46–50, 52, 86, 147
al-Nasir Muhammad (al-Malik al-Nasir), Mamluk sultan, 59, 62, 65
Nasir, sharif, 249. *See also* Faysal, emir; Sharifian forces
National Bloc (al-Kutla al-Wataniyya), 257, 260, 261, 262
Niebuhr, Carsten 3–4
nişan (order of merit), 197
Nizaris, 8, 28, 34–35, 53–54, 157. *See also* Ismailis
North Africa, 18, 41, 179
Nuh al-Hanafi al-Dimashqi, 76
Numaylatiyya, 40
Nusaybin, 23
al-Nuwayri, historian, 62–64, 66–68
Nuzin, 83

Oğuz Turks, 265
Orontes River, region, 45, 79, 144, 232
Osman Paşa, of Tripoli, 183

Palestine, 183, 184, 186, 257
Paris, 138, 261
Payas, 232
Persians, 13, 17, 22, 25. *See also* Iran
Platanus: castle, 28, 35, 62, 64, 80, *107*, 143–44; district of, 63–64, 80–81, *82*, 88, 100–101, 105–106, 133, 136. *See also* Muhalaba
Poincarré, Raymond, French prime minister, 255
Poujoulat, Baptistin, 186
Presbyterians, 203, 204
Protestants, 170, 202–3, 204–5, 220, 222–23, 261

Qabr Shaykh Qar'ush, 45
Qadmus: castle, 28, 35, 54–55, 79, 88, *91*, 115, 127, 133, 135, 157, 169, 247–48, 249; tax district of, 80, *82*, 88, 91, 92, 94–95, 132, 239–40

Qal'at al-Husn, 197, 206. *See also* Hisn al-Akrad
Qal'at al-Madiq, *82*, 142–43, 193, 206
Qalawun, Mamluk sultan, 52
al-Qalqashandi, historian, 62, 68
Qamari sect (a.k.a. Kalaziyya, Qibliyya), 121, 209–10, 217
Qansuh al-Ghawri, Mamluk sultan, 71, 77
Qarahala tribe, and district of, 200, 234
Qaraja al-Salahi, Zayn al-Din, 46, 52
Qaratala tribe, 121
Qardaha, 28, 64, 79, *82*, 100, 140, 143, 190, 204, 232–33, 240, 242, 271; tax district of, 133, 143, 165, 167–68, 189, 194–95, 196, 214, 228
Qarmatian sect, 19, 25, 27, 58
Qarqafta, 95
Qatarba, 83
al-Qawuqji, Fawzi, 259
Qirtya'us, 64, 100
Qom, 20
Qulay'a: fortress, 50, 88, *91*; tax district of, 80, *82*, 86–90, 124, 127
Qulay'at, 87–88
Qurn Hulya, 81, 83, 99
Qusayr, plateau and tax district, 30, 79, 131, 186, 195, 230, 247, 253n140
Qutaylibiyya, *91*, 95
Qutriyya, 83

Ra's al-Basit, 100, 115
Rabi'a, shaykh, 46, 50, 52
al-Radufi. *See* Ibn Mushraf
Rafi'i, 'Umar, 235–36
Ragıb Mehmed Paşa, 146
Rahba, 20, 23
Rama, 146
Raqqa, 20, 23
Rashid al-Din Sinan, 35–36
Râşid Mehmed Paşa, 199, 202, 205
Raslan family, 149, 151, 152, 156, 158, 192, 260; Darwish ibn Sulayman, 149; Muhammad ibn Idris, 128, 149; Mulham ibn Sulayman, 149; Raslan ibn 'Alan, 149; Sulayman ibn Muhammad, 151; Sulayman ibn Raslan, 149
Rassafa castle, 35, 157
Rayhanat Mutawwar, 81
Raymond de St.-Gilles, 36
Reyhani, Mahmut, 191
Rhodes, 112, 212, 230

Rumelia province, 178
Rumkale castle, 186
Rusiyya, 99
Russia, Russians, 162, 173, 178, 181, 186, 199, 200, 206, 207
Rustum Agha family, 131–34, 136, 140; Rustum Agha, 127; Hasan ibn Rustum, 131–32; Musa, 133; Rustum ibn Hasan, 132–33

Sabeans, 22
Safad, province of, 85
Safavids, 32, 61, 75–77, 117
Safita, 29, 54, 70, 79, 82, 86, 88, *91*, 124, 125–26, 150, 171, 173, 183, 189, 190, 193, 194, 196–97, 198, 206, 216, 223, 231, 239, 241, 255, 259, 271, 273; tax district (*nahiye* or *müdirlik*) of, 80, 82, 86–91, 124–30, 133, 146–56, 164, 165, 173, 183–84, 192, 196–97, 199, 217, 234, 240–41, 248; schools in, 227
Sahyun: castle, 35, 39, 62, 106, *107*, 178, 187; highlands of, 30, 63, 231, 249; tax district (*nahiye*) of, 80, 82, 88, 100, 106, 108, 109–111, 114, 130, 133, 134, 136, 140, 177–78, 186–87 (see also Jabal al-Akrad); municipal district (*kaza*) of, 200, 206, 211; schools in, 208, 222–23, 227, 228; anti-French resistance in, 249, 252, 253n140
Salaghno, 63
Salah al-Din al-Ayyubi (Saladin), 36, 46, 52
Salamya, 18, 29, 33, 157; province (*sancak*) of, 135
Salih al-'Ali, 219, 230, 240, 243, 244–50, 252–56, 260n162, 262, 268, 272, 273
Salih ibn Yahya, historian, 59
Salih, Ilyas, historian, 137, 139, 174, 180, 210–11
al-Salihiyya, 59
Saljuqs, 20, 22, 25, 34, 39
Salma, 132, 134
Salman al-Farisi, 13, 64–65
Salman, 'Ali 'Abbas, 240, 243
Salonika, 206n185
Samandağ. See Suwaydiyya
Samt al-Qibli district, 143, 168, 175–76, 185, 194
Saqr ibn Mahfuz. See Shamsin family
Saqr, 'Ali ibn Darwish, 234
Saraj al-Din, 48
Saramita, 200

Sarmin, 29
Sayda (Sidon), 30, 32, 69, 242; province and governor (*vali*, *müşir*) of, 137, 155, 157, 160, 163–64, 173, 193–95, 196–97
Sayf al-Dawla al-Hamdani, 19, 21
Sayfa family, 113, 124
al-Sayyaf, Ahmad Nihad, 262
Schoeffler, Ernest, 260
Seetzen, Ulrich Jasper, 31
Selim Bey, Egyptian commander, 183–85, 187–88
Selim I, sultan, 75–78, 169, 221
Selim III, sultan, 179
Semt-i Qibli. See Samt al-Qibli
Şexan tribe, 131
sexual misconduct, accusations of, 3, 24, 33–34
Seyhan province, 263
şeyhü'l-islam, 132, 222, 225
Sha'ra district, 128, 150
Shaddad, 49
Shafi'i school, 60
Shalfutiyya, 131
Shamsi sect (a.k.a. Haydariyya, Shamaliyya), 121, 209–10
Shamsin family, 86, 120, 124–30, 133, 136, 146–47, 149–56, 158, 192, 196, 198, 271; and conversion of, 171–73; Abu Qasim al-Shibli, 127; 'Ali ibn Shibli, 128; Darwish ibn Shibli, 127–30, 133, 149–51, 153; Husayn, 128; Muhammad, 124–26; Muhammad Muhsin, 151, 153; Mulham Husayn, 127–30, 149–50; Mustafa ibn Shamsin, 150, 151; Shamsin ibn Muhammad, 150–51; Shibli, 127, 159; Zaydan, 124–25; and al-Shibli lineage, 124, 128, 130, 151; 'Ali ibn Husayn, 150–51; Mahfuz ibn Darwish, 151, 152, 153; Saqr ibn Mahfuz, 147, 151–56, 158, 159, 164–65, 171, 271; and al-Mahfuz lineage: Safi Saqr al-Mahfuz, 173; Dandash Saqr, 164–65, 171, 173, 183; Darwish Saqr, 153, 183–84; Khidr Saqr, 183–84; Zahir Saqr, 183
shar'iyya court records, 130, 172; of Antioch, 119, 144, 178, 271; of Tripoli, 6, 119, 124, 132, 133, 139, 140, 146, 148, 152, 164, 171–72, 175, 184, 192, 271
Sharifian forces, 247–48, 254, 256. *See also* Faysal, emir; Husayn, sharifs
Shaykh Badr, 245, 248, 253, 255

Shi'ism. *See* Druze, *ghulat*, Imami, Ismaili, Ishaqi, Kızılbaş, Zaydi Shi'ism
Shibli lineage. *See* Shamsin family
Shihabi emirs, 86, 123, 131, 138, 152, 154–56, 159, 163, 164; Bashir, 155–56, 169, 183, 184; Hasan, 155; Khalil, 184–87;Yusuf, 155
al-Shihabi, Haydar Ahmad, historian, 155, 156, 173, 183
Shillif (village), 259
Shillif family (Bayt al-Shillif), 120, 130–36, 140, 143, 158, 195, 271; Ahmad ibn Muhammad, 134–35; 'Ali ibn Muhammad, 133–35, 159, 273; Hafiz, 136; Hassun ibn 'Ali, 135; Mahfuz, 136; Muhammad ibn Ahmad (Ibn Shillif), 130–34. *See also* Bayt al-Shillif district
Shin, 86, 200
Shu'ayb family, 113
Shu'ba family, 21
Siffin, 12, 23
silk (and mulberry leaf) production, 124–25, 126, 131, 136, 138, 140, 142, 145, 163, 182
Sinan Qazhal, 48
Sinjar, 38–41, 121
Sinop, 193
Sivas, 186
Siyano, 146
Sqaylbiyya, 253
Stanhope, Lady Hester, 168
Subhi Paşa, 205
Sudayda, 126
Sulayman al-Adani, 204–5
Sulayman al-Ahmad. *See* al-Ahmad family, Sulayman
Süleyman Paşa (al-'Adil), 165–66, 167–69, 171–72
Süleyman Paşa al-'Azm, 175–76. *See also* al-'Azm family
al-Sulh, Rida, 212
Sunnism, 8, 18, 20–21, 41–42, 43–44, 61, 63, 69, 157, 170, 219, 222, 271; conversion to, 158, 171, 215, 216, 219, 224; Sunnis, 42, 170, 171–72, 221, 237–38, 239, 257, 265; position toward 'Alawis of, 2, 5, 6, 8, 16, 73; 'Alawi claims to be, 146, 170, 266; as state officials, 15, 17, 18–19, 20, 27, 36, 52–53, 56, 72, 77, 130, 222, 239, 242–43, 258, 270; of Aleppo and Euphrates valley, 22, 25, 76–77; of Damascus, 14, 76; of coastal cites (Jabala, Tartus, Tripoli), 67, 130, 159, 211, 248; and Latakia, 133–34, 166, 180, 185, 202, 210, 243; of Adana, 205, 226; of Alexandretta and Antioch, 195, 202, 205, 224–26, 252, 265; of coastal highland region, 106, 129, 134, 171, 175–77, 195, 200, 211, 241, 248, 252; Kurdish, 106, 134, 177
Sur. *See* Tyre
al-Surayfa, 66
Sus, 179
Suwayda (Homs region), 46
Suwaydiyya (Samandağ), 137, 144–46, 178, 236, 252; district of, 227; schools at, 223
al-Suwayri, 'Ali, 50, 52
Sykes-Picot accord, 250
Syria, Ottoman province (*vilayet*) of, 199, 228, 233, 235, 203, 211–12, 213. *See also* Damascus
Syrian National Congress, 248
Syrian nationalists, 219, 243, 245, 248, 257, 260–61, 266

al-Tabarani, Abu Sa'id Maymun, 27–28, 31, 45
Tabarja, 133
taife-i hüdaiye, 229, 255
Tal'afar, 39
Tall Kalakh, 82, 192, 241
al-Talla, 177
Tamerlane, 53
Tanukhi dynasty, 8, 26, 42, 59
taqiyya, 4, 5–6, 11, 13, 15, 24, 38, 225, 244
Tarikh al-'Alawiyyin, 5, 26, 53, 64, 241, 251, 255
Tarsus, 26, 77, 146, 205, 226, 237, 240, 251, 262, 265
Tartus, 28–32, 35–36, 79, 82, 88, 91, 95, 128, 153, 155, 206, 239, 245, 248; *muhafaza* of, 30; district (*nahiye*) of (Antartus), 80, 82, 86–87, 89–90, 124, 128–29
Taurus mountains, 182, 250
al-Tawil, Muhammad Amin Ghalib, 5, 27, 36–37, 45, 54, 76–77, 121–22, 141, 143, 146, 182, 191, 211, 235, 238, 241, 251, 255
Tayshur, and *hilla* of, 150–51
Thamina sect, 16, 18, 44, 49–50
Tiberias, 31
Tikrit, 20
tobacco production, 6, 9, 120, 131–32, 137, 138, 139–41, 142, 152, 159, 163–64, 166, 169, 183, 188, 271; tobacco Régie, 179
Toprakkale, 249

tribalism, tribalization, 9, 38, 40, 42, 83, 99, 120, 121–24, 143–44, 159, 194–95, 237, 243, 270, 271
Tripoli, 1, 28, 32–33, 36, 58n48, 62, 66, 70, 78, 79, 82, 112, 113, 116, 125, 127–28, 129, 130, 139, 147–49, 152, 157–58, 163–65, 167, 171, 176, 181, 183, 184, 189, 210, 224, 229, 234, 235–36, 250, 269; Mamluk province (*niyaba*) of, 52, 62–63; Ottoman provincial division (*sancak, eyalet, kaza*) and governor (*sancakbeyi, beylerbeyi, vali, mutasarrıf*) of, 70–71, 75, 80, 85–86, 88, 106–107, 111, 113, 115–16, 117, 124–25, 130, 132, 134–38, 142, 143, 149, 150, 153, 154–55, 156, 160, 161, 163–65, 168, 169, 173–74, 183, 190, 194, 197, 200, 212, 223, 231; *shar'iyya* court of, 6, 86, 119–20, 124–25, 127, 128, 130–32, 134, 140, 143, 146–48, 151–53, 158, 164, 171–72, 175, 184, 192, 271; French vice-consul at, 138, 154, 158, 164, 173, 196, 206
Troupes spéciales du Levant, 258
Tuffaha, 129
Tümkaya, Yunus, 76
Tunisia, 18, 179, 207
al-Turkmani, 'Ali, 129
Türkmen, Abdülgani, 266
Turkmen tribes, 75, 116; in coastal highland region, 86, 100, 124–26, 129, 130–31, 154, 243
"Türkmen Dağı," 100
Turks, ethnic, 7, 226, 264–65, 266, 268. *See also* Hittite Turks
Twelver Shi'is. *See* Imami Shi'ism
Tyre (Sur), 30, 32, 36

Ubin, 86, 147; *hilla* of, 147–48, 150–51
al-'Ulayqa: castle, 35, 66; tax district, 80, 82, 88, 91, 65, 95–96, 98
'Umar, caliph, 13, 65, 131, 172
al-'Umari, historian, 67
'Umraniye district, 234
United States, 161, 224. *See also* Americans
'Urfa, 186
Ushmunayn, 21
Üstüvani Mehmed Efendi, 61
'Uthman, caliph, 172

'Uthman, Hashim, 26, 182–83, 191

Vamık Paşa, 195, 196
vatandaşlık (compatriotism), 215–17
Vitalé family, 208

Wadi Qandil, 100
Wadi al-Taym, 34, 69
Wadi al-'Uyun, 29, 88, 189, 194, 246
Wahhabism, 56, 61, 157, 160, 170, 179, 182
waqf foundations (*vakıf*), 84, 138, 140, 143, 165, 177; of 'Alawis, 55, 146, 154, 258, 265
wine, use and production of, 15, 33, 46, 58, 64, 65, 70, 117–18, 131, 271

al-Yafi'i, historian, 67
Yahmur, 87
Yemen, 18, 20, 222, 225, 226
Yeni İl confederation, 116
Yezidis, 22, 222
Yıldız palace, 162, 222, 227, 231, 233
Young Turks, 9, 216, 218, 236, 250, 267. *See also* CUP
al-Yunus, 'Abd al-Latif, 245, 247, 262
Yunus (Yunso) Agha, 186
Yusuf ibn 'Abdallah shrine, 154–55

Za'ura, 31
Zaghrano, 99
Zahir al-'Umar, 163
zandaqa, accusations of, 69, 80, 175
Zangids, 33, 36, 42, 77
Zanniyya district, 32, 58n48, 154
Zarzur, Faris, 246
al-Zawi, 'Ali Hamdan, 240–41
Zayadin (Zayadiyya) faction, 113, 114, 149
Zaydi Shi'ism, 69, 114, 222, 225
Zeytuniye, 145
Ziraat Bankası, 241
Ziya Bey, Mehmed, 214, 222–23, 226, 239, 273
Ziyarettepe, battle of, 262
Zoroastrianism, 11, 14, 22
Zuhrawi family, 78
Zuq Barakat, 152
Zuq Sulayman al-Turkman, 66